A Certain Realism

D1596261

A Certain Realism

Making Use of Pasolini's Film Theory and Practice

Maurizio Viano

UNIVERSITY OF CALIFORNIA PRESS
Berkeley / Los Angeles / London

This book is a print-on-demand volume. It is
manufactured using toner in place of ink. Type
and images may be less sharp than the same
material seen in traditionally printed University
of California Press editions.

University of California Press
Berkeley and Los Angeles, California

University of California Press
London, England

Copyright © 1993 by The Regents of the
University of California

Library of Congress Cataloging-in-Publication
Data
Viano, Maurizio Sanzio, 1950–
    A certain realism : making use of Pasolini's
film theory and practice / Maurizio Viano.
       p. cm.
    Includes bibliographical references and index.
    ISBN 0-520-07854-3 (acid-free).—
    ISBN 0-520-07855-1 (pbk. : acid-free)
    1. Pasolini, Pier Paolo, 1922–1975—Criticism
and interpretation.
    I. Title.
PN1998.3.P367V5   1993
791.43′0233′092—dc20   92-28189
                         CIP

Printed in the United States of America

The paper used in this publication meets the minimum requirements
of ANSI/NISO Z39.48-1992 (R 1997) (*Permanence of Paper*). ∞

Contents

Preface

Suppose a man is working at Democritus. The question is always on my tongue, why precisely Democritus? Why not Heraclitus, or Philo, or Bacon, or Descartes? And, then, why not a poet or orator? And why especially a Greek? Why not an Englishman or a Turk?

F. Nietzsche

Pier Paolo Pasolini's literary and cinematic oeuvre is quietly becoming canonical in the field of Italian Studies. As essays, papers, colloquia, and books on his works unquestioningly multiply, I cannot help remembering the reciprocal hatred that existed between Pasolini and Italian academics while he was alive. While rejoicing at the light that all this interest has shed on Pasolini, I also fear his transformation into yet another academic commodity. Happily haunted by the echo of Nietzsche's contemptuous laughter, I can only write this preface as a string of answers to a few Nietzschean *whys*.

Why Pasolini?

In addition to illuminating my prefatory strategy, the initial quote from Nietzsche suggests the German philosopher's pertinence to my argument, for Pasolini took up Nietzsche's legacy in several ways. Like Nietzsche, Pasolini had a strong humanistic background that he later questioned but did not reject. In fact, the work of both authors utilized tradition and high culture in a nontraditional way. Both Nietzsche and Pasolini asked questions unremittingly, ruthlessly, and with an intellectual honesty that exposed them to lacerating contradictions. They thus both preempted the notion of objective Truth, but nonetheless kept alive the idea of an ephemeral truth as that which *must be said* at a given time.

The internal dissonance that characterized Nietzsche's and Pasolini's thinking was nothing but forthright adherence to the contingent needs of a shifting philosophical horizon, what Peter Carravetta called "the horizon of the modern/postmodern debacle."[1] Nietzsche and Pasolini traveled through contemporary discursive positions, pillaging whatever they thought was worth keeping and discarding the rest. Their practice of permanent dissent made them occupy several subject positions at once, giving their ideas a halo of dangerous unreliability: they can always be appropriated by the wrong party. If Hitler claimed Nietzsche, Italian neofascists have recently reclaimed Pasolini as a forerunner of their "New Right."

When Pasolini entitled his collection of short essays in cultural criticism *Scritti corsari* (Pirate Writings), he provided us with a splendid definition of what both he and Nietzsche were: supreme craftsmen in the art of intellectual piracy, that is, the art of having no stable discursive identity. Indeed, *Scritti corsari* ought to be the overall title for Pasolini's production, for he sailed across disciplines, refusing allegiance to a master discourse and practicing the art of contradiction, first deceiving friends and foes by means of a familiar flag and then parading the black of piracy at the last minute. By turning from literature to cinema, Pasolini gave us the unique opportunity of seeing what a Nietzschean pirate would do with images. This book is an attempt *to use* the film theory and practice of a twentieth-century pirate.

Why Pasolini's Film Theory?

Written *en poète*, Pasolini's essays did not exhibit the rigor associated with Theory and, at the time of their publication, they were harshly criticized as "semiological heresy." But those were the days of semiotics' scientific pretensions. Today, as the future of Theory is jeopardized by the crisis of its very own premises (duty of objectivity, disembodied rationality, etc.), the poetic and down-to-earth quality of Pasolini's theoretical endeavors provides an alternative. Purposefully and precariously situated at the crossroads of several discursive tensions, Pasolini's theory has the kind of openness that demands interlocutors rather than interpreters, dialogue rather than exegesis. Once tackled by a reader who does not shun the responsibilities of an active reading, some of his intuitions provide a useful way of thinking about cinema. For example, he often repeated that cinema was "the written language of reality." By this he meant that cinema changed our idea of reality in the same way that writing changed our perception of oral language. When it was just oral, the word seemed to have a biological necessity. It is only by looking at the written word that humans have grasped the arbitrariness inherent in the linguistic sign. Likewise, Pasolini suggested, audiovisual technology (what Benjamin called "mechanical reproduction") made us realize the extent to which everyday reality is a spectacle. Read with scientific expectations, this hypothesis was first criticized and later ignored. What formerly sounded like a most outrageous statement today turns out to be an intriguing way of thinking about the impact of one hundred years of motion pictures. Most of us would agree that there is no fixed reality "out there." Much postmodern theory claims that all we see are the simulacra of what once was "the real." Baudrillard and Eco have announced the advent of "hyperreality," the feeling that something is real only if it is validated as a media image. The Italian philosopher Gianni Vattimo, too, argues that the end of modernity entails the disappearance of reality and its replacement with a series of images in competition with one another. My contention is that such an epochal change was illustrated in a considerably less specialized, and therefore more accessible, way by Pasolini's analogy of cinema as the written language of reality.

Because I am convinced that the wish for a scientific film theory was an unfortunate episode in the history of film criticism, I have written this book as an attempt to use Pasolini's poetic insights into film theory.

Why Pasolini's Film Practice?

When Bernardo Bertolucci remarked that being an assistant to Pasolini's filming of *Accattone* was like witnessing the ritual of inventing cinema anew, he was not exaggerating. Pasolini came to filmmaking after years of literary practice, with no technical knowledge of the new medium. As a result, his films were stylistically very different from both mainstream *and* countercinema. Just as he did not have a precise knowledge of the technical devices typical of "classic" cinema, so he did not have any preconceived notions as to how one should subvert them. In this respect, Pasolini represented the purest celebration of filmmaking: something we all could do if we had the means or the desire. I recollect independent filmmaker Alfred Guzzetti once saying that Pasolini's cinema is something of a blessing for independents because of the stylistic anarchy and technical freedom it exudes.

Personally, I must confess to disliking some of Pasolini's films. I do, however, find all of them unique in their ability to force viewers to confront relevant sociohistorical issues. Pasolini brought to the screen the wealth of his pirate intellect, the fascinating sights afforded by his will to permanent transgression, and the despair of the self-mutilation imposed on him by heterocracy. He enthusiastically engaged in the representation of sexuality and marginality, of the emergence of the Third World on the Western scene, and of myth—the sacred, the religious, and, more generally, the nonrational—all subjects with which progressive thinking has some hard reckoning to do.

This book is also an attempt to use these films that never lost sight of reality.

Why "A Certain Realism"?

Unlike the champions of postmodernity, Pasolini did not liquidate the notion of reality, nor did he resent images/simulacra for the alleged murder of the real. To be sure, he expressed vitriolic contempt for television images and for the dominant forms of representation, but he never attacked audio-visual technology per se. On the contrary, his entire theoretical edifice was a hymn to the mystery of being alive in a labyrinth of audio-visual signs. Cinema, for him, was not "the evil demon" (as Baudrillard defined images)[2] who spoils our metaphysical dreams, but a precious friend who encourages our symbolic activity inside and outside the theater.

There is a sense in which Pasolini's aforementioned contradictory tensions were neatly encapsulated in his use of the word *reality*. While admitting—like a good postmodernist—to the ultimate meaninglessness of such a term, Pasolini kept using it, in the most diverse ways, with and without quotation marks. This did not earn him the respect of other theorists, who were too sophisticated to be caught employing the word *reality* seriously. Certainly Pasolini understood the reasons of his detractors; he was extremely aware of the problems inherent in the term *reality*, but he continued to use it nonetheless. Pasolini was, moreover, perhaps the last filmmaker and theoretician to argue cinema's privileged relationship with reality.

Pasolini's fetishistic use of the word *reality* led him to frame his own cinematography within the discourse of realism. To be sure, he did not approve of the existing models of cinematic realism, and his films were often a far cry from what we conventionally associate with that term. Yet he kept using it, stubbornly, running into contradictions and stumbling into insights. He knew that his cinematography was motivated by the desire to enhance cinema's reality-value—that is, the amount of knowledge that films may generate about their authors and the society in which they and their spectators live. Pasolini did not just want to "represent" reality. Rather, his films aimed at putting spectators in the position of asking themselves questions about reality. As there was no word to express the way in which his films pursued reality while avoiding the pitfalls of classic realism, Pasolini once coined the expression "a certain realism" to illustrate his position within Italian cinema. Intrigued by his stubborn use of the words *reality* and *realism*, I have written this book as an attempt to use that "certain realism" that permeates Pasolini's films.

And *Why* "Use"?

In his landmark assessment of reading as textual cooperation, *Lector in fabula*, Umberto Eco strove to ground semiotically—which in his case meant scientifically—the distinction between interpretation and use of a text.[3] Interpretation implies an ideal reading, one that presses the exact same buttons that the text was envisioned to set off. It is a relationship between a "model author" and a "model reader" who are not actual people but constructions of the text—"textual strategies," as Eco calls them. For Eco, "using" a text is, instead, a freewheeling appropriation of the text by an empirical reader who often has an ax to grind and who just as often makes assumptions about an equally empirical author. Needless to say, Eco has more respect for interpretation than for use.

On closer inspection, Eco's distinction is hard to maintain, for every interpretation is a use that aspires to a higher status by virtue of its claim to being the canonical form of textual cooperation. Together with *biased* and *partial*, the word *use* is often employed to discredit any reading that does not seek to efface its subjectivity. Ideal interpretations are those which bear no trace of the subject and let the object shine in its purity. The problem is, of course, that ideal interpretations are subjective but stem from a perspective inured to think of itself as *the* perspective. Differently put, it is easy to be objective when your subjectivity is that of the traditional Subject of History: white, male, heterosexual. It is no accident that the following passage, which I quote in its entirety because of its marvelous pertinence to my discourse, was written by a gay critic—that is, by someone who gained his status as subject only in recent times. In "Responsibilities of a Gay Film Critic," Robin Wood writes,

> I do not believe that any theory exists in a vacuum or as truth. Every theory is the product of needs of particular people within a particular culture at a particular stage of its development, and can only properly be understood within its context. Our gravitation, as human individuals within, and determined by, our culture, toward one or other of the available critical positions, will depend upon our personal needs, on the way we wish to live our lives, on the sort of society we would like to build, on

the particularities of our involvement in the social process. Such a view presupposes a constantly developing, dynamic relationship between criticism and art, between individual and work. There is in a sense no such thing as "the films of Ingmar Bergman," existing as an entity that criticism could finally and definitely describe and interpret and place in the museum. Rather the films exist as experienced and perceived by the viewer, with the precise nature of experiencing depending on the viewer's position in society and within ideology. Our sense of the *use* of art, generally, and of the particular uses to which particular works allow themselves to be put, will vary from generation to generation, shifting in accordance with our sense of personal and social needs.[4]

"Political correctness" can be boring, idiosyncratic, and counterproductive—and on the verge of being passé. Still, I think it is the responsibility of all film critics, and especially of white, heterosexual men like myself, to become aware of the personal foundation of their readings, to see through the determinants of their positions, and, above all, to account for all this. A first, if small, step in this direction would be the recognition that we *use* a text.

In this book, I will use Pasolini's film theory and practice in order to ascertain the extent to which they allow for a better grasp of certain realities. By saying that I use Pasolini's films, I also intend to honor one of the few Marxist concepts to be salvaged from the collapse of historical materialism: *use-value*. As opposed to exchange-value, which denotes the opinion of the market, use-value alludes to the usefulness that things may have for individuals, who are thereby entitled to appropriate these things in view of their needs. A reading no longer justifies itself merely on the basis of how correct it is, but also of how useful it is. Of course, if the use of a text is too free and bears no relationship to the original, it will attract very few followers and will dig its own grave.

My use of Pasolini does not claim to have found the right keys in his film theory and practice. It claims instead to be honest in prefacing its subjective bent and hopes to be, well, useful to you. Other readings are certainly possible, especially with a director like Pasolini. One could select passages in his work, or phases in his career, that support and celebrate, for example, the Western canon. I thereby invite other critics to account for the subjectivity of their readings more openly than they normally would and I stress the active side of my spectatorship. Readers of this book will occasionally ask themselves the question, "Is this Pasolini or is this Viano?" My answer would be, this is Pasolini used by Viano. Or, better yet, this is the result of a relationship between a series of texts copyrighted by Pier Paolo Pasolini and an Italian academic animated by the desire to revive the spirit of "a certain realism." And the decision of whether or not I have committed violence against his films will ultimately be up to you.

This question is nowhere more likely to crop up than in my reading of the homosexual content in Pasolini's films. With *very* few exceptions, critics have thus far been too reticent about Pasolini's homosexuality. This is not to say that they do not acknowledge it—how could they not? Indeed, they all talk about Pasolini *il diverso* (the different one), and they all mention crotch shots and the aestheticization of male figures when they cannot do otherwise. Nevertheless, they often refrain from weaving the fact of his homosexuality into the very texture of their analyses. They often act as if the emphasis on the evident traces of a homosexual subtext in, say, *Mamma Roma*, somehow detracts from the film. My argument will take the opposite stand: *Mamma Roma* is exceptional *because* it cleverly inserts a homosexual subtext in a film made at a time when the representation of homosexuality was forbidden.

My eyes were alerted to the homosexual paradigms in Pasolini's films by two sets of considerations. The first has to do, precisely, with "a certain realism." Realistically speaking, it is unlikely that such a key factor in Pasolini's life would not leave constant traces in his work, especially in view of the self-repression that gay critics have detected in his relationship to his own homosexuality. Realistically speaking, the subject of the enunciation in Pasolini's films is no mere textual appendix; it has a body, a homosexual body, in one of the most heterosexist countries in Europe. There is a sense in which Pasolini *had to* hide his homosexual feelings in subtextual notations, in the folds of homosexual narrative paradigms. The act of retrieving the homosexual dimension from the depths to which Pasolini relegated it is a tribute to "a certain realism": the desire to say what *must be said*.

This leads into the second set of observations. The current state of sexual politics in Italy is so regressive—Pasolini called it "false tolerance imposed from above"[5]—that the pervasive silence concerning the possible homosexual paradigms at work in his films would amount to indirect complicity with the state of things. While I am aware that to many readers I may seem "too reductive," I will raise the issue of the narrative, thematic, and stylistic consequences of Pasolini's homosexuality as much as I can. The danger of going too far in this direction is justified not only by the need to rescue the criticism on Pasolini from its aphasia but also by the need to wrest theory from its rationalist premises. Much of the existing discourse stems from the conviction that the body can somehow be excluded from the picture, as if art and poetry were not engendered and embodied. But, again, it is a matter of "a certain realism."

This much said, only a few more words are needed to facilitate the reader's use of this book.

I concerned myself only with cinema. Pasolini's poetry and prose entered the book only to the extent that they shed light on his film theory and practice. As to Pasolini's life, I provided an essential biography at the end of this preface. For more information regarding the historical circumstances of Pasolini's death and the ambivalence of his life, the Anglo-American reader is referred to Siciliano's biography and to Naomi Greene's recent book, *Pier Paolo Pasolini: Cinema as Heresy* (1990). The latter is, indeed, quite complementary to my book, for she contextualizes Pasolini both within a historical framework and within his literary production. Greene's book stems from the conviction that "Pasolini's films cannot be separated either from the body of his work or from the stage of European intellectual and artistic thought on which he himself was a prominent player."[6] While agreeing that situating Pasolini's work within its European context is of paramount importance, I would argue that knowing the rest of Pasolini's works is *not* necessary for a *use* of his films. It goes without saying that if you know his poems and novels, if you are familiar with the idiosyncratic events of the fifties and sixties in the Italian cultural milieu, you get a good idea of what Pasolini was, which is to say, you get to know Pasolini as he emerged and emerges in the Italian context. But is this *the real* Pasolini? There is another Pasolini, the one "appropriated" by the non-Italian public, those who read his film theory, rent his films (almost all of which are now available on video), and automatically situate him in a different context. These viewers/readers might actually profit by their ignorance of *some* contextual information and be free to explore other intertextual links. Less tied to the duty of uncovering the real Pasolini, these readers/viewers might well discover new uses for Pasolini which an excessively philological approach would conceal.

I have tried to circumvent the risk involved in an *auteurist* approach—that is, the risk of reifying and canonizing an imaginary entity, the-author-Pasolini. Important doubts about thinking in terms of authorship have been raised by Foucault and Barthes, among others. By granting privilege to the discourse on realism, I have sought to decenter the-author-Pasolini, or better, to create two centers. *Auteurist* readings are, by definition, centripetal. The information they mobilize is all subsumed under the duty of explaining the author. Here, I have attempted to use Pasolini's film theory and practice in a centrifugal way, as points of departure for "a certain realism."

Chapter 1 examines the various major discourses within which Pasolini positioned himself: Marxism, psychoanalysis, and so forth. It will concurrently establish the theoretical horizon within which the rest of the book proceeds. Chapter 2, introducing the reader to Pasolini's semiotics, dissects his notions of reality as language and of cinema as "the written language of reality." Chapter 3 introduces Pasolini's film practice, articulating it within the discourse on realism and attempting a theoretical clarification of "a certain realism." Finally, Chapters 4 through 21 treat Pasolini's films individually and in chronological order. Old-fashioned though it may be, such a film-by-film structure allowed me to verify the extent to which each film may or may not be a contribution to "a certain realism." Moreover, this organizing principle will facilitate the reader's use of the book, for Pasolini's films are likely to be viewed, taught, or considered separately. Ideally, this is the book you will go to when you have just watched a Pasolini film on your VCR. Of course, the film-by-film treatment is not without its problems, the most serious of which is the danger of losing sight of the major themes at work. A book centered around a main point of analysis would have allowed me to say all there was to be said about each theme all at once. I would have given some key notions (a certain realism, the partially obscured vision, the area of the signifier death) my unconditional attention, instead of dispersing them throughout the treatments of several films. The price I have had to pay for a fragmented treatment of the main themes is that of repetition. On more than one occasion I repeat arguments that appear in other chapters. Still, I feel this is a small price to pay, if we consider the advantage of giving each text its own space.

Essential Biography[7]

1922   Pier Paolo Pasolini is born March 6 in Bologna, son of Carlo Alberto, a career officer, and Susanna Colussi, an elementary school-teacher of peasant origins. His parents would never get along, and Pier Paolo, who sided with his mother, would develop an intense and loving relationship with her.

1925   Moves from town to town in northern Italy as Carlo Alberto is restationed. Pasolini's brother, Guido, is born in Belluno. This is also the year of the famous "teta veleta" episode, that is, his "first pangs of sexual love"—the object of several subsequent recollections (see "Psychoanalysis," chapter 1).

1929   A third-grader, Pasolini writes his first love poems for his mother and illustrates them with drawings.

1930–1936   A model student, he quickly moves from reading Salgari's adventure novels to Homer, Pascoli, D'Annunzio, Shakespeare, and Dostoyevski.

1938   Back in Bologna since 1937, he discovers the French poet

Rimbaud, which, according to his personal mythology, causes him to change his views on fascism and initiates the corrosion of his humanistic formation.

1939 Attends classes at the University of Bologna, studies art history under Roberto Longhi, and plans a thesis on the Italian twentieth-century painters Carrà, De Pisis, and Morandi.

1942 To seek refuge from the war, Susanna and her two sons evacuate to Casarsa, in Friuli. Pier Paolo publishes *Poesie a Casarsa* (Poems in Casarsa), in Friulan dialect, which is favorably reviewed by Gianfranco Contini, a well-known literary critic and philologist.

1943 Has furtive homosexual experiences with some young peasants: "the most beautiful year of my life" (Maldini, 54).

1944 His brother Guido joins the partisan guerrillas. "The war stinks of shit" (Maldini, 64).

1945 Guido is murdered by Communist partisans. Pier Paolo starts teaching peasant children, fulfilling his pedagogic vocation.[8]

1947 Reads Gramsci and participates in peasant struggles. In his letters to his friends, he confesses his homosexuality. His collection of dialectal verses is now entitled *Ciants d'un muart* (Songs of a Dead Man).

1948 Completes his doctoral thesis on the Italian poet Pascoli and joins the Italian Communist party (PCI), thus provoking the resentment of the local authorities.

1949 Denounced by the local carabinieri for "obscene acts in public," he is fired from his job and expelled from the PCI.

1950 Leaves for Rome with his mother; finds a poorly paid teaching job and low-income housing in the slums around Ponte Mammolo.

1951 Meets Sergio Citti (invaluable source of information on "street-wise" youth) and his brother Franco, who will star in six of his films.

1954 First collaboration on a film script, Mario Soldati's *La donna del fiume*. In these years, the friendships that will last throughout his life take shape with the writers Giorgio Bassani, Alberto Moravia, Elsa Morante, Attilio Bertolucci (Bernardo's father), and, later, with the actress Laura Betti.

1955 Publishes the novel *Ragazzi di vita* and is tried for obscenity immediately afterward. Together with Angelo Romanó and Gianni Scalia, he founds *Officina*, a journal engaged in a struggle against both ends of the contemporary literary spectrum, neorealism and hermeticism.

1956 Collaborates on Fellini's *Le notti di Cabiria* (Cabiria) as the expert on street jargon, and publishes his first film article, "Notes on *The Nights*" (in the published film script), welcoming the return of dialectal, everyday reality in the Italian cinema. As correspondent for the leftist journal *Vie Nuove* (New Avenues), he goes to Moscow's Youth Festival.

1957 Publishes the poetry collection *Le ceneri di Gramsci* (Gramsci's Ashes), which confirms his heretical position within the Left.

1959 Publishes his second novel, *Una vita violenta* (A Violent Life), which will run into trouble with the law the following year. His father dies.

1960 Plays the role of a partisan fighter in Carlo Lizzani's *Il gobbo* (The Hunchback). Makes it to the final round of the Strega Prize—Italy's most prestigious literary prize—but loses to Tomasi di Lampedusa's *Il gattopardo* (The Leopard). On this occasion, Pasolini reads aloud the long poem "In morte del realismo" (On the Death of Realism), which prefigures his work on the realist tradition in the cinema.

1961 After Fellini's refusal to produce Pasolini's first film, *Accattone*, the director Mauro Bolognini introduces him to Alfredo Bini, who will become the producer of his films through *Edipo re*. *Accattone* is presented at the Venice Film Festival and is favorably reviewed by critics. First trip to the Third World (India and Kenya) with Moravia and Morante.

1962 Appears in court to defend *Accattone* against charges of "immorality" (most of his films will cause him similar problems). Second trip to Africa (Egypt, Sudan, and Kenya), whence he returns with the idea of making a film entitled *African Resistance*. *Mamma Roma* is released.

1963 Buys an apartment in Rome's new residential area, EUR. Travels to Palestine and returns to Africa (Kenya, Ghana, Nigeria, and Guinea) for the third time. Writes the script for a film he will never make, *Il padre selvaggio* (The Savage Father), the story of a relationship between a white teacher and a black student. *La ricotta* and *La rabbia* are released.

1964 Publishes *Poesia in forma di rosa* (Poetry in the Form of a Rose), which contains several poems inspired by filmmaking. *Il Vangelo secondo Matteo* is released. The latter receives a special prize at the Venice Film Festival (Antonioni's *Red Desert* won the Golden Lion).

1965 Participates in Pesaro First International Film Meeting, where he reads the initial draft of his first film theory article, "Il cinema di poesia" (A Cinema of Poetry). Meets Roland Barthes. *Comizi d'amore* (made in 1963) is released.

1966 Hospitalized for an internal hemorrhage; writes the tragedy in verses *Orgia* (Orgy), which will later become half the film *Porcile*. Travels to New York and meets Ginsberg as well as some Black Panthers, forming the impression that America is pervaded by a revolutionary tension. *Uccellacci uccellini* is released.

1967 Begins his years of activity as film theorist/semiotician. *La terra vista dalla luna* and *Edipo re* (his first color film) are released.

1968 Writes the notorious "Il PCI ai giovani" (Give the PCI to the Young), a poem in which he criticizes the student movement, although sustaining its reasons. The sensationalist weekly *Espresso* publishes it under the treacherous title "Vi odio cari studenti" (I Hate You Dear Students). References to this piece will thereafter be (ab)used by many commentators. *Teorema* and *Che cosa sono le nuvole?* are released. *Appunti per un film sull'India* is broadcast on Italian television and subsequently presented at the Venice Film Festival in the documentary section.

1969 Returns to New York and finds it changed: it is "Nixon's America" (Naldini, 334). *La sequenza del fiore di carta*, *Porcile*, and *Medea* are released.

1970 Publishes *Trasumanar e organizzar* (To Transfigure, To Organize), a collection of deliberately "ugly verses." Furthering his critique of Italy's progress, he becomes increasingly critical of the Left and becomes an uncomfortable presence (*una presenza scomoda*) in the contemporary debate. *Appunti per un'Orestiade Africana* and *Il Decamerone* are released.

1971 "I tend more and more towards anarchy" (Naldini, 358). *Il Decamerone* is awarded the Silver Bear at Berlin Film Festival and becomes a blockbuster hit, making Pasolini rich.

1972 Collaborates on the documentary *12 dicembre* (December 12th), a project by the extraparliamentary leftwing group *Lotta Continua* (a proof that, however ambivalently, he *was* on the protesting students' side). *I racconti di Canterbury* is released and wins first prize at Berlin Film Festival.

1973 Starts writing for *Il corriere della sera*: vitriolic articles against consumerism, leftist conformism, and abortion (which will later form the core of *Scritti corsari* (Pirate Writings). "What is a feminist? An extremist, with all the defects of extremists" (Naldini, 370).

1974 *Il fiore delle mille e una notte* is released and awarded the Grand Prize at Cannes Film Festival. By now, leftwing critics have given up on him.

1975 Writes *Lettere Luterane* (Lutheran Letters), in which he proposes to put Christian Democrat leaders on trial for treason. Co-writes with Sergio Citti the script for *Porno-Teo-Kolossal*, a visionary work on "the comet of ideology."[9] On November 2, Pasolini is murdered by a male prostitute under murky circumstances. *Salò o le 120 giornate di Sodoma* is released on November 22 at Paris Film Festival, while Italian authorities veto its release for one year and bring the producer to court for "corruption of minors."

1976 While many denounce Pasolini's murder as a political conspiracy (was the assassin alone?), the hagiographic rereading of his work begins. Of all the voices that criticized and held Pasolini in contempt while he lived, only a very few are left. Critics start calling him Pier Paolo. Everyone was his friend and admirer. The canonization is under way . . .

1

Authorial Intertext

Once the connection between homosexuality and coded references to it was established, the fact of homosexuality had entered, however vaguely, the public consciousness. It was mainly to prevent the focusing and exploration of this awareness that the censors acted.

Vito Russo

The richness and openness of Pasolini's work is the result of his intellectual piracy—that is, of his highly personal appropriation of different, seemingly contradictory, discourses. As a preliminary step, then, I propose to identify such discourses, to define the role they had, and to manifest the traces they left. I will call the set of discourses that came together and interacted in Pasolini's essays and films his *authorial intertext*. Authorship, from a discursive point of view, is an intersection of texts, a relay of discourses. Every author, every body, incorporates texts and discourses. With the exception of authors drawing their energy from only one discourse (e.g., the work of a dogmatic Marxist), every oeuvre originates in an authorial intertext. Yet an authorial intertext as complex and inherently contradictory as Pasolini's is difficult to find.

The identification of Pasolini's authorial intertext is bound to be partially arbitrary and reductive. One could argue, for example, that linguistics, phenomenology, and cultural anthropology were all somehow present in it. The point, however, is not to determine Pasolini's familiarity with and occasional borrowings from certain disciplines. Rather, it is a matter of identifying the ultimate and continuous foundations of his texts. While taking responsibility for the arbitrariness of my operation, I invite the reader to think of the strategy implicit in it, the strategy of regarding Pasolini's textuality as the shifting intersection of some key discourses.

As a point of fact, Pasolini himself suggested the composition of his authorial intertext in *Edipo re* (*Oedipus Rex*, 1967), his most explicitly autobiographical film. The last segment of *Edipo re* is set in modern Italy and depicts blind Oedipus's (Franco Citti) final wanderings. Accompanied by Anghelos (Ninetto Davoli), Oedipus plays the flute— Pasolini's symbol for poetic activity—first on the steps of the cathedral in Bologna, and then near a factory in industrialized Milan. The last images of the film show Oedipus returning to the meadow where Jocasta used to take him as a child. Commenting on the significance of this ending, Pasolini remarked, "First Oedipus is a decadent poet, then a Marxist poet, then nothing at all, someone who is going to die."[1] On closer inspection, and in perfect keeping with his contemporaneous interest in allegorical representation (those were the years of *Teorema* and *Porcile*), this brief sequence brilliantly illustrates the five major discourses from which Pasolini's work drew its intriguing complexity: Bologna, the city in which he was enrolled as a university student, and its cathedral indicate both the humanism of his early years and his adolescent Catholicism; the factory represents his Marxism; and the return to his childhood and to the relationship with his mother indicate his interest in psychoanalysis. The concurrent replacement of Antigone with Anghelos as the person who accompanies Oedipus suggests Pasolini's homosexuality.

Humanism, Catholicism, Marxism, psychoanalysis, and homosexuality: the polycentric character of Pasolini's film theory and practice was the result of his participation in these discourses as they circulated in Italian culture during his lifetime. Of course, it was not a matter of a clean slate between different phases, with one discourse replacing the other, as *Edipo re* seems to imply. More often than not they all coexisted, forming an authorial intertext whose nearly infinite permutations gave his work its "volcanic" uniqueness.

Humanism, Catholicism, Marxism, psychoanalysis, and homosexuality endowed him with rational strategies, cognitive gestures, and discursive needs. They provided his theory with epistemological foundations and acted as archives of images and rhetorical figures, representations and self-representations. In addition, these five discourses offered him a multiplicity of different subject positions. One could even say that Pasolini shaped and apprehended his subjectivity thanks to the tools offered to him by this authorial intertext. This is not to say that he was mechanically determined by these discourses, nor that he was "spoken" by them, as a structuralist account would have it. Rather, Pasolini interacted with them, modifying them, subjecting them to strenuous tensions, provoking ruptures, engineering serendipitous findings.

What follows is a tentative charting of Pasolini's authorial intertext. As if on the black vault of a planetarium in a museum of science, I will light up the five textual constellations across which Pasolini's film theory and practice shed their lights and cast their shadows.

Humanism

There is no doubt that Pasolini's intellectual development was shaped by the humanism at the core of the Italian school program, indeed of Italian culture *tout court*, at least until the sixties. After the *liceo classico* (a high school which emphasizes the study of the classics through a five-year program in Greek and Latin), he attended the University of Bologna, where he studied Italian literature, Romance philology, and art history. Originally he intended to write his dissertation with Longhi on twentieth-century Italian painting. He eventually wrote it on Pascoli, a "decadent" poet known for his love of rural life, his linguistic experimentation, and his poetics of the *fanciullino* (little child), a poetry that taps the *puer* in our souls.

Unlike his later struggles with Catholicism, Pasolini never really questioned his humanistic education. To be sure, on some occasions he used the term to describe the stale culture of Italian academics and state bureaucrats. And we shall see that his passage from literature to cinema was, among other things, an attack on humanist ideology. But the foundations of Pasolini's thought always bore the trace of humanism. More often than not, he gave the term "humanist" a positive connotation, relating it to the idea of history as the continual process of perfecting an abstract humanity. He regretted the advent of technocracy and consumerism with its concomitant loss of humanistic values. Humanism, in other words, was for him a signifier of "human" resistance against the postindustrial nightmare. The role played by humanism in his authorial intertext was varied and is not always acknowledged as such. Pasolini's humanistic formation brought along a canon, a set of paradigms, to be kept in mind during the discussion of his theory and films.

The word *humanist* belongs to a complex group of words (including *human*, *humane*, *humanity*, and *humanitarian*) derived from the root *homo*, which metonymically signifies both men and women. Not only is sexual difference effaced from the start, but, since the model for *humanitas* is Western man, ethnocentrism is often part of the game too. In spite of occasional surges of gender awareness, Pasolini used the word *Uomo* (Man) in a way that a feminist critique would find problematic. And, in spite of his declared love for the Third World, he just as often betrayed a Eurocentric perspective.

The acquisition of humanistic cultural "capital" also implies an investment (of time, values, and desire) in the classical tradition and in the "The Great Books." Pasolini often tried hard to prove the unconditional worth of his cultural capital (for example, by reading contemporary situations in the light of references to ancient Greece), without asking himself the question of whether "The Great Books" might not be "Great" just for him and those like him. This explains his constant adaptation of past "masterpieces" as if they were intrinsically modern and, now and then, his myopic disregard for the avant-garde, modernism, feminism, and situationism, even when these could have been mobilized as allies rather than fought as enemies.

Furthermore, humanist discourse involves subject positions in relation to the past (seen as the locus of timeless achievements), the present (seen as the best of possible worlds—that of liberal humanism), and the future (seen as the teleological site of a progressing Mankind). History becomes evolution. Together with Marxism, humanism provided Pasolini with a sense of history as *telos*, as the progress of *one* collective subject (Man or the proletariat). Fortunately for him (and for us), his authorial intertext harbored a discourse, homosexuality, which countered the belief in *one* perspective by exposing the violence implicit in it.

In the field of psychology, humanism presumes the unity of the transcendental subject of consciousness as well as the rational presence of the self suggested by the Cartesian "*cogito.*" Although Pasolini acted out his contradictions in a way that confirmed de facto the hypothesis of a fragmented subjectivity, on certain topics he adamantly clung to the humanist ideal of a subject in total control. Nowhere is this more evident than in his belief in authorship as the expression of individuals who are in control of the meaning they create. Even when he turned to cinema, he underestimated the collective potential expressed through filmmaking and jealously claimed total authorship for his work.

Finally, humanism endowed Pasolini with notions of Beauty and Form which he may have violated at times but which he never forgot. The allegorical ingenuity of Dante's poetry and the centrality of Man in fourteenth-century Italian painting left lasting impressions on his artistic sensibility, gave rise to formal imperatives, and became aesthetic pathos. Humanism contributed to Pasolini's lifelong self-perception as a "poet" and to his unflinching use, always in positive terms, of the word "poetic." As to his identity as a "poet," one must point out that it underwent three phases, as shown by the last segment of *Edipo re*. Until his encounter with Marxism, poetry was for him an almost sacred territory of refined perceptions and expressions. Leftwing ideology brought him to confront the contradictions inherent in such an attitude, and he bent his poetry to a political, "civil" use. By the mid-sixties, he stopped believing in poetry altogether, and, although he never stopped writing verses, he always maintained the sharpest awareness of the loss of poetry's halo.

Ironically, there is a tendency among critics today to revive the early connotations of the word "poet." By resorting to the formula "Pasolini was a poet," critics somehow wish to carve out a special place for Pasolini *and* for themselves as the happy few in a position to savor the implications of "poetry." Differently put, "Pasolini was a poet" has become a convenient catch-phrase for all those who wish to suggest the nuances that "poet" took on in classical humanism, especially that of belonging to the aristocracy of the spirit.

As for the word "poetic," Pasolini used it to allude to the superior status of any signifier that is not straightjacketed into one signified. In fact, "poetic" was the adjective that according to him best described the language "spoken" by reality and by cinematic images.

Catholicism

Until I was fifteen I believed in God with all my adolescent intransigence, which increased the rigidity and the seriousness of my false faith. I was particularly devoted to the Mother. I would provoke fake effusions of religious sentiment in myself, so much so that several times I convinced myself that I had seen the Holy Mother move and smile. In my brief discussions on religion, I would take clearcut stands. The greatest religious anxiety and my first sins coincided. In Reggio Emilia I experienced libidinal desire in all of its violence and I committed my first "impure acts" (I was only fourteen). I would submit to my tendencies without judging them. At night, before going to sleep, I would repent of my sins, reciting hundreds of Holy Marys. . . . In Bologna, at fifteen and a half years old, I took my last communion, because of my cousin's pressures. But it already seemed useless to me. Since then I could never even conceive the possibility of believing in God.[2]

In spite of this declaration, Catholicism continued to exert its influence over Pasolini's thought. It was ingrained in him. Upon his first trip to India, Pasolini remarked, "It will seem absurd, but for the first time I had the impression that Catholicism does not coincide with reality; yet the separation of the two entities was so unexpected and violent that it constituted a kind of trauma."[3] This was in 1962, at the peak of his Marxist commitment, some twenty-five years after he ceased to believe in God. It could be argued that Pasolini's artistic and existential itinerary was, among other things, a struggle to extricate himself from the weaknesses of Catholic belief while preserving its originary moment of faith in the face of mystery. Thanks to the presence of secular discourses in his authorial intertext, he explored the heretical margins of Catholicism, so that Christ became a signifier of passion and God Himself became a feeling, a bodily need, for which no appropriate name existed.

The most visible consequence of the Catholic discourse was, perhaps, Pasolini's guilt for his own "sin." In 1944, for instance, when T., a boy whom Pasolini had loved, fell sick, he wrote, "I was so scared that for the first time I was taken by the scruple of God."[4] Pasolini formed the idea of God as an overbearing presence that thwarts an individual's instinctual life—a Master-Super-Ego—and most effectively dramatized it in the short film *La sequenza del fiore di carta* (The Sequence of the Paper Flower, 1968). And just as Catholic guilt was a constant presence in his life, so was guilt's complementary by-product, the desire for transgression. All of Pasolini's work was traversed by the double gesture of both visualizing a limit and wanting to transgress it.

From the standpoint of artistic influence, Catholicism constituted a strong gravitational pull toward certain *topoi*, such as the mystery of death, the representation of rituals, and Christological imagery. Religious painting provided Pasolini with an iconographic storehouse of images, frames, and compositions. In addition, the Catholic taste for baroque rituals intensified Pasolini's penchant for symbolism and for allegorical representation. The graphic emphasis on Jesus' martyrdom, the visions of blood and thorns, were Pasolini's first encounter with images of physical pain and certainly fueled his future tendency toward the imagery of pathology.

Catholicism's messianic fervor prepared the terrain for Marxism, and Pasolini dedicated much time and energy to the reconciliation of the two. From a political perspective, Pasolini's most fertile intuitions came precisely from the combination of a religious outlook with a radical ideology. In the second half of his life, thanks to the beneficial influence of his travels in the Third World and his readings in cultural anthropology, the mystical strand in the Catholic discourse (e.g., the Desert Fathers) emerged powerfully in his work. Especially in his last decade, when Catholicism confronted the pantheism of Oriental religions, Pasolini attempted to create syntheses that are still bearing fruit.

He began to conceive of religious feelings as the authentic antagonist to bourgeois materialism. He was led by his interest in mythology to revive premodern values and broach the discourse of postmodern spirituality. As an enlarged notion of the sacred made him perceive the spiritual bond that connects humans to the Earth, Pasolini came close to articulating his Marxist anger with an ecological consciousness.

Catholicism also nurtured Pasolini's famed myth of innocence, according to which the peasantry, subproletariat, and Third World represent existence outside of Western history. As these subcultures' resistance against cooptation would consist of ignorance rather than knowledge, of indifference rather than struggle, Pasolini's idea of innocence owes much to the Catholic myth of *beati pauperes spiritu*. At its best, this idea caused Pasolini to challenge leftist conformism and to shun the rhetorics of the proletariat. It also enabled him to debunk dialectics, for it suggested that there are only oppositions, theses and antitheses, history and what lies outside of it, and that any synthesis is nothing but the colonization of the margins by the center. Differently put, this idea contained the seed of a non-Marxist form of political opposition. It suggested that the outsider's autonomy is better than a dialectical synthesis, for the latter would effect the reduction of differences to one ruling model.

At its worst, the myth of innocence is a mere projection. It projects an ideal alterity onto the backs of people who do not have the chance to understand, appreciate, negotiate, or refute the role into which they are forced, and thereby creates the impression that radical difference is something falling on us from above and not the result of a choice. In other words, Pasolini's mythology of innocence suffered from his condescending superiority complex so clearly evinced by occasional comments such as this: "Quite incredible is the inner disorder, the unawareness and shamelessness of these peasant kids. Their impure laughter kept resounding amidst senseless words—a bunch of apes."[5] Like the idea of the good savage, the Pasolinian mythology of innocence betrayed its essential Catholic (humanist, intellectual) conceit: the sense that we have been blessed by truth and by the duty to administer it.

All things considered, the presence of Catholicism in Pasolini's authorial intertext had a beneficial influence, for it opposed the secular tendencies of humanism, Marxism, and psychoanalysis. Thanks to his religious leanings, Pasolini became a fierce opponent of the dialectic of the Enlightenment. In fact, the Catholic discourse was perhaps his most controversial, since it led him to emphasize values and cognitive modes for which academic secularism and progressive thinking have no tolerance.

Marxism

In 1944, under the combat name of Partisan Hermes, Pasolini's younger brother Guido joined anti-Fascist fighters in the mountains. A touching example of a far-gone past, he left home on a clear morning in May carrying a backpack loaded with bread, a hollow dictionary concealing a pistol, and a book of poetry, Dino Campana's *Canti Orfici*. Once in the mountains, Hermes took the side of the non-Communist *Partito d'azione*. As the German defeat seemed more and more inevitable, the disputes among the various factions intensified. And Partisan Hermes was killed, at nineteen, by Communists associated with Tito's army, people who equally opposed the Nazis but had a different view of Italy's future.

Two years later, in the tense climate of postwar reconstruction, Pasolini participated in the struggle waged by Frioulan day laborers against landowners and decided to join the Communist party (PCI), his ideological convictions largely due to the influence of reading Gramsci. His membership ended abruptly in 1949 when he was expelled from the party because of his homosexuality:

> Faced with the facts which have determined a serious disciplinary action against the poet Pasolini, we wish to denounce once again the dangerous consequences of certain ideological and philosophical currents by Gide, Sartre and other decadent writers, who pride themselves as progressives but are in fact the catalysts of the most harmful aspects of bourgeois depravity.[6]

In spite of such first-hand experience of what he would later call "leftwing fascism," Pasolini was to stay close to the Communist party throughout his life. In the 1975 elections he gave his vote to the PCI, and the articles that he wrote before his death reiterated his faith in the moral superiority of Italian Communists. Indeed, Pasolini's unorthodox and highly personalized Marxism represented the most prominent discourse in his authorial intertext, the one that provided him with the public subject position from which he couched his ideological views as well as most of his theoretical writings.

Why such dedication to an ideology in the name of which so much harm had befallen him? Perhaps the main reason for Pasolini's clinging to a Marxist identity lies in his conviction that we all must reckon with tradition. And for the politically committed and culturally prominent, Marxism was the tradition. To operate outside a fruitful and, of course, critical relationship with the past was neither possible nor desirable for Pasolini. Hence, he assumed a discursive Marxist identity to ensure that his ideas would end up enriching the most serious tradition we have in cultural antagonism.

Of course there were other reasons. In postwar Italy, the Left had succeeded in forming a cultural bloc that included the most capable intellectuals and artists of the time (Vittorini, Pavese, Fortini, Visconti, and Zavattini, to name but a few) and produced works of undisputed value. It was virtually impossible not to feel the spell of such a collective effort. Moreover, in Marxism, Pasolini found an ideology that gave him the tools to think through the problems of oppression. His Gramscian version of Marxism endowed him with a large umbrella under which even some of the humanistic and Catholic principles dear to him could gather. For example, he often pointed out that by postulating a socialist future, dialectical materialism prevented the disintegration of "History" and thus, like humanism, saved the past of "Man." And just as often, he stressed the contiguity between Marxism and Christianity. Finally, in addition to the promise of a paradise on earth and the offering of a metahistorical episteme legitimizing knowledge, Marxism gave artists and intellectuals an identity and a role. By providing artists with what Fortini called a "mandate," Marxist *engagement* actually offered the best possible answer to the crisis tainting the self-images of those engaged in merely intellectual labor.[7]

On the subject of self-identity, I already remarked that the word Pasolini used most frequently to describe himself was "poet." Not only did the encounter with Marxism subject this self-image to the imperative of engagement, but it also offered him the tools to think and speak of himself as a member of a social class. Thanks to Marxism, Pasolini was able to grasp the basic contradiction at the heart of his social position: He was ideologically against the class to which he belonged and which gave him the means of production. To use Pierre Bourdieu's terminology, Pasolini became aware of belonging to the dominated fractions of the dominant class.[8] He began to see himself as a product of the "petty bourgeoisie." Readers of Pasolini's essays are struck by the frequency with which he employed this term, accusing other directors, writers, and himself of being petty bourgeois. During the last years of his life, Pasolini visualized the end of the humanistic world as he knew it as the transformation of all mankind into a mass of petty bourgeois. At the same time, he often maintained that the fundamental characteristic of the petty bourgeoisie was its idealism. Far from being employed with Marxist rigor, the adjective *petit-bourgeois* was, for Pasolini, an open signifier, a signifier of both idealism and narrow-mindedness, a signifier, above all, of contradictions. Pasolini's reiterated definition of himself as a petty bourgeois should be taken as an indication that for him the term harbored contradictions. He found himself couched in the middle of a vertical social spectrum and was therefore open to the ambivalent tensions of what was above and what was below.

To be sure, the hegemonic role that Marxism had in his authorial intertext exacted its toll: it acted as guilty conscience (a replacement for God); it forced participation in the game of detecting who was being more politically correct; it set forth a series of obligations to be honored on every discursive outing (e.g., the duty of historical optimism); it even created delusional fantasies whereby perceived Reality was in fact marred by the most unrealistic idealism (such as when militants waste away while attempting to visualize the collapse of capitalism).

Perhaps the best way to picture the toll exacted by Marxism is to call to mind the figure of Valentin, the middle-class revolutionary in Hector Babenco's *Kiss of the Spider Woman* (1984). Since the two epithets used most often to qualify Pasolini in Italy or abroad were "Marxist" and/or "homosexual," it is tempting to understand the interaction between his Marxism and his homosexuality by way of the relationship between Valentin and the "queen" Molina in Babenco's film: revolutionary reason and deviant passion are forced into the same prison cell. *Kiss of the Spider Woman* portrays their mutual lack of comprehension and exaggerates Valentin's inability to accept Molina as a comrade fighting a common enemy in his own way. Because he is incapable of understanding the reality of the struggle in terms other than armed militancy, Valentin fails to appreciate the genuinely subversive quality of Molina's difference. Not only did the Communist party act like Valentin, but Pasolini himself gave voice to an orthodox Marxism like Valentin's in his authorial intertext, a voice that followed the party line on private matters and refused to seek out a common strategy with the homosexual thrown in the same jail cell.

Psychoanalysis

Toward the end of the linguistic essay "Dal laboratorio" (From the Laboratory, 1965), Pasolini made one of his customary autobiographical detours and recounted a childhood episode. After confessing "a desperate love" for his mother, he wrote,

> In that period at Belluno, precisely between three and three and a half years, I experienced the first pangs of sexual love: identical to those that I would then have up to now (atrociously acute from sixteen to thirty)— that terrible and anxious sweetness that seizes the viscera and consumes them, burns them, twists them, like a hot melting gust of wind in the presence of the love object. I believe I remember only the leg of this love object—and exactly the hollow behind the knee with its taut tendons. . . . Naturally I did not know what it was about; I knew only the physical nature of the presence of that feeling, so dense and burning that it twisted my viscera. I therefore found myself with the physical necessity

of "naming" that sentiment, and, in my condition as only an oral speaker, not a writer, I invented a word. This term was, I remember perfectly, TETA VELETA (*HE*, p. 66).[9]

This memory had such a special place in his mind that he referred to it on two other occasions: in *Quaderni rossi* (1946), and during an interview with Dacia Maraini (1971).[10] Interestingly, the 1946 version does not speak of the *teta veleta* feeling as overtly sexual, but merely calls it "sensual," stressing the melancholy sensation of an unreachable object, the bittersweet emptiness of a desire "for which no name exists as of yet," a sort of romantic *Sehnsucht*. By 1965, then, two key changes had occurred. The idea of infantile sexuality, the lynchpin of Freudian theory, makes its unquestioned appearance: the *teta veleta* feeling is now redefined as "pangs of sexual love." And, more important, the recollection of such "pangs" is coupled with the confession of a "desperate love" for the mother. These two changes will be reiterated in the 1972 version, in which Pasolini tells Maraini that the *teta veleta* feeling is the same as that which he felt for his mother's breast.

This new perspective reveals the extent to which, by the mid-sixties, Pasolini had enthusiastically subscribed to the Freudianism that had been widely, if superficially, circulating in Italian culture since the fifties. The advantages that Pasolini may have derived from accepting Freudian discourse are obvious. In the first place Freudianism, like Marxism, constituted an attack on bourgeois ideology, so much so that a reconciliation between the two approaches was being thought possible at the time (e.g., Sartre's *Search for a Method* and Marcuse's *Eros and Civilization*). Furthermore, Freud's emphasis on biological drives appealed to Pasolini's interest in "physical necessities" as the source of cultural phenomena. Grounding the higher functions firmly in the flesh, Freudian psychoanalysis suited Pasolini's project of giving sexuality and the body their due. In this respect Freud's theory of the *id* as something to be salvaged from the discontents of civilization runs parallel to the Marxist mythology of the heroic proletariat. Most important of all, Freud offered Pasolini a clear and coherent "scientific" theory of the etiology and phenomenology of homosexuality.

Couched within psychoanalytic discourse, homosexuality stopped being a sin or a decadent vice and became the unfortunate result of a protracted love for/by the mother and a faulty resolution of the Oedipal complex. Although Freud changed his mind several times on the relationship between homosexuality and psychopathology, it is safe to say that he never regarded homosexuals as perverts and that on more than one occasion he showed the utmost respect for their achievements (e.g., in his monograph on Leonardo da Vinci).[11] Still, homosexuality remained for Freud a matter of inhibited normal functioning, which is precisely the theory that Pasolini assimilated. Indeed, of all the discourses in his authorial intertext, Freudian psychoanalysis is the one in which Pasolini was the least creative, for he accepted it as science.

Pasolini's relationship with the psychoanalytic discourse was not limited to Freud but extended to Jung, especially in the 1965–1975 decade. The 1965 version of the *teta veleta* recollection contains Jungian overtones that partially undermine Pasolini's militancy in the Freudian camp. In the paragraph following the one cited above, Pasolini reports that literary critic and philologist Gianfranco Contini once told him that *teta veleta* "was a matter of a reminder of an ancient Greek word, *Tetis* (sex, be it masculine or feminine, as everyone knows)." As Pasolini himself had noted at the outset of the section on *teta veleta*, this new piece of information casts a Jungian shadow on the entire argument: How can a child utter Greek mnemonics if a collective unconscious is not somehow at work? Not a rigorous thinker, Pasolini may have peacefully reconciled Jung and Freud; but the question then becomes: Just how much Jung is present in Pasolini almost unnoticed, in the background and yet supporting the entire discursive thrust? This is one of the few times in which Pasolini lets himself mention Jung, even though, as his friend and collaborator Zigaina reports, he knew Jung's works extremely well.[12] Zigaina goes so far as to postulate an alchemical secret behind Pasolini's reticence. I content myself with suggesting that because of the ban on Jung imposed by the leftist culture around Pasolini, his fecund appropriation of Jung's ideas took place undercover. In fact, there is a sense in which Jung was more congenial to Pasolini than was Freud. Like Pasolini, Jung never severed his ties with Christianity and always maintained that we need to distinguish between religiousness and organized religion. He was also at some point convinced that the only truly realist perspective is the one afforded by mythology, and he did not regard Thanatos as the perennial opponent of Eros but as the first and last metaphor, the most powerful mythical presence in the psychic underworld. Furthermore, the Jungian theory of *anima* as a feminine component in every man's soul well suited an individual who felt guilty about not living up to masculinity's requirements.

Homosexuality

I want *to kill* a hypersensitive and sick adolescent who is also trying to contaminate my life as a man; he is almost moribund, but I shall be cruel, even though at bottom I love him, because he has been my life until today. As to girls, I spend hours of desire and vague dreams alternating with inane, or, better, silly attempts at action as well as with periods of extreme indifference: three days ago Paria and I walked to the threshold of a brothel, where the bad breath of naked, fat forty-year-old mamas made us look back at innocent childhood with nostalgia. We then urinated hopelessly.[13]

As this excerpt from a 1941 letter to his friend Farolfi makes clear, nineteen-year-old Pasolini was still trying to pass for straight and "to kill" his "sickness." He knew, however, that this was not possible: "In my individual development I have been very precocious; and I was not like Gide who suddenly screamed 'I am different from anyone else!' with unexpected anguish. I have always known."[14] By 1949 his closest friends were informed of his homoerotic tendencies and he himself thought he had overcome, "all bloody and scarred," the trauma of his "rot." Still, he certainly was not ready to come out of the closet.[15] But on October 15, Pasolini, then a teacher and a political activist, was accused by the carabinieri of Corcovado of having enticed minors on the occasion of the feast in Ramuscello, a hamlet at the outskirts of San Vito al Tagliamento. As a result of the scandal, he was fired from his job and had to leave Friuli. He moved to Rome, where he did not know anybody. With his homosexuality forced out of the closet, what had thus far been a soliloquy nurtured by guilt and secret wishes became a public discourse. From then on Pasolini had to defend and explain his sexuality before the state, his family, his friends, and his actual readers as well as the readers in his head. He also had to renegotiate his self-image, for he no longer had the relative protection of invisibility. He was now more vulnerable to the concerted attacks of an opponent whose overwhelming majority cast him against nature, against himself, and on the road to self-loathing. All this was standard fare for many homosexuals who grew up before the days of the gay liberation movement, and Pasolini's adventure was less personal than it sounds. In fact, his was a personal way of living a preordained text, a discourse which ran in the interstices of Italian culture much like Marxism and Catholicism, albeit with much less legitimacy and visibility.

According to so-called social constructionists, the categories homosexual/heterosexual are not rooted in some universal syntax of sexual desire but are the product of a recent conceptual turn in thinking about sex and deviance. Sexual activity among members of the same sex has of course always existed, but the term "homosexuality," argues David Halperin in the wake of Foucault, is only one hundred years old.[16] Although it is a seemingly bland clinical term, homosexuality as a discourse carries along an ideological baggage, that is, a network of pseudomedical representations and self-representations. Active participation in the homosexual discourse involves a subject position and a scopic regime, a way of being and seeing that is historically specific and is located at the intersection of individual responses on one side and the constraints of a sociocultural grid on the other.

The homosexual discourse in Pasolini is a hard one to trace in all of its manifestations, and the critical apparatus has not helped much. There is no agreement as to the importance that the homosexual discourse had in his authorial intertext. On the one hand, the majority of straight critics, especially the Italian ones, chose to downplay the issue, either through recourse to a few psychoanalytical formulas or through euphemisms. Paradoxically, in Italy it was the district attorney, the criminal anthropologist, the sensationalist tabloid who emphasized the importance of Pasolini's homosexuality. It is as if those in the ranks of high culture were afraid of diminishing the "artistic" status of Pasolini's work. More important than being a homosexual, Pasolini was "a poet." In a sense, by purifying his image, many critics robbed him of an essential part of himself. This is nowhere clearer than in the attempt to see a fascist plot in his murder. Pasolini's murder was political in that the condition in which homosexuals in Italy were (and are) forced to live their sexual lives is part of a sociosexual structure. But, as Dario Bellezza has knowingly pointed out, the murder carried all the marks of a specific subculture.[17] One must have the courage to see that Pasolini was a great artist, not in spite of his homosexuality but in part because of it—because of what he saw from his particular position inside the homosexual discourse.

In open contrast to all this, gay critics gave his homosexuality the utmost importance. They acknowledged Pasolini as yet another one of their martyrs while voicing reservations about his lack of gay awareness and pride. As Richard Dyer noted, Pasolini's homosexual discourse "is deeply scarred" by the fact that he "tried to think and feel" his "gayness in terms of heterosexual norms, which means in terms of guilt, sin, sickness, inadequacy, perversion, decadence."[18] Pasolini internalized many of the norms of heterosexist patriarchy and conceptualized his homosexuality within the restrictions and shadows imposed by the other discourses in his authorial intertext. While this could be the subject of a book in itself, it is worth at least outlining the effects of the homosexual discourse in Pasolini's authorial intertext.

Pasolini was keenly aware of the importance of the body and sexuality. This had momentous consequences for his film theory and practice. It led him to downplay the role of the mind and to counter the rationalist tendencies of the other four discourses in his theoretical writings. If psychoanalysis provided him with the tools to talk about the body *rationally*, homosexuality gave him the certainty that the body is a purveyor of knowledge. Moreover, the homosexual discourse had inevitable repercussions on the way Pasolini regarded the oppressor/oppressed dialectic. It exposed Marxism's inadequacy in addressing sexual oppression and led him to highlight the private sphere as a terrain for struggle. As to his film practice, the emphasis on sexuality and the body resulted in the frequent depiction of sexual encounters and, more generally, in what goes by the name of the "physicality" (*fisicità*) of his images.

Marked for life by the events of 1949, he engaged in a tireless struggle with state censorship, striving to transgress the limits imposed by the existing codes of what was representable. He thus had to face the humiliation of being brought to court because of the allegedly "obscene" quality of virtually all of his novels and films. He was tried thirty-three times—once even after his death—in a grotesque ritual in which power merely aimed at reinforcing its (self)image as power.[19]

The homosexual discourse forced him to occupy an ambivalent position in gender relations. Extending Bourdieu's definition of the lines of power traversing and overdetermining each individual's life, we can say that Pasolini belonged to the dominated fraction of the dominant sex. As a result, his position in both economic (petty-bourgeois) and sexual (homosexual) relations bore the mark of ambivalence, of a simultaneous participation in what is "above" and what is "below." This in turn explains why Pasolini so often chose to situate his art in the middle ground between "high" and "low," a mixture of high art and low imagery, of high culture and subculture.

But the most crucial consequence of the homosexual discourse lay elsewhere. As Pasolini's homosexual self was practically coerced into a situation of obligatory silence, he could refer to his sexual oppression only by allusions and circumlocutions. This, in turn, fostered a metaphorical tendency in his works through the desire to find groups or individuals whose condition could function as an analogical correlative to his own. Hence arose his identification with those who are outside history (peasants and the subproletariat), those who are the victims of history (Jews and Blacks), and those who are in the margins of society (thieves).

Finally, it is tempting to see Pasolini's lifelong obsession with reality in light of his homosexuality. The constant experience of the real Pasolini (what he felt he was), as opposed to the Pasolini as perceived by others, convinced him of the existence of a gap between reality and representation, reality and the mask. Inevitably this led to the desire to pursue reality as what lies beneath the mask. Critics have often pointed out that Pasolini's conception of reality was quite undifferentiated and visceral. They sensed that the word "reality" did something for him which exceeded the boundaries of theoretical discourse. Perhaps they felt that in some obscure, emotional way Pasolini's use of the word "reality" was not pure, but carried with it the weight of a vague allusion to his homosexuality. What is certain is that while Pasolini openly and publicly situated himself in relationship to the other four discourses, he rarely spoke of his homosexuality. He relegated his homosexual discourse to the bottom, as it were, of his multilayered authorial intertext. As with dreams, where the latent content surfaces after the requirements of representation have been satisfied (through displacement, condensation, and censorship), homosexuality surfaced by means of "poetic" signifiers, those which were capable of carrying a surplus of personal signification. It is therefore plausible to assume that "reality" became one of such signifiers through which the homosexual text would emerge from the depths. Pasolini himself suggested the psychosexual tensions implicit in his treatment of "reality" through frequent allusions to his "hallucinated, infantile, and pragmatic love for reality" as something that is "religious in that in some way it is fused, by analogy, with a sort of immense sexual fetishism" (*HE*, p. 225).

The hypothesis of a connection between the mask and what lay behind it on the one hand, and the problematic of reality and representation on the other, is confirmed by a 1946 entry in his diary.

> Once I entered puberty, drawing acquired another meaning: the "average" aspirations instilled by family and teachers merged together with the fantastic ones deriving from the reading of Homer and Verne. Together, they would offer me a world, *another* world, which I, totally anguished, would try to comprehend on those ugly drawing sheets. Here I should talk about Achilles' shield, about how much I suffered because of that tremendous shield. In fact, that was the first time in which I felt anguished because of the difference between reality and representation.[20]

The advent of puberty, that is of sexuality, brought along an anguish related to the representation of a reality that could not be totally contained. Pasolini felt the need for a more realistic representation. But more than informing us about what he actually thought when drawing as a boy, this 1946 recollection indicates that twenty-four-year-old Pasolini still thought of reality and representation in terms of anguish. Let us not forget that these were the years of his passing as a heterosexual and of his struggle against the dominant representations of homosexuality: the years of the mask. The desire for realism would then be primarily inscribed as an effect of the homosexual discourse.

Existing outside a visible and open social text, Pasolini's homosexual discourse could not receive rational articulation per se. It sought an outlet through analogical representations. The homosexual discourse was like a dark presence operating at a sentimental and sensory level. It made him *feel* the existence of a painful discrepancy between reality and representation. It made his discourse on reality more viscerally felt. It made for a theory ignited by need, fueled by desire.

> It has been said that I have three heroes: Christ, Marx, and Freud. This is reducing everything to formulae. In truth, my only hero is *reality*.[21]

Seen from the standpoint of realism, it is certainly no accident that Pasolini's authorial intertext comprises three discourses that are founded on the desire to exorcise and express the discrepancy between reality and appearances. Catholic discourse posits the existence of an unseen beyond, an ultimate reality that cannot be verified but merely accepted by a leap of faith. The entire edifice of Marxism is based on the attempt to pierce the crust of ideological representations (appearances) and to expose the economic base (reality). And psychoanalysis, positing as it does the existence of a more authentic self made of unconscious drives, is equally implicated in maintaining the split between what appears to be and what really is. If he was, so to speak, "breastfed" on humanism and Catholicism, the adult Pasolini chose Marxism and psychonalysis as two discourses capable of furthering and enhancing his "pragmatic love."

2

Extravagantly Interdisciplinary

In order to be truly alive, philosophy cannot but contain light, sounds, energy, vibrations of the soul and the body: when all of these are weak, philosophy stops being the plan of a grand flight and becomes an academic discipline. Philosophy is not a system of thought; it is, instead, a castle of light. And if philosophy has a place of its own, it is not the mind alone: it is mind, heart, skin, cells, neurochemical receptors, senses.

Franco Bolelli

To understand the nature of Pasolini's theoretical production, it may be useful to recall Richard Rorty's distinction between "the informed dilettante, the polypragmatic, Socratic intermediary between various discourses" and "the Platonic philosopher-king who knows what everybody else is really doing whether *they* know it or not because he knows about the ultimate context."[1] Partial to the former and sarcastic toward the latter, Rorty reminds us that, whereas Philosophy constantly strives for an ultimate anchor of rational purity, philosophy is a "conversation on how things hang together" with no special method. "Pragmatists are saying," he argues, "that the best hope for philosophy is not to practice Philosophy."[2]

Pasolini was an "informed dilettante." While film specialists and full-time semioticians paraded the methodological rigor and the selective language so typical of Theory, he merely practiced theory, and consciously so. The opening sentence of his most controversial film essay, "The Written Language of Reality," is absolutely exemplary in this respect:

> I am listing a few points, not in strictly logical correlation among themselves, which must be kept in mind while reading these pages (as usual so extravagantly interdisciplinary) (*HE*, p. 197).

This might well be the preface to all of Pasolini's writings on cinema, for they always proceeded by leaps and repetitions, eschewing logical rigor and providing, at their best, uncanny intuitions. At their worst, they sounded like a pretentious concoction of personal obsessions. Whatever their value, all his essays were "extravagant" and "interdisciplinary," incorporating discourses that no "serious" scholar would have dreamt of pulling together. For many of his critics, this was intolerable. Systematic thinkers objected to Pasolini's bricolage of heterogeneous fragments, to his quick changes of discursive register, to his wandering among conceptual frameworks, to his poetic and diaristic incursions into the space of rational analysis—in short, to his practice of "pirate intellect."

Twenty-five years later, in the wake of postmodernism and feminism, his theoretical "extravagance" bears scrutiny. Much of what goes by the name of postmodern thinking seeks to undercut the standard oppositions between logos and mythos, logic and rhetoric, concept and metaphor. Postmodernism has also exposed the ideological fragility of any distinction between "high" and "low" cultures. Feminism, by showing that Reason's traditional aspiration to universal objectivity rests on the systematic repression of sexual difference, has brought about a so-called crisis of reason and has often effected a return to "irrational" intuitions as viable theoretical strategies.[3] Meanwhile, an extended critique of disciplinary boundaries has enhanced experimentation and contamination across different fields. The birth of "Cultural Studies" as a legitimate academic discipline has sanctioned the practice of "interdisciplinary extravagance." In the light of these epochal changes, what appeared to be a weakness in Pasolini's mode of theorizing now turns out to be its strength.

Not only did Pasolini contaminate the purity of theoretical discourse but he also removed it from its canonical sites. Newspaper articles and poems stood side by side with his "serious" essays, often functioning as a practical test for the use-value of theory. In fact, Pasolini's theoretical practice gave wider scope to Gramsci's notion that "all men are intellectuals, although only a few do it as a profession."[4] Surreptitiously, Pasolini's mode of theorizing proved that all signifying practices are theoretical, although only a few theorize explicitly. Everyone is involved in theory, formulates theory, because even the most elementary feelings and observations stem from a more or less conscious theoretical grid, of which they are the expression. Theory, then, can and must be practiced through a wide variety of textual modes, of which the canonical essay-form is just one, and not even the most effective. No sooner did Pasolini acknowledge the crisis of rational, written argumentation than he tried new outlets for his reflections. As I hope to demonstrate, he even sought to formulate theory through the medium of cinema, with the film *Teorema*.

An inevitable and somewhat unfortunate consequence of Pasolini's mode of theorizing was the wide dispersion of his ideas on either cinema or semiotics, a dispersion that occasionally makes it necessary for us to turn to a poem or to a newspaper article to retrieve the best formulation of a problem. Things are further complicated by the fact that the essays collected in *HE* are only a part of Pasolini's writings on cinema. The rest of them are, at least in Italy, still scattered in the various sources where they first appeared.[5]

The most conspicuous group of articles on film outside *HE* resulted from his short-lived collaboration with the magazine *Reporter* in 1959–1960. This was a "pre-semiotic" Pasolini who, astride literature and cinema, tested the possibility of doing film criticism by means of literary tools. If such a habit was often irritatingly reductive and somehow confirmed the ancillary role that cinema had vis-à-vis more pedigreed arts, it did have a redeeming quality: it stressed the common denominator between film and literature and therefore opposed the isolation of film studies. In "The Catholic Irrationalism of Fellini," which, incidentally, is the only article from his earlier output available in English, Pasolini complained about the "profound separation between literature and cinematic criticism," which are like "two rivers that flow parallel and never merge as though there were two cultures or two histories in Italy."[6] As a remedy to "this absurd situation," he proposed the practice of "critically basing the study of a book or film on the same aesthetic and ideological principles, keeping in mind that their difference is simply technical." Rudimentary though this statement may have been (and Pasolini himself would later change his mind about the "simply technical" difference between the two media), it emphasized his effort to base literary and film studies on something outside the text, which at the time he called "aesthetic and ideological principles." But it was not until he discovered semiotics that Pasolini found the ideal tools to turn film theory into a philosophical endeavor, which is what *HE* did.

HE collects essays that Pasolini wrote in the period 1964–1970 and later re-ordered for publication in 1972. Although it is divided into three sections—Linguistics, Literature, and Cinema—*HE* exhibits a common, obsessive concern: the effort to rethink the discourse on social and cultural reality by means of semiotics and film theory. *HE* can be read, ought to be read, as a long, multifaceted essay revealing the extent to which film theory and semiotics—as practiced by Pasolini—are philosophy's most logical outlets. Semiotics, by transforming everything into a sign, is the most useful tool in the ongoing "conversation on how things hang together." And film theory, thanks to cinema's proximity to "the language of reality," is a necessary step in any philosophical conversation.

The cultural backdrop of the essays in *HE* extends from phenomenology to cultural anthropology, from structuralism to existentialism, all in Pasolini's "extravagantly interdisciplinary" mode. For all of its "extravagance," however, *HE* does provide a few remarks betraying its author's position. On one occasion, Pasolini openly states that he does "not have and never will have an alternative other than Marxism" as "the only ideology that protects me from the loss of reality" (71–72). Elsewhere, he reminds the reader of the crisis of Marxism, which he blames on its excessive rationalism. Or he professes the intent of contributing to "the renewal of Marxism" by means of "extravagant" borrowings from other thought systems. Seen in this light, *HE* is something like a homeopathic cure for Marxism's disease, a typically Gramscian attempt to reinvigorate our ideology by incorporating whatever we find useful in our opponents' ideas. It may be argued that the film essays rarely mention Marxism; rather, they exemplify Pasolini's detachment from it and must be read separately. Still, while spanning the years of his disillusionment with the Left, the film essays are remarkably consistent in contributing to the project of disempowering rationality, according to Pasolini the main cause of Marxism's crisis. In fact, it seems to me that no sooner does Pasolini stop declaring the need for "the renewal of Marxism" than he actually sets out to expand its horizons by means of an exemplary theoretical practice.

The films essays in *HE* tackle several issues, such as the "cinema of prose/cinema of poetry" distinction, the "pregrammatical" nature of film images, and the comparison between death and montage (I will speak of these in the course of the film analyses). Pasolini's main concern, however, as well as the source of his most useful intuitions, lies in his treatment of the relationship between cinema and reality and in his notion of reality as a language. It is to this set of theoretical problems that the present chapter is dedicated.

The Written Language of Reality

Pasolini's ideas on cinema ought to be read against the backdrop of the contemporary debate on the question of whether or not cinema is a language and on the status of the iconic sign (do images represent their referents in a natural way or through less obvious but no less operative cultural codes?). Both questions were a symptom of the credibility that semiotics (then semiology) was acquiring through Bettetini, Eco, and Garroni in Italy, Barthes and Metz in France. Their work accomplished the much-needed task of showing that virtually no aspect of our reality is "natural" but depends instead on petrified cultural conventions. As psychoanalysis had done with minor psychic occurrences, semiotics transformed everything into a signifier. Paraphrasing Freud's famous dictum, the battle cry of semiotics back then was "where nature (id) was, there shall culture (ego) be."

As the purveyor of the infamous "impression of reality," cinema soon became the target of semioticians' attention. The commonsensical notion that film images are objective reproductions of profilmic reality (what is in front of the camera) was ruthlessly stamped out in all of its manifestations. Situated within this context, some of Pasolini's statements in the essay "The Written Language of Reality" outrageously flaunted the critical current:

> *Reality is, in the final analysis, nothing more than cinema in nature.* If reality is therefore nothing more than cinema in nature, it follows that the first and foremost of the human languages can be considered action itself, as the ratio of the reciprocal representation with others and with physical reality. (HE 198)
>
> Metz speaks of an "impression of reality" as a characteristic of film communication. I would say that it is a question not of an "impression of reality" but of "reality" itself. . . . *The various real objects that compose a shot are the smallest unit of film language.* (200)
>
> It is well known that what we call language, in general, is composed of oral language and written language. They are two different matters: the first is natural and, I would say, existential. Its means of communication is the mouth and its means of perception the ear: the channel is thus mouth-ear. As opposed to written language, oral language brings us without historical discontinuity to our origins, when such oral language was nothing more than a "cry," or a language of biological necessities, or, better still, of conditioned reflexes. . . . Written language is a convention that fixates this oral language and replaces the mouth-ear channel with the graphic reproduction-eye channel. (203)
>
> In reality, we make cinema by living, that is, by existing practically, that is, by acting. *All of life in the entirety of its actions is a natural, living film: in this sense, it is the linguistic equivalent of oral language in its natu-*

ral and biological aspect. By living, therefore, we represent ourselves, and we observe the representation of others. The reality of the human world is nothing more than this double representation in which we are both actors and spectators: a gigantic happening if you will. (204) It [cinema] is, therefore, nothing more than the "written" manifestation of a natural, total language, which is human action in reality. (205)

Pasolini's unencumbered use of such words as "natural" and "reality" was indeed striking. And so was his simultaneous self-positioning across linguistics and phenomenology (reality as double representation to self and others), tinged with a Marxian-Vichian perspective (human action as history-making), poststructuralism (the notion of written language as inscription), and religious mysticism ("natural total language," the book of God). All this while doing film theory! Pasolini's visionary "extravagance" climaxed with the idea of a General Semiology of Reality as the investigation of all the systems of communication regulating the semiotic exchange between subject and object, between self and other, a General Semiology which would, of course, rely on cinema as its prime tool and support.

What is necessary, therefore, is the semiology of the language of action or, in simplest terms, of reality. That is, to expand the horizons of semiology and of linguistics to such an extent as to lose our heads at the very thought or to smile with irony, as is proper for specialists to do. (204)

Before analyzing Pasolini's propositions and suggesting a possible use for them, it may be worth briefly considering the specialists' reactions to the ideas espoused in "The Written Language of Reality." At the time of its publication, specialists did more than smile "with irony." They first attacked and later ignored Pasolini.[7] According to Eco, his ideas contradicted "the most elementary principles of semiology, which hold that facts of nature become cultural phenomena, and do not reduce cultural facts to natural phenomena." Eco also criticized Pasolini's idea that human action is a natural language, "for kinesics (the study of human gestures) has proved it to be the result of cultural conventions." With respect to the suggestion that reality is a total language, Eco was firm in rejecting it as unscientific.[8] In *Segno*, then, he placed Pasolini together with Scotus Eriugena and Pseudo-Dionysius the Areopagite as representatives of a pansemiotic metaphysics.[9] Garroni criticized the idea of the universality of cinematic language as an outdated attempt to revive a neorealist fallacy. Likewise, Garroni felt that Pasolini assumed cinema's transparent rendering of reality and denied its specificity as a language. Accusing him of "spiritualism"— indeed the ultimate sin in those years of enthusiastic faith in a secular and semiotic Enlightenment—Garroni stated clearly that "reality, as the material presupposition for every possible code, cannot itself be the code" so that "the assertions made by the Italian writer and director do not make sense" unless "they are interpreted in the light of Pasolini's artistic work, as a poetic statement."[10] Metz leveled similar criticisms at a semiological project that was so unrigorous, poetic, and ultimately misleading, an opinion that he still holds some twenty years after the diatribe. "Pasolini had truly genial intuitions," he says, "but did not know how to formulate them on a scientific plane and this has discredited him among other semioticians."[11] Bettetini (purely a film theorist, unlike Eco and Garroni) rejected Pasolini from his horizon of interlocutors, for in his three important books he scarcely took Pasolini's theories into consideration. On the last occasion in which he acknowledged Pasolini's presence, he grouped him together with Bazin and Kracauer as believers in the ontological realism of the film image.[12] And once in the company of Bazin—along with Lukacs, *the* strawman of antirealist arguments—Pasolini and his theories were hopelessly relegated to their role as exemplary aberrations. It was on such grounds that Heath went so far as to argue that Pasolini was not a Marxist.[13] And it is on such grounds that film students are scarcely ever asked to plow through *HE* for reasons other than to explain Pasolini's films.

Of course, the critics' reaction to Pasolini's ideas was not entirely unjustified. In addition to their "interdisciplinary extravagance" (a suspect trait in discourses that were discovering and celebrating their own specificities), Pasolini's essays did lend themselves to superficial misreadings. He often capitalized the word "reality," indulged in repetitions, gave the impression of seeking provocation at all costs, and often neglected areas where his ideas would give rise to legitimate doubts, thus failing to spell out a defense acceptable to his critics. And yes, his theories were animated by a sense of ontological mystery which could find no tolerance *then*; in fact, they seemed to exemplify the persistence of old religious paradigms cloaked in new approaches.

Still, more often than not, his critics read him superficially, as if looking for what they knew they would find. They picked on his weakest points and did not really pay attention to the numerous places that evince a different awareness and an intriguing potential. The Pavlovian punctuality with which they reacted to the "irrational" and "poetic" streaks in Pasolini's essays essentially betrayed what Pasolini called "the dogma of secularism" (*HE*, 278): in refusing to see that mystery and death—the passing of time and the dust of history—ought to bring scientific hubris down to size. In the eyes of Pasolini's critics, theoretical discourse required brushing aside our fragility as human beings. Whereas Pasolini's essays vibrated with oblique references to their author's existential search and philosophical panic, Eco's and Metz's revealed nothing of their authors. It was ironic that these theorists, so dedicated to the unmasking of the cultural determinants behind seemingly natural events, would ignore the sociohistorical embeddedness of *their own* sites of enunciation. Their voices reaffirmed the illusion of neutrality so typical of the self-appointed spokes*men* of Reason; and, however deconstructive, their theories often gave the impression of seeking the universalist positions of the Enlightenment. Campy though it often was, Pasolini's inclusion of the personal register fared better than the impersonal and unquestioning rationality of his critics.

Mutual responsibilities aside, the main cause of misunderstanding was the difference in the theorists' discursive levels. Whereas Eco, Metz, and Bettetini were professionals in their respective fields, had quasi-scientific expectations of their disciplines, and were practicing Theory, Pasolini was an "informed dilettante." His mixture of discursive registers and his constant references to personal situations positioned his words on a different plane, one that could only be appreciated later, by theorists who regarded "the personal" as a sine qua non of discourse.

It is no accident that the first theorist to argue the useful potential of Pasolini's ideas came to them from feminism. In *Alice Doesn't*, Teresa De Lauretis argued that

> ironically, from where we now stand, his views on the relationship of cinema to reality appear to have addressed perhaps the central issues of cinematic theory. In particular his observation that cinematic images inscribe reality as representation and his insistence on the audiovisuality of cinema bear directly on the role that cinema's imaging has in the production of social reality.[14]

Although compressed in a few pages, De Lauretis's reappraisal was the first genuine attempt to use Pasolini's idea of reality as inscription. Then it was Gilles Deleuze's turn to show interest in and develop Pasolini's ideas on the free indirect subjective (a type of shot which I will discuss in the chapter *Mamma Roma*) and the "prerational" nature of images.[15] More recently, Naomi Greene has dedicated a chapter in her book to Pasolini's theory, contextualizing his notion of "a cinema of poetry" and briefly defending Pasolini's semiology against Eco and Co.[16] Finally, Giuliana Bruno's article, "Heresies: The Body of Pasolini's Semiotics," significantly published in the *Journal of the Society for Cinema Studies*, has sanctioned Pasolini's return to the limelight of theory.[17] The effect that Bruno's article may have on the contemporary debate reminds me of a "goose bump" sequence in Pasolini's first film, *Accattone*. During an unsettling dream, the protagonist Accattone attends his own funeral and, once inside the cemetery, begs the undertaker to bury him "a little further over, in the sun." Bruno's article does just that: It removes the body of Pasolini's theory from the obscurity in which it has been buried and brings it into the arena of contemporary film theory.

Bruno argues that Pasolini's semiotics foreshadows "poststructuralist concerns" and "puts a stress on notions such as 'discourse,' 'process,' and 'writing'," with the result that "the body itself of Pasolini's semiotics is work-in-progress, and produces a similar notion of the cinematic sign."[18] More specifically, "Pasolini's formulation of cinema as the 'written language of reality' assumes, on the one hand, that the real itself be considered a language (the discourse of action), and, on the other hand, that cinema be considered as *scrittura*, in a sense that approaches the now widely used notion of *écriture*, writing."[19] My analysis below follows, complements, and I hope amplifies Bruno's reading of the notion of cinema as the written language of reality.

As a first step, I would like to turn to the distinction that Pasolini made between cinema and film, a distinction that, in its general outline, was typical of early semiotics. "It is probably incorrect to speak of cinema," Pasolini argued, and "it would be more correct to speak of audiovisual technique, which would therefore also include television" (*HE*, 197). Cinema, then, is an almost abstract concept indicating (that humans have perfected) a technology capable of capturing on film the shapes and sounds of profilmic material. Films, instead, are the actual texts made through that particular "audiovisual technique." Metz drew a similar distinction, but Pasolini's notion of cinema soon acquired a certain philosophical/mystical flavor: "Cinema is an infinite sequence shot—I have already said it dozens of times—it is the ideal and virtual, infinite reproduction made possible by an invisible camera which reproduces as such all the gestures, the actions, the words of a man from his birth to his death" (*HE*, 249). Cinema thus became a sort of God's eye, an "ideal and virtual" long-take from an "invisible camera." It was the mysticism contained in this idea, together with Pasolini's use of the word "reproduction," that caused the critics' indignation. He often reiterated, however, the purely theoretical plane of his argument: "Cinema in concrete terms does not exist: in concrete terms only the film that I am looking at exists, and therefore I never forget completely that I am in the presence of a fiction of reality since it is a 'reproduction'" (288). Ignored by his critics, passages like this one made it clear that Pasolini was aware of the dangers contained in his discourse and that he simply was not interested in deconstructing the notion of "reproduction," for he wanted to tackle the larger picture—that is, the philosophical implications of his notion of cinema.

To understand such implications we need to look now at his proposition that "cinema [as audiovisual technique] is the written language of reality." Such a proposition renounces scientificity from the start and establishes a discursive level where the demands of rational discourse give way to practical, I would say almost pedagogic, concerns. With this catchy phrase, Pasolini intended to capture the multifaceted relationshlp between cinema, reality, and language. On closer inspection, "cinema-is-the-written-language-of-reality" rests on an equivalence: Cinema is to reality what written language is to oral language. Let us write this equivalence in such a way that the possibility of vertical analogies is emphasized:

$$\text{cinema: reality}$$
$$\updownarrow \quad = \quad \updownarrow$$
$$\text{written language: oral language}$$

The epigram "cinema is the written language of reality" thus harbors four statements:

1. Cinema is to reality what written language is to oral language.
2. Cinema is like written language.
3. Just as written and oral languages are different modalities of the same linguistic system, so cinema and reality belong to the same linguistic system, speak the same language.
4. Reality is like oral language.

Each of these statements deserves attention.

1. With the equivalence "cinema is to reality what written language is to oral language" Pasolini retraced Benjamin's steps and highlighted the revolution in perception brought about by the advent of audiovisual technology. Just as the invention of writing "revealed to man what his oral language is" (*HE*, 231), so cinema enhanced our self-consciousness of our daily acts of audio-vision: "the language of reality, as long as it was natural, was beyond our consciousness: now that it appears 'written' through cinema, it cannot fail to demand a consciousness" (*HE*, 231). It was our experience with cinema as "audio-visual technique" that made us aware that our decoding of real events was not natural but cultural, not an immediate perception of "what is there" but a discursive event subjected to the pragmatics of communication. It follows that "the written language of reality will cause us first of all to know what the language of reality is, and it will end up modifying

our idea of it—at least transforming our physical relations with reality into cultural relations" (*HE*, 231). This last sentence alone ought to dispel any doubt regarding Pasolini's allegedly naive belief in a "natural reality." For Pasolini was saying that cinema would finally make us realize that physical relations (*physis* = nature) are in fact cultural. Pasolini knew, no doubt, that nature must be replaced by culture, but he also knew that in certain situations the word "nature," like "reality," is useful and should not scare us a priori. Seen in these terms, the statement that "reality is cinema in nature" stops being outrageous; for it implies that both reality and nature—these pillars of Western metaphysics—are transformed by cinema into cultural relations; they are subjected to semiosis; they *are* semiosis.[20]

2. Cinema is like writing. As Bruno suggested, this idea lends itself to be read in the light of the widely used notion of *écriture*, writing as inscription of traces and difference, *differance*. Reading Pasolini's ideas in a Derridean light, however, poses certain problems. Pasolini's ideas on oral language as being more natural than writing most definitely opposed the work of Derrida, who painstakingly deconstructed the speech versus writing opposition. Once regarded from a Derridean standpoint, Pasolini's ideas indeed seemed to rely on the logocentric tradition, but he did not bestow any *metaphysical* privilege on speech. He merely maintained the usefulness of the speech versus writing distinction, with speech somehow being more "natural" because it is physically related to the "primitive cry" and to what animals do.

Peter Brunette and David Willis's recent book *Screen/play* dedicates a chapter to the question of "cinema as writing."[21] Applying Derridean deconstruction to cinema, they show that, insofar as it relies on spacing, distancing, and deferral, cinema is writing. Brunette and Willis thus take issue with those who claim that cinema is like speech, closer to reality than writing. Again, Pasolini's position in this respect would be, at once, with and against them. Like Brunette and Willis, he saw cinema as writing, but he also regarded it as closer to reality than they would be willing to admit. The question then becomes: How could Pasolini regard cinema at once as writing and yet something closer to reality?

Cinema "writes" with "the various real objects that compose a shot" which are "the smallest units of film language" (*HE*, 200). Pasolini did not mean that cinema transcribes a fixed reality which is the same for everyone. Nor did he mean that cinematic images lose their linguistic specificity and become transparent stand-ins for the profilmic material. Cinema "writes" reality because it uses real people or objects in front of the camera.

> If I want to represent Sanguineti [a poet of the *Neo-Avanguardia* with whom Pasolini had a rancorous polemic], I do not resort to magical evocations [poetry], but I use Sanguineti himself. Or if Sanguineti is unwilling I choose a long-nosed seminary student, or an umbrella salesman in his Sunday best; in other words, I choose another Sanguineti. In any case, I do not go outside the circle of reality. I express reality—and therefore I detach myself from it—but I express it with reality itself.

Cinema has a privileged relationship with reality because it forces the director to use fragments of reality, real bodies, real objects. On the spectators' end, this means that if we see a dog on the screen we know that there was a real dog in front of the camera. Pasolini was not saying that we all see the *same* dog, but that the director has to place a real dog in front of the camera and that we can "read" the dog "written" on the screen *if* we know what dogs are in real life.

3. Since it is our familiarity with dogs in real life that permits us to see a dog on the screen, Pasolini argued that reality is cinema's code and, going one step farther, that cinema and reality speak the same language. In the past, critics chose to read this statement as saying "cinema = reality." That is, cinema, by virtue of the iconicity of its signs, is a transparent, immediate reproduction of the real. Was Pasolini so "naive" as to regard the dog on the screen as the objective stand-in for the real dog? We have seen that this was not the case. I propose, then, that we interpret the sense of Pasolini's analogy backwards, not "cinema = reality," but "reality = cinema," or, as he himself put it, "reality is cinema in nature," it is a cinematic spectacle. "This view," Bruno suggests, "is a direction of thought that has largely been explored by postmodernism" and "it is by now a common assumption that we live in a 'society of the spectacle.'"[22] Pasolini then *chose* neither to challenge nor demystify cinema's "impression of reality." He *wanted* spectators to think of reality when watching a film, hoping that such an analogy would backfire and would make them think of reality as spectacle. Differently put, Pasolini hoped that the "impression of reality" experienced at the movies would have a ricochet effect and produce an "impression of cinema" in everyday reality.

4. Perhaps the most revolutionary use to which Pasolini's epigram can be put is contained in the idea that reality is itself a language. By this, Pasolini, with Saussure's notion of *langue* in mind, meant two things, exemplified by the following equivalence:

Langue: *Parole* = Reality: Cinema
Speech: Writing = Reality: Cinema

According to the first, reality is to cinema what a linguistic system (Saussure's *langue*) is to an individual utterance (*parole*); that is, the precondition of its intelligibility. We recognize the dog on the screen because a dog is part of a sign system called "reality." By comparing reality to a Saussurean *langue*, by suggesting that reality is a linguistic system whose speech acts are made of people and actions, gestures and words, Pasolini unmasked the very notion of objective reality. The physical reality that cinema "writes" on film has no objective existence to begin with: it is a language, a differential system itself. Gone is the idea of reality as a fixed, stable entity. Gone is the reassuring self-evidence of reality. Everything we see is subject to the laws of discourse. Not even in real life do we see the same dog, because a dog is a "living sign" whose meaning depends both on its position within the overall system (What is the status of a dog in a particular context?) and on the person "reading" it (Are we familiar with dogs? Did we have experiences with them?).

According to the second equivalence, reality is analogous to speech, to oral language. It is, as a point of fact, the most natural, oldest form of language:

> Man, intent on life, caught in the cycle of pure pragmatism, continuously deciphers the language of Reality: the savage in the presence of an animal is in the presence of a "sign" of that language—if it is an edible animal, he kills it; if it is ferocious, he runs away, etc. Eating, running away, are other "signs" of that Language. Living, therefore, is expressing oneself through pragmatism, and said expression is nothing more than a moment of the monologue which Reality holds with itself concerning existence. In fact, both the eaten animal and the savage who eats it are part of the entire body of the Existing or of the Real, physically without a break of continuity. (HE 293)

The excess of capitalized words in this passage indicates the unease and the courage of a theorist who wanted to be able to investigate reality's living signs "without the hesitations of specialists" (*HE*, 293). I would argue that the idea of reality as a total language in which we are at once "the decoder and the decodable" (*HE*, 257) is useful in that it stresses the interdependence between us and the environment. Reality is a constant process of signification, a "double representation in which we are both actors and spectators" (*HE*, 204).

Pasolini's idea of reality as a "pragmatic dialogue between us and things" (*HE*, 258) stressed the relationship between subject and object and implicitly took issue with semiotics, which emphasized either one or the other. I find his notion of reality as language appealing in that it implies that reality is not just the "world out there," as it is normally conceived, but is always-already a relationship. The subject, in other words, is involved in the making of the object. And although "the development of the theory of this pragmatic relationship between the decoder and the decodable" remained "a frustrating lacuna in my work" (*HE*, 257), it is worth extrapolating Pasolini's extravagant contributions to a theory of reality as a language, that is, of reality as an ongoing, semiotic exchange between "us" and "things."

Empire of Signs, Empire of Passion

In order to tease out a viable theory of reality as language I propose to turn to the passionate, when not rabid, pages of the pedagogical treatise *Gennariello*, which Pasolini started writing for the weekly *Il Mondo* in 1975, a few months before his death. As an aging man, he had lost the sense of a future ahead of himself. As a filmmaker, he was about to repudiate the joyous physicality of "innocent" bodies such as those paraded in his *Trilogia della vita*, and embark on the production of one of the most inconsumable films in the history of narrative cinema: *Salò*. As a leftist, he had lost all hope, for the "new fascism" of consumer society was effecting an "anthropological revolution" in Italy and was effacing the difference represented by marginal (sub)cultures. As the social space was being increasingly "homogenized" to one image, Pasolini felt the times were ripe for desperate moves. He began to write a series of short lessons aimed at providing his beloved subcultures with the tools necessary to resist assimilation into the dominant culture. And he addressed his lessons to Gennariello, an imaginary representative of the Neapolitan subproletariat (for him, the quintessential icon of innocence). However wishful, *Gennariello* was his only attempt to actually write a "General Semiology of Reality." Pasolini tried to wrench semiotic discourse away from the abstraction of specialized tomes and to offer it to an audience that actually needed it. The use-value of semiotics was thus being tested.

Significantly, Pasolini did not begin his cautionary treatise by deconstructing the "educative sources" most likely to come to mind, that is "your father and mother, school and television," and not even "your peers who clearly are your true educators."[23] Rather, his first lesson intended to warn Gennariello against the language that indoctrinates us without having the appearance of doing so, a language that is capable of addressing us regardless of our will to listen: the language of things. Aptly entitled "The first lesson was given to me by a curtain," this chapter opens with two memorable paragraphs that deserve to be quoted in full.[24]

Our first memories are visual ones. In memory life becomes a silent film. We all have in our minds an image which is the first, or one of the first, in our lives. That image is a sign, or to be exact a linguistic sign. So if it is a linguistic sign it communicates or expresses something. I shall give you an example, Gennariello, which to you as a Neapolitan may sound exotic. The first image of my life is a white, transparent curtain which hangs—without moving I believe—from a window which looks out on to a somewhat sad and dark lane. That curtain terrifies me and fills me with anguish: not as something threatening and unpleasant but as something cosmic. In that curtain the spirit of the middle-class house in Bologna where I was born is summed up and takes bodily form. Indeed, the images which compete with the curtain for chronological primacy are a room with an alcove (where my grandmother slept), heavy, proper furniture, a carriage in the street which I wanted to climb into. These images are less painful than that of the curtain, yet in them too is concentrated that element of the cosmic which constitutes the petty-bourgeois spirit of the world into which I was born.

This first paragraph introduced Gennariello to the notion of images (in memory and in films) as linguistic signs. As a linguistic sign, the image of the curtain communicates two things: a referential content (that particular curtain) and a signified (the spirit of the middle-class house). Insofar as the image of the curtain expresses more than its referent, images communicate more than they seem. They communicate something intangible, which cannot be pinned down rationally and yet is there. For all their new-age connotations, the twice-repeated adjective "cosmic" and the word "spirit" suggest that communication through images exceeds rational explanation. Of course, it would be possible to chastise Pasolini for his unrigorous terminology, but to do so would be missing the fact that he was recasting semiotics into a more accessible form. He was putting into practice his idea that theory must substantiate its validity through the personal experience of the author.

After explaining the notion of images as linguistic signs, Pasolini proceeded to argue that the curtain itself (and not just its image) was a linguistic sign—*res sunt nomina* (things are nouns/names), as he had argued in *HE*.

They are, in fact, linguistic signs which, if for me personally they evoke the world of middle-class infancy, nevertheless in those first moments they talked to me objectively and demanded to be deciphered as something new and unknown. In fact, the content of my memories did not superimpose itself on them; their content was only their own. And they communicated it to me. So their communication was essentially instructional. They taught me where I had been born, in what world I lived, and above all how to think about my birth and my life. Since it was a question of an unarticulated, fixed and incontrovertible pedagogic discourse, it could not be other—as we say today—than authoritarian and repressive. What that curtain said to me and taught me did not admit (and does not admit) of rejoinders. No dialogue was possible or admissible with it, nor any act of self-education. That is why I believed that the whole world was the world which that curtain taught me: that is to say, I thought that the whole world was "proper," idealistic, sad and skeptical, a little vulgar—in short petty bourgeois.

This is not the place to examine the intriguing parallel between *Gennariello*'s curtain and the film screen. A discussion of this will have to be postponed until *Edipo re*, the openly autobiographical "first movement" which includes an image of the curtain of his childhood. What interests me here is the crux of Pasolini's argument: things too, and not just images, are linguistic signs. Physical reality, the world "out there," speaks a language, is a language whose constant flow of messages constitutes, like Barthes's Japan, an empire of signs. Everywhere we turn we find signs. This omnipresent sign-system performs a double operation on us, the addressees. In the first place, the presence of things/signs around us "demands to be deciphered." Children must interrogate every "new and unknown being." We must somehow establish a semiotic relationship with our surroundings because things imperiously demand our interpretive efforts. Pasolini argued this point already in *HE*, referring to "a world to be signified, or more simply, with a daring neologism, a *Significando* (a word with which it would always be right to humbly indicate Reality)" (206). To appreciate the intriguing potential of the term *significando*, it is necessary to bear in mind its Latin meaning more than the Italian one. In Italian, *significando* is the gerund of the verb *significare* and thus means "to be signifying." Here, however, Pasolini had in mind what in Latin is called "passive periphrastic," a verbal form that conveys the notion of something that *has* to be done, as in Cato's motto "Cartago delenda est" (Carthage must be destroyed).[25] A notion of reality that is both suggestive and difficult to contradict thus emerges: reality is the *must* entailed by the constant presence of what is other. Pasolini's use of the capital letter for "Reality" would then be an indication of his humble respect for the "thou shalt interpret me" by which the outer world simultaneously becomes the object of knowledge and constitutes us as the knowing subject. Reality dissipates in its purely external dimension and becomes a questioning attitude, a subjective gesture and desire.

In the second place, not only does reality push the subject on the semiotic path but also speaks a language of its own. The wondering subject, in other words, is not entirely free to give *il significando* just any meaning. In fact, in the case of an infant, the language of things/signs is authoritarian, that is, it imposes its meanings on the subject. Reality's authoritarian language placed the infant Pier Paolo into a system of values and expressed a world that presented itself as *the* world, so that images from other social worlds "seemed to me to be extraneous, anomalous, disquieting, and devoid of truth."[26] With adults, however, the language of things is less authoritarian, for adults have their own semiotic histories that resist the authoritarian language of things/signs. For example, Pasolini's experience with that curtain overdetermined each of his subsequent encounters with curtains. In the case of adults, every encounter between "the decoder and the decodable" is less an authoritarian lesson than a relationship, a semiotic negotiation. Still, the subject's semiotic history is largely dependent on those primal encounters whose formative role can hardly be overemphasized.

Gennariello's analysis of the language spoken by things exemplifies Pasolini's approach to all the other signifying layers that make up the empire of signs and that ought to be considered in a General Semiology of Reality:

> A character in cinema, as in every moment of reality, talks to us through signs or *living syntagmas* of his action, which, subdivided into chapters, could be: (1) the language of physical presence; (2) the language of behavior; (3) the language of written-spoken language—all, exactly, synthesized by the language of action, which establishes relations with us and with the objective world. In a General Semiology of reality each one of these chapters should then naturally be subdivided into an undefined number of paragraphs. (HE 238)

Pasolini's classification of the various layers underwent several changes, testifying to the impossibility of ever achieving scientific rigor. The bottom line, however, did not change: the dialogic relationship between subject and object is a continuum of semiotic strata "synthesized by the language of action." The language of physical presence is part of the language of action, because things, by the mere fact of being there, *act* upon the subject.

It may be wise to stop for a moment and ask ourselves: Was Pasolini prey to the so-called metaphysics of presence, whereby a privileged and unmediated access to some essential reality is granted to seeing and hearing, to presence? The example of the curtain in *Gennariello* would suggest that the language of things appears as natural. In spite of the occasionally ambiguous use of the term "nature," Pasolini was aware that the language of presence is ideological, characterized by the social intonations through which it gains historical specificity (a curtain can be petty bourgeois). It is true that in *HE* Pasolini often argued that oral signs are not merely arbitrary (like written signs) but retain the necessity of the primal scream of terror with which the first humans expressed their reactions to the sight of a dangerous wild animal. And it is equally true that for him the communication taking place through the sense of sight was somehow more revealing than, say, written communication. However, Pasolini's argument never intended to be metaphysical; he did not say that presence makes us know what the other *really* is. He simply appealed to a commonsensical truth: We *feel* that we know something better when we are in its presence, when we see it.[27] By choosing to avoid the terrain of metaphysics and by refusing to bring the discussion to the heights of Derridean abstraction, Pasolini investigated the question of presence in a down-to-earth manner, which is exactly what a deconstructionist philosophy would not, or could not, do. To put it differently, Pasolini preferred running the risk of seeming philosophically naive rather than forsaking the capacity of talking about the political aspects of the language of presence.[28] His essays intentionally relied on a commonsensical notion of presence and implicitly asked us to suspend its metaphysical overtones, in the attempt to broach the more pressing subject of a politics of presence.

In the article "What is Neo-Zdhanovism and What Isn't," Pasolini argued that nothing has the power of scandalizing the bourgeoisie as much as "the FACE of a black, or the SMELL of a poor person, or the BEWILDERMENT of a Jew, or the PROVOCATION of a homosexual" (HE 159). Apparently a matter-of-fact observation, this argument accomplished many tasks in one stroke. By lumping homosexuals, Jews, and blacks together with the poor, he challenged the Marxist notion of the primacy of the class struggle: anything violating the codes of dominant ideology is an instance of struggle. In turn, this entailed redefining the bourgeoisie as more than just an economic category: bourgeois are those who cannot cope with the presence of scandalous otherness. Furthermore, Pasolini's argument had the devastating effect of placing the weight of political awareness on physical presence, on how we look, for "in the picture of a paroxysmally invoked pansemiology, the language of one's action or simply of one's scandalous presence can count as an aspect of prerevolutionary confrontation" (*HE*, 160). What kind of idiom do we speak in the language of presence? Or, better still, how do we act upon others through such an idiom? Pasolini's reflections anticipated the recent trends in cultural studies that investigate symbolic transgressions achieved through clothes, makeup, hairstyle, and even bodily mutilations (punks and skinheads, subcultures whose physical appearance acts out the desire for an antagonistic presence). The importance of one's artificial look in the eighties ought to be seen as a consequence of the discovery of the language spoken by presence.

The mere sight of a scandalous body represents a (voluntary or involuntary) speech act in the language of presence. People's bodies send out messages that exceed the intentions of either the sender or the addressee. It is for this reason that Pasolini argued that, after all, the scandal provoked by an avant-garde narrative was politically less relevant than the scandal provoked by a scandalous presence, because it "takes place at a cultural and not existential level" (*HE*, 159). When talking of the signified of the curtain, Pasolini had recourse to the words "spirit" and "cosmic." Here, the idea of *another* level of communication was conveyed by the adjective "existential" (as opposed to "cultural"). In both cases, he was urging us to look beyond the rational level of communication.

There can be no theory of the image without a realistic understanding of how this "existential level" of communication works. We must, in other words, take the body that is sending the message into account, for it complements and/or alters, when it does not contradict, the conscious intentions of the sender. This is something that feminists have been stressing in the last twenty years: because of the different positions that patriarchy assigns to the subjects of enunciation, the same words uttered by a man or by a woman have different meanings. We should bracket the question of what is being communicated in order to pose the question: by whose body? And it is here that Pasolini performed a Marxian gesture. Just as Marx revealed the extent to which we overlook the labor relations contained in commodities and think of exchange as a clean activity between two free subjects, so Pasolini's notion of presence as an inevitable and yet ignored part of communication revealed the extent to which we like to investigate linguistic exchanges within the safe boundaries of an idealist semiotics. Communication between two or more human beings, however, can never be rid of the dark presence of bodies interfering with the ideal speech situation. The very notion of an ideal speech situation is, in fact, the product of a philosophical tradition that has neutralized sex, race, and class—the body—in the name of an abstract human mind. Bodily presence is like a specter haunting the messages we exchange.

From the standpoint of film studies, the most interesting development of Pasolini's "extravagant" reasoning lies in the notion that the first and foremost layer in the empire of signs is the language of physical presence—that is, the language which things and people "speak" by the mere fact of being on the screen and looking the way they do. Does the presence of certain objects reinforce what one would normally see from a middle-class positioning? What are, for example, the ideological implications of the overbearing presence of cars, chase scenes, and collisions in Hollywood films? Moreover, Pasolini's emphasis on the body as a powerful signifier urges us to consider the way people on the screen look as a prime purveyor of meaning. If reality is a socially coded language, it has its good words and its bad words—words to be censored. We should then investigate what are reality's dialects and its swearwords, the expressions that official grammar and syntax regard as improper. For example, the neorealist strategy of using nonprofessionals was valuable in that it sought to sidestep the consequences of having a star on the screen. The bodies of professional actors do carry connotations that alter whatever intention the film may have. Political filmmakers are now more willing than before to make concessions to cinematic pleasure and thus employ famous actors in their films. If this strategy is valuable in that it enhances the mass appeal of a film, one should not forget the danger of a homogenized cinematic look. It is of course no accident that Pasolini intended to wage war on mainstream cinema on this level rather than on the narrative one. In his films, subproletarian faces and deformed, toothless mouths stood as powerful reminders that other "living signs" existed in the language of reality which were normally excluded from the screen.

I have argued that, nonscientific though they were, Pasolini's views on the empire of signs contained several points of interest. I explored the language of presence to substantiate his concern with the politics of bodily appearance. And I have suggested that Pasolini's imputed naiveté was in fact his conscious choice for a more down-to-earth level of discourse. I will now examine what happens on the subjective end of the semiotic relationship.

The discussion on the language of things in *Gennariello* suggested that objects, which surround children and demand to be deciphered by them, have a crucial role in the formation of the subject. Pasolini regarded himself marked for life by those first semiotic encounters. To appreciate the way in which Pasolini formulated his ideas on the formation of these archi-traces, let us return to his memories. Just a few lines below the description of how household objects provided him with his future parameters of "cosmic" truth, we read,

> The education given to a child by things, by objects, by physical reality—in other words, by the material phenomena of his social condition—make that boy corporeally what he is and what he will be all his life. What is actually being educated is his flesh as the mold of his spirit.[29]

Objects qua linguistic signs make an impression on the body, and corporeality seems to constitute the first instance of subjectivity. The flesh is slowly being branded by a sedimented pile of marks and traces which will constitute the subject's *semiotic history*. And the flesh, Pasolini argued, is "the mold of the spirit." The body, then, constitutes a reserve, an archive that will inform and overdetermine every semiotic act to come. The point is important and deserves attention. Pasolini is not merely saying that signs affect the body. He is also suggesting that, as "the mold of the spirit," the body is educated and/or indoctrinated; it learns how to read and later on engage in semiotic transactions with "the world out there." In short, the act of decoding is also physical. The flesh lodges a reading regime and contains a powerful way of seeing, through invisible eyes.[30]

It is now clear why Pasolini called his theoretical practice "heretical empiricism." It was an empiricism because of the primary role assigned to bodily experience, a role which, according to him, contradicted Marxist rationalism.[31] It was heretical, however, in that Pasolini challenged the value-neutral premises of empiricism and regarded experience as taking place within historically specific contexts and assumptions. If the word "empiricism" evoked the Anglo-Saxon philosophical tradition that opposed idealism, the adjective "heretical" brought along a halo of religious pathos and suggested an attack against hierarchical structures from below. Thus, in the short space of an oxymoronic alliteration, *empirismo eretico* evoked the heresy of a Marxist who, by re-evaluating personal experience, aimed at providing Marxism with the theory of the subject which it sorely lacked.

By stressing the body *of* the subject and the body *as* subject, Pasolini took issue with the disembodied, rational subject of the Enlightenment. The subject is not autonomous, nor is his/her activity located in the mind. In fact, Pasolini's remark that "the flesh is the mold of the spirit" suggested that he was not merely prompting an inversion of the traditional body/mind relationship, but that he was pointing toward the much-needed supersession of their dualism. We are, however, so inured to thinking within the framework of this binary opposition that to disclaim it often amounts to a self-deceiving act of will. This was certainly true for Pasolini, who often revealed his faith in the mind/body dichotomy by attacking the former and celebrating the latter as the repository of unbridled vitality. Nevertheless, in the context of his notion of the body as subject (traditionally the body is the object), he did something quite different. He counterbalanced the power attributed to the mind, disempowered reason, and set a limit to the imperialism of rationalist epistemologies. The body is something with which we must reckon intellectually, and yet it escapes the control of reason. Pasolini's implicit invitation to heed the epistemological role of the body was thus also a plea for a knowledge that did not aim at scientific neutrality and recognized the inescapable role played by nonrational factors. The question then becomes: How do we frame, conceptualize, and refer to such nonrational forces at work in the subject? In the course of his extravagant theorizing, Pasolini fabricated a concept that we can use to refer to the subject's semiotic history in a manner that takes the body into account: the concept of passion.

It has often been repeated that Pasolini's entire work, be it films, poems, or essays, hinged on the polarity of passion and ideology. Without exception, each of Pasolini's critics looks back at the poem "Le ceneri di Gramsci" (The Ashes of Gramsci) as the first symptom of an opposition that would subsequently animate all his output. In a poetic monologue addressing Gramsci's unpretentious tombstone, Pasolini confessed to his own "schizo-self":[32]

> The scandal of contradicting myself, of being
> with you and against you; with you in my heart,
> in light, but against you in the dark viscera;
> traitor to my paternal state
> —in my thoughts, in the shadows of action—
> I know I'm attached to it, in the heat
> of the instincts and aesthetic passion;
> attracted to a proletarian life
> that preceded you; for me it is a religion,
> its joy, not its millennial
> struggle; its nature, not its
> consciousness.

This often-quoted passage evoked a dichotomy between, to use the language of *HE*, the "existential" and the "cultural." Pasolini took the side of the proletariat on a "cultural" level but did not belong to it "existentially." Conversely, the proletariat attracted him for its "existential" ("its joy," its living in the body) rather than for its cultural qualities ("its millennial struggle"). The dichotomy between these two planes often found expression through the terms "passion" and "ideology." Critics seem to agree as to what "passion" and "ideology" signify. Passion is associated with irrational desire and is often qualified as a regressive symptom by left-wing critics. Ideology implies the faith in Hegel's dictum that the real is rational as well as the subjective commitment to understand and change the world. Antonio Costa's assessment may be considered paradigmatic:

> With these terms, Pasolini himself drew attention to the opposite poles
> underlying the basic contradictions in his work: on the one hand an un-
> ashamedly visceral kind of love for reality, urging him to regress towards
> the individual and collective phases constituted by infancy and the primi-
> tive culture of the subproletariat; a reality perceived as an undifferenti-
> ated totality, the source and stimulus of pure vital energy; on the other
> hand, a need to understand reality without it ever becoming a lucidly
> adopted intellectual stance, because it is nourished by mysticism and
> irrationality.[33]

There are two problems with such a view. First, by regarding passion
as the opposite of ideology, critics prevented themselves from grasping
the actual value they both had in Pasolini's universe. Passion did
not oppose ideology but reason. The dichotomy expressed in the poem
did not pit passion against ideology, but passion against reason, visceral against mental. Entitling his collection of literary essays *Passione e
ideologia* (Passion and Ideology), Pasolini himself specified that the
"and" in the title did not imply dualism, nor did it suggest simultaneous acceptance of both terms. Rather, it signaled supersession,
whereby passion, after coupling with reason, would be transformed
into ideology. It was not an either/or matter between passion and
ideology. In order to be effective, ideology, for Pasolini, *had* to include
passion. In the light of his Gramscian Marxism, this is hardly surprising, for Gramsci himself often condemned impassive, purely intellectual endeavors as ineffectual.

> The intellectual's error consists in believing that one can know without
> understanding and, even worse, without feeling and being impassioned
> (not only for knowledge in itself, but also for the object of knowledge):
> in other words, that the intellectual can be an intellectual (instead of a
> pure pedant) even if distinct and far removed from the people-nation,
> that is, without feeling the elementary passions of the people, under-
> standing them and therefore explaining them and justifying them in a
> particular historical situation.[34]

The second problem lies in the critics' habit of regarding "passion"
exclusively as something that explains Pasolini's poetics. By using it as
a cipher to his oeuvre, they overlook exploring the potential that "passion" might have as a theoretical tool. This is a great loss, since feminism and postmodernism have recently attempted to restore the cognitive value of passionlike states.[35] Undoubtedly, the task of exploring
the concept of passion according to Pasolini is complicated by the fact
that he did not test "passion" theoretically. Mostly absent from his
semiotic essays, the word "passion" appeared frequently in his poems

and novels as well as in his "less serious" articles. It is as if Pasolini had internalized the critics' censorship and respected the requirements of serious discourse. But we know, by now, that some of his best ideas hatched in the secret of never-renounced idiosyncrasies. And it is of course no accident that Pasolini "wrote" his best essay on passion in the language of cinema, with the film *Teorema*. Made at the time of his partial disillusionment with the difficult language of semiotics, *Teorema* explored the role of passion in the process of signification.

Pasolini's earliest associations with the word "passion" are quite revealing. In his posthumously published *Amado mio* (written in the 1940s), "passion" signified the irresistible call of the protagonist's homosexual flesh. In his poetry of the same time, it referred to Christ's passion. This semantic ambivalence reflected the Western tradition, according to which passion could signify the seemingly opposite poles of sublimity and vulgarity, Christ's superhuman suffering as well as the urge to be dominated of the protagonist of *Venus in Furs* (allegedly masochism's founding text).[36] Alternately condemned as submission to baser instincts or celebrated as the romantic key to a higher state, "passion" well suited Pasolini's desire for ambivalent signifiers capable of conveying the deepest knots in his authorial intertext. It is very likely that Pasolini's love for the figure of Christ originated in an identification with His unflinching obedience to something higher. Just as Christ obeyed a call that set Him against human nature, so Pasolini obeyed his call and went "against nature." If we keep in mind that violent death—largely self-inflicted—was a homosexual narrative paradigm, then we see how Christ and homosexual martyrdom came to overlap and how the word "passion" came to connote something that one *must* do, a necessity forcing itself on human beings and separating them from others, all the while giving them the narcissistic joy of feeling in harmony with a higher order. On the one hand, passion enslaves the subject through compulsive desires often at odds with the rational ego; on the other, it exalts the subject's freedom from compliance with the dominant semiotic script. The impassioned subject brings his or her passions to bear in the semiotic transactions with the language of reality.

Passions of a different sort and intensity make up our semiotic histories. The more our semiotic histories are impassioned—that is, the more the marks on our flesh are allowed to influence our sign-reading—the greater are our chances to resist the authoritarian language of things. What Pasolini called "the pragmatic relationship between the decoder and the decodable"—the semiotic relationship between subject and object—is the result of an encounter between the decoder's transfiguring passions and the potentially authoritarian language of the decodable. If reality, from the point of view of the object, is, like Barthes's, Japan, "the empire of signs," then from the point of view of the subject it is also, like Oshima's tragic love story, "the empire of passion." The empire of signs is the empire of passion because signs act on the body which, in turn, reacts to and reads them. The empire of signs is the empire of passion because the subject is at once the somewhat passive construct of primal semiotic encounters and the passionate reader of subsequent signifying situations.

The concept of passion according to Pasolini, then, alludes to the subject's bodily semiotic history, to the active memory in the flesh, which overdetermines our readings to some degree. As a descriptive term, "passion" has the advantage of referring to the subject's bodily activity in a mundane, intuitive way that can be understood by all. Used by everybody, everywhere, "passion" is not a suitable word for Theory, so that by using it, one automatically takes issue with the idea that theoretical discourse must employ difficult language. Indeed, the use of the word "passion" parallels the decline of Reason and indicates an openness to nonrational elements. "Passion" does not have a clear denotation in and of itself. It merely "points at": it suggests an agency that in a strict sense is extradiscursive and yet informs and permeates discourse. I would like to suggest that "passion" modifies the traditional conception of subjectivity and inaugurates the domain of subjactivity, the subject as activity, the subject as compelling action.

The idea of passion as the semiotic history written on a body that reads signs has momentous implications in film studies, for it alludes to the body of the viewer, the viewer as body. We could even say that cinema made it impossible for us to keep ignoring the bodily aspects of all artistic consumption, because from its inception, film aroused physical reactions in an unprecedented way. Linda Williams has recently established the category of "body genres": melodrama, horror, and porn.[37] Not only have these genres indulged in graphic descriptions of bodily excess, but they have attempted to affect the spectators' bodies, occasionally taking pride in the promise of spectacles not suitable for everyone. There have been films that explicitly dealt with the corporeality of vision. Stanley Kubrick's *A Clockwork Orange* (1970) literally played out Pasolini's intuition by having Alex develop a series of bodily reactions to the sight of protracted film images of sex and violence. The most brilliant visual translation of the interface between body and image, however, was Cronenberg's *Videodrome* (1982), in which videotapes were directly inserted into the protagonist's stomach in order to substantiate Dr. O'Blivion's idea that "the TV screen is the retina of the brain."

Recent trends in film theory have echoed *Gennariello*'s idea of the body as the subject of vision. The role of optic nerves is being explored to restore the subj*a*ctive dimension of looking—visuality rather than vision.[38] In film criticism, the focus has shifted from textual analysis in a vacuum to an examination of what movies do to us. More specifically, reception theory, feminist film theory, and psychoanalytic semiotics have furthered Pasolini's recognition of the viewer's body. Reception theory started by conceiving the viewer as someone who is inscribed in and constructed by the text, thus disregarding the spectators' capacity to read a film against its grain, in accordance with their passions. More recently, however, the spectator in the text has given way to audiences divided by gender, class, age, and race. Feminists have long singled out the body as the site of productive interactions that are gender specific and thus divide spectators by their sex. Teresa de Lauretis argued that "spectators enter the movie theatre as either men or women, which is not to say that they are simply male or female, but rather that each person goes to the movies with a semiotic history, personal and social."[39] A number of feminist theorists also exemplified the psychoanalytic-semiotic approach within the parameters of a post-Freudian, post-Lacanian discourse (e.g., Mulvey, Penley, Silverman, and, more generally, the *Camera Obscura* group). Indeed, psychoanalytic semiotics seemed to be best equipped to examine spectators as bodies in the dark. A massive amount of criticism concentrated on the spectators' entrapment in a mirrorlike situation, on their giving in to dream states, on the suturing processes through which narrative constructs subjectivity (e.g., Metz, Bellour, and much of the work in *Screen*). It is through psychoanalysis that the discourse on visual pleasure began, and film studies certainly contributed a great deal to a cartography of pleasure in popular culture. Still, the body of the spectator was often theorized within a conceptual and linguistic framework that in many ways signaled the triumph of ultrarational discourse. In my view, an authentic reappraisal of the body's role ought to keep such discourse at bay. I intend neither to condemn psychoanalysis nor to deny its potential. I merely wish to point out a possible drawback: psychoanalytic criticism has been responsible for some of the most difficult language in film studies, creating a caste of insiders and throwing the discipline into disrepute among outsiders (practically the whole world). The very language that one used to describe primary processes and the libidinal economy was so far removed from the everyday experience of the body that only interpretive elites, a small percentage in the academic body, were able to relate to it.

Perhaps the best way to think about the physicality of artistic consumption is that of the French sociologist Pierre Bourdieu, whose book *La Distinction* has founded a sociology of taste away from essentialism.

> To different degrees, depending on the art, the genre and the style, art is never entirely that *cosa mentale*, the discourse intended only to be read, decoded, interpreted, which the intellectualist view makes of it. This product of an "art" in Durkheim's sense, i.e. "a pure practice without theory," and sometimes of a simple mimesis, a sort of symbolic gymnastics, always contains also something ineffable, not through excess, as the celebrants would have it, but by default, something which communicates, as it were, from body to body, like the rhythm of music or the flavor of colors, that is falling short of words and concepts. Art is also a bodily thing, and music, the most "pure" and "spiritual" of the arts, is perhaps simply the most corporeal. Linked to *états d'âme*, which are also states of the body or, as they were once called, humours, it ravishes, carries away, moves. It is pitched not so much beyond words as below them, in gestures and movements of the body, rhythms—which Piaget somewhere says characterize the functions located, like everything which governs taste, at the articulation of the organic and the mental— quickening and slowing, crescendo and decrescendo, tension and relaxation.[40]

Like Pasolini, Bourdieu sees artistic consumption as the site of something ineffable, a dialogic "pragmatic relationship" in which the spiritual dimension is inseparable from the corporeal. Spelling out what Pasolini did not (Pasolini's humanism prevented him from calling the reader/spectator "consumer"), Bourdieu's argument has the merit of flatly stating that the intellectualistic view of art is deceptive, because it preempts art's effect on the body, and nonrealistic, because it conjures up the dream of a purely mental, disembodied space. In order to substantiate his anti-intellectualistic point, Bourdieu assimilates states of mind to states of body and has recourse to the old-fashioned word "humors." Conflating Bourdieu's notion of humoral states with that of semiotic history, Pasolini's concept of passion can be used to fabricate the prolegomena to an "extravagant" theory of spectatorship.

Two out of the three times that the word "passion" appeared in *HE*, it referred to artistic consumption. In "The Written Language of Reality," Pasolini argued that "poetry is nothing more than another form of action" and that "in the instant in which the reader listens to it or reads it, in other words perceives it, he frees it again from linguistic conventions and re-creates it as the dynamic of feelings, of affections, of passions, of ideas" (204). As suggested by De Lauretis, "the emphasis on the subjective in three of the four terms" defining the activity of the reader "points to the current notion of spectatorship as a site of productive relations, of the engagement of subjectivity in meaning, values, and imaging."[41]

In "The Unpopular Cinema," Pasolini directly addressed the question of the film spectator and took issue with all the sociopolitical approaches that regarded the spectator as passively constructed by texts (267–275). Suggesting that the relationship between author and spectator resembles the one taking place "between democratically equal individuals," Pasolini concluded that "for the author, the spectator is merely another author," someone "who understands, who sympathizes, who loves, who becomes impassioned" (269). Again, three of the four terms referred to humoral states. The spectators' passion is the element that allows them to re-create the message in accordance with their subjactivity. A viewer is never free to fulfill the role of ideal spectator that the text in isolation seems to construct. Under the sway of one's passions, images are appropriated in ways that only a social pathology might fathom; the viewer is unable to exorcise the nonrational elements contained in bodily affairs.

To summarize Pasolini's contribution to semiotics: Reality is "that which must be made sense of," a call to semiotic warfare, a structuring absence that demands efforts while promising no rewards. As such, it must always comprise the subject who is called to make sense of it. The relationship between "the decoder and the decodable" is pragmatic, in that it obeys no transcendental law and is determined by the context; and it is empirical, in that it is communicated from body to body, "the mental" being just *one* function within a larger corporeality. Decoding, then, is not the discovery of a meaning that is already there, but an activity whereby the subject modifies the real in accordance with his/her passions: subjactivity. The external world, however, does act on the subject: first by branding his/her flesh in the course of primal scenes which demand semiotic intervention, and later by attempting to force its own meanings on him/her. This two-way interaction is not apolitical, as it often appears in the classical works of empiricism/ pragmatism. Both the subject and the object, "the decoder" and "the decodable," are territorialized within a larger picture, the language of reality, a linguistic totality in which they rank as living signs. Seen in this light, ideological pragmatism would seem the best definition of Pasolini's semiotics.

As to film studies, the first of Pasolini's contributions regards cinema's historical role: as an audio-visual technique, cinema made us aware that reality is produced, constructed, and decodable, just like a film. To be sure, in the darkness of the theater or in front of the television screen, we do not watch cinema but films, that is, aesthetic statements made in the language of cinema under sociospecific market circumstances. Even in this case cinema's potential as the written language of reality is not lost, but permeates the film experience, acting on spectators' passions, on their bodily humors. Film images, qua visual linguistic signs, tend to address the spectator with an authoritarian voice. But film spectators are those who were once subjected to the authoritarian first lessons of the language of things, so that their reactions to the images of a film will be overdetermined by their semiotic histories. Paradoxically, then, the more spectators are enslaved by their past, the more freedom they will have in contradicting the language spoken by the images in a film.

3

An Explosion of My Love for Reality

*What counts is the depth of feeling, the passion I
put into things; it isn't so much the novelty of the
content, nor the novelty of the form.*

Pier Paolo Pasolini

Pasolini's conviction that cinema, as "audio-visual technique," was
"the written language of reality" was undoubtedly the main reason for
his dedicating the last fifteen years of his life to filmmaking. In the
1968 book-length interview with Oswald Stack, Pasolini remarked that
"the passion that had taken the form of a great love for literature" gradually turned out to be "a passion for life, for reality, for physical, sexual, objectual, existential reality around me. This is my first and only
great love and the cinema in a way forced me to turn to it and express
only it."[1] Such a "passion for reality" was, of course, the driving force
behind a "certain realism" in Pasolini's film theory and practice.
Before exploring, however, the theoretical foundations of "a certain
realism"—and in the hope of practicing its tenets—I would like to investigate Pasolini's transition from literature to cinema a little further.

Pasolini was fond of repeating that cinema had been a childhood
dream and that filmmaking was his true vocation. He collaborated on
the scripts and/or the subjects of several films throughout the 1950s,
and critics have often noted the extent to which his literary style, so
rich in visual details, was, in a sense, already "cinematographic." In

47

short, it would seem that by turning to cinema, Pasolini chose what best suited his authorial needs. I would argue that such a continuity in his career is the result of hindsight. What now appears to be a natural turn in a seamless artistic trajectory had, back in 1961, different connotations, both for Pasolini and for the intelligentsia around him. More specifically, Pasolini's decision "to make movies" had an anti-literary, antihumanistic slant.

In an interview at the time of his first film, *Accattone*, Pasolini noted that "while writing a book, you are always closed up in a room with a typewriter, while in making a film you are out in the street, in the sunshine, with people all around you, laughing and arguing."[2] Seven years later, after semiotics had given him the chance to think through his transition to cinema, his explanations ran along quite similar lines: "When I make a film I am always in reality, among the trees and among people like yourself; there is no symbolic filter between me and reality, as there is in literature. So in practice cinema was an explosion of my love for reality."[3] In both of these instances, Pasolini was discussing literature as a mode of production. Literature is a job and, as such, has its own *deformazioni professionali* ("professional deformations")—a term with which the Italian language aptly defines the physical, mental, and behavioral consequences of one's profession. For Pasolini, literature's *deformazioni professionali* were being forced to sit at your desk, being separated from the world, having fewer opportunities to be exposed to the language of things, suffering a greater confinement within the mind at the expense of the body. Thus, by choosing cinema, Pasolini rejected the relationship with the world inscribed in literary production.

Humanist ideology regards the writer's forced separation from the world as something ultimately positive, at once the cause and the effect of nonparticipation in ephemeral, mundane concerns. Pasolini's attack on literature was an implicit rejection of the humanist discourse that formed the backdrop to Italian culture, so much so that his decision to make movies upset the Italian intelligentsia. Naomi Greene notes that "his transition from novelist to director evoked a great deal of comment" and she quotes Turigliatto's perceptive remark that "it was the first time that an intellectual of Pasolini's importance took on a completely different medium from that of literature, a medium whose origins and evolutions were linked to the culture industry."[4] It was the first time that someone empowered by formal recognition from the humanist world (albeit in its Marxist manifestation) decided "to divest" himself of high culture and invest in a domain hopelessly, chronically tainted by its intimacy with "industry."

Until his cinematic debut, Pasolini had published three novels, four collections of poetry, and one volume of literary essays. His collaboration with cinema as a screenwriter was regarded as a "part-time" occupation, the source of that extra money of which most writers are constantly in need. But there was no doubt that he was a writer. I cannot help smiling at the frequency with which major Italian writers (Calvino, for example) denounced Pasolini's transition to cinema as a capitulation to the lure of money and worldly success, away from the depth of the *humanitas* that is best expressed through the practice of writing. Siciliano entitled a section of the chapter dedicated to Pasolini's transition from literature to cinema "Le tentazioni del cinema," the temptations of cinema. In the preface to the catalogue of the retrospective of all Pasolini's films, the late Moravia, then the president of the Pasolini Foundation, conceded that "indeed his work in the cinema must be ranked immediately after his work as a poet." Official high culture always wished for Pasolini's return to full-time literary activity. For most of the Italian intelligentsia, Pasolini, by choosing cinema, had stepped down, as it were, from purity and had accepted contamination with industry.

In the first chapter of this book, I argued that Pasolini occupied an ambivalent position characterized by his stepping down from legitimate values (intellectual *but* Marxist, man *but* homosexual). It is tempting to see Pasolini's transition to cinema as the choice of an activity that best suited the ambivalence of his sociosexual position.[5] Speculating on and knowing why Pasolini chose cinema is important; equally important, although much less explored, is the reverse question: Why did cinema and/or the culture industry choose Pasolini?

If Pasolini "stepped down" by turning to cinema, the latter, by choosing Pasolini, "stepped up." In 1960, cinema had not yet been allowed to forget its low origins as pop culture and was still striving to prove itself as the "seventh art." In academia, curricula did not include film studies; literary artifacts (backed by six of the Muses) monopolized the study of "Italian." It is hardly coincidental that the late 1950s saw the rise of auteurism in theory, according to which film demanded a complex critical apparatus quite similar to that of literature. As Peter Wollen put it, "the *auteur* theory does not limit itself to acclaiming the director as the main author of a film. It implies an operation of decipherment; it reveals authors where none had been seen before."[6] By employing someone like Pasolini who was already an author of literary merit, cinema gained cultural legitimacy.

In Italy, to be sure, cinema had already acquired *some* legitimacy in the 1940s. Neorealist films had made Italian culture known abroad more than had all the Italian literature of the twentieth century, and there seemed to be no doubt about the films' artistic merit. In the

1950s, however, pink neorealism, the attempt of some producers (e.g., De Laurentiis) to transform Cinecittà into Europe's Hollywood with its star system (the Lollobrigidas, the Lorens, the Pampaninis all boomed in this decade) certainly tainted Italian cinema's aspirations to artistic status. But the work of Fellini, Visconti, and Antonioni was also emerging in these years (indeed, Fellini's *La strada* of 1956 earned both critical and commercial acclaim, even winning an Academy Award). And in 1960, Fellini's *La dolce vita*, Visconti's *Rocco e i suoi fratelli* (Rocco and His Brothers), and Antonioni's *L'avventura* reestablished Italian cinema as Italy's chief contribution to the international artistic panorama.

In the early 1960s, a few young Italian producers (Goffredo Lombardo, Alfredo Bini) initiated a trend aimed at increasing cinema's cultural legitimacy through a return to the values of neorealism. What critic Lino Miccichè called *l'operazione "nouvelle vague" italiana* (the Italian "new wave") was born—the attempt by "some enlightened producers" to revive the national market and emulate their French counterparts.[7] Alfredo Bini, the producer of Pasolini's first seven films, thus summarized the situation facing Italian cinema:

> The two roads that Italian cinema ought to take are, on the one hand, the *cinema d'autore*, which can count on a public beyond the national boundaries, and, on the other, films with a potential for high spectacle (*film di alta dignità spettacolare*) possibly realized in cooperation with other European countries, so as to reduce the risks and cover production costs, since the Italian market cannot bear the average cost of a spectacular film all by itself.[8]

Defined in opposition to commercial cinema—those films that Bini euphemistically called "films with a potential for high spectacle"—the *cinema d'autore* would consist of low-budget films abjuring escapism and appealing to the intellectual public both in Italy and "beyond national boundaries." Many *films d'autore* were made in the early 1960s, some of them soon forgotten. In 1961, the Venice film festival presented the first films of four "young" *autori*: Vittorio De Seta's *Banditi a Orgosolo* (Bandits of Orgosolo), Ermanno Olmi's *Il posto* (The Sound of Trumpets), Giuliano Montaldo's *Tiro al piccione* (Pigeon Shooting), and Pier Paolo Pasolini's *Accattone*. In 1962 came Petri's *L'assassino* (The Lady Killer of Rome), the Taviani brothers' *Un uomo da bruciare* (A Man for Burning), and Bertolucci's *La comare secca* (The Grim Reaper, with a script by Pasolini). The *operazione "nouvelle vague" italiana* failed as an attempt to create a unitary movement with a stylistic and theoretical identity of its own. It nevertheless launched the *autori* who, together with the triad of mature *auteurs* from the previous generation (Antonioni, Visconti, and Fellini) and Bellocchio, who debuted in 1966, contributed to the "decisive decade" of Italian cinema.[9] Pasolini's directorial debut ought to be seen within the framework of a larger investment that the Italian film industry was making to enhance its own image.

Realistically speaking, however, there were additional reasons that prompted producer Bini, and with him the culture industry, to invest in Pasolini. Pasolini's notoriety was of a peculiar kind: he was immensely more popular than any other writer because his "perversion" assured that his name was regularly dragged through the pages of national newspapers and tabloids. If nothing else, Pasolini's films would always guarantee a *succès de scandale*. A joke that I personally recollect hearing a few times in the early 1960s captures the kind of notoriety enjoyed by Pasolini better than any description could:

> A Rolls Royce and a small Fiat 500 are waiting side by side at a red light. The British vehicle's engine is virtually silent. Inside, an elegant and austere gentleman patiently waits for the green light. The driver of the Italian car, instead, nervously pushes on the gas pedal, getting ready for a quick, screeching start. Vroooom! Vroooom! Visibly annoyed, the gentleman rolls down his window and exclaims: "'Patience is the virtue of the strong,' quote William Shakespeare." To which the other guy replies (the window of his car, of course, is already down): "'Fuck you,' quote Pier Paolo Pasolini."

Pasolini's name could safely be used in jokes with the assurance that everyone, even those who had not read a single word by him, would be familiar with it. Everybody had heard Pasolini's name as the writer who used obscene language in his novels and was brought to court for "obscene behavior." Pasolini's name, then, indicated more than a poet. He was a pawn in a struggle between progressive and conservative groups, a struggle that marked the 1960s in all Western, capitalist countries but was particularly virulent in Italy because of the country's backwardness.

Italy had just commenced upon what sociologists and historians called "the economic miracle," that is, the transition from a poor, mostly rural economy into an industrial power. If Bini and the film industry needed a public "beyond the national boundaries," so too the major industrial employers aspired to an international market. The ascending fractions of the Italian ruling class—what Bourdieu would call "the new bourgeoisie"—wanted to introduce a consumer ethic in Italy. This meant changing Italians' attitudes about sex and morality, encouraging permissiveness rather than repression, and opposing the Catholic mentality and the Fascist ideology which had been the rule of the Italian state in the 1950s. In this political climate, different sections of Italian society fought a sort of civil war through certain symbolic pawns—much like America's current controversies about record labeling, NEA funding, and Mapplethorpe exhibits. Pasolini was one such pawn. He was defended, or at least given a fair chance to speak, in leftist journals as well as in the new economic groups' press (Mattei's *Il Giorno*, for example). In the right-wing press he was lynched as "the apostle of mud" and as the exemplar of corruption that called for conservative reaction. As cinema was a prime vehicle for symbolic struggles and an arena where opposite ideologies would clash (Italian TV was then firmly in the hands of the State), the film industry could not ignore Pasolini. It is no accident that Miccichè described the *operazione nouvelle vague* as a "neo-capitalist renovation of the rather primitive and clumsy national cinematographic capitalism."[10] The progressive forces in the film industry saw in Pasolini the opportunity both to appeal to the curiosity of a public titillated by the press and to contribute to the struggle for freedom of expression.

This brief analysis of Pasolini's transition from literature to cinema has emphasized three factors. First, Pasolini's decision to make films originally antagonized the Italian literary establishment and, in a sense, Italian culture *tout court*. Second, he was part of the *cinema d'autore* movement, which meant that his cinema, by definition, followed in neorealist, antispectacular steps. And third, the culture industry looked at him with political expectations. Once inside the film industry as a director, Pasolini occupied a position of his own which in a way reflected these three factors. He soon declared that his cinematic models were not Italians but were Dreyer, Chaplin, and Mizoguchi. He did, however, greatly respect Rossellini, himself a solitary figure. He was critical of Fellini who, in turn, never appreciated Pasolini's technical simplicity. Pasolini also liked Visconti's realist works, above all *Rocco e i suoi fratelli*, but criticized his penchant for grandiose theatricality. Of the three *grandi*, Antonioni was certainly the one who most appealed to Pasolini, for his films enhanced the notion of reality as a language to be deciphered in astonishment.

As to the *cinema d'autore*, Pasolini never betrayed the expectations of the "enlightened young producers." With the possible exception of his commercial hits like *Il Decamerone*, his films enhanced Italian cinema's artistic aspirations at home and abroad. As a point of fact, Pasolini, together with Olmi, was the *autore* who most effectively reworked the neorealist legacy. From a political point of view, too, Pasolini fulfilled the expectations of those who had invested in him: his films did contribute to the change in moral and sexual attitudes in Italy.[11] Although situated within the Left, his films were never political in the conventional sense. Pasolini never participated in and always expressed contempt for political fiction films à la Costa Gavras, a popular genre in those years with *autori* like Rosi, Petri, Maselli, and, to some degree, Bellocchio.

On the subject of political cinema, it would be interesting to explore the relationship between Pasolini and Godard, for they represented two highly individual ways of rethinking cinema's capacity to engage spectators in political reflections. At the time, Godard was immensely more influential. Pasolini often engaged in an oblique debate with him through Bertolucci, who, at least until *Il conformista* (The Conformist, 1971), manifested sympathy for the French director. Pasolini himself had a brief Godardian phase with *Porcile* and, arguably, *Teorema*. In retrospect, however, Pasolini left a mark on film history and politics that is equal in importance to Godard's, a mark that pertains less to his style—although there are followers of his style too, like the Georgian director Serguëi Paradjanov—than to his critical rewriting of the realist tradition, to "the passion I put into things," in short, to the practice of what he once called "a certain realism."

In the Stack interviews, answering a question on the realism of *Hawks and Sparrows*, Pasolini remarked:

> Realism is such an ambiguous and loaded word that it is hard to agree on its meaning. I consider my own films realist compared with neorealist films. In neorealist films day-to-day reality is seen from a crepuscular, intimistic, credulous, and above all naturalistic point of view. . . . Compared with neorealism I think I have introduced a certain realism, but it would be hard to define it exactly.[12]

If we keep in mind Pasolini's theoretical writings and his passion for reality, it is surprising that nobody has thus far attempted a reading of his films in the light of cinematic realism. While his theory was often labeled "naively realist," his films are normally regarded as the initiators of the *cinema delle metafore*, a cinema of metaphors rather than reality.[13] "Myth" is the word usually associated with Pasolini's cinema. Only *Accattone*, *Mamma Roma*, and *Il Vangelo secondo Matteo* are taken as tributes to neorealism. After these films, the question of realism is dropped, as if Pasolini himself had dropped it, as if he had not wished to change and improve, develop and enhance cinema's realistic potential in the light of new historical needs; or as if realism could not undergo changes, as if realism and metaphors/myth were intrinsically incompatible, and as if realism were not the result of a "passion for reality."

To be sure, the critical view of Pasolini's career as a progressive break with realism is partially justified by some declarations of his. His occasional repudiations of realism, however, must be seen in the context of his "love for reality," as symptoms of his critical stance vis-à-vis traditional realism. For example, speaking to a French journalist after the release of *Teorema* in Paris (thus around the same time as the interviews with Stack), he declared:

> The only expression which still interests me is poetry, and the more a meaning is complex the more poetic it is. I am discovering a reality which has nothing to do with realism. And it is precisely because this reality is my only great concern that I am increasingly drawn to the cinema: it apprehends (*il appréhende*) reality even beyond the will of the director and the actors.[14]

At the time, Pasolini was no longer writing the legitimate kind of poetry for which he was famous among literary critics; *Trasumanar e organizzar* (1970) was unanimously criticized as bad poetry. Most of the essays in *HE* expressed his dissatisfaction with literary creation and the state of literature. By "poetry," then, he meant a film style, a cinema of poetry, which better highlighted the director's subjectivity. Evidently, at this point in his development as a film director and theorist, Pasolini regarded traditional realism as a cinema made in the language of prose, a cinema characterized by invisible style and narrative conventions, a cinema that had to be renovated.

Pasolini's relationship with realism is summarized by his two statements above. On the one hand he strove to enhance cinema's capacity to deal with reality, and on the other he was critical of the style that traditionally had aspired to do so. Hence "a certain realism," the project of recasting realism in a problematic and open form. The central argument of this book is that in order to appreciate Pasolini's role in film history, one should use his films as examples of a self-critical realism, "a certain realism," which preserves whatever was good in the tradition while rejecting its burden. Millicent Marcus has recently paved the way for such an enterprise in her book *Italian Cinema in the Light of Neorealism*. Herein, she argues that several Italian films of the 1960s and 1970s continued the spirit of neorealism, in spite of their stylistic differences from it. In her reading of *Teorema*, she suggests that the moral commitment to a constant reassessment of reality is the key to Pasolini's work.[15] Different though the bent of her discourse is from mine, I do acknowledge her work on *Teorema* as being the first significant step in the direction that my use of his films will take. What follows is an attempt to ground the question of "a certain realism" theoretically.

A Certain Realism

There is of course a sense in which a realist position was a cultural duty for Pasolini. Not only had neorealist cinema represented the most significant artistic production of his formative years, but the word "realism" had been and in some ways still was the battle cry of the Left. In Italy, the fifties were characterized by interminable debates about the essence of realism and about the need to overcome the limitations of neorealism to achieve the ideological and artistic proficiency of critical realism—a not-so-distant relative of the socialist realism that many indicated as the role model for artistic commitment.[16] In France, the work of Bazin voiced the claims of a phenomenological kind of realism based on the ontology of the film image and on the potential reproduction of the ambiguity of the real via a repudiation of montage. Finally, the *cinema d'autore* was expressly meant as a return to a neorealist attitude.

In spite of what is commonly held, nearly everyone in the realist camp was aware that there was no one "realism," but "realisms." By 1960, the realist tradition included such theorists as Aristarco, Barbaro, Bazin, Kracauer, Zavattini, and arguably Eisenstein. Oversimplifying, the word "realism" had three, variously overlapping, meanings: (*1*) the rendering of minute details—that is, photography's perfection that "redeems" physical reality (Kracauer, the various documentary schools); (*2*) the respect for and fidelity to real time and space so that representation mimes reality's perceptual coordinates (Bazin, Zavattini); (*3*) a socially progressive portrayal of the reality beyond appearances that aims to teach the spectator how things really were/are—often assuming the lower classes as its objects (Eisenstein, Aristarco, Barbaro). From the point of view of film practice, the realist tradition recognized its antecedents in Lumière (the by now mythical portrayal of the train arriving at the Ciotat station); Stroheim (total fidelity to detail and dawn of the realist fiction film); Flaherty (the idea of documentary); Eisenstein and Vertov (opposite and yet complementary examples of "extravagant" and progressive filmmaking in the name of a Marxist reality); Grierson and the British school of documentary (photographic truth in the service of social problems and the downtrodden); Renoir and the so-called French poetic realism (social subjects treated in a way that exudes the melancholic pessimism often associated with realism); and, finally, neorealism (nonprofessional actors, shooting on location, "anti-Hollywoodism," social concerns).

Nearly all realist theories and practices before Pasolini can be grouped under the heading of *mimetic realism*.[17] Not only do they stress the power of photographic mimesis and cinema's role as a window on the world, but, more important, they all assume that there is a reality in the traditional sense—a sort of noumenal kernel to be reached by means of proper methods. Pasolini never subscribed to a belief in mimetic realism, for he undermined its very basis by denying the existence of objective reality. Cinema, yes, uses real objects in front of the camera but they are always-already linguistic signs, so that the concept of perfect mimesis can have no grounds—not even in real life do we see things as they are. In fact, Pasolini consistently called naturalism the style seeking to represent things the way they are as well as the accurate rendition of minute details; and he abhorred such a style, devising a film form as distant from naturalism as possible. His reputation as a naive realist, then, was mostly due to the bad timing of his theoretical stance. For the sixties brought a vehement and sophisticated attack upon realism; this was most definitely the wrong time to defend cinema's relationship to reality.

Although the results of the antirealist wave became a fait accompli only after Pasolini's death, the first, massive attack took place in the decade 1965–1975. It started with the deconstruction of the "impression of reality" (Metz), of the "reality effect" (Barthes), of the very notion of an outside of the text (Derrida), and of the false transparency of iconic signs and the open work theory (Eco). *Cahiers du Cinema* and *Screen* initiated a systematic demolition of representation and realism from a leftist point of view. Blurring any distinction between naturalism and realism, exposing the dangers contained in the idea of representation, and highlighting the complicity of realist cinema with the classic antecedent of the nineteenth-century novel, numerous critics slowly forced realism to signify what Bazin and the neorealists regarded as its very opposite: illusionism. Crowning such attacks, Colin MacCabe detailed the notion of the "classic realist text" as a formal organization that fosters the idea of a fixed reality waiting to be objectively perceived. It treats the sign as transparent, privileges representation instead of signification, reinforces the passivity of the spectator, and fails to portray the real as contradictory and articulated.[18] Furthermore, such a mode of textual organization would be so powerfully deceptive as to override any progressive intent that the author might have had. Thus practically every narrative film—from *Bicycle Thief* to *Rambo*—falls into this category. There certainly was something unfair in calling films "realist" when they had not been conceived as such by their makers. Still, much of the criticism against realism succeeded in exposing the cinematic conventions that Pasolini ascribed to the cinema of prose (continuity editing, reverse field, etc.). Since the attack upon mimetic realism originated from a leftist standpoint, most critics at first hesitated to dismiss the notion of reality altogether. As one could no longer speak of something outside the text, however, the only reality that one was allowed to postulate was that of the text itself. *Semiotic realism* was thus born of the attempt to combine Marxist commitment with the poststructural shift from representation to signification. According to Gianni Scalia, this definition would include all those films that foreground their material reality by means of a self-reflexive, modernist textuality. The referential function was then supplanted by the self-referential one. Brecht's theater became the model for a realist practice that aimed at distancing the spectators rather than at encouraging their identification with the narrative. Pleasure and feelings were ruled out; truly subversive films were supposed to make the spectator work. But by the late seventies, the disastrous effects of the critics' agreement on calling Hollywood films realist could no longer be contained. With a few exceptions, the term "realist" was no longer used to designate progressive and critical films. Today, to my knowledge, nobody attempts a revival of the positive connotation of realism; the proclamation of the evils of realism/representationalism has become a ritual that nearly every piece of theory feels compelled to celebrate. Although some now have pointed out the one-sidedness of the antirealist attack, the general mood is that realism is, at best, a useless term.

And perhaps it is. But the question then becomes: What do we call texts *animated by the desire* to refer to a reality that, however problematic and elusive, nonetheless is there to haunt us as "that which must be made sense of"? It seems to me that once we have all agreed on the fact that there is no objective reality, we can then proceed to map out the possibility of talking about it again. The refusal to do so amounts to leaving the discourse on reality in the hands of those who have the power of truth, those who are not inclined to deconstruct the notion of reality because they are too busy constructing it through the control of what Adorno called the "culture industry" and Enzesberger the "consciousness industry." In this respect, I think that "realism" is still the best term, provided that we submit it to the critical revision indicated by Pasolini, or better, by his-work-as-I-use-it.

From the standpoint of theory, Pasolini's contributions do *not* have the capacity to rescue the word "realism" from its disgrace. We have seen that he himself had mixed feelings about it and occasionally felt compelled to keep it at a distance. Only through his film practice can one appreciate the extent to which he surreptitiously worked at keeping a positive connotation of the term in sight. It is nonetheless possible to reconstruct a sense of his theoretical orientation by using the only text in which he extensively dealt with the subject, tellingly a poem rather than an essay. In 1960 he wrote an eight-stanza, Shakespearean remake of Anthony's rousing speech over Caesar's dead body, which he entitled "On the Death of Realism."[19] A perfect example of Pasolini's "extravagant" theorizing, this poem expressed his worries for the future of realism which, let us not forget, was then the *mot d'ordre* of the leftist intelligentsia. Vulnerable as he was to their criticism, Pasolini could not just say that realism was better dead and had to start anew. He thus imagined that realism, like Caesar, had been treacherously murdered by "respectable writers" (Cassola and Lampedusa, whom he labeled "neopurist") and that it had left "seventy-five liras of renewed sense of history," a legacy of which Pasolini himself was the self-appointed executor. In so doing, he killed two birds with one stone, for he attacked the opponents of realism *as well as its enemy within*. Ironically, the enemy without turned out to be the same as the enemy within: formalism, that is, the excessive preoccupation with formal prescriptions which reduce writing to its literary function alone and "purify" the text from "vulgar" concerns with reality. If the attack against formalism from a realist standpoint was nothing new, the idea that realism had itself become a formalism was. And, even more interestingly, Pasolini did not suggest that realism heed content alone, but that it should subordinate *both* form and content to something else, for in and of themselves neither form nor content is a guarantee of realism. What then is the mark of a realist practice?

In the seventh stanza, Pasolini admits to being "involved with that massacred style because of passion," thus implying that realism is bound to desire and the subject. The entire edifice based on the notion of realism as impassive observation and dispassionate portrayal from an objective point of view crumbles. Fueled by passion, realism becomes a subjective force, a bodily humor circulating in the veins of people rather than in the crevices of a text. To crown this suggestion, in the eighth and last stanza Pasolini describes the realist legacy as a series of authors (Moravia, Morante, Calvino, and Gadda) who can be appreciated only "*individually*." The emphasis on "*individually*" (the only italicized word in the entire poem) obviously reinforces the irruption of subjectivity in the realist domain. But there is more. The list of books and authors that Anthony-Pasolini recommends as the legacy of realism is heterogeneous and idiosyncratic; the line separating the "neopurist" murderers from the "good guys" is so flimsy that it is as if Pasolini were saying: "After all, I, the reader, am the measure of all realism. Read as I do and you'll live up to Caesar's legacy." Realism then becomes an act of reading. Differently put, Pasolini is surreptitiously saying what his fidelity to the Party li(n)e prevented him from stating right out: mimetic realism is better off dead, and no resurrection is possible unless one starts by reconsidering the role of the reader/viewer. It is a powerful argument that could neither be fully understood nor fleshed out back then, not even by Pasolini himself. Thirty years later, however, our familiarity with reception theories allows us to find a use for Pasolini's dawning awareness of realism's disease *and* of its possible cure as well.

The argument that realism is essentially a mode of reading anticipates the later developments of the antirealist wave. In *Visible Fictions*, for instance, John Ellis argues that realism is "a complex network of conventions of portrayal and audience expectations alike," that it is "a powerful regime of reading sounds and moving images" which, for him, constitutes an equally "powerful block to the development of new forms of use of the two media" (cinema and TV).[20] Although the virulence of his rejection of realism is similar to that, say, of MacCabe, the problem is no longer seen exclusively in the text. Realism is a powerful regime of reading images and sounds, a set of active operations performed on a text. Whereas the early antirealist attacks strove to find the seed of illusionism in the text itself, now the complicity of the audience is taken for granted. Pasolini reached these conclusions some twenty years before Ellis, for he had too high a sense of how passions literally inform artistic consumption ever to ascribe a rigid and exclusive power to the text. Although Pasolini never actually tackled the question of what a realist reading would/should do, it is safe to assume that for him it did not have the negative connotations that it has for Ellis.

An uncertain category, realism as the viewer's responsibility cannot be defined once and for all. Since my reading of Pasolini's films will presumptuously attempt to both exemplify and flesh out such a category, suffice it here to sketch its main traits as I infer them from Pasolini's discussions on realism. Informed by passion, a realistic reading acknowledges that artistic consumption is not an exclusively mental thing, concerns itself with the feelings provoked by the text, and is constantly aware of the subj*a*ctive nature of interpretation. A realist spectator first lets his/her bodily humors be moved by the text and then allows reason to enter the scene, rationally asking him/herself how and why s/he could have been moved like that. Thus, as a mode of textual consumption, realism transforms viewing into an experience with a reality-value, that is, an experience which increases the subject's awareness of his/her position within the language of reality. An example: quoting Vito Russo's statement that "the men in Hawks's buddy films spend an inordinate amount of time preventing each other from actually getting laid or even spending too much time with women," Bertrand

Philbert astutely remarks that "where 'normal' spectators will see nothing but a celebration of virility and misogyny, the gay ones will certainly read something else."[21] Let us follow Philbert's suggestion and imagine two possible readings: the "normal" and the gay. It is very likely that the "normal" reading, qua "normal," will lack the awareness of itself as being just one of the possible readings and will think of itself as "natural." Obversely, it is just as likely that the gay reading will be aware of itself as different from the "normal." Hence, the gay reading is more realistic, *not* because it uncovers what the text really says but because it uncovers a textual dimension that is normally overlooked *and* stems from the viewer's positional awareness. The gay reading turns interpretation into an experience yielding information about the differential constitution of the public *and* of the text, for the text too, offering as it does different footholds for different readers, is divided. In Pasolinian terminology, the gay reading stems from a forceful combination of passion and reason. And since according to him the combination of passion and reason results in ideology, we can assume that the main trait of a realist reading is *ideological awareness*. Responding to a reader of the weekly *Vie nuove* who had accused his poem "On the Death of Realism" of superficiality (or naiveté, as it would later be fashionable to say), Pasolini wrote that he did "not consider realism a formal but an ideological fact. Whenever the ideological dimension is realistically faced, any formal solution is valid."[22] The point is important and deserves attention, for it implicitly takes issue with a mistake made by mimetic and semiotic realisms alike (although the latter was not yet born): they both consider realism as a formal fact. If the former strove to define the essence of realism as a mode of textual organization (long take, deep focus), so did most of its critics take it to be a set of technoformal arrangements (narrative sutures, 180 degree rule, reverse field, etc.). Of course, the mapping of the *potential* effects of stylistic devices and of the technological apparatus is extremely important, but one cannot discount the power of ideological awareness, of realistic passion and reason. For Bazin and MacCabe the form of the text flattens out content and nullifies the spectator's intentions. But, Pasolini seems to be suggesting, when the act of viewing is realistically faced, every text will offer information about its reality. There is no Hollywood illusionism that can narcotize an ideologically aware viewer. Similarly, there is no modernist self-reflexiveness that will ensure that the ill-famed "large public" will become conscious of the productive apparatus behind the film. Indeed, the most that an avant-garde film can do is to force the average viewer to leave the theater and thereby decree its commercial failure (taken as a sign of quality in many circles, and perhaps *not* without good reason).

The thrust of Pasolini's argument, of course, aims at leaving the realist author free of formal constraints. This is not to say that he disregarded formal questions. Quite the contrary, they had a primary role for him. But he did not tolerate stylistic prescriptions, consistently refused to ascribe rigid meanings to this or that form, and thought that the question of realism had to be solved "individually." The passion with which the author transforms his/her material may imbue the text with "a certain realism" that, in its turn, may affect the spectator in such a way that s/he feels motivated to adopt a realistic attitude (ideological self-awareness). By arguing that the decision of whether or not a text is realist cannot be made on formal considerations alone, Pasolini cuts across all the diatribes on the essence of the realist text and joins the voice of two solitary realists whom he admired: Brecht and Rossellini. The former did more than just preach the method of distancing the viewer. In his polemics with Lukacs, Brecht argued that "our conception of realism must be broad and political, free from aesthetic restrictions and independent from convention."[23] Unwittingly preempting Bazin's statement of the opposite, Brecht argued that realism is not at all a matter of means but of ends, for "the means must be asked what the end is."[24] And Rossellini also often remarked that neorealism had no a priori stylistic prescriptions, for it was above all a moral fact. Brecht, Rossellini, and Pasolini thus displace the discussion of realism as method and push it on the uncertain road toward Roy Armes's "realism as attitude," which he distinguishes from "realism as style."[25] Realism, then, is first and foremost an attitude of both authors and spectators. Although the details and vicissitudes of Pasolini's realistic attitude will be examined in the context of individual films, it may be useful to introduce its fundamental polarities here.

At its best, Pasolini's realism is the result of an interaction between two fundamental semiotic attitudes which I will define as (1) ideological and (2) mystical.

Fueled by Marxism and Freudian psychoanalysis, the ideological attitude does not trust the world of appearances and therefore treats reality suspiciously. It is an interpretive strategy reminiscent of what Paul Ricoeur felicitously called a "hermeneutics of suspicion" to describe the attitude Marx and Freud shared vis-à-vis their object of inquiry, an attitude characterized by distrust of the given as dissimulation of the real.[26] Immediate physical reality (e.g., *Gennariello*'s curtain) and the subject's consciousness (e.g., his perception of the curtain) are *not* to be trusted, for something more real is going on behind and beneath them, something which determines their actual meaning and which must be uncovered if knowledge is to prompt effective action. Interestingly, then, Pasolini accepted Marx and Freud more for the cognitive gestures they suggested than for the actual picture of reality they proposed (and often imposed, at least through their dogmatic followers). The realist gesture par excellence, the desire to reveal what lies behind the deceptive mask of appearances, has been criticized on the score that it would consider reality as made up of progressive layers, and knowledge as the act of digging up the deepest of them, a sort of Kantian noumenon. In fact, ideological suspicion, at its best, has nothing metaphysical about it. *There are*, undeniably, realities that are misrepresented and/or silenced by the hegemonic information system; *there are* social groups and practices that, as it were, get little or no coverage; *there are* instincts and feelings that we are not supposed to acknowledge. In this respect, Pasolini did not need Marx or Freud to learn the need for suspicion. Since his own libidinal economy was the object of repressive strategies and he knew that a different kind of reality lay behind the words and images used conventionally to depict homosexuality, mistrust for the given was only "natural" to him. In this respect, realist suspicion is/should be the daily bread of the oppressed. It is never a question, however, of discovering an ultimate essence or of arguing that what power hides is intrinsically more substantial than what it reveals. True, he often believed that the subproletariat and the peasants, *il popolo*, were somehow more real than the upper classes, but this was only because traditionally they had been excluded by dominant representations. In this light there will always be a reality to be unveiled by realists, because the majority has the tendency to create the world in its own image. To refuse suspicion on the basis that it has a metaphysical underpinning would be missing the point altogether. It would be suspect.

Thus, the ideological view of reality prompts the subject to investigate what cannot be seen, the dark side, the forbidden. As historical changes modify the politics of representation and tend to repress certain things more than others, so will different periods have different hidden realities to be rescued from the limbo of social oblivion. Each epoch has its realists who seek to give visibility to what is socially invisible. The hidden reality need not be a social group. It can be sexuality in a time of repressive censorship, as it certainly was for Pasolini. Or it can be an aspect of the ruling classes which is not emphasized by standard representations. Seen in this light, some of the films by Antonioni were realistic in that they uncovered truths of the bourgeois condition which were generally disregarded.

But one cannot be suspicious all the time. Reality is also what is visible, the realm of appearance and the sense that there is no unmasking that will get us to the core of things. It is hardly coincidental that

Pasolini's mystical attitude is reminiscent of what Ricoeur called "interpretation as recollection of meaning," an attitude which opposes suspicion and is based on trust and respect: driven by "care or concern for the *object*," the subject seeks "to dis-implicate that object" from sociohistorical questions and surrenders "to the movement of meaning which, starting from the literal sense, points to something grasped in the region of the sacred."[27] Fueled by Jung's and Eliade's works on myth as well as by his own readings in existential phenomenology, Pasolini's mystical attitude eschews logical thinking, exalts the enigmatic quality of life, and celebrates death as the purveyor of *the* mystery that "makes Man great." Unlike rationalism (which for Pasolini included both bourgeois and Marxist scientisms), it regards enigma less a block to understanding than its very key. Unlike the philosophies variously deriving from the Enlightenment, it values myth and the sacred, for they both rely on metaphor, bear witness to the multiplicity of meaning, and enhance the subject's disposition to wondering. And wandering. According to James Hillman, the most "Pasolinian" of Jung's followers, deviance and "extravagance" are the passions of a soul that "sees through the hypocrisies, the fixed positions of every convention" and thus is "always at variance with the point of view of the others."[28] By adopting a mythical perspective, Pasolini thus took issue with both Marxism and with Freudianism, which saw deviance as decadent and regressive.

The mystical attitude was responsible for the capital "R" which Pasolini often used when referring to "Reality" as an impersonal Being in constant soliloquy. The idea of this global entity, which so much irritated Pasolini's critics, is obviously reminiscent of Spinoza's God and of the serene immanence of Brahma endlessly playing with its own fragments. It is my contention that Pasolini's mystical attitude helped him to think of his homosexuality. Burdened with the dominant view that his own existence was a crime against nature, Pasolini found relief in the notion of a Reality that "plays at questioning its own rules by means of anomalies which have the effect of creating the infinite chain of meaning."[29] In the idea of Reality as a global language playing with its signs, there is no room for hierarchies: everything under the sun is worthy of existing because it is a fragment of the whole, everything is necessary and beyond good and evil. Moreover, such Reality needs "transgression" and "anomalies" for meaning to exist. It is only through opposition and deviance that meaning is created. "Transgression," then, is a necessary (when not sacred) state in the order of things: opposing nature is part of nature too.

In Pasolini, the ideological and mystical attitudes were intimately connected in various ways. They both presuppose a totality which gives meaning to individual cases. They both grant primacy to wondering and questioning. Pasolini himself was often tempted to regard both attitudes as one, for he did not regard Marxism and the sacred as irreconcilable. Critics, however, are fond of emphasizing his development as a transition from ideology to myth, thus preventing the possibility of exploring the points at which the two intersect. If it is true that during the years 1968–1973 Pasolini emphasized his mystical leanings, it never was a matter of a clean slate, of a replacement of one attitude with another. The mystical attitude became prominent in a moment of historical crisis and must be viewed in this context. Confronted with the Marxists' increasing blindness to myth and death, to the irrational in life, Pasolini, *when addressing a leftist audience*, chose to emphasize his mystical leanings. In fact, Pasolini's double attitude was the best proof of the dialogical nature of discourse. Discourse is never just the position of an isolated subject of the enunciation but is always a positioning with respect to some interlocutor. Whenever addressing the public at large, Pasolini couched himself within the ideological/Marxist attitude, for the most urgent task in those circumstances was (is) that of demythologizing, demystifying. When his interlocutor was the progressive intelligentsia—that is, a public that had gone too far in the duty of demystifying and had forsaken the oppositional nature of the sacred—then Pasolini felt the need to adopt a different position which countered leftist conformism. Pasolini's emphasis on a mystical attitude represented his strongest statement on the improbability of Italy's renewing itself in the wake of the superficial *gauchisme* of those years. Pessimistic and cynical though this view may have been, history proved him right. His diagnosis was realistic (in both the common and philosophical meanings of the word) and he was prophetic: since then Italy has quickly buried its openness to change, restoration is under way, and the Left slowly discovers the need to reestablish its discourse on a less dogmatic basis, a discourse capable of incorporating the irrational and the religious.

By regarding realism above all as a question of attitude, Pasolini shifted the focus toward the two realities previously overlooked by mimetic and semiotic realisms alike: the subjactivities of, respectively, the author and the spectator. This, to be sure, dissipates the category of realism, but such is the price to pay if we are to live up to the demands of the epochal change we are experiencing. Dissipated and fuzzy, realism is still viable as a discourse on the various realities at work in the process of artistic consumption. It is possible to imagine each film as an event involving four variously articulated realities:

1. the reality of the author
2. the reality of the text, as the material format with which it circulates
3. the reality alluded to (represented/signified) by the text
4. the reality of the spectator

Mimetic realism concerned itself almost exclusively with (3). The author had to disappear to let nature be the artist; the text had to deny its signifying status in order to convince an unrealistically conceived spectator of its reality-value. Semiotic realism, instead, dissolved (3) as a by-product of (2), which thus acquired an inordinate prominence. The author him/herself was not so much a reality to be accounted but an effect of a signifying organization that left visible traces of its production. And the viewer was either a passive, statistical entity constructed by the film or a politically correct subject willing to work at the rewriting of the text. In both cases, a primary place was being assigned to the two realities lending themselves to objectification: text and referent; realism was the discourse of the object alone. Pasolini's initial move indicated the spectator as the arbitrator of the question. His/her reality regulates the fate of the others. A reminder of the impossibility of ever fixing what a successful realist text *is*, the viewer can hardly be accounted in a theoretical paradigm. Will s/he cooperate? Who is s/he anyway? A director with a realist aim ought to be prepared to see his/her entire project dependent on the viewer's cooperation. The idea of a totally uncooperative spectator is of course a bit farfetched, but it has the merit of "de-objectifying" realism. Simultaneously, Pasolini privileged the reality of the author as the subjective filter which alone can guarantee that realism will not repeat its past errors (formalism, rationalism). After its death, realism is born again as "a certain realism," a discourse which can only be broached by making it hinge on the element whose repression caused the demise of all previous realisms: the subject. It is only after paying this tribute to the subject's formative role in the constitution of the object that one can proceed to map out what Pasolini thought of (2) and (3), the two realties on which previous realisms were based.

Pasolini's refusal to define *the* means in order to leave the author free from prescriptions as to how reach the end makes a general discussion of realist poetics impossible. One can only see what he did in each film and whether or not he may have succeeded. Suffice it to say here that Pasolini agreed with semiotic realists that a text should leave visible traces of its production, but he disagreed with them as to how this should be done. Whereas they would opt for a metadiscursive textuality, he thought that a text ought to inform the spectators about the author rather than about itself. He criticized avant-garde texts on the score that they reveal nothing about their authors (*HE*, 130). Pasolini was not saying that a text should expose the author's intentions. In fact, he never dealt with the subject of intentionality at all. He was merely suggesting that a poem or a film is so much more effective if it manages to offer an idea of how its author lives, what his/her relationship to the text is. In other words, the awareness of the production of meaning is not to be entrusted to the difficulties of a film on filming but to a film poetically bent upon revealing the author's subj*a*ctivity. For example, the spectators of *Accattone* are obliquely informed of Pasolini's relationship to the material so that they find themselves in the position of evaluating *the relationship* between a particular author and the Roman subproletariat. We are still within the realm of the Godardian refusal of cinema as "reflection of reality" in favor of "reality of the reflection." The reality that is doing the reflection, however, is that of the author, lest we fall prey to yet another version of realism's mortal enemy: formalism. Ideally, then, Pasolini aimed at modifying the mirroring theory of mimetic realism by changing the shape of the mirror. The truly realistic mirror is bent around the edges in order to include a fleeting picture of the author who is holding it up, all the while exhibiting its distorted shape—its style—as a memento that the reflected reality will be distorted accordingly.

On the subject of (3), too, it is possible to understand Pasolini's position as a simultaneous acceptance and refusal of antirealist positions. He would totally agree with their attack upon a simple-minded notion of reality represented by a text, but would not go so far as to deny the possibility of some referential function. In the article "The End of the Avant-garde," he completely agreed with Barthes's plea for a "suspension of meaning" but he refused to draw antireferential conclusions from it: "To suspend meaning," comments Pasolini, "here is a stupendous epigraph for what could be a new description of commitment" (*HE*, 138). Citing the internal revolution of the bourgeoisie (Pasolini's own definition of the sixties) and the emergence of the Third World as events upsetting Western mental habits, Pasolini suggests that it is because of reality's fragility that meaning is to be suspended. Rather than in the name of an omnipotent textuality, referentiality should be questioned in order to better mime reality. "It seems to me, in short, that in any case a 'reality' to be evoked is not lacking and, on the contrary, we are guilty if we do not do so" (*HE*, 138). The text must somehow evoke reality, albeit within the framework of a problematic referentiality, which is what most of Pasolini's films do.

I hope I have provided the reader with a theoretical introduction to

Pasolini's cinema from the standpoint of "a certain realism." The rest of the book is dedicated to the analysis of his films, one by one, chronologically. To anticipate my overall thesis, I shall argue that Pasolini contributed to the creation of "a certain realism" with varying success up until *Medea* (1970). Here and in the films of *La trilogia della vita* his realist vein failed. He became aware, however, of such a failure, repudiated *La trilogia della vita*, and attempted a return to a realist ideology with what, in many ways, was to be his best film: *Salò*. Once seen from the point of view of his last film—his cinematic death—Pasolini's oeuvre, I shall argue, must be read in the light of the need to rearticulate cinema with a discourse on reality.

4

Accattone

Vittorio, nicknamed Accattone, is a pimp supported by Maddalena, a prostitute who turned in her former pimp, Ciccio, in order to stay with Accattone. The latter spends his time lounging with his cronies (pimps, swindlers, loafers), talking and arguing (the first sequence shows Accattone diving into the Tiber on a full stomach to prove that he is not afraid of death). After Maddalena is first beaten up by Ciccio's friends and then thrown in jail, Accattone turns to his ex-wife Ascenza for help. She and her brother reject him, but while looking for Ascenza, Accattone meets Stella, a naive, virginal figure. He plans to make her into a prostitute, but when she is finally willing to sacrifice herself for him, Accattone feels remorse and decides that he will provide for her. He gets a job loading scrap-iron, but he finds it too hard—"What is this, Buchenwald?"—and quits. Meanwhile, in jail, Maddalena finds out about Accattone's new girl and squeals on him, and the police start watching him. Finally, Accattone turns to a thief, Balilla, and, together with another *buono a nulla* (good for nothing), they go out looking for something to steal. No sooner do they steal a load of meat from a truck than the police arrest them. Accattone manages to escape on a motorcycle but dies when he crashes into a car.

> *Realism is the explicit search for a new frame to make us see better, or to see something else, or to see the same thing differently. . . . Every realism is the anti-realism of another realism.*
>
> Dominique Noguez

Shortly before beginning the filming of *Accattone* (1961), Pasolini
wrote a brief, enlightening piece for an issue of *Films and Filming* dedicated to Italian cinema.[1] Entitled "Intellectualism . . . and the Teds,"
it reveals the extent to which realism was on his mind. As if taking
issue with Aristarco, whose influential journal *Cinema Nuovo* had
been supporting the Lukacsian, socialist yet classic realism best exemplified by Visconti's *Senso* (1954), Pasolini categorically denied that the
cinema could parallel nineteenth-century realism and concluded:
"There is no absolute Realism that is valid for all epochs. Every epoch
has its own realism. And this is because every epoch has its own ideology." Having thus declared the historicity of realism, Pasolini proceeded to distance himself from the artistic ideology which had pre-
ceded and formed him: neorealism. In the same article, he reiterated
the conviction that in its day neorealism had lifted the mask from
Italy's face and revealed what fascism could not show; but he also
accused it of being too humanistic and rational. Something different
was needed, Pasolini suggested, in order to broach the "New Realism"
for which the times were ripe. Such a "New Realism," which "is the
feeling behind my work," would still perform neorealism's unmasking
operation, but it would rely on different ideological and cinematic
assumptions.

In the best realist tradition, Pasolini argues that what had seemed
realism in 1945 no longer held up in 1960, and that only by understanding where neorealism had gone sour could one hope to keep up the
realist spirit: every epoch has something to unmask; for power, by
definition, only tends to produce representations instrumental to its
reproduction. *Accattone* picked up the realist trail where neorealist-
realists had left off. While this seemed evident to contemporary critics
(the French coined the expression "neo-neorealism"), more recent
accounts of Pasolini's cinematic debut have ignored the question of
realism and have preferred to analyze *Accattone* in the light of traits
which would characterize Pasolini's subsequent production, such as his
mythical populism and antinarrative style. Although such an auteurist
reading of *Accattone* has generated interesting thematic insights (as
well as wishful projections) into Pasolini's oeuvre, my concern with
realism prompts me to revert to the question of *Accattone*'s relationship with "the undisputed glory of the Italian cinema."[2]

There is no doubt that in many ways *Accattone* resurrects the spirit
of early neorealism. Thematically, the film purports to show the reality
of those social groups (pimps, whores, marginals) which even neorealism had often kept at bay. The stark quality of the images, the pre-
cariousness of conventional suturing strategies (match-cutting and
screen direction are often shaky), and the use of nonprofessionals are

all evident examples of Pasolini's intention to follow in the tracks of the cinematic tradition with which he was familiar. In *The Altering Eye*, R. P. Kolker quite aptly entitles the chapter in which he discusses neorealism's role in the history of cinema "The Validity of the Image." In it he argues that by opting for unembellished narratives and by reducing plot devices to the bare bone, neorealists sought to enhance the significance of the individual image. In effect, from watching neorealist films one gets the impression that their directors strove to eschew a too artificial mise-en-scène because they believed that the images possessed the power to speak in and of themselves. Undoubtedly, Pasolini's cinema is a tribute to the validity of images. But while retaining the neorealists' faith in single shots and frames, he thought it necessary to question the sense of plenitude which seemed to be its corollary.

Due perhaps to the self-evident drama of postwar landscapes and situations, neorealists assumed that images could have the same meaning for everyone. Theirs was a common assumption that all spectators would be affected by the images of, say, a homosexual (Rossellini) or a distressed child (De Sica) in the same way because of the inherent meaning of that image, because of the necessarily common human reaction in the face of an unequivocal signifier of either depravity or pitiable unhappiness. Put another way, neorealism relied on the plenitude of the represented image, that is, on its hoped-for monosemic status. Inevitably, the audience was also thought of as unified, as an undifferentiated mass bound to experience a common (because natural) reaction in the face of a universal signifier. Most of the ideological assumptions behind this attitude were not questioned. For example, as Pasolini suggested, the faith in a human matrix that *must* be the same for all (humanism) and the belief in ecumenical Reason as the stand-in for God (rationalism) were the theoretical linchpins of neorealism. The basic values of the very society criticized by neorealists were unwittingly reinforced: honesty, heterosexuality, the work ethic, socioeconomic aspirations. Most neorealist marginals aspire to an honest job, and society's failure to provide them with one is the root of and justification for their deviation from the norm. Typical was the example of *Ladri di biciclette* (*Bicycle Thief*, 1948), where the hapless protagonist is caught by a menacing albeit good-hearted crowd that represents the code he should not have broken, no matter how justified his actions may have been: Thou shalt not steal.

As for children, neorealist directors never suspected that the pity we are forced to feel for a child roaming the streets reinforces the conventional image of childhood as the age of cozy and innocent fun, an image that, in its turn, universalizes the condition of bourgeois children as well as *our* (middle-class) type of social contract. This is not to say that disenfranchised youth should be kept off the screen. Bunuel's *Los Olvidados* or Babenco's *Pixote* reveals what is needed to portray subproletarian kids without falling into neorealist sentimentalism and ideological bad faith: a keen sense of and acceptance of difference. These children do not implicitly long for a middle-class Christmas tree; they have their moments of happiness *within* their world.

Accattone takes on the ideological and cinematic assumptions outlined above and drives the wedge of difference into neorealist plenitude. *Accattone* makes the image the site of an ambivalent decoding. With the typical passion of a writer who is setting out to make his first film, Pasolini cleverly encapsulates *Accattone*'s entire operation in the four Dantean verses which preface it:

> The angel of the Lord took me and Satan
> cried out: why do you rob me? You take
> for yourself the eternal part of him for
> one little tear which takes him from me.

On a formal level, a prefatory quotation from Dante, whom Pasolini always praised for his realism, serves the purpose of legitimizing the "low" subject matter as well as placing the film under the aegis of an Italian realist tradition which dates back to the Middle Ages (an indirect reminder of the historicity of realism). Taken from *Purgatory*'s fifth canto, these verses relate the climax of Buonconte's tale of his own salvation. In the final moments of a sinful life, Buonconte bursts into tears and is thus saved by God, who takes the tear as a sign of commendable repentance. Satan feels deprived of a soul to which he thought he had all the rights, and is scorned "for one little tear!"

Besides reminding us that one's life can be judged only after one's last breath (a crucial notion for Pasolini to which I will return later), Buonconte's story offers us a preliminary parable of the ambivalence of the image. Although the devil regards a certain man as hopelessly damned, he is proved wrong by another interpretation. And we have a tear which the devil sees as meaningless and which God, as opposed to the devil, normatively interprets as a sign of repentance. Critics took this quotation as a sign of Accattone's repentance, as if Pasolini had accepted God's judgment unquestioningly. I would like to use the quote from Dante as a sign of Pasolini's awareness that the image of the tear is always-already interpreted by opposite, antagonistic readings. It is only by virtue of an act of interpretive force that the tear image comes to have one meaning. That the image in question is a tear is no less significant. Neorealists easily assumed that tears had a univocal meaning, and indeed many of their films were geared for tear-jerking.

As did God in Buonconte's tale, so did they believe in the redemptive value of tears; their realism was a search for images which, like tears, would elicit a compassionate response from the audience. Thus the role of the quotation is less to emphasize the intrinsic ambivalence of the image than to suggest that there is no image beyond the eyes of the beholder. Moreover, the beholders are ordered like God and Satan, in a vertical spectrum, *within power relations*. An image, any image, is a bone in a struggle between conflicting visions, between, on the one hand, a higher position which is endowed with the power of truth, and on the other hand, a lower position which must comply with the resolutions made in the higher spheres, however unwillingly. The cinematic implications of this are all too evident: images are subjected to antagonistic readings; there is no universal human position from which to look. To claim that such a position exists amounts to reconfirming the phallo-ethnocentrism of the dominant gaze which subsumes everything to one perspective. There are always different readings and—Pasolini's Marxist touch—they are subjected to the dominant/dominated dialectic.

It is of course no coincidence that the film's first image after such a prescription of ambivalence is a visual translation of vertical duality. We see a frontal close-up of a man holding a feathery bunch of flowers next to his bony, lower-class features (somewhat reminiscent of Pasolini's). Even if we leave aside the absence of an establishing shot informing us where we are, this image is perturbing. No sooner does the man open his mouth than the typically Pasolinian row of devastated teeth peeks through his lips. The words he utters (we still do not know to whom he is talking) indicate that he belongs to the uneducated. By mixing together a signifier of beauty with a visual translation of social lowliness, the first image in the film illustrates the quotation and reveals images to be the locus of a vertically ordered ambivalence: Are the flowers being "dragged down" by the low-class man, or is he "pulled up" by the flowers? Eventually, by the end of the film, we realize that he is Fulvio, an honest flower vendor, quite unlike *Accattone*'s pimps and loafers. Thus, by restricting our access to information and by means of an artificially constructed shot worthy of Eisenstein, the film's first frame begs to be taken as a signifier of ambivalence if not *coincidentia oppositorum*. The rest of the film will follow this track against plenitude and for dualism, against unity and for difference.

The Dual Vision

Atop the bridge on the Tiber from which he will dive, Accattone is flanked by a solemn marble angel. "Sculpturesque, he lingers"[3] in the suspension of time preceding the solution of the first narrative enigma: Will he win the absurd wager? A visual climax of the first episode which individuates Accattone among his friends, the frame with Accattone and the angel reinforces the notion that he does not really belong to his own world. It is a shot that nobody can miss and that many remember, as attested by the critics' frequent reference to it. Is Accattone the "real" angel? Or is this a premonition of his salvation? Or, again, is it an indication that he will stoop low and that the angel will fly high? Whatever the meanings generated by such a contrast, one thing is beyond doubt: the angel is there as a conventional sign of loftiness against which we are to measure Accattone. The frame is the site of a bipolar tension along the axis angel/Accattone. Reminiscent of the shot of Fulvio with the flowers, this is another example of blatantly dual framing that will recur at least twice in the film.

The first instance occurs when the starving Accattone and three of his friends ask Fulvio for permission to use his stove to cook some pasta. While everybody is anxiously waiting around the steaming pot, Accattone draws Fulvio aside in order to contrive a confidence scheme at the expense of the others. It is the first instance of Accattone's intentional rejection of his cronies. While explaining his plan to Fulvio, Accattone tries on a woman's hat and puts a wicker basket on Fulvio's head. The camera then isolates Accattone by means of a cut. On the wall behind him is a portrait of a woman. Besides stressing the polarity already introduced by the woman's hat, this frame singles out gender as an omnipresent set of relations that Accattone (and perhaps *Accattone*) has thus far systematically misrepresented. Since most women in the film are exploited as prostitutes and all of them figure in dominated positions at the mercy of men, the woman on the wall establishes a polarity against which Accattone's image is to be evaluated. Does his putting on of a woman's hat indicate that he is equally exploited? Is it suggesting that Accattone wants to abandon the sex of the exploiters? Is the wish to become a woman Accattone's, *Accattone*'s (in the sense of *écriture feminine*), or Pasolini's? Be that as it may, we are again confronted with a single frame whose unambiguous interpretation is undercut by vertically ordered tensions.

Accattone will never eat the spaghetti he has so cunningly secured for himself. On his way back to Fulvio's house, he meets Stella and sets out to corrupt her, albeit with a heart full of remorse. Although externally transformed into a lower-class sexual object, Stella retains her innocence and thus embodies the ambivalence (angel/whore) which women have long symbolized. Accattone has created an icon of ambivalence next to whom he will continue his textual trajectory. Significantly, his romantic stroll with Stella begins in a square dominated by a chalk-white, modern church. Again the camera isolates Accattone via a cut, so that he is contrasted with the towering figure of a saint painted on the church. Is this polarity a sign of what Accattone is leaving behind by initiating Stella's seduction? Or, quite the contrary, is it an indication that by making love to his ambivalent "star" he will embark on the road to heaven?

The importance of dual frames such as these does not lie in some ultimate meaning that each of them might disclose. They are peculiar instances of Pasolini's attempt both to highlight the validity of the individual image and to show it as the site of an unsolvable ambivalence. Within *Accattone*'s textual economy, dual frames interrupt the flow of seemingly naturalistic images and jolt spectators into the acknowledgment of the artifice of mise-en-scène. Differently put, one becomes aware that framing is the author's choice rather than the best and most natural position for the camera to be looking at things. The distancing effect that these shots achieve is not as extreme as in modernist texts, but is more subtle and therefore more subversive. Furthermore, dual frames confront us with a set of possible relations (high/low; salvation/damnation; dominant sex/dominated sex) and surreptitiously force us to take a position somewhere along the vertical axis. Our assessment will ultimately depend on how we view the opposites in the frame and in the film. For example, many regard *Accattone* as a story of redemption and read Accattone's affair with Stella as a sign of his salvation.[4] For them, Accattone's movement is upward. He is, so to speak, "pulled up" by the angel, and the initial quote from Dante is an anticipation that Accattone will be saved. I do not deny that this is a plausible reading. It is the film itself that constructs this possibility, *along with another*, which I happen to prefer: the question of salvation is irrelevant, for Accattone drags the angel down to earth. The film is not about what will happen after death, but what happens before.[5] Finally, dual frames are the climactic result of a dual vision which constructs visual space antagonistically. By juxtaposing images that a conventional iconography sees as contradictory, dual frames act as catalysts in the narrative, like practical signals disseminated along the textual path to invite the audience to see the film in the light of a blatantly heralded ambivalence. Spurred by the overbearing presence of dual frames, many viewers (at least those who want to "read" the film) are likely to notice that *Accattone* does indeed hinge on duality.

A sacrilegious mixture of "high" and "low" permeates the film and constitutes a primary level of duality, for *Accattone* mobilizes high culture to sustain and accompany a story of thieves and pimps, whores and lowlifes.[6] One need only think of Bach's music—which for Pasolini was "music with a capital M"—played over the image of the beating of Maddalena by the four Neapolitan pimps and the fight between Accattone and his brother-in-law.[7] Besides adding an epic quality to these scenes of bodies rolling in the dust of sun-drenched suburban alleys, such a use of Bach snatches "timeless" classical music away from its "natural"—but really only conventional—signification and forces it to come into contact with characters who traditionally do not "deserve" noble musical accompaniments. Similarly, the film contains several pictorial references to Masaccio, to fourteenth-century Florentine painting, and to Morandi, signaling the author's investment in high culture and his desire to mix it with his passionate portrayal of a transfigured underworld. Such a legitimate/illegitimate dialectic comes as no surprise, for Pasolini's own social position straddled both sides of the divide (dominated faction of the dominant sex) and represented an intolerable mixture of cultural refinement and sociosexual "turpitude." Moreover, the mixture of Bach's music and the pimps' language, of epic tone with low subject matter, adapts for the screen the *contaminatio* of *sermo sublimis* (sublime, tragic style) and *sermo humilis* (low, comedic style) which Auerbach found at the heart of European literary realism and which Pasolini enthusiastically took up.[8]

The main character's trajectory can be described as an uneasy balance between opposites. "Accattone," for example, is no real name, but means "beggar." *Accattonaggio* is the word by which Italian law designates and condemns the practice of beggary. Accattone's "real" name is Vittorio, a name that is onomastically antipodal to Accattone.[9] Significantly, only Stella will call him "Vittorio" and, on one occasion, he rebukes her for doing so: "Call me Accattone, because there are many Vittorios, but only one Accattone." If "Accattone" stresses his difference from everybody else, "Vittorio" somehow implies the acceptance of a sociolinguistic contract and the desire to rank high in its order. As a result of this, the main character is precariously suspended between a nickname and a name which both oppose and presuppose each other.

An image of incorporated ambivalence, Accattone moves in a narrative which variously articulates his (often physical) conflicts with the groups portrayed in the film, which, not surprisingly, are situated along a dominant/dominated vertical axis. On the socioeconomic level Accattone fights the ruling class (significantly present only via the police) and the working class (Ascenza's brother and Ascenza; though not proletarians in the Marxist sense, they both display the characteristics of a neorealist working class). On the sociosexual axis, he ends up opposing the pimps/exploiters, but he never ceases to regard the women/exploited as prostitutes. Accattone fights each of these groups, albeit with varying degrees of fervor. He rejects work whenever he is given the chance to become an honest proletarian, and he rejects pimping after his chance encounter with Stella. He wants neither to be exploited nor to exploit. The text does everything in its power to indicate that he is an outsider, even in his own milieu. Thus, while articulating a sociosexual space around the polar opposites dominant/dominated, *Accattone* visualizes an interval between opposites within which the main character positions himself. Repudiating both opposites, he turns to thievery. An exploration of thievery in the film will allow for a tentative charting of Accattone's/*Accattone*'s third route between opposites.

Thou Shalt Steal

The professional thief Balilla confirms that thievery marks a scandalous mixture which, in the context of values and activities shown in *Accattone*, somehow escapes the dichotomy exploiter/exploited. We first see him when the four Neapolitan pimps get Accattone drunk to loosen his tongue. In tears, Accattone launches himself into a bitter invective against pimping, so that Balilla's appearance at this moment qualifies him as the locus of a possible alternative. We then see him standing by a fountain "as if in a dream,"[10] while Accattone plods by. On this occasion, Balilla runs after Accattone, joins him, and, while reproaching him for his hopeless condition, suggests thievery as a way out. Finally, we see Balilla a third time during the crucial dream sequence in which Accattone prefigures his own death and *Accattone* its own ending. The text, here, will do everything in its power to contrast Balilla with Accattone's friends. He is the only one not wearing black; he stands by himself by the same fountain where we saw him before and mouths soundless words. It is as if Accattone could not listen to him yet. In order to be able to hear Balilla properly, Accattone must forsake pimping, which he does the morning after when he decides to try to provide for his woman by means of thievery. Together with the young Cartagine and Balilla himself, Accattone embarks on his first day as a thief. As if to christen the new course, they all stop at the flower stand where Fulvio throws some flowers on the cart that the three are pulling. Balilla sits on the cart, a thief amidst grace and beauty, an illegitimate mixture. But the eyes of the law are on them, and Accattone's first day as a thief will also be his last.

From the very moment Accattone repudiates the codes of his low world and Maddalena denounces him, the narrative is punctuated by recurrent close-ups of a policeman's eyes. Irregular and unpredictable in its recurrence, this shot gives a new tempo to Accattone's story. His life is reduced to segments, the length of each measured by the eyes of

the law, of power. The significance of this shot goes beyond its narrative and thematic function, for it opens up the vital question of
looking or, better yet, of the possible ways of seeing. Dominant
and dominated, exploiters and exploited, high and low, the opposites
which are visualized by the film and between which Accattone's/
Pasolini's ambivalent gaze situates itself connote ways of seeing as
well. Lost in the desolate dust of the Roman hinterland, lowlifes have
only peripheral vision which prevents them from actually seeing things.
It is as if they live in permanent darkness—Fulvio's opening remark to
Accattone and his friends suggests just that: "It must be Judgment
Day! Let me see your faces in the daylight! I have always seen you by
night!" In the "night" in which they live, one does not see things; one
is simply informed of them. Accattone is told of Maddalena's accident
by Pio; the Neapolitan pimps are informed of Maddalena's role in the
jailing of their friend Ciccio by Accattone; and Maddalena herself is
told of Accattone's affair with Stella by another prostitute. The low-life
characters seem to live in a prison which bars them from active sight.
They see only themselves and, what is worse, they seem not to have
any interest in wanting to see more. Power, on the other hand, demands absolute clarity of vision. The extreme close-ups of the policeman's eyes indicate power's conviction that all must be seen, monitored, and recorded. It is the ruling class's dream of panoptical vision,
an invisible surveillance which becomes so threateningly ubiquitous as
to force the social subjects to assume "a state of conscious and permanent visibility that assures the automatic functioning of power."[11] The
thief's way of seeing is opposed to both power's paranoid will to plenitude and to the marginals' lack of visual ambition.

A thief looks at the world from behind a mask, a screen which functions as a constant reminder of the individual position orienting the
gaze. There can be no illusion of an impartial and objective view, for
the world is seen, as in the cinema, through an "arbitrary rectangle."
By necessity, a thief is always aware of the interest which motivates
his/her gaze as well as the possibility of being, at any given moment,
subjected to an overpowering Gaze.[12] Shortly before their unsuccess-
ful theft, Balilla enters a sidewalk urinal made of a solid metal sheet
topped by a grating at eye level. After Balilla steps into it, Pasolini
cuts to a close-up of his eyes peeping through the grating. In blatant
and striking contrast to the policeman's eyes, Balilla's eyes look at us
through holes. His vision (and ours with it) is determined by the holes
in the gratings as much as by the full spaces between them; for him
(and us) the image will be the result of a pattern of light and dark,
presence and absence, objective properties and subjective filling in.
Drawing constant attention to the fact that something is left out,

the gaze through holes stimulates the self-reflexivity of the viewing subject. This is what we are shown in the scene in which Accattone steals the necklace from his son's neck. It is the first theft in the film, and it is significant that Accattone steals in order to buy Stella a pair of high heels, that is, in order to facilitate her conversion to that position of ambivalence by which he, in turn, will be increasingly affected. Accattone sneaks behind a wall in front of his ex-wife's dwelling. Through a hole in the wall, he first watches his brother-in-law, then Ascenza, going off to work. With its idyllic musical score, this portrait of early rising workers presents neorealist iconography at its most sentimental. Perhaps there is even some nostalgia for this world, but a cut to Accattone's face signals the impossibility of adhering to it. Accattone reflects on what he has seen through the hole and excuses himself for what he is about to do—he excuses himself for not respecting the proletarian idyll. The thief's vision—here Pasolini's vision—breeds division, a dissociation from a reality too full to be real: a reality from which something *must* be stolen.

In sum, Accattone's trajectory culminates in an activity and a vision which set him against all the other options and positions in the film. This is not to say that the film proposes thievery as a universal panacea, even though in the fettered world of Accattone it does seem the best way out for anybody who sees work as slavery. Upon careful scrutiny of the two opposite positions and viewpoints through which Accattone wriggles his way, thievery is symptomatic of both Pasolini's homosexuality and his realism.

In 1961, homosexuality could not be the object of Pasolini's realism. Even if his desire for a "New Realism" had screamed for a portrayal of homosexual sociosexual marginality, Pasolini would not have had the freedom to embark on such a project. Homosexuality could only surface after "considerations of representability" (to use the expression brilliantly coined by Freud to describe one of the dream-work's main principles) had been met with censorship's approval—not just State censorhip but also Pasolini's own. Hence, displacement and condensation: the prostitutes' world as a metonymical displacement of sexual deviation, and Accattone's marginality and relative invisibility as a metaphor for the nonbeing of the homosexual. Indeed, only the critics' ignorance of the hiways and byways of the "screen closet" has made it possible for them to miss that Accattone is in many ways a metaphor for homosexuality and that *Accattone* was obliquely lifting the mask from Italy's heterosexist face.[13] This is not to say that the character Accattone is gay, but that strong elements from the homosexual discourse coalesce around him as a textual knot.

Accattone himself brings the idea of the mask violently to the fore when, on the night of Stella's initiation into prostitution, he runs to the river's bank and casts his face into the sand. The ensuing shot, depicting Accattone's face totally transfigured by sand, has been the object of much critical attention but has never been linked to the presence of homosexual paradigms in the film. Accattone's penchant for a tragic ending and his violent death are nothing if not representative of the treatment of gay characters in films until the sixties. Moreover, he never seems to be interested in sex, not even with Stella. Indeed, although dealing with illegal sexuality, *Accattone* never once hints at sexual intercourse or arousal—quite the opposite of what the other Italian directors were doing. And Accattone's trying on of a woman's hat—emphasized by Pasolini's camera work—is, of course, another indicator of Accattone's unconscious denial of his masculinity, his wish to explore a position which will set him "against nature." But the clearest evidence of Accattone's status as metaphor for a homosexual subjectivity lies in his ambivalence. The film constantly delineates a set of opposites which are granted a socio-ontological existence by the status quo and which are ordered hierarchically: they suggest the two genders. Between them, the protagonist carves his own precarious and death-bound path. Since in 1961 Italy there could be no talk of there being more than two genders, it comes as no surprise that *Accattone*'s illustration of a third way, a third position, was portrayed through a figure of illegality (homosexuals steal pleasure) who ended in nonbeing. The homosexual/thief's survival is perilously based on his/her success in stealthily acquiring what others seem to have by virtue of natural right, be it sexual pleasure or gender identity.[14]

On the subject of ways of seeing, *Accattone* suggests a position from which the holes in the texture of reality can be seen, a gaze conscious of itself which eschews the dream of total vision (old-fashioned realism) as well as the nightmare of total subjectivity (modernism). Astride the opposites of full sight and blindness, *Accattone* suggests that realists should be like thieves. Nothing has been said about the thief's vision which does not apply to realism as conceived by Pasolini in 1961. Like thieves, realists look at the world with interested eyes: they want to derive meaning from what they see. As they are not willing, however, to pay the price set by the existing system of values, they discard the meaning conventionally attributed to each sign and seek new ways of looking. Realist practice entails stealing images away from their seemingly natural value/meaning in order to appropriate them to another regime of signification. Furthermore, like thieves, realists must always change their ways of appropriating reality because, as Brecht said, "reality alters and in order to represent it, the means of representation must alter too. . . . the oppressors do not always appear in

Accattone: *Accattone (Franco Citti), with a woman's hat on, puts a wicker bas-ket on the flower vendor.* Courtesy of the Museum of Modern Art/Film Stills Archive.

the same mask. The masks cannot always be stripped off the same way."[15] But, as suggested by the metaphor of the thief's vision through holes, realists also know that they are looking at a world rich in mean-ing from behind a mask. Everybody has one, even the policeman who wears the mask of power, a mask that keeps him from seeing his own. Pasolini's "New Realism," then, relies on the traditional notion of un-masking but puts forward the condition that the viewing subject be aware of his/her own mask.

The Will to Realism

Although set in a radically different milieu, Fellini's *I vitelloni* (1953) portrayed a world adrift reminiscent of that in *Accattone*. Male camaraderie and machismo, lack of activity and ideological concerns define the space in which *I vitelloni*'s petty bourgeois and *Accattone*'s subproletariat vegetate. In both films, moreover, there is a main character who signifies dissatisfaction with that world, a character whose vision is privileged by the narrative.

At the end of *I vitelloni*, Moraldo (Franco Interlenghi) is disgusted with his previous life and leaves town on an early morning train. A beautiful young boy runs after the train, a boy who works at the railroad station and is in some respects a modified version of the neorealist child. Instead of being the "tear-jerking" witness to a world in ruins, the railroad child here points at a romantic opening beyond the suffocating limits of provincial life: he is the *puer*, the figure of innocence which, according to Jung, is rooted in the Soul of Man. The boy cries out to Moraldo: "But. . . weren't you happy here?" Hurled in a Felliniesque wind, these words are the last of the film and well epitomize Fellini's progressive distancing from neorealism. The connection with the *puer*, the ending with a question, and the mystery of Moraldo's destination suggest the existence of an autobiographical parallel between Moraldo's departure and what Pasolini called "Fellini's refusal of rationality and criticism." Realistic though they seem, the events in the film are episodic observations of a restless mind: "But weren't you happy here?"

As if to make clear that his plea for the ambivalence of the image had nothing to do with Fellini's passion for ambiguity, Pasolini chose to have *Accattone* end in a way which calls *I vitelloni* into question. Accattone also quits his world but does not leave for an imaginary land: instead, he dies. There are no eternal figures of the Soul next to him, but policemen in uniform and handcuffed thieves. And as if answering the question thrown at Moraldo by the railroad boy, he says: "Now I am happy." Besides indicating that Accattone, qua metaphor for homosexuality, cannot rest content except in death, his happiness harkens back to the initial quote from Dante and exemplifies Pasolini's will to realism.

The story of Buonconte, whose soul was saved at the last minute, is less a hint of Accattone's final redemption (as argued by critics who desperately looked for a "little tear" in his eyes) than a cogent example of a theme dear to Pasolini: human life can be judged only after it is finished. Pasolini's fascination with this idea derived from his belief in death as the ultimate event which alone can give meaning to life: "It is absolutely necessary to die, because *while living we lack meaning*" (*HE*, 236); or: "*Death effects an instantaneous montage of our lives*; that is, it chooses the truly meaningful moments (which are no longer modifiable by other possible contrary or incoherent moments) and puts them into a sequence" so that "a life, with all its actions, can be completely and truly deciphered only after death; at that point its rhythm is compressed and the insignificant is eliminated" (*HE*, 242).[16] Differently put, we cannot make sense of people's lives until their deaths have put a halt to the possibility of changes: there can always be a life-saving tear or a fatal mistake altering the sense of someone's trajectory. It is easy to think of how our idea of Pasolini himself was indeed changed by his death; how his filmography was changed by *Salò*. But the importance of this quote exceeds biographical considerations, however intriguing they may be. By suggesting that death is the final "linguistic moment" in a chain of symbolic gestures and that, as such, it inaugurates the possibility of a retrospective reading, this quotation offers an intriguing explanation of the film's obsession with death. Starting with Accattone's initial dive in the Tiber on a full stomach and ending with his happy death, the film abounds with instances of his proximity to, when not longing for, death. If we keep in mind that characters are not real people but textual knots, Accattone's will to die signals the film's attempt to generate a clear-cut judgment on its trajectory. After reaching an ambivalent status astride opposites—his mixture of and dissociation from both opposites—Accattone must die, lest we wonder about his future. Or (which amounts to the same thing), Accattone, as a sign, is so full of possible and ongoing significations that it is only when his signifying potential is brought to a halt by death that sense can be made of him. Taken as a discursive event, death exemplifies the text's will to realism, its desire to put the spectator in the position of effecting a closure: "Now I'm happy."

The initial quotation is not the only means the text adopts to make us see Accattone's death as a *discursive* event. The glaring, over-exposed dream that prefigures his death works as a prescription as well. The dream occurs at a moment when the narrative is obsessively punctuated by the close-ups of the policeman's eyes. Accattone is under strict surveillance. Moreover, he is not the kind of man who can consciously assess his own position; rather, his existence unfolds on an instinctual, preverbal level. Hence, a dream is the most logical space in which he may unravel his desires and rearrange his choices far from the eyes of Power.

The dream begins with Accattone walking on the parapet of a bridge, the stage of his previous displays of theatrical bravery. Summoned by the four Neapolitans who sit by an old building, Accattone reaches them only to find them dead, crushed by a collapsed wall. He then turns around and sees all of his friends (with the already mentioned exception of the thief Balilla) dressed in black and with flowers in their hands. They call him "Vittorio" and urge him to follow Accattone's funeral. But there are no women in the cortege. What Accattone had repressed in life is conspicuous here by its absence. Such absence, moreover, may well indicate that Accattone is dying for his male friends only (another suggestion that he is a metaphor for homosexuality). Be that as it may, when the procession arrives at the cemetery, Accattone is denied entrance. After climbing the wall and seeing an old undertaker digging his grave in the shade, Accattone begs, "Why don't you dig over there in the sun?" After repeating his demand, Accattone is finally granted his wish and thus symbolically displaces the locus of his afterlife.

The dream constitutes an intriguing prescription for a productive reading of the signifier death as a discursive event. There is no question that in most films death is portrayed in a naturalistic fashion. However symbolic, death is usually presented as such an unfortunate event befalling a character that there is seldom room for considering its textual functions. Here, just as Accattone displaces his own grave from the shadow to the sun, we are invited to wrench his fatal accident from the gray zone of a naturalistic reading (Accattone is dead. . . . poor Accattone. . . . He deserved it after all . . .) and graft it onto the terrain of realist discourse. Death in a film is also a discursive event indicating the conclusion of a signifying trajectory. In addition to displacing the signifier death from its univocal meaning and thereby showing that it too can be ambivalent, the happy death of Accattone acts as a corrective to Moraldo's indecision and becomes a symbol of Pasolini's first realist steps—indeed of his "certain realism," for many of his films will end with a death.

5

Mamma Roma

Mamma Roma's days as a prostitute are over when her former pimp, Carmine, gets married to another girl. She leaves the streets, rents a vegetable stand at a local market, and is, at last, in a position to take her son Ettore back home (Ettore grew up in the country with some relatives of hers). Together, Mamma Roma and Ettore move to another flat in a suburban housing project. Here Ettore joins the local gang of street kids and has his first sexual experience with Bruna, an easy neighborhood girl. Mamma Roma schemes to take Ettore away from both Bruna and the streets. Blackmailing the owner of a restaurant, she finds Ettore a job as a waiter. Carmine's unexpected return, however, forces Mamma Roma into prostitution again and Ettore is now teased by his friends about his mother's profession. Ettore quits his job and turns to thievery. Feverish and out of luck, he is caught while stealing a portable radio from a patient in a hospital and winds up in jail. He has a nervous fit in the prison hospital and is tied to a bed in an isolation cell, where he dies. (There was a "true story" in this ending: a Roman youth, Marcello Elisei, had died in an isolation cell the year before.)

> *Neorealist reality is incomplete, official, and altogether reasonable; but the poetry, the mystery, everything which completes and enlarges tangible reality is completely missing from its work.*
>
> Luis Buñuel

Mamma Roma (1962) completes the liquidation of neorealism initiated in *Accattone*. Critics have focused mostly on its similarities with the previous film and on the fact that Pasolini, by his own admission, had repeated himself somewhat. As a result, Pasolini's second film was and is considered a bad copy of the first. To be sure, *Mamma Roma* seems a more contrived film than its predecessor because it tries too hard to prove a political thesis that would be pleasing to leftwing critics: no sooner do marginal cultures come into contact with the center than they are destroyed. But it is nonetheless surprising that no one has addressed *Mamma Roma*'s exemplary role as Pasolini's final tribute to and rejection of neorealism. Indeed, he could not have been more explicit in drawing the viewers' attention to the film's relationship to neorealism and in particular to one of its founding texts: *Roma città aperta* (Open City, 1945).

To gauge the weight of what Pasolini did with *Mamma Roma*, a brief digression on its background may be useful. Perhaps no other film had at once touched and represented postwar Italian collective consciousness as did *Roma città aperta*. Some of its images ended up signifying the entire Resistance period as well as the hope for a brighter future. The figures of the priest, Don Pietro (Aldo Fabrizi), who stood up to the Nazis, and of Pina (Anna Magnani), who was machinegunned to death in a memorable scene, had become symbols of good Italians and their yearning for a more just society. Fifteen years later, many intellectuals and artists thought that these hopes and yearnings had turned sour. In a 1958 poem, Pasolini recounted having gone to see Rossellini's film in a little suburban theater and being crushed by a mixture of nostalgia and frustration: "Almost an emblem by now, Magnani's cry" resounds "in the cold theatre. . . . I am overwhelmed and carried away by *l'intermittance du coeur*."[1] With this intriguing French expression borrowed from Proust, Pasolini expressed his inability to feel unconditional sympathy for a picture that had turned out to be nothing but a Catholic dreamer's wishful projection. Hence his intermittent heart, now with Rossellini, now against him.

One year later, Rossellini made *Il generale della Rovere* (General Della Rovere, 1959), a film which returns to the theme of the Resistance. Although still drenched in the rhetoric of "the good Italian," this film was less optimistically clear-cut than *Roma città aperta*, for the protagonist (played by neorealist hero De Sica) was a petty swindler, and his heroic change at the last minute did not completely efface his previous display of cynicism. In a contemporary article written for the magazine *Reporter*, Pasolini defined 1959 as "the year of *Il generale della Rovere*," and wished that Rossellini's film would herald a return to politically committed cinema.[2] At the same time, he stated bluntly that "Rossellini *is* neorealism." But Pasolini's feelings for Rossellini/ neorealism were by now "intermittent," and a few lines later he added that "there is something forced, conventional, and faded" in Rossellini's realism, something which ought to prompt new directors to find new ways "to strip Italy of its mask and see again its real face as in 1945."

To some extent, Pasolini's wish was fulfilled, for *Il generale della Rovere* was the first in a long series of films about fascism/resistance. Between 1960 and 1962—thus in the middle of the Italian *nouvelle vague* period—several Italian directors revisited what, during the "white" fifties, had been a taboo subject. Some examples: in 1960, De Sica's *La ciociara* (Two Women), Puccini's *Il carro armato dell'8 settembre* (The Tank of the Eighth of September), Comencini's *Tutti a casa* (Everybody Home!), Vancini's *La lunga notte del '43* (The Long Night of 1943), and Lizzani's *Il gobbo* (The Hunchback); in 1961 Loy's *Un giorno da leoni* (One Day as a Lion), Salce's *Il federale* (The Federal), Lizzani's *L'oro di Roma* (The Gold of Rome), and Montaldo's *Tiro al piccione* (Pigeon-Shooting); and in 1962 Del Fra's *All'armi siam fascisti* (We Are Fascists!—a documentary), Loy's *Le quattro giornate di Napoli* (Four Days in Naples), Prunas's *Benito Mussolini* (Mussolini—a documentary, reportedly with Rossellini's collaboration), and Zampa's *Anni Ruggenti* (The Roaring Years).

The result, however, was uneven, and the generation gap between old masters and new directors became apparent. Of the newer generation, only Vancini and Montaldo (and later De Bosio with *Il terrorista*, The Terrorist, 1964) made films about the Resistance, and, not surprisingly, their films were the most uncompromising from an ideological standpoint. The other young directors (Bertolucci, De Seta, Olmi, and, of course, Pasolini), suspicious of a popular revival that froze fascism into a finite historical period and overlooked its persistence in contemporary Italy, chose to stay away from the subject. As to the old guard, fascism and resistance were often seen in the same sentimental vein as during early neorealism. In many cases, commercial goals were clearly overriding intellectual and political rigor (e.g., Sophia Loren in *La ciociara*). Rossellini himself, in the wake of the success of *Il generale della Rovere*, made *Era notte a Roma* (It Was Night in Rome, 1960), another film on the Resistance which recalls *Roma città aperta* by reproposing the motif of Rome as the emblem of Italian hopes. Responding to pressing commercial demands, however, Rossellini's new film displayed high drama and the usual clear-cut distinction between good and bad guys, with the novelty, however, of having an ex-seminarian as the bad guy.

It is in this context of a more general and flawed return to political cinema that Pasolini made *Mamma Roma*, his heart fraught with *inter-*

mittance and his mind bent on "stripping Italy of its mask." In fact, he must have decided that the time had also come to strip neorealism of its deceptive ideology once and for all. He thus took Anna Magnani and had her star in a film whose title contained the word "Roma," a clear enough reference to Rossellini's tribute to the *città eterna*. As if that were not enough, he shot a sequence in which Magnani repeated her emblematic cry in circumstances (her son's death) that constituted a commentary on *Roma città aperta*'s idealism. Moreover, he made the image of a church dome the paradigmatic shot in his new film, just as Rossellini had twice employed St. Peter's dome as the emblem of Rome/Italy. Finally, to indicate that his attack was not just against one film, he cast Lamberto Maggiorani, *The Bicycle Thief*'s protagonist, as the man from whom Ettore steals a radio. Taken together, all these elements seem to indicate that Pasolini intended to create a powerful subtext in *Mamma Roma* capable of addressing the question of neorealism. Ironically, no one picked up on this and he himself was not explicit about it, leaving us to doubt whether or not his choices were intentional. Be that as it may, *Mamma Roma* now stands as an unequivocal critique of neorealism from both an ideological and formal point of view.

Mamma Roma Città Aperta

Roma città aperta, it will be remembered, pitted Pina (Anna Magnani) against both her sister and Marina, who did not hesitate to lower their moral standards to improve their social conditions. An icon of proletarian strength, Pina was pregnant at the moment of her death, but her unborn child lived through the actions of Romoletto and the other children with which the film ended. It is as if Pasolini had changed Pina's fate, as if she had not died and had instead given birth to a son, Ettore. And, more important, it as if her wartime idealism had subsequently turned into petty ideals. Seventeen years later, Anna Magnani played a prostitute with dreams of social ascent. Once freed from the exploitative relationship with her former pimp Carmine (Franco Citti), Mamma Roma gets into small business, leaves her previous neighborhood for a new apartment in a modern housing project, and nurtures the brightest hopes of upward mobility for her son Ettore. But her lack of loyalty to her social background will prove fatal.

By showing Mamma Roma's petty dreams, Pasolini makes a rather harsh commentary on the idealism with which *Roma città aperta* had portrayed the lower classes as basically immune from greed. In Rossellini's film there was no question that Italians were good at heart and that the rot was coming from outside: Marina was corrupted by Ingrid; Pina was shot by the Germans. Mamma Roma, instead, outlives her son, who is not killed by a foreign occupying force but by the Italian police, the strong-arm of the very State which ensued from the hopes of 1945. The enemy, Pasolini suggests, is within. Gone is the good-natured, kindly disposition which Rossellini had once ascribed to Italians—even the fascists. Gone is the Renoirean forgiveness which permeated Rossellini's film—a pessimism à la Stroheim has taken its place. Gone is the warmhearted, working-class humor with which *Roma città aperta* began (the riot at the bakery) and which sustained it throughout. In *Mamma Roma* jokes do not establish solidarity among people; they are mean and cutting, as in the opening scene at Carmine's wedding banquet which, in many ways, sets the tone for the film's humor (or lack thereof). Jokes are bitter parodies made at another's expense: everyone for himself and all against the idealized Italy of the Resistance. As a point of fact, Pasolini begins the film with the image of Mamma Roma pushing three little pigs, which Carmine ironically calls *Fratelli d'Italia* ("Brothers of Italy," the title of the national anthem). By first associating pigs with national pride, and then by showing a microcosm of pimps and whores celebrating a wedding, Pasolini creates a biting polemic on Italians as prostitutes. Everyone has his or her price—a grim statement that neorealism was almost by definition unequipped to make.

The casting of Lamberto Maggiorani as the hospitalized man from whom Ettore unsuccessfully steals a radio yields intriguing considerations on stealing and point of view, a discourse that Pasolini had initiated in *Accattone*. In *The Bicycle Thief*, we saw the first theft from the point of view of Ricci, who had himself been robbed. We are led to sympathize with his search, and we are subtly forced to feel at once supportive and scornful of his own decision to steal. In *Mamma Roma*, we see things from the point of view of the thief. As with *Accattone*, it is less a celebration of thievery than a plea to accept difference. We are not asked to understand Ettore's theft. There are no special extenuating circumstances behind it. Thieving is simply a part of the subproletarian way of acquiring the money for which we of the middle class feel obligated to work (or to engage in legalized forms of theft). Ettore's thievery, in this respect, is a violation of *our* norms, a transgression for which neorealism implored the kind of understanding that confirms the rule. By attacking *The Bicycle Thief*, Pasolini strips the mask of the universal, monocentric perspective from which neorealists saw reality.

Stylistically, *Mamma Roma* radicalizes Pasolini's departure from neorealism, already evident in *Accattone*. Neorealists believed in minimizing the filmmaker's intervention so as to let viewers perceive the whole picture and not be guided by the director's choices. "The assemblage of the film must never add anything to the existing reality," said Bazin, and this was, indeed, neorealism's credo.[3] Rossellini's humility; Zavattini's idea that "the most irreplaceable experience comes from things happening under our eyes from natural necessity"; De Sica's aphorism "reality is there, why change it?": all were indications of a belief in the director's self-effacement.[4] Thus, long takes were unanimously held to be the best stylistic translation of this wholesome attitude toward reality. Although neorealists and Bazin were never as naive as their detractors portrayed them to be, their emphasis on immediacy undeniably engendered a dangerous conflation of realism and empiricism: reality is what we see, and what we see is real. Knowledge, then, becomes a matter of passive reflection, and objective recording and cinema becomes "a window on the world." This minimization of syntactical intervention on the director's part brought some neorealists very close to adopting the invisible editing of the conventional cinema that they set out to oppose. By advocating a "zero-degree" style, they fostered the commonplace notion that realism is styleless or transparent.

Seeing through the stylistic conventions of his predecessors, Pasolini created his own figurative style that owed more to painting than to Bazin's idea of realism. Admittedly, he drew inspiration from Masaccio, the painter who opposed Beato Angelico's stylization and painted the human figure in a more realistic way.[5] In *Mamma Roma*, Pasolini defined and perfected a style of brief, frontal, medium close-ups linked together by "unprofessional" editing that subverted the ideological implications of the reverse-field figure. In fact, his repudiation of long-takes caused him some problems with Anna Magnani, for he would not give her enough space for her virtuoso pieces.

Pasolini's attitude toward acting differed from that of the neorealists. Although they often chose nonprofessionals, neorealists expected good performances from them. It is never evident that *The Bicycle Thief*'s or *Umberto D.*'s protagonists are nonprofessionals. In fact, one can say that in neorealist films nonprofessionals were "beginners," people chosen from the street who aspired to a cinematic career. One recalls Visconti's *Bellissima* (1951), a pungent satire of the spirit with which "nonprofessionals" approached cinema. In Pasolini's films things were quite different, for he did not demand professional acting from anybody (except with *Salò*). With the exception of a few professional actors (always employed for specific iconographic reasons), none of Pasolini's nonprofessionals was ever a "beginner" starting out in a cinematic career. Indeed, most of them only acted with Pasolini. As a result, the viewers of Pasolini's films are often aware of some actors' inability to act, a fact that once again threatens narrative flow and emphasizes textuality. A splendid example of this happens in *Mamma Roma*, when Magnani and Garofalo fall after trying a tango step. While Magnani's laughter is a perfect replica of the bravura pieces which we expect of her, Garofalo's laughter is self-conscious, and for a split second his eyes wander towards the camera as if seeking the director's approval. Clearly, Pasolini made the conscious decision neither to reshoot nor to cut the scene but to leave it like that, an uncomfortable memento of the real relationship between the director and the actor, an implicit step outside the fiction.

Finally, *Mamma Roma* contains a subtle indictment of the Bazinian argument in favor of the inherent realism of long-takes. Far from bespeaking the absence of authorial intervention, the twice-repeated long-take of Mamma Roma walking in the night presents yet another example of artifice. Singled out by virtue of its unusual length, its darkness, and its duplication in a later sequence, this shot acquires an emblematic status. It is as if Pasolini had wanted to show that one can have a long-take and yet achieve a most expressionistic effect.

Mamma Roma takes issue with *Roma città aperta* on the subject of Rome, too. Rossellini's film begins with a location shot celebrating the famous *Piazza di Spagna* and ends with an image of Romoletto and friends walking towards the city against a sky dominated by the dome of St. Peter's. As the city in many ways is the collective protagonist, the shot of the dome, evoking as it does the film's hero, Don Pietro, stands for the belief in a brighter future for Italy.[6] Like *Accattone*, *Mamma Roma* denies viewers any familiar sight of the Rome for tourists, except perhaps for a popular restaurant in Trastevere. Far from representing the glory of Italy, the word "Roma" is at first uplifted by its association with "mother"—indeed one of the sacred signifiers in Italian culture—and then degraded as the nickname of a prostitute. Aside from being an obvious reminder of the mother/whore dichotomy, the reduction of Rome to an individual—and a social outcast at that—is symptomatic of the petty individualism which Pasolini saw on the rise during the years of so-called economic boom.

But it is on the signifier "dome" that Pasolini centers his confrontation with neorealism. Mamma Roma's dream of upward mobility is epitomized by her new apartment in a modern housing project on the outskirts of the city. Against the background of ancient ruins scattered like ghosts in a littered hinterland, the white buildings of the projects signify the paucity of her dreams. Turned into an emblem by a shot recurring seven times, the view from her apartment is dominated by the shining dome of a modern church. It is inside this "house of God" that Mamma Roma compares her old neighborhood with the new and

Mamma Roma: *Mamma Roma (Anna Magnani) is prevented from committing suicide after Ettore's death.* Courtesy of the Museum of Modern Art/Film Stills Archive.

spots the restaurant owner whom she will blackmail into giving Ettore a job. Needless to say, *Mamma Roma* also ends with a shot of the dome, after a sequence which is worthy of detailed attention.

The sequence begins in the market, with Mamma Roma finding out that Ettore is dead. Pasolini films the sequence from afar; we do not hear what Mamma Roma is being told; we just understand from her cry. At this point the resemblance with *Roma città aperta* is striking, for Magnani wriggles out of the other vendors' grip just as she had struggled with the Nazi soldiers in the earlier film. Her voice resonates loudly, "Ettore! Ettore!" just as it had resonated "Francesco! Francesco!" seventeen years before. Mamma Roma then starts running, and we get a point-of-view shot (POV) of the tenement building where she lives: the signifier of her dream of upward mobility is now an image of punished hubris. Cut to a frontal, medium-long shot of her running with other vendors in pursuit, and then to a similar shot of her pursuers alone. Brief tracking shot of her entrance into the projects—the exact replica of the shot which celebrated her triumphant arrival at her new flat with Ettore. Cut to an image of her opening a door and barging into her apartment. We remember that shots of opening doors were plentiful indeed in *Roma città aperta*, where they served as evocative punctuation and indicated the overall mood of the film: an opening towards the future. Conversely, in *Mamma Roma*'s final sequence, the opening of her apartment door signifies the tragedy of an impending suicide attempt.

At this point, Pasolini cuts to a shot of her pursuers going through the same door—typically, he did not hold the shot on the door but preferred to cut. We then see Mamma Roma entering Ettore's room, rushing toward the window but changing her mind at the sight of Ettore's bed. Cut to a shot of the bed with Ettore's clothes lying on it. Cut to Mamma Roma frantically hugging the clothes, followed by a cut to her pursuers entering the room, stopping, and seeing a mother crying over the sacrifice of her son. A cut to Mamma Roma turning around and looking at the camera signifies that she returns their/our gaze. She then rushes to the window and opens it, but four people, a man and three women, hasten to grab her. Prevented from hurling herself from the apartment that meant so much to her, Mamma Roma concludes her textual trajectory by exchanging glances, as it were, with the dome. Pasolini starts by simulating the most common POV structure, what Branigan calls the closed POV: shot A of the point/glance (Mamma Roma), shot B of what she is looking at (the dome), and then a repetition of shot A.[7] Upon the second shot A, Mamma Roma intensifies her gaze, and she is now staring, so much so that the other four characters all look in that direction too. The expression on their faces is one of astonishment, as if they are all trying to comprehend the meaning of that dome. Here, Pasolini opens up the closed POV structure, for he cuts again to a shot of the dome, this time taken with a shorter focal length. At the same time, he questions the reliability of POV shots. Let us see how.

Like Rossellini's *Roma città aperta*, but with a totally different bent, *Mamma Roma* ends with an image of a faraway dome. Given the resemblance to Rossellini's film, the adoption of a different, shorter focal length in the last shot is important and opens up intriguing questions. Semantically, of course, it may indicate that the more Mamma Roma looks at the view from her apartment, the more she gets the whole picture. She sees how petty she had to become in order to be part of the petite bourgeoisie. From a technical standpoint, Pasolini forces us to ask other questions: Was Mamma Roma's first view of the dome—the one we see throughout the film—taken with a telephoto lens, and the second taken with a 50–55 mm lens (so-called normal)?

In this case, we would get a progression from magnified to "normal" vision. Or did he use the "normal" lens throughout and then take the last shot with a 35 mm or a 28 mm lens? Or, perhaps, are both shots distorted by either long or short focal lengths so that in neither occasion do we see exactly what the characters see? Two things are certain: we cannot determine what the characters have seen, and POVs are unreliable. This is what the film tells us with its very last image, an image which, by hearkening back to one of neorealism's founding texts and suggesting that shots are not to be trusted, shakes realism's foundations.

Never had a neorealist film questioned what a character sees to this degree. And, above all, never had it posited the question of what the "normal" image looks like: "reality is there, why change it?" In *Umberto D.*, for example, De Sica gives us a vertiginous zoom on the street pavement from Umberto's window to indicate that he is thinking about suicide, but we are given the "normal" perception to begin with. The psychological function of the zoom is explicit, and "normal" perspective is ultimately reinforced. In *Mamma Roma*, by contrast, the distinction between psychologically altered and normal perception is blurred. What is normality of vision? How does this affect realist representation? It should be noted, at this point, that out of the seven times in which the shot of the dome occurs, three are objective shots: no character is shown looking at the dome. Thus, *Mamma Roma*'s last image threatens the reliability of objective shots as well. All this indicates that Pasolini, while working towards creating a film style which would overcome traditional realist assumptions (e.g., the reliability and normality of vision), finds the objective/subjective shot dichotomy along the way. Convinced that the objective shot is nothing but another subjective shot from the director's point of view, Pasolini mixes the terms. He thus arrives at a poetic realism in which the image is both objective and subjective, a cinema of poetry which, as he would theorize three years later, relies on what he called "the free indirect subjective."

A Cinema of Poetry

Buried within all of his other attempts to bring literary categories to bear on film studies, the idea of a free indirect subjective is one of Pasolini's finest and is slowly getting the recognition it deserves. Recently, Metz called it "a truly genial intuition" which his next book will explicitly take up, giving it, of course, "the theoretical rigor which Pasolini was unable to bestow on his poetic insights."[8] Gilles Deleuze, for his part, already put it to use in his *Cinema 1*, finding it

an extremely useful tool to overcome the often useless objective/
subjective shot dichotomy.[9]

Pasolini derived the notion of free indirect subjective from that of
free indirect speech, a literary category brilliantly assessed by Volosinov and Bakhtin in *Marxism and the Philosophy of Language*. Calling
it "quasi-direct speech," the two Russian authors offer this example
from Pushkin to substantiate their point: "All, all, the dreadful sound
betrayed. The world of nature dimmed before him. Farewell blessed
freedom! He is a slave!"[10] In this passage, both of the final exclama-
tions are the author's, and yet they may be interpreted as part of the
hero's internal speech. "From the point of abstract grammar," they
argue, "it is the author who speaks; from the standpoint of the actual
sense of the whole context, it is a character who speaks."[11] Since "its
specificum is precisely a matter of *both* author *and* character speaking
at the same time," Volosinov/Bakhtin see "quasi-direct discourse" as
being "double-faced, like Janus."[12]

A double-faced technique could not but intrigue Pasolini, who avid-
ly read the literature on the subject and dedicated a lengthy essay to
"free indirect discourse" (*HE*, 79–101). In it, he saw the possibility of
rendering in one and the same stroke the point of view of the author-
and-the-character, a Janus-like figure that would force the reader into
an acknowledgment of the subjective nature of all objective narration.
In addition, he gave free indirect discourse the political dimension
which had thus far been missing. Arguing that it combines the mimetic
value of direct speech with the freedom of indirect narration, Pasolini
maintained that the presence of free indirect discourse "implies a
sociological consciousness, clear or otherwise, in the author" (*HE*, 82)
who would thus attempt to reconstruct the characters' linguistic reality
by imitating the way they speak. He regarded this technique to be the
quintessentially realist literary strategy, and, after adopting it in his
novels, he asked himself: What would its cinematic counterpart be?
Equating direct speech with POV, Pasolini concluded that it was possible to have a free indirect subjective, a shot that technically is objective (the camera's) but does in fact belong to the character's visual regime. Conversely, he argued, there may be shots that are technically
subjective (relating what the character sees) but are *also* objective, because some directors use a character's way of looking to express their
own vision. According to Pasolini, an extensive use of the free indirect
subjective is the stylistic feature characterizing the "cinema of poetry"
in which the authors no longer efface their presence with an invisible
style, but imbue the characters with their vision. Partly critical of the
technique that he had theorized—to live up to the requirements of
Marxist discourse *he had* to condemn any concession to form—and

partly intrigued by it, Pasolini limited himself to identifying the directors who used the free indirect subjective extensively: Antonioni, Rocha, Bertolucci, and Godard. Not only did he forget to put himself on the list, but he did not pursue his intuition any further.

Deleuze investigated the figure of the free indirect subjective, which Pasolini had abandoned, in a cogent and clear way, arguing that "the camera does not simply give us the vision of the character and of his world; it imposes another vision in which the first is transformed and reflected." Some directors impose their own vision more than others, and that's where Pasolini's cinema of poetry/cinema of prose distinction comes in handy, the former signifying, precisely, a cinema in which directors impose their ways of seeing on characters more than it is normally done in classic cinema. "We are no longer faced," Deleuze argued, "with subjective *or* objective images: we are caught in a correlation between a perception-image and a camera consciousness which transforms it (the question of knowing whether the image was objective or subjective is no longer raised)." The doubts cast on the subjective/objective shot dichotomy should not surprise us, for contemporary theory is presently questioning the very notion of an object separate from the subject. This does not mean that Branigan's painstaking work to classify subjective shots is useless. It is just that subjective and objective shots are not all there are. Indeed the majority of shots in *cinema d'autore* are of the kind described by Pasolini, a mixture of character's and author's vision.

In *Accattone*, "a certain realism" in the text expressed Pasolini's own vision through the thieves Accattone and Balilla. *Mamma Roma* reinforces this tendency and creates a paradigmatic instance of a cinema of poetry where its director merges his vision with the protagonist's. Not surprisingly, the character with whom Pasolini blends his gaze is not Mamma Roma, but Ettore.

Ettore takes up and perfects Accattone's legacy. He refuses work and integration; he is an outsider everywhere he goes, even among his own friends. More blatantly than Accattone, Ettore lives in a perennial dreamlike state, as if between sleep and waking, night and day, nightmare and reality. Critics have often defined Ettore as an embodiment of "innocence," for indeed he is another Pasolinian character outside historical consciousness. This definition, however, obscures the subtext of his sexual deviance. Of course Ettore is diegetically heterosexual, for he covets Bruna and makes love to the prostitute Biancofiore. But something in his behavior indicates detachment and apathy, even toward sex. The Canadian critic Stephen Snyder quite rightly shifted the focus from innocence to the body by calling Ettore's attitude "a disaffection from reality."[13] "He sleepwalks through most of the movie,"

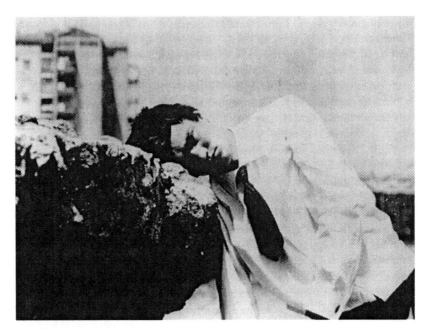

Mamma Roma: *One of the many instances in which Ettore (Ettore Garofalo) is portrayed in a "somnambulistic" state.* Courtesy of the Museum of Modern Art/Film Stills Archive.

says Snyder, "with an incredible passivity and lack of awareness about the necessities of life." I would argue that Ettore's disaffection from reality is a clear enough indication that he cannot feel genuine affection for *that particular reality* in which he has to act normal. Pasolini has Ettore "sleepwalking" throughout the film because "sleepwalking" is the best visual translation of a state of nonparticipation in normal, waking life. The great novelty of *Mamma Roma* is that Pasolini starts emphasizing the body by means of visual signifiers. Not only is Ettore's rigid "sleepwalking" a visual metaphor for a body caught between two realities, but his feverish state at the end clearly indicates an abnormal body temperature, an excess, a passion causing his difference from the rest.

There is yet another dimension in which Ettore emulates and even goes beyond Accattone: thievery. More so than Accattone, Ettore is presented as someone who resorts to stealing. The sequence in which he first appears is paradigmatic of his condition. At first, he is all alone on a spinning merry-go-round, a grown-up boy protecting a childhood he perhaps never had. The audience is invited to look at him through Mamma Roma's eyes, that is, with a mixture of compassion and guilt, ready to justify whatever he does because of his loveless life. Ettore suddenly disappears, and we next see him in the act of stealing a chocolate bar. He soon joins four friends whom he accuses of having stolen his cigarettes from him. As they all deny it, he asks them to open their mouths so that he can smell their breath. This sequence goes further than *Accattone* ever did in clarifying the figure of the Pasolinian thief. It suggests that Ettore cannot trust his friends and that perhaps he has previously been robbed by them. The Pasolinian thief is then someone who feels that something has been stolen from him, someone who is getting back at a society that has done something to him.

Ettore will steal two more times in the film (the records from his mother and the radio in the hospital), and he will die as a result of it. In the previous chapter, I argued that the role of thief in *Accattone* stood as a metaphor for homosexuality and that the thief's gaze through the holes of a urinal grating visually suggested Pasolini's "certain realism." *Mamma Roma* strengthens both of these associations. For one, the film blatantly repeats the shot of the thief's vision through holes, by having feverish Ettore look out from a urinal *just* before entering the hospital where he will steal for the last time. As his vision is altered by fever, the connotation of a highly subjective gaze is reinforced. Ettore dies because he is a thief and because his body is altered. As the thief with an altered body, Ettore cannot but die, cannot but reach the state of nonbeing which already qualifies him.

In fact, Ettore's actions, his "sleepwalking," his bodily affections, all make sense once we see them for what they are: a metaphor for the homosexual subtext in the film. Whereas *Accattone* left this subtext more undefined, *Mamma Roma* brings up homosexuality by means of precise and yet furtive textual clues. It is as if *Mamma Roma* wanted the spectators to lift the mask from Ettore's superficial heterosexuality in the same way that Pasolini's "certain realism" was trying "to strip Italy of its mask." When Ettore first arrives at his mother's apartment, she asks him whether or not he likes to dance. With his usual unenthusiastic expression, he replies, "A little. The cha cha cha." Mamma Roma laughs at him, puts a record on the turntable and grabs Ettore: "Come dance the tango with your mother!" She then proceeds to teach him some tango steps. Their dancing becomes overtly sensual, cheek to cheek, body to body. They are soon interrupted by Carmine, Mamma Roma's old pimp, who is in need of money and wants Mamma Roma to resume her job. After such a powerful reminder of ambivalence—the mother is a whore; the sacred mother of Italian iconography is also a figure to despise—Mamma Roma goes back to

Ettore, who has in the meantime locked himself in his room and is practicing the cha cha cha step with a zeal quite unusual for him. The implicit refusal of his mother's dance—later reinforced by the fact that he will sell the record she played for him—will be clarified in the next sequence.

After a night of work, Mamma Roma leaves her friends in the park and walks away, the camera obediently backtracking before her. It is the first of two long tracking shots in which she is progressively flanked by different people who walk a bit with her and then vanish in the dark of the night. The last group to emerge from the darkness and walk next to Mamma Roma includes at least two homosexual men. They are the stereotyped homosexuals of conventional, heterosexist cinema, with high-pitched voices and affected mannerisms. It is as if Pasolini *needed* the audience immediately to identify them as gay, without any shadow of doubt. While Mamma Roma dominates the scene and the conversation, a muffled and yet quite discernible Latin American rhythm can be heard on the soundtrack. Then one of the gay men, indeed the most stereotypically so, follows Mamma Roma, who is leaving the group behind. All of a sudden, he breaks into a cha cha cha in front of her. It is a pivotal moment that inaugurates the film's most important subtext by linking Ettore metonymically with homosexuality via the cha cha cha. After this, Ettore's love/hate relationship with his mother, his sexual awakening clouded in a mist of despair, his doomed affair with Bruna, his trouble with his friends because of her, his lonely "sleepwalking" amidst the ruins, all acquire a different texture. And so does Ettore's death, shot in a way which resembles the crucifixion and thus introduces the Christ theme to Pasolini's cinema.

By means of Ettore's character, then, Pasolini creates the ideal terrain for an extensive use of the free indirect subjective shot which, "as I have repeated several times, is pretextual. It serves to speak indirectly—through any narrative alibi—in the first person singular" (*HE*, 185). *Mamma Roma* is a film shot in the language of poetry. Unlike neorealist films, where the poetry, if any, was inherent in the things being filmed, here it means the bivalent quality of the images, their capacity to openly express the vision of the author, who molds a character into being a perfect vehicle for his vision.

6

La ricotta

Stracci is a professional extra playing the good thief in a commercial movie about Jesus Christ. As he has a large family to support, he gives them his lunch basket, but then manages to get another one for himself. He cannot eat it, however, because the director calls him on the set for the scene of Christ's deposition from the cross (shot in color, after a painting by Rosso Fiorentino). Upon returning to his lunch basket, he finds that the "primadonna's" little dog ate it. Meanwhile, a journalist interviews the director, asking him broad, conventional questions and getting venomous answers (e.g., Italy has "the most illiterate people and the most ignorant bourgeoisie in Europe"). The journalist is finally dismissed by the director as "an average man," that is, "a monster; a dangerous criminal, a conformist, a colonialist, a racist." Wandering about the set, the journalist sees Stracci weeping over his stolen lunch basket, next to the dog. Stracci promptly sells the dog to the journalist and runs to buy a wheel of ricotta cheese. After being summoned again to the set for another take of the deposition from the cross (equally in color, this time after a painting by Pontormo), Stracci can, at last, run to a nearby cave and eat his ricotta. Some crew members, however, tease him and throw the food used on the set at him. He gobbles it all up. Nailed to the cross again, for the crucifixion scene, Stracci fails to recite his lines. Everyone looks up and realizes that Stracci died, of indigestion, on the cross. In the astonished silence following this discovery, the director remarks, "Poor Stracci! He had to die to show us that he was alive."

> *How could I know that it was real if somebody*
> *was not watching?*
> (Georgine to Richard in Peter Greenaway's
> *The Cook, the Thief, His Wife & Her Lover*)

After settling accounts with neorealism in *Accattone* and *Mamma Roma*, Pasolini initiated a thorough examination of the cinematic medium which resulted in three important works in the same year (1963): the short, tragicomic *La ricotta*, the montage-film *La rabbia*, and the *cinéma-vérité Comizi d'amore*.[1] For all their formal differences, these three films all investigate cinema's potential for unmasking, a practice which Pasolini believed to be at the heart of realism. The *revelation* of a reality beyond the realm of appearances was his major goal; in a sense, he suggests this in a quotation from the Gospel according to Mark which prefaces *La ricotta*: "For there is nothing hid, which shall not be manifested; neither was anything kept secret, but that it should come abroad. If any man have ears to hear, let him hear" (Mark 4:22–23).

Hailed by most critics as a masterpiece, *La ricotta* is, above all, a refreshing example of a film about filmmaking which resists the temptation to indulge in cerebral metacinema. In effect, it exhibits such clarity, it is so adamant in pursuing its point, that Maurizio Ponzi spoke of it as an example of "didactic cinema."[2] Essentially, the film shows that Stracci (Mario Cipriani, the thief in *Accattone*), a seemingly vulgar man with a gargantuan appetite, is in fact a Christ figure. *La ricotta* reveals the extent to which appearances (Stracci deserves contempt and ridicule) conceal a quite opposite truth (Stracci is sublime), dramatizing at once the existence of the mask and the discovery of what lies beneath it. Pasolini's third film, then, simulates a modernist self-reflexiveness with its film in a film, only to locate this modernist perspective within realist concerns.

La ricotta is constructed as a visual counterpoint, alternating between the activity of the director (played by Orson Welles) and that of Stracci. The beginning and the end of the film suggest that, although seemingly unrelated, both the director and Stracci belong to the same visual field. Their relationship is like the one between the observer and the observed. The first sequence—through means of what was becoming, by then, Pasolini's stylistic cipher, his portraitlike shots and countershots—shows feverish Stracci being mocked by other members of the film crew. Abruptly, on a medium close-up of a "saint" laughing at Stracci, we cut to a frontal, medium shot of the director sitting in his chair. Slowly, the camera starts zooming out. The director takes his glasses off and squints, as if trying to focus on something. For a moment we believe that he is about to do what we may have felt like doing, that is, intervening in the outrageous spectacle of the crew teasing poor Stracci.

We soon discover, however, that the director was not looking at all this; we were. He was getting ready to direct the scene of the deposition. The illusion fostered by the juxtaposition of shots faking a reverse field warns against the eye-line matches of classic realism at the same time that it suggests the visual relationship between the director and Stracci. It is a clever device, revealing that Pasolini, after the dome-sequence that ended *Mamma Roma*, is exploring the possibilities inherent in the reverse-field figure.

Eventually, the film's end will confirm our first, deceptive impression. The director's remark that Stracci had to die in order to prove that he was alive proves that, although seemingly oblivious, he had observed more than anyone else. Thus, the film's structure allows Pasolini to show two different characters who exist in their own right, all the while suggesting the existence of a visual relationship between them: one observes the other suffering.

Stracci's Passion

The first image of the film is a close-up of Stracci lying on the ground, his head framed horizontally—an unusual shot for a film's beginning. In retrospect, it will suggest that in some sense Stracci was already dead. The rest of the first sequence confirms this hypothesis. It intercuts between Stracci and other actors/crew members and sketches the dynamics of a life-denying relationship. Everyone ignores Stracci's fever, as well as his needs. They all mock him and dismiss him as a comic figure not to be taken seriously. Later in the film they will treat him like a hopeless glutton, unaware that he donated his lunch bag to his large family and that the star's dog ate his food. In short, they look at him without seeing who he really is and thus exemplify those who deny life by seeing only the surface of things.

By all appearances, Stracci is full of life. We see him bustling about, feverish and restless, trying to secure some food to satisfy his unnatural hunger. The visual linchpin of his life, the fast motion with which the text twice portrays him, sets him off from the other characters. The fast motion in *La ricotta* achieves a multiple effect on both formal and semantic levels: it disrupts narrative naturalism and exposes the authorial presence as the source of formal manipulation; it establishes a connection with silent comic cinema and more specifically qualifies Stracci as a passionate human being à la Chaplin; it graphically illustrates the paradox of Stracci's life, for the more he moves, the more his existence goes unacknowledged; and it enhances the sense of Stracci's bodily excess already conveyed by his fever, tears, and hunger. It is precisely the exaggeration in Stracci's endeavors that exposes him as a person whose needs are frustrated and whose life is denied.

Although Stracci is defined by compulsive hunger, the scene in which he is tied to the cross and teased by the others suggests that he only craves what he is being denied. First, they dangle a sandwich before his mouth; then, a bottle of cold water; and, finally, they urge a voluptuous, if vulgar, actress (the film's Mary Magdalene) to strip next to him. The camera soon abandons the cheap spectacle of her undressing and concentrates on Stracci's impotent gaze. In addition to suggesting that he represents a desire that is first tantalized and then frustrated, this scene unveils an essential dynamic: Stracci's needs are not merely a private question; rather, they are played upon and magnified by society's false promises of fulfillment. A contradictory duality emerges: Stracci is both nailed down in a lifeless position and yet asked to move, castrated and yet aroused, repressed and yet forced to desire a life that he cannot have.

In the scene in which Stracci stuffs himself to death in a cave, the text makes it clear that we ought to see the others as a single force, the collective embodiment of the life-denying gaze. It is a climactic moment, more so than Stracci's death on the cross. The text conveys this point through the music (the *Dies Irae* played on the accordion) and another clever use of the reverse-field figure. First we see Stracci eating his cheese in fast motion and we are thereby invited to laugh. Then we hear laughter off-screen. A cut to the actress playing the role of Jesus' mother identifies her as the source of the laughter, as well as of the gaze which frames Stracci as a comic figure. We then cut again to Stracci and then back to the mother who has been joined by another actor. They are both laughing. Intercutting between Stracci and the others who double in number at each cut, the scene ends with a frame filled with sixteen mocking spectators who throw food at him and treat him like an animal to be fed in the darkness of its lair.

After denying him gratification under the sun, the others provoke his fatal excess underground. But, unless there is a witness to the scene, no one will know the extent of the others' responsibility, for it took place underground. On the surface, Stracci will appear like a bestial glutton who, after all, warrants his destiny. The film, however, shares the underground truth with us, and thus invites us to see beneath the surface and unmask the appearances: although full of energy, Stracci is dead to the others. He is dead to history and discourse, and his death on the cross is but the last act of the passion of

La ricotta: *Stracci's (Mario Cipriani) bodily excess occurs underground.* Courtesy of the Museum of Modern Art/Film Stills Archive.

invisibility struggling to be seen. With such a surface/underground dialectic, *La ricotta* literally dramatizes the spatial metaphor at the heart of an ideal realist observation.

We are now in a position to notice that the inversion of appearances characterizes *La ricotta* in other ways. It is a comic film, but, in fact, it tells a tragic story of thwarted passion. Pasolini's film may seem the impious vision of a blasphemous eye when, in reality, it aspires to denounce commercial speculation just as Christ denounced the moneylenders in the Temple. The main instance of inversion, however, concerns the film that the director (Welles) is making. Whereas the expensive production of Christ's Passion fails to reproduce the feeling of its alleged object, the ridiculed Stracci is the true inheritor of the cross. We did not need the film's ending to know this, for the music in *La ricotta* had already indicated the locus of the authentic passion. Opposed to both the pompous Scarlatti and the modern twist music defining the film within the film, the Gregorian *Dies Irae* reveals where true holiness is. It is in the frugal meal shared by Stracci's family. It is in the image of the empty cross on which the camera briefly lingers after following Stracci's frantic perambulations. And it is in the previously mentioned scene of Stracci's underground excess. *La ricotta* does not deny the Passion. It just shows that it is not where we normally look for it.

Stracci is a type: the subproletarian without consciousness, much like Accattone and Ettore. And, like his two predecessors, he is also set against the group which he seems to represent. On the one hand, Stracci confirms the standard, populist idea that the body and passion, as well as the lower classes and reality, are all aligned on one side of the spectrum. On the other hand, Stracci's body is too excessive, his passion is too close to death, his lowness is just too subterranean, his reality is too invisible to be acknowledged as such. Stracci's hunger finds satisfaction underground, in a place secluded from public view. Long repressed, the fruition of his desire will be so excessive as to bring about his death. Thus another set of meanings condenses in the figure of Stracci, that of bodily deviance. It is a deviance that is connected to death and resumes the homosexual discourse initiated with Accattone and Ettore (who was killed, feverish, in a cruciform position). It is this new set of meanings, loosely centered around homosexuality, which appears in this film when Stracci's young sons follow the lecherous "saints" into the bushes. As in *Mamma Roma*, homosexuality appears as prostitution, as illicit sex. Equally apparent in the two films, the stereotype serves the purpose of introducing a theme which will then be picked up under different circumstances by the protagonist. Stracci, who on one occasion dresses like a woman in order to appear to be someone else and thus have the right to another lunch bag, is also a vector for Pasolini's autobiographical impulse.

The Director's Reason

As I mentioned earlier, the director enters the narrative in an abrupt way, by means of a shot suggesting that he may be observing Stracci and the others. It is a reverse zoom, which slowly reveals the director's visual field. Repeated four times, this particular shot is his visual theme. In contrast to Stracci, who is defined by frantic motion, the director sits in utter isolation (only once do we see three children in the same frame with him), surrounded by black jackets draped across the backs of empty chairs. Undoubtedly, someone wore those jackets and sat on those chairs, but they are now signifiers of absence. If Stracci is in the grip of a social death that prevents him from being seen, the director portrayed in *La ricotta* represents the type of artist who, like Pasolini, "sits" next to the signifier death in all of its ramifications (invisibility; absence; negation of and opposition to established re/productive values). This explains why the director can understand Stracci's fate and encapsulate it in the final remark: "He had to die to show us that he was alive." However commercial and uninspired the director's film may be, he is not the kind of Hollywood craftsman who is unaware of his position. In fact, Pasolini chose Orson Welles, a Hollywood *maudit*, and wanted him to play himself, a director who worked within and yet against the productive machinery.

Clearly reminiscent of how Pasolini saw himself as a leftist and bourgeois intellectual, the director in *La ricotta* can understand the wretched of the earth because of a structural homology between his and their sociocultural position. Caught between his real position in the relations of production—qua established author, he enjoys bourgeois privileges—and his no-less-real ideological beliefs, the director has the doubtful gift of self-consciousness, which, in his case, results in cynicism. He knows that the producer of the film is also the owner of the newspaper for which he is being interviewed. He knows that everything he does (the film) or says (the interview) is heavily mediated by such private ownership. He knows that, after all, he is a mere administrator in the industry of cultural commodities. The director's cynicism, through a rigorous exercise in self-awareness, does not really abdicate the faith in reason but generates a critique of conventional modes of reasoning.

The interview with the silly journalist is quite revealing in this sense. To the question "What do you think of death?" the director replies, "Death is something that I as a Marxist do not take into consideration." *La ricotta* thus informs us of the director's political beliefs but also puts Pasolini's finger on one of Marxism's weak points, its refusal to acknowledge death as a worthwhile subject for theoretical reflection. In a similar vein, when asked the question, "What do you intend to express with this film?" the director replies, "My intimate, deep, and archaic Catholicism." The grin on his face leaves no doubt: He know his words will be taken at face value and will therefore be seen as contradicting his Marxism. At the same time, the director's grin suggests that the opposite is true, that a certain Catholicism and a certain Marxism could coexist. Both statements allow Pasolini to express his discontent with Marxism all the while positioning himself within it, in the attempt to reform Marxist reason.

The director's cynicism offers more than just bitterness. He has something to say and says it by reciting a poem to the dumbfounded journalist. Poetry had already appeared in *Accattone*, where Buonconte's story at once articulated and enriched the film's meaning, and in *Mamma Roma*, where a prison inmate reciting a few lines from Dante's *Purgatory* acted as an oblique reminder of the film's aspirations to high culture. Together with such other elements as classical music and references to fine art, poetry raised Pasolini's films to the status of *cinema d'autore,* which is what his producer and the intelligentsia wanted/expected from him. The poetry in *La ricotta* is Pasolini's and thus is charged with yet another role: self-expression. In effect, it is Pasolini's first *explicit* autobiographical reference in his cinema.

> I am a force of the Past.
> Only tradition is my love.
> I come from the ruins, from the churches,
> from the altarpieces, from the villages
> abandoned on the Apennines, the Alpine foothills
> where my brothers lived.
> I rove the Via Tuscolana like a madman,
> or the Appia like a dog without a master.
> Or I look at the twilights, the mornings
> over Rome, Ciociaria, the world,
> like the first acts of post-history,
> which I witness, thanks to my date of birth,
> from the far edge of some buried
> age. Monstrous is he born
> from the womb of a dead woman.
> And I, adult fetus, roam,
> more modern than any modern,
> seeking brothers who are no more.[3]

A close reading of the poem is beyond the scope of my project. What interests me here is the type of vision that Pasolini saw fit to ascribe to the director in *La ricotta,* "a force of the past" who is "more modern than any modern." The love for the past was nothing new; it was inscribed in the humanist discourse in his authorial intertext. What was new was the notion that recovery of the past could make one advance beyond modernity, which is to say that Pasolini gave his director a postmodern outlook (in 1963!). Far from being a hindrance to be sublated within the dialectic of the Enlightenment, the past—archaic Catholicism—must be reckoned with. The director in *La ricotta* wants to be free of the sense of history as a forward march which forces intellectuals to move in accordance with its progressive tempo. He declares his brotherhood with figures that "are no more," figures that modernity, in its progress, has effaced. It is an intriguing position, one which values tradition—then a conservative gesture—through a Marxist mouthpiece.

The vision of life deriving from his position between modernity and its postmodern aspects does not make the director a very happy person. It fosters his detachment and cynicism. But, as I noted above, it is a cynicism of a different kind; rather than causing a distancing from life, it profits by its contiguity to Marxism and becomes *engagé*. In his introduction to Peter Sloterdijk's book *The Return of Diogenes as Postmodern Intellectual*, Andreas Huyssens notes that the postmodern intellectual revives "the tradition of *kynicism*, from Diogenes to Schweik, as a counterstrategy, as the only form of subversive reason left after the failures and broken promises of ideology critique in the tradition of Western Marxism."[4] The director played by Orson Welles in *La ricotta* is a perfect example of that *kynical* eye.

The emphasis on the director's *kynical* postmodernism defines the nature of "a certain realism." When reality goes through "the first acts of post-history," the realist director can only be a "witness," and not a very reliable one at that. Like the narrating subject in the poem, the director roams, like a loose dog without a master (narrative). His vision is "monstrous," its origins in death, a vision "from the far edge of some buried age." Postmodernism, Pasolini suggests, is a historical condition characterized by the removal of the metaphysical backlighting from History, which then becomes history, his story, a story among others. It is a hard blow for his Marxism and for humanism. In the postmodern condition, a realist "witness" has no foundation on which to ground his witnessing. But Pasolini's urge for realism seeks a way out of the impasse by means of "a certain realism," that is, a realism which must pass through the yoke of lost metaphysics. It is a realism which must forsake the strength with which it used to deliver its illustrated sermons about the real. It is a "weak" realism, but a realism nonetheless, for the *kynical* director in *La ricotta* has witnessed Stracci's life and has *used* what he witnessed to make a statement about reality.[5]

It may be argued that the director's film is not a courageous act of witnessing the reality of Christ's Passion. But on closer inspection, the visual quotations from Pontormo and Rosso Fiorentino mitigate an otherwise harsh judgment on the director's film. The director has to obey the producer, but within the constraints imposed on him by the productive apparatus he inserts his own interpretations. As both paintings portray the same subject, Christ's deposition from the cross, we are invited to think less of what they represent than how they do it. They are instances of Italian Mannerism. Mannerist painters often agreed to paint religious subjects, but their angels had blackish wings and estranged faces, revealing not seraphic bliss but rather doubt and torment. Both Rosso and Pontormo worked in a period of crisis, which explains "the sense of tragic isolation, intellectual anarchy and formal extravagance that we find in their work."[6] Discussing the rational proclivities of such Mannerists, Arnold Hauser wrote,

> On the one hand, they took fully into account the inadequacy of rational thought and appreciated that reality, everyday reality, was inexhaustible and defied rational synthesis. On the other, in spite of their fundamental irrationalism and skepticism, they could not give up the art of reason, playing with problems, throwing them up and catching them again. They despaired of speculative thought, and at the same time clung to it; they had no high hopes of reason, but remained passionate reasoners.[7]

Having witnessed the decentering of "Man" brought about by the Copernican revolution, Mannerists no longer regarded harmony with nature as a self-evident goal and questioned the idea of objective representation altogether. In the age that saw the triumph of linear perspective and naturalist representation, the Mannerists' convoluted figures and gyrating rhythms evoked the simultaneity of points of view. Their spaceless works undermined the idea of linear perspective. Their choice of colors did not aim at verisimilitude but at modulating a sort of expressionist dissonance. The intellectualist *maniera*, opposing as it did the Classical doctrine of imitation, "marked a revolution in the history of art," that is, "for the first time art deliberately diverged from nature."[8]

The director in *La ricotta* may not be a rebel, but he has refused to draw his inspiration from a more canonical tradition. In his search for "brothers who are no more," the director has found the antinaturalist painters within and yet against the tradition, figures through whom he can convey his *kynicism*, his aggressive detachment. By choosing two paintings by Rosso and Pontormo, the director does what he can to be a brave witness to the "first acts of post-history." And Pasolini, by choosing two paintings by Rosso and Pontormo, confirms that his "brothers" are "passionate reasoners."

The Observer and the Observed

I have argued that Stracci and the director may be seen as social types and as two autobiographical projections of the author. I have also argued that the film suggests that the two protagonists belong to the same field of vision, more specifically, that Stracci is the target of the director's gaze. I shall now examine the relations ensuing from this scheme, starting with Pasolini's autobiographical projections.

As is to be expected, Pasolini sees himself as split in two parts: the director and Stracci. Together, they elucidate the dynamics inside the by now familiar partnership of reason and passion. *Kynical* reason and deviant passion are intimately related. Theirs is a visual relationship, where the former gazes at and frames the latter. The *kynical* subject sees himself acting, and this occasionally entails an unpleasant self-consciousness. But self-consciousness has its good points. It is by virtue of the rational eye that passion becomes a visual object. In and of itself, passion is bodily vitality unaware of itself, and it has no discursive existence. It takes a gaze, an observer, for passion to become an object, for it to have a reality. It is the director's final comment that brings Stracci to life; it is Pasolini's self-consciousness that understands the mechanisms of his own passion and oppression.

The visual relationship between the director and Stracci as social types follows a similar pattern. The director's gaze is the mechanism by virtue of which Stracci becomes visible. In fact, the director embodies the new, weak realist gaze. He is a realist in that his observation brings the subproletariat into discourse, an area in which they normally do not exist, or rather, they exist as dead, like Stracci. He is a weak realist in that he makes no claim to objectivity.

Pasolini starts from the reality of his own self, from the perception of himself as divided between "reason" and "passion." He then scans the social horizon in search of "brothers." In the course of his exploration of the social text, Pasolini finds the deviant subproletarian and the unorthodox Marxist, the *kynic*. He then establishes an analogical link between these two social types and the two parts of his self that demand expression. This mechanism provides a good example of the metaphorical tension inscribed in his homosexual discourse, whereby he has to look for "brothers" through whom he can express himself. Such metaphorical tension has a realistic value, for it allows him to be sincere, to tell the truth about himself, all the while engaging in the portrayal of social types and situations (the ideal of Lukacsian realism).

Pasolini's realism does not give us minute details, nor does he reconstruct the environment in search of neorealist fidelity. His portrayal of the director and Stracci does not aim at making us see their surface but rather suggests their essential position in society. It may be argued that the director and Stracci are nothing but projections of the author. This is so, and herein lies the nature of "a certain realism." Pasolini is aware of the subjective filter which colors everything we observe and makes his realism start from the subject, from his own self, from the one thing which he can best know. One might doubt the validity of the portrayal of the world out there, as critics have often done, but it would be beside the point. What counts is that Pasolini is motivated to represent the "brothers" existing out there and knows that such a representation cannot prescind from the subject. He is proposing an expressionist realism wherein reality is always already observed from a specific (i.e., the author's) position.

This representation by analogy expresses one reality by means of another, and, in so doing, it articulates them both. Once the analogical link between the self and the world is established, once one's inner microcosm becomes commensurate with the macrocosm, the relationship works both ways, in a reciprocity that makes it hard to detect which came first. The question of what came first—Pasolini's desire to represent reality or the narcissistic urge to know himself—is irrelevant. Likewise, it is hard to detect which comes first between the observer and the observed. In fact, self and world, reason and passion, the observer and the observed, all exist in one and the same gesture. They presuppose each other. The realist gaze starts existing only at the moment in which there is something gazed upon in a realist fashion. Conversely, the observed needs the observer to become visible. Realism then is the product of a relationship between a gaze and a gazed upon, and every attempt to sever the two, that is, to produce only the gazed upon as if it existed alone, is epistemologically false and, realistically speaking, preposterous.

7

La rabbia

La rabbia (The Rage, 1963) is a collage of documentary footage.
Pasolini selected the images and also wrote a commentary on a double
register: poetry and prose. The former was read by the novelist Giorgio Bassani, the latter by the painter Renato Guttuso. As this film is
still unavailable to the American public, my synopsis here is more
detailed. I will indicate the events chosen by Pasolini and I will add,
in parentheses, a few key sentences. from the commentary. Needless
to say, the film is a seamless continuum. Demarcations, here, are arbitrary and motivated by my desire to achieve a clearer exposition.

- Disquieting images of atomic explosions. (Guttuso's voice proposes the question which motivated the film—"Why is our life
dominated by discontent, by anguish, by the fear of war, by
war?"—and adds: "To answer this question I've written this film,
following no chronological nor even logical line perhaps, but only
my political reasoning.")
- Soviet invasion of Hungary. (Bassani: "Black Hungarian winters,
the counterrevolution has erupted; black Hungarian sun, Stalin's
mistakes are our mistakes. . . .")
- Anti-Communist demonstrations. Parisian crowds burning the
French Communist party headquarters. (Bassani: "Black Parisian
boulevards, your leaders march like colonels; black Parisian forebodings, freedom has become suffering. . . .")
- Italian refugees after World War II; the 1956 Suez crisis; Congo,
1961, the death of Lumumba; crowds in India and Indonesia.

111

(Bassani: "A new problem bursts out in the world: it is called color. The new dimension of the world is called color. We must incorporate the idea of thousands of black or brown children, with black eyes and curly heads; we must accept the infinite spectacle of real lives that want to enter our reality with ferocious innocence. . . .")

- Israel's attack against Egypt. Cuban freedom fighters rejoice and die on dusty roads. Latin music on the soundtrack. (Bassani: "Fighting in Cuba! Perhaps only a song can tell us the meaning of the Cuban fights. . . .")
- Sarcastic visual and aural quotation of newsreel snippets: Sophia Loren's visit to an eel-fishing village; Ava Gardner's arrival in Rome.
- Images from the Italian "economic miracle": the unions sign an agreement with the government. (Bassani: "It is easy to buy a worker. It is enough to lure him with the recognition of nobility. He, too, wants to be spirit, to be part of the banquet of those who do not live by bread alone. . . .")
- Coronation ceremony of Elizabeth II. Nomination of presidential candidate Eisenhower. (Guttuso: "The joy of the average American who feels equal to other millions of Americans united in their love of democracy: this is the disease of the future world! When the Classical world is exhausted, when artisans and peasants are all dead, when industry makes the cycle of production and consumption unstoppable, then our history will be over. . . .")
- Fleeting images of the atomic mushroom cloud in the Nevada desert. (Guttuso: "In this unrecognizable sun the new prehistory begins. . . .")
- Death and funeral of Pope Pius XII. Election of Pope John XXIII.
- A Soviet village. (Guttuso: "Only revolution can save the past. . . .")
- Exhibition of socialist-realist paintings. (Bassani: "Look at these beautifully painted miners, look at these wonderful women comrades. . . and yet something else weighs on my heart. . . these paintings contain our mistake. We must take them down from these walls!")
- *Color* shots of Guttuso's drawings (Bassani: "We must start anew, from where there is no certainty, and signs are desperate, and colors are strident, and the figures are all twisted like the dead in Buchenwald, and a red flag trembles with a victory which must never be the last. . . .")

- Long sequence on the Algerian war. Shots of bombings and fighting, enlargements of newspaper stills, dead bodies. (Bassani: "People of color, Algeria is given back to history! . . . On my first brother, the bandit; on my second brother, the cripple; on my third brother, the shoeshiner; on my fourth brother, the beggar, I write your name. On my lowlife friends; on my jobless friends; on my working comrades, I write your name: freedom!")
- Atomic mushroom cloud. Marilyn Monroe sequence, quick montage of stills. Bach on the soundtrack. (Bassani: "Of the ancient world and of the future world, only beauty had remained, and you, you, little younger sister, had that beauty upon you, humbly; and your soul, as daughter of humble people, was never aware of it, because otherwise it would not have been beauty. It vanished, like a golden dust. The world taught you about it, so your beauty became the world's. . . .")
- Atomic explosions (Guttuso: "Reality is nothing but these shapes in the sky. . . . ")
- Contrast between images of the bourgeoisie (Guttuso: "The class that warrants beauty and riches. . . .") and the disenfranchised. (Bassani: "The class of the black, wool shawls, of the cheap, black aprons. . . .")
- Gagarin's return from space, welcomed by Khrushchev and the Russian people. Revolutionary song on the soundtrack. (Guttuso: "Revolution demands one war only, the one within the spirit. . . .")

> *Yo! Man! There is a lot of brothers out there flakin' and perpetratin', too scared to kick reality.*
>
> Niggers With Attitude

When producer Gastone Ferranti asked Pasolini whether he would be interested in making a compilation-footage film in response to the question "Why is our life dominated by discontent, by anguish, by the fear of war, by war?" Pasolini saw in this project the opportunity to do something new. He thus watched all the documentary footage from the archives of *Mondo libero* (the *cinegiornale* that Ferranti had been managing throughout the fifties) and found it to be "a depressing parade of international conservatism (*qualunquismo*)."[1] Still, here and there, "in the middle of all that banality and squalor," he caught sporadic glimpses of "beautiful images: the smile of an unknown person, two eyes brimming with either joy or sorrow, and sequences full of historical meaning." Attracted by the "visually fascinating black and white of these images," Pasolini accepted Ferranti's offer "on condition of being able to write my own poetic commentary" to the images. "My ambition was that of creating a new cinematographic genre, of making an ideological and poetic essay with new sequences." Although he fully succeeded in his ambitious effort, the film ran into distributional problems which kept it from achieving the notoriety it deserved.

In order to enhance his chances for commercial success, Ferranti decided to ask someone from the Right to work on similar premises, the intention being to pit two world views against one another. Ferranti chose Giovanni Guareschi, the author of the *Don Camillo* series, a well-known representative of Italian conservatism. After seeing Guareschi's part, Pasolini decided to withdraw his signature from the project. Guareschi's film was indeed racist, full of colonialist nostalgia and facile anticommunism. It was the product of an aging petty bourgeois attached to the notion of white, European supremacy. Still, the contrast with Pasolini's work was so intense, so revealing, that it would have been worth risking being linked with Guareschi in order to let the viewers take their stands. But in those days, the Left did not even want to talk to fascists.[2]

La rabbia (The Rage, 1963) was released nonetheless, with both Guareschi's and Pasolini's sections. However, because of bad press and its own objective difficulty—it is, after all, an extremely political, non-narrative document—it failed at the box office. After a few runs in Italy's major cities, it was withdrawn from circulation and it has been sitting on some dusty shelf in Rome ever since, only to be resurrected on the occasion of Pasolini retrospectives, a sad fact since *La rabbia* is one of Pasolini's highest achievements. It is a stunningly beautiful and moving visual poem which deserves to be known outside the circle of specialists.

The Poetics of Anger

La rabbia is Pasolini's many-faceted experiment with the signifying power of montage, both as linkage of images and juxtaposition of images with sound and spoken commentary. The newsreel images, which were originally meant as visual evidence of documentary truth, are grafted by Pasolini into new sequences where they acquire different meanings. Postmodern in its idea of reworking already existing material, *La rabbia* represents an exercise in the art of semantic highjacking. For instance, the image of a butler closing a door behind a bejeweled woman, originally intended as tabloid-like "who's who" reportage, becomes in *La rabbia* a signifier of the lower classes' exclusion from beauty. Likewise, the tribute to Marilyn Monroe—inserted between two nuclear explosions and alternating images of boxers in a ring, a self-flagellating Christ in a religious parade, and burning wax statues—relocates a sex symbol into the melancholia of lost beauty and missed opportunities. The sight of Monroe's body in sensuous poses introduces the ineffable frenzy of the senses into the streamline of political history.

As was unanimously noted by the critics and by Pasolini himself, the Marilyn Monroe sequence is the highest achievement in *La rabbia*. The viewer is almost taken by surprise, so striking are her images and the montage of the visual and aural components. In effect, Marilyn Monroe perfectly fits Pasolini's intentions in this film. Her suicide offers a sublime example of refusal: Her death "showed us the way," the way to a radical rejection of the mechanisms co-opting body and desire. A rebellious, shooting star in a celluloid firmament, Monroe is, according to Pasolini, an unwitting martyr, in the etymological sense of "witness."[3] In the imaginary tribunal of the new prehistory that Pasolini was theorizing in these years, Monroe's martyrdom amounts to bearing witness to the wreckage of the culture industry.

La rabbia explores more than just the effect of montage. Its nonnarrative nature permits Pasolini to verify the potential that images have to convey a meaning which exceeds verbal and logical discourse. As attested by his transition from literature to cinema a couple of years earlier, Pasolini senses, at this stage, the existence of a truth which no word, not even the poetic word, can evoke. His interest in facial expressions as vectors of an otherwise untransmittable meaning begins to have conceptual legitimacy precisely with *La rabbia*. Entire chains of events are encapsulated in carefully chosen and edited close-ups. Political and philosophical arguments gleam through black and white, moving images. The energy of anger is suggested by shots of dying soldiers. All this is important, for Pasolini is testing the possibility of writing an essay in a cinematic form in order to convey a different kind of message than that which we expect from words. His intention is to establish a communication that exists apart from the verbal spectrum, escapes definition, and yet *is* there, thus opposing the logocentric tradition in which nothing exists which is not definable. In fact, by analyzing its images, I am doing a disservice to *La rabbia*.

At the time of *La rabbia*, Pasolini was asking himself questions which he would address later in his semiotic writings, such as: Are not images used to document historical and factual truth because they speak a language? What is the part played by the image and what by the commentary? And how can a viewer inured to the "atrocious banality" of predigested images be jolted from his/her acquiescence?

Although these questions had no answers at the time of *La rabbia*, the film shows evidence of the direction Pasolini would take. For example, his taste for shocking visuals (e.g., close-ups of tortured Algerian bodies) initiates a strategy which would last throughout his entire work: to push both images and spectators to the limit, where reality raises its ugly head and realism becomes an imposed medicine.

In fact, within the scope of "a realist and visionary cinema," as noted by Maurizio Liverani, *La rabbia* contains a meditation on the ideas of both reality and realism.[4] Towards the end of the film, the often-repeated image of the atomic mushroom cloud blazing in the sky finds, at last, a spoken explanation in Guttuso's remark: "This is reality." Such a visual rendition of a most loved word/concept suggests more than apocalypse and frustration; it gives an image to the epistemological break characterizing the postmodern condition. Reality *is* overdetermined by those shapes up there. The historical and existential horizon within which we must live and think has been irreparably altered by nuclear power. One might even argue that postmodernism was set off by Hiroshima and Nagasaki. In the face of the caustic lights of atomic explosions, the past grows pale, or, rather, it demands revision: Is this the progress of *humanitas*? As a sign whose meaning cannot be highjacked, as a sign that, Pasolini thinks, ought to evoke the same response in all of its interpreters, the image of a nuclear explosion *is* postmodernity's transcendental signifier. Pasolini's anger is aimed at those who think and act as if all this had not happened.

There is of course a contradiction between postmodernism and the existence of a sign whose meaning is stable. Postmodernism tolerates no pivot, no center. Not even the image of a nuclear explosion can function as cornerstone of a notion of reality. But this is the healthy contradiction at the heart of "a certain realism." On the one hand, Pasolini moves within the boundaries of conventional realism, in which meanings are ordered hierarchically and reality has a central signifier that can be discovered and imaged. On the other, he acknowledges and incorporates the epistemological break set off by the advent of postmodernity. In this respect, it is only logical that Pasolini's next major project was to be the filming of the Gospel; Jesus, like the atomic explosion, is yet another transcendental signifier. But one has to wait until *Teorema* in order to find Pasolini's theoretical assessment, *through images*, of the contradictory dialectic which founds "a certain realism."

On the subject of realist representation, *La rabbia* contains a sequence that takes up the idea of reality as redefined by nuclear explosions: the socialist realism art exhibit followed by Guttuso's drawings shot in color. Inviting the spectator to forget the craftily painted images of a healthy proletariat, Pasolini urges us to dismantle the system of representation according to which realism unquestioningly takes the lower classes as its objects. The notion of the proletariat as *the* subject of history and representation is now (1963!) a mistake, Stalin's mistake. Paired with the nervous lines of Guttuso's color drawings, the poetic image of a red flag fluttering over "a victory which must never be the last," reiterates the idea that no stopping point can be provided, that realist passion must reinvent itself all the time.

The use of Guttuso's work has yet another point of interest within the scope of this book. In 1962, the Sicilian painter had an exhibit in Rome, for which Pasolini wrote the catalog introduction.[5] Therein, Pasolini focused on the analysis of *Operai in riposo* (Resting Workers, 1945), a black and red ink drawing that *La rabbia* carefully emphasizes (out of the ten color shots, four are of this drawing). Contrasted with the magniloquent imagery of socialist realism, the image of a worker sitting at the center of the drawing haunts Pasolini. "Now," he noted, "this worker's face is bereft of the entire left side: no eyebrows nor eyelashes, no eyelids nor pupils, no cheekbone nor cheek." This is the first indication of Pasolini's fascination with the image of one-eyed vision, which will constitute a recurrent shot in his films to come. A discussion of the implications of such a predilection must be postponed until later (see *Edipo re* and *I racconti di Canterbury*). Here, I would like to suggest that Pasolini's description of the drawing is reminiscent of the theme of partially obscured vision initiated by Balilla (*Accattone*) and Ettore (*Mamma Roma*) peeping through the holes of a urinal grating. A visual metaphor for an absent totality, the one-eyed worker suggests a visual regime which cannot dream of plenitude. Just as in *Accattone* the thief's vision was positively contrasted with the eyes of power, the worker's split face, here, is defined by its juxtaposition with a perfunctory realism that admits neither gaps nor void. Monoscopic vision is not a negative trait, but is a courageous adequation of vision to historical circumstances, to the new reality of the atomic mushroom cloud.

Transposing Adorno's and Horkheimer's brilliant definition of Sade and Nietzsche as the "black writers of the bourgeoisie"—writers who mercilessly exposed the dream of progressive *Ratio* as a nightmare—I would argue that *La rabbia* is the political and aesthetic manifesto of Pasolini, "the black film-maker of the bourgeoisie."[6] As the most often employed color in the poetic commentary to the images, black implies a chromatic counterweight to the red implicit in Pasolini's declared ideological stand. The use of black occasionally represents the "no future" feeling that inevitably overcomes anyone who looks at nuclear explosions—the "no future" of punks who appropriately chose black as their color. But black is not just the color of despair and death. It is also the color of anarchists—which fits well with the antirationalism in Sade, Nietzsche, and Pasolini—and of pirates. Inevitably, however, Nietzsche's and Pasolini's methodological anarchism and intellectual piracy has the effect of situating *some* of their work beside the black of fascism. Although very few Italian critics want to hear of this, it nonetheless is a fact. On a few occasions, Pasolini himself confessed to his attraction to propositions coded as reactionary, such as the mythology of action and ultra-libertarian ideology.[7]

La rabbia celebrates the complexity of Pasolini's blackness. For in this film, as in another "forgotten" masterpiece, *Appunti per un'Orestiade Africana*, the color black ultimately symbolizes a kind of hope that no fascist would have: the irruption of the black race into the Western, white scene. In perfect keeping with its postmodern outlook, *La rabbia* makes it clear that Western reality—thus far thought of as *the* reality—is too narrow and must be renegotiated: "We must accept the infinite spectacle of real lives that want to enter our reality with ferocious innocence." In spite of the contradictions marring Pasolini's relationship to the Third World, one must credit him for theorizing in *La rabbia* the double bind which Western culture faces vis-à-vis the rise of black cultures. On the one hand, as a white progressive, Pasolini cannot but welcome the decentering of the West and the proliferation of discourses. On the other, he also expresses the unavoidable nostalgia for a moribund master discourse. As a white, male humanist, Pasolini feels a sense of loss at the reduction of his own world; as a homosexual and an anarchist, he is pervaded by a feeling of Messianic elation at the sight of the wretched of the earth on the threshold of History. He knows that once blackness makes it into History, the latter will become history, and his own white identity will have to come to terms with such a dramatic reduction. But he also knows that History, the splendid age of the fathers, had no place for deviants like him. Seen in this light, the color black functions as an oxymoronic signifier of both apocalypse and redemption, of the end and a new beginning. And *La rabbia*, in the stunning alternation of contradictory images, conveys this dual sense, the Janus-like gaze of someone at once depending on and rejecting the white hand that feeds him.

8

Comizi d'amore

Comizi d'amore (Love Meetings, 1963, released 1964) consists of interviews on the subject of sexuality conducted by Pasolini all over Italy. It is divided into four sections: (1) "Big Italian-style Mixed Fry" (*Gran fritto misto all'Italiana*), in which Pasolini asks general questions on "the sexual problem"; (2) "Disgust or Pity" (*Disgusto o pietà*), in which he sounds out the interviewees on the topic of sexual deviance; (3) "True Italy" (*La vera Italia*), in which he asks "more practical questions" regarding marriage, divorce, women's rights; and (4) "From Below and from the Depths" (*Dal basso e dal profundo*), in which he investigates people's reactions to the *Legge Merlin*, the law which abrogated state-run brothels in 1959. Before the first section and between the second and the third, Pasolini asks novelist Alberto Moravia and psychoanalyst Cesare Musatti for their opinions on the enquiry. The film ends with the staged sequence of a marriage in a rural town in the north of Italy. Each section is framed by an ironic, off-screen commentary. As Pasolini did not want to have his own voice heard twice, in both the interviews and the frame, he chose for the latter Lello Bersani, a TV anchorman with "perfect" Italian diction and an impersonal voice.

> *I believe that the world continues to evolve towards evil because we do not know the truth: we remain unaware of reality.*
>
> Cesare Zavattini

119

The 1950s were not good years for documentary. The line separating it from fiction films was blurred, partly because documentary elements were present in neorealist films and partly because documentaries used feature-film equipment, shooting scripts, and situations manipulated by the filmmakers. The doubts concerning the specificity of documentary seemed to vanish when, in the early 1960s, new technology, including light, portable cameras, battery-driven tape recorders, and fast film requiring minimal lighting became available. Documentarists could entertain, once again, the Griersonian dream of fidelity to the actuality of events. This happy season for documentary saw the birth of direct cinema in the United States and *cinéma vérité* in France. The main difference between the two concerned the filmmakers' attitudes about their own roles. Whereas the authors of direct cinema (Leacock, Pennebaker) strove to be as self-effacing as possible—no commentary, no interviews, no staged situations—their French counterparts (Rouch, Rozier, Marker) favored the filmmakers' contact with their subjects.[1]

In Italy, too, the early 1960s witnessed a resurrection of documentary, mostly as *cinéma vérité*, of which Cesare Zavattini was a precursor. Zavattini had advocated a complete absence of fiction in film since the heyday of neorealism, and he proposed *pedinamento* ("tailing" someone) as the ideal technique for the pursuit of reality in the cinema. As early as 1953 he supervised the multidirectorial project *Amore in città* (Love in the City), in which various aspects and consequences of the mythology of love were investigated.[2] What then seemed a rigorous experiment, however, is today appreciated for its intent rather than for its documentary validity. All of the five episodes now seem too staged and make spectators think of docudrama rather than *cinéma vérité*. In 1961, Zavattini again supervised the work of several directors (among them Ferreri, Vancini, Maselli, and Nelo Risi) in *Le Italiane e l'amore* (Italian Women and Love), a rather interesting example of an all-male documentary on women. And, in 1963, he presided over a similar project entitled *I misteri di Roma* (The Mysteries of Rome). Each director was supposed to document a slice of daily life (e.g., the collection of garbage) in Italy's capital. But the input of too many individuals (twelve directors!) harmed this film, and it turned out to be more uneven than the previous one.

The best of the Italian documentaries adhered to the spirit of *cinéma vérité*. Gregoretti's *I nuovi angeli* (The New Angels, 1962), produced by Pasolini's producer, Alfredo Bini, mixed sociological rigor with staged happenstance, and provided a cutting portrait of Sicilian youth. Caldana's *I ragazzi che si amano* (Boys and Girls in Love, 1963) described the crisis in the love and friendships of two couples. Caldana's film achieved an unusual level of intensity by violating the total passivity rule which then reigned supreme in direct cinema. Astutely, Caldana first interviewed each of the youths separately, confronted them all together afterwards, and finally edited the material in a way that best suited his dramatic purposes.

Even a cursory look at the titles of the prolific Italian documentary production in the sixties reveals that love and sex were the preferred foci. On the side of commercial and exploitative cinema one finds the many "sexy documentaries" such as *L'America di notte* (America by Night, 1961) and *Sexy al neon* (Sexy in the Neon Light, 1962). True predecessors of the pornographic films of the seventies, they all claimed to show what had never been shown before—a twisted realism of sorts. On the side of the *documentario d'autore*, in addition to Zavattini's and Caldana's films, one finds Biagi's *Italia proibita* (Forbidden Italy, 1961), Sabel's *In Italia si chiama amore* (In Italy They Call It Love, 1962), and Pasolini's *Comizi d'amore*. To be sure, sexuality had been a major interest and a commercial decoy practically since the beginning of cinema. But the early sixties were shot through with an unprecedented desire to talk about sex, to find out how people lived their sex lives.

As I suggested in the third chapter, the Italian "economic miracle" of the early 1960s initiated the country's transition from old-fashioned capitalism to consumerism. Whereas the economic expansion called for a market geared to consumption, pleasure, and freedom, the State's ideological apparatuses, in many ways tied to the Vatican, retained a "clerical-fascist" mentality. The legal space for the representation of sexuality was extremely narrow, and censorship of "obscene" material was a routine matter. The gap between where many Italians actually were and where they should have been according to those who governed them was particularly acute in the northern cities, where a neocapitalistic ethos had already replaced old patriarchal models. As television was in the hands of the State, it was largely through the press and the cinema that the new bourgeoisie strove to bring "the real Italy" to public attention. It is no accident that the magazine *Espresso* and the newspaper *Il giorno* were founded in those years when the "enlightened" classes emerged. Of course, film producers were willing to back up "enlightening" projects because they knew that sex would sell. Sexuality became the object to be investigated, the reality to be unveiled. It is as if the lower classes, once the privileged object of a realist gaze, were slowly being replaced by sexuality.

Pasolini's cinema had already pointed to sexuality as the hidden agenda of his "certain realism." Not only did *Accattone* and *Mamma Roma* deal with prostitution and sexual awakening, but they also contained a subtextual dimension in which Accattone and Ettore connoted the homosexual condition. *La ricotta* portrayed the passion of frustrated instinctual life. And in *La rabbia*, the most poignant sequence—the sequence that attained the kind of artistic perfection that only ensues from the treatment of deeply felt subjects—was the one dedicated to Marilyn Monroe, a tribute to desire, albeit in its heterosexual, male form. Eager as he was to keep probing the subject, Pasolini convinced Alfredo Bini that their travels in search of locations for *Il Vangelo secondo Matteo* constituted a wonderful opportunity to interview Italians and make a documentary on their attitudes about sex.

Shortly before making *Comizi d'amore*, Pasolini saw *Chronicle d'un été* (Chronicle of a Summer, 1960), the French documentary which initiated *cinéma vérité* (the phrase itself was recorded for the first time in this documentary). In it, the anthropologist Jean Rouch and the sociologist Edgar Morin interviewed several Parisians and, at the end, invited the participants to watch a rough cut of the filmed material. The reactions to the cut were filmed and discussed by the authors in the final sequence. Intrigued by the potential of *cinéma vérité*, Pasolini embraced Morin's and Rouch's suggestion that the only possible documentary truth was one that included the filmmaker's presence. In addition, he derived from *Chronicle d'un été* the idea of discussing the methods and results of the enquiry *in* the film. In order to achieve the desired self-reflexiveness, he asked for the collaboration of his friend Alberto Moravia (a champion of rationalism and an advocate of libertarian stands in sexual matters) and of Cesare Musatti (an orthodox Freudian analyst and the so-called "father of Italian psychoanalysis"). With them Pasolini set out to offer his contribution to *cinéma vérité*.

A Crusade against Ignorance and Fear

Comizi d'amore opens in an emblematic way. Pasolini asks some children in the streets of Naples and Palermo: "Do you know where babies come from?" Long a symbol of the pious lie that we tell our children to protect their innocence, this question anticipates the film's pessimistic conclusions: Italians are immature and live in a fantasy world. The need for serious sexual pedagogy is reinforced by the next sequence, in which Pasolini, Moravia, and Musatti talk on camera about the project of finding out what people really know. Moravia gives his unconditional support, because "sex is taboo everywhere in Italy." Musatti, however, is skeptical, because, as a psychoanalyst, he foresees that people will either avoid answering or will lie. When sexuality is at stake, ignorance and fear prevent them from coming to terms with themselves. But Pasolini is full of passion and accepts the challenge: "A crusade against ignorance and fear, then!"

Such a beginning reveals the particular nature of Pasolini's documentary. He wants to document a certain reality, but, at the same time, he also wishes to fight and leave a mark on that reality. He sees himself as a crusader, a soldier of God fighting to liberate the Holy Land (the body and society) from the infidels (ignorance and fear). In this respect, *Comizi d'amore* is the chronicle of Pasolini's mounting frustration at the sight of people's refusal to acknowledge sexuality as a problem.

As has often been observed, *Comizi d'amore* does not have much sociological value. As an interviewer, Pasolini talks too much and ends up suggesting what the "correct" answer should be. Most interviews take place in a group situation—point-blank questions on a sunny afternoon—with the result that the interviewees conform to what they think is expected of them. As one of them (the actress Antonella Lualdi) suggested, Pasolini should have taken the time to get to know the participants beforehand and thus earn their trust. As a point of fact, the value of Pasolini's documentary lies in its immediacy. In a splendid 1977 article, Michel Foucault captured the essence of *Comizi d'amore* by arguing that "the faces of these kids" with whom the film begins "do not even try to give the impression that they believe what they say."[3] This extends to virtually all the people interviewed: they lie without trying too hard to conceal the lie. On one occasion, for example, Pasolini approaches the popular singer Peppino di Capri and asks him whether or not "the sexual problem" is important to him. Faced with di Capri's reluctance, Pasolini puts his own crusader attitude on and charges: "Isn't it a problem which for you has a different mask?" "That's it!"—the singer hastens to agree without concealing his desire to get rid of Pasolini. This brief sequence encapsulates both the success and the failure of *Comizi d'amore*. Pasolini's documentary obviously fails in its attempt to provide a document of "the true Italy"; it succeeds, however, in documenting the mask. The value of *Comizi d'amore* is to be found in the documentary representation of men and women, young and old, wearing masks.

This is not an entirely fortuitous effect, for Pasolini wrote in the preparatory notes:

> The questions must be stinging, malicious, impertinent, and fired point-blank (they can be toned down in the dubbing if necessary), so as to wring from those interviewed, if not the truth in the logical sense, at least psychological truth. An expression in the eyes, a scandalized angry reaction, or a laugh, can say more than words.[4]

Comizi d'amore: *Pasolini fires his "point-blank questions" that make most of the interviewees lie on camera.* Courtesy of the Museum of Modern Art/Film Stills Archive.

Pasolini begins to have a sense of what he can do with cinema that he could not do with literature: he can "wring" a particular kind of truth from the image of "an expression in the eyes." The distinction between a verbal and visual truth, "truth in the logical sense" and "psychological truth," makes its first, explicit appearance in Pasolini and foreshadows the direction that his film theory and practice will take. In order to allow this "psychological truth" to be wrung out from those interviewed, the camera stares at their faces. In *Comizi d'amore* Pasolini's obsessive frontal close-ups begin to show their realistic function. They aim at wringing out "at least psychological truth" and allow the viewer to perceive the physiognomy of lying. In fact, lying is nothing but the obedience to codes of self-representation, the codes of the mask. The upper-class student in Bologna who claims to be totally free from taboos and prejudices is clearly complying with a hidden script. He is dead serious, all wrapped up in his role as enlightened Italian. Lower-class kids, instead, do not pretend to be telling the truth, and lie with an awareness of lying. They know that (we know) they are merely seeking the funniest answer, the one that most enhances their status among their friends.

As with *La rabbia*, Pasolini's use of words belonging to the semantic area of the term "reality" is worth analyzing. Exploring the north-south dichotomy, the voice-over commentary concludes that

> there in the south ideas on sex are clear. The north is modern but ideas on sex are confused, the wreckage of an old ideology unable to explain reality as a whole. The south is old but intact: woe to hussies, woe to cuckolds, woe to one who does not kill for honor. These are laws of people poor but real.

The use of the word "real" in this context poses obvious problems. Are northerners "unreal"? Of course, Pasolini means that southerners know what the "natural" laws are and live by them. There is no doubt that Pasolini disagrees with the southerners' views. He thinks, however, that they do not wear a mask and are more authentic. They are not trying to be something different. We can understand what he means by this, and perhaps even sympathize with his preference for southerners' spontaneity. Still, the problem of thinking that one group of people is the ontological bearer of reality remains, and, as a matter of fact, it would surface in more contradictory terms at a later time (see *La trilogia della vita*).

"Reality" and "real" are used once again in the commentary, this time more in tune with "a certain realism." After discovering that people from the north and south alike are incredibly united in their contempt for the *Legge Merlin*, Bersani's voice vents Pasolini's despairing conclusion:

> So ends our enquiry shouted from the bottom of the social classes and the depths of the instincts. Workers in Milan, Florence, Naples, and Palermo united against a modern democratic law . . . forced to admit the pressing (*pressante*) reality of certain desires in the face of which we would all like to act like ostriches. Or else, if we discuss them, we do so with a disarming simplification and desperate confusion. This we ascertained in the economic miracle of Italy, naively hoping to discover signs of a cultural and spiritual miracle. If this enquiry has a value, it is a negative one of demystification. The Italy of prosperity is contradicted by these real Italians.

Pasolini could not be more paradigmatic. The adjective "real" connotes what contradicts appearances; and reality is what is deep and below, the lower classes and the instincts. It must be noted, however, that Pasolini is not really blaming these men. Or, better yet, Pasolini the rational utopian may be outraged at their rejection of modernity, but one also senses a Pasolini who understands their obedience to "certain desires." Such an ambivalence is underscored by the camera's affectionate pan over the faces of southern Italian men—an image most dear to Pasolini, the visual symbol, in fact, of his passion. Pasolini's rage is not aimed at those who submit to desire but at the ostrich who pretends that certain realities are not there. The crusade, again, is against ignorance and fear.

The parallel that Pasolini establishes between human body and social body—two similarly structured organisms, with "deep" layers— prompts the question: What is the "pressing reality" in society which corresponds to "the pressing reality of certain desires" in the body? Or, differently put: Does the social body harbor "pressing" realities which "shout" to be "admitted" to the surface and "in the face of which we would all like to act like ostriches"? Thus, obliquely but no less clearly, the enquiry's conclusion harkens back to the section in which Pasolini had his first, most frustrating experience with the ostrich, the section on homosexuality.

Astutely, Pasolini begins this section with Giuseppe Ungaretti. To the question, "Does sexual normality or abnormality exist?," the old poet replies that "every man is made in a different way," so that "all men are in their own way abnormal. All men are in contrast with nature, and the act of civilization is an act against nature." Faced with more personal questions, Ungaretti extricates himself with a coy answer: "I am a poet, I transgress all laws just by writing poetry." Pasolini does not succeed in legitimizing "the pressing reality" of homosexuality through an open confession by Ungaretti. Only those among the viewers who know of Ungaretti's homoerotic tendencies are able to understand what Pasolini is trying to do. For the rest, this interview is just a sign of respect for a Nobel Prize–winning poet.

The rest of the section brings nothing but grief. In a Milanese discothèque, outside a café in the southern town of Catanzaro, and in a first-class train compartment, Pasolini tries to ascertain whether the sight of a homosexual inspires pity or disgust. Significantly he never asks, "What do you think of homosexuality?" but, rather, "How does the idea of homosexuality make you feel?" or "What do you feel when in the presence of a homosexual?" As compassion or revulsion are the most common answers, Pasolini presses on: "How does such pity/ disgust manifest itself?" Not only does Pasolini seem to be chasing his old obsession of naming feelings, but he is also laying the foundations for what would later become his theory of physical presence as a political subject.[5] Concurrently, he pursues the idea that truth emerges from one's body, from the guts: All the interviewees are convinced that their feelings of contempt towards a homosexual *mean* homo-sexuality's objective vileness. At the end of the section, Pasolini sadly reports his findings to Moravia and Musatti, who agree in explaining both disgust and compassion as two defense mechanisms.[6]

The film's ending—the staged sequence of the marriage of Tonino and Graziella in a northern farm town—epitomizes the attitude behind *Comizi d'amore*. Pasolini's own voice now comments upon the images against the background of an American pop love song. Reiterating that "to be silent is to be guilty," Pasolini's greeting for the newlyweds is "may your love be further blessed with the knowledge of your love." Passion and reason loom large again, needing each other. Only a rational distance ensures that what is deep and below will receive its proper treatment. As is argued by Jean Delmas, *Comizi d'amore* is a corrective to the widespread idea that Pasolini is the director of myth and the irrational.[7] In the field of sexuality, Pasolini may have enter-tained a nostalgia for a mythically innocent, spontaneous, and pre-rational vital energy, but he suffered too much from social prejudices ever to abandon his crusade on behalf of "those who are suffering, directly or indirectly, from the burden of ignorance, of hypocritical in-hibition or, in a wider sense, from the prejudices that regulate sexual relations."[8]

9

Sopraluoghi in Palestina

Sopraluoghi in Palestina (Seeking Locations in Palestine, 1964) is a direct record of Pasolini's and Father Andrea Carraro's travels through the Holy Land: Galilee (Lake Tiberias, Mount Tabor, Nazareth, Capernaum), Jordan, Baram, Jerusalem, and Bethlehem. We see Pasolini's reactions to the places, hear his reflections and his questions to Father Carraro.

> *Like Paolo at the end of* Teorema, *the realist filmmaker must remain in the desert, ever seeking, but never achieving, the promised land of stylistic and ideological certainty.*
>
> Millicent Marcus

Between June 27th and July 11th, 1963, Pasolini traveled to Palestine. Together with Father Andrea Carraro in the role of biblical expert, he attempted to evaluate the possibility of shooting *Il Vangelo secondo Matteo* in the Holy Land. *Sopraluoghi in Palestina* is the chronicle of Pasolini's gradual disillusionment with the Israeli landscape (too modern for his purposes) and the slow emergence of his decision to make *Il Vangelo secondo Matteo* in southern Italy. Pasolini virtually disowned this film, for "he never took any part in the camera set-ups or the shooting or anything else."[1] Nevertheless, *Sopraluoghi in Palestina* is worthy of attention for what it anticipates about his next film and for what it discloses and clarifies within his filmography.

Along with the observation that Israel, for the most part, is too modern to be the ideal setting for *Il Vangelo secondo Matteo*, Pasolini's most recurrent comment over the images is his variously expressed surprise at the smallness of the Holy Land. Just a few months earlier, while in India, Pasolini discovered for the first time that "Catholicism did not coincide with reality." Now his idea of what biblical places are like is brought down to size. At the end of the film, Pasolini remarks:

> What impressed me most was the extreme smallness, misery, and humility of this place. I had imagined that this world of the "Beatitudes" would be one of the most fabulous places of the film, and I thought Palestine would have offered a wonderful spectacle. But the reality was an incredible impression of smallness. And, I repeat, of humility. A great lesson in humility.

Evidently, the story of Christ that existed in Pasolini's mind before his trip to Palestine had mythical proportions. It is as if his idea of the Holy Land had been molded by omnipresent Italian Catholic imagery, which, if it included the realism of Masaccio and Caravagggio, mostly abounded with Renaissance magniloquence and Baroque splendor. Above all, it is as if his imagination had been shaped by biblical films, always so full of stately palaces and open vistas.

Pasolini is not disappointed but impressed by the visit. By the end of *Sopraluoghi* he confesses to having received not only a "great lesson in humility" but also "a profound aesthetic intuition": small is beautiful. The point, now, is to re-create this smallness somewhere else. It is here that the idea of the analogy with southern Italy comes in. Pasolini decides to transpose Christ's story to a setting which physically resembles the Holy Land and even carries vague historical parallels with the Gospels. According to him, only in southern Italy could one still find masses of poor, naive believers willing to embrace the wonder of miracles. And, with a bit more imagination, one could even find the presence of a conflict between a central Roman power and a silent, subproletarian population.

The visit to Palestine allows Pasolini to focus on three principles of his "certain realism." The first is the revelation of a small reality behind the false representation of dominant culture. The second is Pasolini's determination to make *Il Vangelo secondo Matteo* refer analogically to Italian contemporary reality. The third concerns his burgeoning idea of cinematography as the opportunity to scrutinize the human face and the mysterious traces left on it by culture. For *Comizi d'amore*, Pasolini had spoken of a "psychological truth" to be caught on the faces of the people that he interviewed. *Sopraluoghi*—which was actually shot before *Comizi*—complements and expands upon this idea. As instructed by Pasolini, the cameraman focuses on the faces of poor Arab girls, of nomadic Palestinians. While these shots indicate his mounting interest in the icons of a premodern mankind and are a prelude to his Third World films, they also have an exceptional value, for they are dubbed with Pasolini's own spontaneous commentary. When the camera stares at the faces of some Arab children, he remarks: "These won't do for the film, because one can see that Christ's preaching has not passed across their faces." Or, speaking of young Israelis, Pasolini notes that "these faces have suffered and bear the mark of all contemporary culture, from Romanticism onward." These typically Pasolinian statements may be puzzling to those who are not familiar with his project that he would later call a "physiognomic realism." As he would most convincingly convey in *Gennariello* (see chapter 3), external reality addresses us, speaks to us, and in so doing leaves its traces on our bodies. As cultural phenomena, Christianity and modernity mark people's features in a perceptible way. One just has to learn how to read the language spoken by faces, the language of physical presence. Cinema, Pasolini begins to understand, transcribes such a language on the screen, and therefore, as he would argue in a year, it is "the written language of reality."

One final subtext in this unusual, if repetitive, documentary is represented by the formula with which Pasolini introduces the main "holy" places to us: "Here Christ must have preached . . . here Christ must have. . . ." One is reminded of the essence of photography which, according to Sontag's and Barthes's frequently similar assessments, is the record of a "here there must have been." The photographic image reassures us that something was really there at the moment of the camera's click. In *Sopraluoghi*, Pasolini is recording an absence (He is no longer here) and postulating a presence (He must have been here), an absence and a presence of nothing less than the transcendental signifier of Catholic culture, the sign which keeps all the others in place. Once seen in this light, we can see why Pasolini's certain realism wanted/needed to confront itself with Christ, with the myth that founded the reality of his never-forgotten Catholic discourse.

Within Pasolini's filmography, *Sopraluoghi* inaugurates, albeit unwittingly, a genre that he would perfect with *Appunti per un film sull'-India* and *Appunti per un'Orestiade Africana*. And, more important, it marks Pasolini's cinematic discovery of the desert as a symbol as well as a series of visual possibilities.[2] At the sight of the Dead Sea, Pasolini notes: "The only landscape that has in and of itself the mark of grandiosity is this cyclopean desert." And just before the end, he marvels at the fact that Christ chose "this desert place" for His Messianic incarnation. Cinematically, the desert is an authentic aesthetic revelation, for it entails the realization of what the camera can do with and in it: slow panning shots over wild, open spaces; long shots which minimize the human figure and make it look like an appendage of the earth. Not only would the desert appear in *Il Vangelo secondo Matteo*, *Medea*, and *Il fiore delle Mille e una notte*, but it would also acquire a structural significance in *Edipo re*, *Teorema*, and *Porcile*.

Pasolini's fascination with the desert, however, should not surprise us, for its figure appeared early in his writing. In a 1946 letter to Sergio Maldini, twenty-four-year-old Pasolini talked about his "experience of absolute, macabre solitude" which led him to "mystical openings" and to "such deep, inner deserts from which the world, once examined, appears in all of its original and tremendous objectivity."[3] One year later, Pasolini entitled a poem in the collection *L'usignolo della chiesa cattolica* (The Nightingale of the Catholic Church, 1947), *Deserto*.[4] Therein, the desert was still an image of solitude, but of a different kind, for "in the heart of the desert" one finds "the barren marble of the urinal which becomes the temple of my dreams." As the desert in this poem was related to forbidden dreams and lovemaking with statues, the solitude it implied was less spiritual than phantasmal: the solitude of the self having submitted to desire.

These two examples are complementary and indicate the desert as a spatial metaphor for a total confrontation with one's self, the place in which one is relieved from having to lie about anything.[5] As the place where silence and temptation meet, Pasolini's desert is most certainly an image derived from the margins of his Catholic discourse. According to the Christian mysticism of the Fathers of the desert, God chose the desert as the arena for His revelation.[6] The image of the desert in Pasolini's films owes much to this idea, but, as usually happens, it blends with the other discourses of his authorial intertext. The desert will then become a visual metaphor for the psychoanalytic process: the regression to one's primal scene (*Edipo re*) and the submission to primary instincts (*Porcile*). And, in *Teorema*, the mystical connotations will be enriched by the presence of a post-Marxist anger that will make the desert the symbol of revelation as much as revolution.

10

Il Vangelo secondo Matteo

Joseph is puzzled by Mary's pregnancy, but an angel explains that she bears the Son of God. Jesus is born, the three wise men bring their gifts to Him, and Joseph and Mary flee to Egypt to avoid the slaughter of the innocents. Some twenty-five years later, John the Baptist prophesies the coming of the Messiah to a crowd of followers. When Jesus goes to him asking to be baptized, John recognizes Him and kneels in front of Him. Jesus then chooses the Apostles and goes around the country with them, preaching and healing the sick. Meanwhile, John the Baptist is decapitated in jail. The Pharisees plot against Jesus and, thanks to Judas's betrayal, have Him arrested. Jesus is tried and condemned to death. Peter lies about his friendship with Jesus three times, as He had foretold. Jesus is crucified. On the third day after His death, His mother and her companions find His burial place empty.

> *Between the idea*
> *And the reality*
> *Between the motion*
> *And the act*
> *Falls the Shadow*
> T. S. Eliot, *For Thine is the Kingdom*

Pasolini's lifelong interest in the figure of Christ emerged in all of its compelling sincerity one night in Assisi, where he had been invited

by a local religious order to attend a workshop on *Accattone*. He
icked up the Gospels by his bedside and, "after six pages," was
truck by the idea that he should make a film on the life and preaching
of Christ, more precisely on Matthew's Gospel.[1] Later, he was to say
that "the key by which I conceived the film" and that "drove me to
make it" was Jesus' sentence:

> Do not suppose that I have come to bring peace on the earth. I have not
> come to bring peace but a sword. For I have come to bring division, a
> man against his father, a daughter against her mother.
>
> (Matt. 10, 34)[2]

This was certainly not the image of unconditional love normally associated with the spirit of the Christian family. The impulse behind the decision to make *Il Vangelo secondo Matteo* (The Gospel according to
Matthew, 1964) was yet another manifestation of the realist desire to
show what lies hidden. Pasolini wanted to reveal that there can be
another side to Jesus and thus strip His preaching of its official mask.
As "in Italy nobody reads the Gospel, really nobody,"[3] the interpretation of Christ's words was left to the officials of the Catholic Church.
As a consequence, the Gospels were either ignored (by atheists) or
taken as the expression of the Absolute.

When Bunuel's *L'age d'or* (1929) portrayed the Duke of Blangis
(one of the four libertines in Sade's *The 120 Days of Sodom*) as Christ,
it did not simply make the point that God is the great sadist who
takes pleasure in people's sufferings. Rather, it touched upon the
nature of absolute principles: just as Sadean libertines conceive themselves outside and above common morality, so absolute truths claim to
exist independently of anything else. The Absolute needs nothing and
nobody to exist. It is the ultimate Object, the Unique, which has always been and always will be. In order to maintain power, Absolutes
must conceal the fact that they are the product of relations, of subjective and historical relations. By suggesting that there was another
Christ behind the absolute image imparted by Catholic education and
by showing that another perfectly legitimate and inspired reading of
Jesus's story was possible, *Il Vangelo* revealed that the story of Christ
the Son of God, far from being the locus of absolute truth, is a quintessentially open text, a set of interpretive strategies which are left to the
reader.[4]

In the early sixties, there were also contingent historical reasons for
which a cinematic translation of the Gospel could be regarded as a
realist project. The relationship between Italy's two major ideologies,
namely, Marxism and Catholicism, constituted a pressing historical

reality, especially since the pontificate of Pope John XXIII had broken with the Catholic Church's militant anticommunism. The times were ripe for an opening on the Left's part. A self-proclaimed Marxist, Pasolini had just been given a four-month suspended sentence for *La ricotta*'s alleged blasphemy and was the ideal figure for such a proposition. Just when the public expected another scandal, he surprised everyone by making what many still regard the most religious film on Christ ever made. As a consequence, *Il Vangelo* ended up having an impact on the very reality which Pasolini wanted to affect with his cinema.

Il Vangelo strove less to *e*voke a specific historical moment (Christ's times) than to *pro*voke the social constellation in which the text was to be consumed. Pasolini's film stirred endless confrontations and forced nearly everyone, from Right to Left, to take a stand. The reactions to the film reflected the different positions within the cultural institution called religion. Unable to dismiss the film, conservative Catholics betrayed their bad faith by perpetrating an *ad hominem* attack against Pasolini and thus revealed their substantive proximity to the positions of the far Right. Progressive Catholics, on the contrary, were extremely pleased, enthusiastically participated in the countless seminars and debates on Marxism and Catholicism following the projection of the film, and were thus forced to heed Pasolini's proposition that the great enemy of Christ is less Marxism than bourgeois materialism.

Il Vangelo raised even more trouble within the secular camp, for most leftists were highly critical of the idea of a serious film on Christ. Attacking the film on the basis that it did not deny Christ's divine nature, Marxists proved to be adoring their own God, Reason, just a bit too much.[5] Forced by their own ideology to repress, deny, or misrepresent the irrational elements in human life, secular and leftist intellectuals were for the most part unable to understand either Pasolini's fascination with the story of Christ or *Il Vangelo*'s cultural impact. In retrospect, the leftist hysteria on the subject of *Il Vangelo* appears to be a mistake, the consequence of forgetting that Christ has no reality other than the various, concrete ways in which faith is *used* by different groups or individuals. Religion can also be the vehicle for social antagonism. If, for the higher spheres in the Catholic Church, the figure of the Redeemer served the purpose of legitimizing the status quo, for many others (*Cattolici del dissenso*, Liberation Theologists, Jesuits) Christ's preaching founded an ethos of struggle against political injustice.

To fully appreciate "a certain realism" in *Il Vangelo*, however, it is not enough to consider the historical context of the film. It is necessary also to examine the cinematographic background against which Pasolini's film situated itself. Shortly after Pasolini's *Il Vangelo*, Hollywood released a star-studded "holy pic" whose title claimed that the story of Christ is *The Greatest Story Ever Told* (Stevens, 1965). Indeed, if not the greatest, the Redeemer's story is the longest-lived, for it still endures. Even if we leave out the Old Testament—the long pre-existing surface from which it emerged—it has been told and retold for two millennia, and there seems to be no end in sight. It is for this reason that Jean-Louis Commolli treats Pasolini's *Il Vangelo* as yet another remake of the narrative that most dominates our collective imagination and argues that Christ's story was a film long before the invention of cinema.[6] Privately projected on the screen of one's mind or publicly shown in *sacrae representationes*, Jesus' story is the longest running film ever made.

The cinematic apparatus took a great interest in Christ from the very beginning, for the first *Passion* was produced in the summer of 1897. Sponsored by the book company *La Bonne Presse* and shot on a vacant lot in Paris, it made enough money to transform a religious publishing house into a production film company. Two months later, the Lumière *Passion* came out, a fifteen-minute version arranged in thirteen *tableaux* scenes, which was immediately offered for sale in the United States to R. G. Hollaman's Eden Wax Museum in New York. As the asking price of ten thousand dollars was too high, Mr. Hollaman thought it better to produce his own Passion. The race for the megaproduction had thus begun. The greatest story ever told kept being retold with an ever larger display of means. Every "holy pic" had to look like a rich gift from above, the offering of *circensem* for a public in need of costly spectacles. Interestingly, it was Italian cinema which made the first long Christological narratives, with Guazzoni's *Quo Vadis?* (1912) and, above all, Antamoro's *Christus* (1916), which were made with the same principles and budgets as the mythological blockbuster *Cabiria* (1914). Then there came, among others, Wiene's *INRI* (1924), De Mille's *King of Kings* (1927) and *The Sign of the Cross* (1932), Duvivier's *Golgotha* (1935), Ray's *King of Kings* (1961), and Fleicher's *Barabbas* (1961). After Pasolini's film, the list continues with Stevens's already cited *The Greatest Story Ever Told*, Zeffirelli's *Gesù di Nazareth* (Jesus of Nazareth, 1977), Sykes's *Jesus* (1979), and, last, Scorsese's *The Last Temptation of Christ* (1987). Regardless of their artistic merit and occasionally inspired moments, all of these films display a disheartening uniformity in more than one respect.

They are all made with large budgets—and the budget is, in a sense, the first stylistic step in a film. Their settings succeed in taking spectators away from their own realities. Whether it is Antamoro's Egypt,

Sykes's accurately reconstructed Palestine, or De Mille's lavish studio re-creation, none of these films ever allows the spectators to establish a connection between where *they* live and the holy places. The feeling of transcendence conveyed by the settings is usually redoubled by the copious use of glamorous stars: familiar, and yet mythical, faces. Not only does the presence of famous professionals lure the public into the "spot-the-star-game," but their acting skills, respectful of mimic conventions, fill the narrative with psychological dramas. The great and "inspired" interpretations by actors playing even minor roles (e.g., John Wayne as the centurion in Stevens's film or Jean Gabin as Pilate in Duvivier's) convey a sense of great individuality—"the Great Men who made History"—for each and every figure, from Barabbas to the Apostles. The psychological characterization of every figure invites the public to feel the "true story" behind each individual. In this respect, the greatest story ever told is nothing but the same story that keeps being told by nearly every commercial film, the only difference being that, in the "holy pictures," the proportions of the spectacle are indeed biblical. As immense crowds of carefully made-up extras are usually employed, the vision of thousands in the frame suggests a mass participation which, in fact, mirrors the box-office hopes of the producers.

There are, of course, exceptions. Dreyer's Christ episode in *Blade af Satans Bog* (Leaves from Satan's Book, 1919) evinces the stylistic originality and the spiritual tension which led Pasolini to cite the Danish director as one of his main sources of inspiration. Virgilio Sabel's *Il figlio dell'uomo* (The Son of Man, 1954) is the true predecessor of Pasolini's film, for it portrays the life of Christ through the eyes of a group of simple believers, and, most important, it employs fishermen and agricultural workers from Peschici and Rodi, two villages in the southern Italian region of Puglie. And Rossellini's *Il Messia* (The Messiah, 1975), with its interest in a logocentric Christ, its emphasis on community, and its didactic and despectacularized style, well deserves to rank with *Il Vangelo*. These exceptions constitute a small, alternative tradition in the Christological filmography. Like all exceptions, they confirm the rule, a rule that the reader should keep in mind during the discussion of Pasolini's *Il Vangelo*.

Analogical Reflections

Free of expensive sets and technicolor embellishments, Pasolini's *Il Vangelo* is a low-budget production that eschews the idea of faithful historical reconstruction and opts for analogical rereading. Whereas reconstruction forgets the present and aims at an absolute past, analogy translates the past into the present and suggests a series of relations of resemblance and difference for the audience to recognize and to judge. If reconstruction ultimately abuses history, holding it up to the paranoid myth of discovering "what really happened," analogy *uses* personal and historical knowledge to gain insights for the present.[7]

Pasolini chose to shoot the whole film in southern Italy. The town of Matera, with its hauntingly beautiful Sassi (the old section, virtually untouched), was a daring visual translation of Jerusalem. Analogical representation thus surcharged the settings with connotations that meant something to an Italian audience: Christological passion happens here and not over there. It may be argued that Stevens's *The Greatest Story Ever Told* also chose a setting familiar to the audience, Arizona's canyons and the lakes in the Rockies. However, while the canyons were chosen for their postcard beauty and thus reinforced the notion of a holy land for religious tourism—in fact, they inevitably remind us of the landscape of so many westerns—*Il Vangelo*'s settings prompt the parallel between Christ's Palestine and the Italian South as colonies of Rome.

Southern Italy was also the ideal follow-up to the "profound aesthetic intuition" that Pasolini had while visiting the Holy Land. Surprised at the smallness and humbleness of the part of Palestine which had not been contaminated by modernity, Pasolini rejected the cinemascopic vistas and the grandiose palaces of traditional biblical cinematography and chose a small space to which the audience could relate: the arid hills of Basilicata. Not only is small beautiful, but it is also more realistic. In sum, "southern Italy enabled me to go from the ancient to the modern world without having to reconstruct it either archaeologically or philologically."[8]

Pasolini did not employ professional actors or extras, but chose faces on the basis of his "social physiognomy." Some writers and intellectuals, that is, people whose bodies bore no trace of manual labor, played certain key roles: the Apostles (Enzo Siciliano, Alfonso Gatto, and Giorgio Agamben), Herod Antipas (Francesco Leonetti), and Mary of Bethany (Natalia Ginzburg). For the most part, however, the film was a gallery of unfamiliar, wrinkled faces, whose southern traits could not escape the Italian spectator's notice. As a result, the actors in *Il Vangelo* carried a second meaning apart from the fictional one: they pointed in the direction of Italian social reality, their presence in this film reminding the public of subproletarian faces normally excluded from the screen. From the point of view of audience reception, moreover, it must be noted that this second meaning was not the same for everyone, for it was inextricably linked to the position of the viewer, whether s/he was a northerner or a southerner, liberal or racist. Finally, if Pasolini was right in detecting the trend of anthropological leveling as a side-effect of consumer society, *Il Vangelo* will remain as an ethnographic document of marginal Italians before such a mutation occurred. The story of Christ the Son of God, of the Absolute, thus became a pretext for a public projection of social differences.

Analogical representation clearly posed some problems for the role of Christ. Pasolini thought of Kerouac—an interesting analogy indeed!—but then realized that the picture on which he had based his decision was an old one and that the American writer was actually unfit for the role. He ended up giving the role to Enrique Irazoqui, a Spanish student whose severe features and Mediterranean beauty contrasted with the iconography of conventional blue-eyed images of Jesus. Irazoqui's voice was dubbed by Enrico Maria Salerno, a famous actor with an easily recognizable voice. A common Pasolinian strategy favored by the Italian film industry, dubbing certainly had its drawbacks, especially if considered from the standpoint of realism. Filmmakers Jean-Marie Straub and Danièle Huillet harshly criticized Pasolini's sound choices as "restrictive," and dubbing as practiced by Italians as "a terrible parasitism" which does not allow "the least rapport between what you see and what you hear."[9] Straub's point, I am afraid, is well taken, especially if we look at the films that Pasolini made in the Third World. Nevertheless, as I argued in the second chapter, realism according to Pasolini is not a matter of adherence to any particular techno-stylistic strategy. It is an attitude circulating in the material, a desire and a feeling which may be obtained through the most diverse means. Each case is different. In *Il Vangelo*, the gap between Jesus' image and voice was less illusionist than Straub thought, for Italians easily recognized Salerno's voice and thus were forced to acknowledge the directorial manipulation. Furthermore, as the character in question was no less than the transcendental signifier of our culture, the unfastening of the image/voice bond was not without its intellectual justification: as the two major signifying registers were stretched wide apart, the Absolute that Jesus represented was cracked, fissured. Finally, Pasolini's choice to dub must be seen in the context of his repudiation of naturalism and his representation of a reality which the director has ostensibly manipulated. The practice of dubbing with voices heavily marked by regional dialects in order to induce analogical associations in the viewer is not without its ideological and artistic validity. Hence, one may dislike, as I often do, how Pasolini created his voice/image counterpoint, but it is also necessary to understand the potential in his use of sound.

Pasolini's desire to force the audience into analogical reflections also required another major change from traditional films on Jesus: characters had to be deprived of individual interiority so as to avoid the pitfalls of psychologism. In order to achieve this, Pasolini had to change his shooting style, which tended to emphasize frontal close-ups exclusively. To be sure, close-ups are plentiful in *Il Vangelo* (among all the films on Christ, it is the only one to begin with an unpretentious and puzzling series of close-ups), but they are motivated by physiognomic rather than psychological reasons. *Il Vangelo* is the film in which Pasolini most experimented with different styles and rapid changes of pace. The memorable twice-repeated zoom in the baptism scene (there are twenty-one zoom shots in the film!), the vertiginous camera movements during Christ's temptation in the desert, and the extreme wide angles of His face in the Garden of Olives were all cinematographic techniques Pasolini used to depersonalize the Redeemer.[10]

While the first part of the film, dealing with Christ's ascending popularity, allows for a certain intimacy with Him, the second part is considerably detached from his sufferings. A technique typical of direct cinema keeps the account of the Passion from becoming a sado-pietistic imposition on the noblest pain ever felt. The Passion is shown mainly through its effects upon His followers. All the scenes that are filmed at their highest dramatic pitch in other Christological films are merely skimmed through by a hand-held camera in Pasolini's version. Pilate's great psychodrama, for example, is merely hinted at, in long shots, from behind the shoulders of a *small* crowd. Occasionally, we are even kept from following Jesus' trial by a head in front of the camera. The Apostles are not fully developed characters; none of them has a personal story, not even Judas who, as a rule, is the privileged locus of psychological interpretations. As to the "bad guys," the representatives of organized religion, they are just visual representations of a power that represents itself with the rigidity of a Byzantine icon. The clumsy, cone-like miters on their heads graphically depict the difference between their real height and the impression of height that they seek to convey: the physiognomy of power. The decision to have Herod's soldiers remind us of Fascist thugs, or the Roman militia of the Italian anti-riot police, bespeaks the realist desire for analogical representation; the story of Christ becomes the terrain for political appropriations.

Before moving to the analysis of *Il Vangelo*'s representation of Christ's message, I should mention the other side of the film's stylistic unevenness. There are shots which drag themselves out to the point of monotony, such as the Sermon on the Mount, a five-minute close-up of Christ's face with a background shifting from white to black and then white again. The miracles are unbearable, "disgusted pietism" Pasolini himself called them, a sign of his failure to offer a viable analogy for such events. Interestingly, the miracles' climax is rendered by means of juxtaposed, extreme close-ups of Christ's and the cured men's eyes, the kind of shot which, it will be remembered, had already represented the policeman's vision in *Accattone*. To be sure, within the context of *Il Vangelo*, this shot has its own raison d'être. It is even a possibly intentional quotation from Ray's *The King of Kings*, in which one miracle is portrayed in just the same way. In the context of Pasolini's total oeuvre, however, the shot carries other nuances. The close-up of two eyes free from any impediment (be it urinal grating, gates, visors, posts, binoculars, holes) will occur only one more time in Pasolini's cinema, in *Edipo re*, where it connotes Oedipus's desire to know his destiny. As all of Pasolini's films seem to emphasize a kind of partial vision, one cannot help feeling that, in *Il Vangelo*, either the lofty subject did after all exact its toll, and made him give a positive value to a type of total vision which elsewhere is negatively connoted, or that the filming of the Absolute from a believer's perspective required this shot.

Finally, Pasolini's analogical representation entailed, here as elsewhere, self-reflexive gestures. It is hardly coincidental that, shortly after *Il Vangelo*, Pasolini theorized the cinema of poetry, a film style which allows the director to mix his/her point of view with that of the protagonist by means of what Pasolini called the "free, indirect POV" (see *Mamma Roma*). When Christ walks by His mother's house and we see him move on with the Apostles without much recognition of her desire for him to stop by, we know that Pasolini found in the story of Jesus the ideal terrain for his "free indirect POV."

Christ the Wrath of God

Hate as well as love can write a life of Jesus, and the greatest of them are written with hate.

Albert Schweitzer

The major difference between *Il Vangelo* and all the other remakes of the longest-running film ever made is that not one word in the film is Pasolini's invention, the whole being a long faithful quotation from the original.[11] True, there is a lot of Matthew that is omitted and the film does not rigidly follow the order of the written text, but it is nonetheless evident that, for the first time, Christianity is being treated like a text. The spectator is then invited to judge a relationship between an objective reality (Matthew's text) and the subjective rendering of it (Pasolini's images). Before examining such a relationship, it is worth considering the reason why, of the four evangelists, Pasolini chose Matthew.

Reportedly, Pasolini declared that he selected Matthew because he is the most "revolutionary" of the evangelists. This statement provoked the reaction of those who "consider him the most counterrevolutionary of the evangelists," for "his main point was to convince the Jews to back Christ, a moderate, against the Pharisees, who were the religious leaders of the national liberation struggle."[12] To this objection, born of an in-depth, specialized knowledge, Pasolini replied with his usual appeal to the viscera: "It is the feeling of the Gospel according to Matthew as a whole when you first read it that is revolutionary." By this, he meant that Matthew's text is the one which most offers unfamiliar glimpses of Jesus. To a larger degree than the other three, Matthew's text allows for an appreciation of the multifaceted quality of Jesus' teachings, which, in turn, explains how Christianity has managed to function as a storehouse of answers to such a wide variety of moral and political questions.

Furthermore, Matthew's Gospel is most concerned with the problem of the relationship to the Law and tradition and, much to Pasolini's liking, suggests an ambivalent attitude towards both.[13] Any reader of Matthew's text is bound to be struck by the recurrence of the formula "you have heard that it was said . . . but I tell you. . . ." Tradition is invoked and corrected, accepted and refused. As a result, Matthew's Christ is the embodiment of a destructive reverence, of an oxymoronic love/hate relationship with the Law. Such a gesture of simultaneous affirmation/negation is cleverly emphasized by a recurrent image in Pasolini's film: Christ's most often-repeated posture shows him walking decisively ahead, with his back to the camera and his face turned towards it, an image which stresses leadership but also conveys the sense of going ahead while looking back. Finally, it is the common understanding of those having even a superficial knowledge of the Gospels that Matthew's Christ is an angry Christ. And anger is precisely the dimension which Pasolini's visual translation wishes to highlight.

The desire to portray an angry Christ can be detected from His very first appearance, when He fades in over the image of a ragged and infuriated John the Baptist. While John's violent words ("You viper brood," Matt. 3, 8–13) are taken from Scripture, the film adds a little visual detail, the image of three scribes casually passing by, which provokes John's indignation, causes him to raise his voice, and sets the mood for Jesus' appearance. His head draped with a dark shawl, Jesus advances slowly, without even a hint of a pacifying smile, his browline giving the impression that He is frowning.

Instead of following the order of Matthew's text and starting Christ's preaching in the fifth chapter, the film gives precedence to the previously mentioned passage from the tenth which so impressed Pasolini: "Do not suppose I have come to bring peace" (Matt. 10, 34). After this initial statement, the film goes back to the skipped chapters, so that the rest of His words are tinged with the previously established sense of antagonism. All of the parables (much of chapter 13) and the eschatological sermons are missing from the film, while not a single word is omitted from His last harangue in Jerusalem. This part of the film is shot with a *verité* style which emphasizes the analogy with the present by evoking a sense of news coverage. Glimpsed from afar through a dodging and peeping camera, Jesus is nothing but a vehement voice thundering against "the blind leaders." The point, of course, is not so much that we are in front of a Marxist Christ, as that He is not the gentle, all-loving Jesus of conventional, Catholic iconography. He is a wrathful Christ who, by virtue of the analogical reference to Italian contemporary reality, legitimizes social hatred rather than universal forgiveness.

Wrath is not only associated with the figure of Christ but also pervades the film in other ways. For example, in Matthew's text, Herod's death is not narrated but merely reported by means of a prepositional phrase with adverbial value: "But *upon Herod's death* an angel of the Lord . . ." (Matt. 2, 19). In the film, the "upon" becomes an entire scene, with Herod shuddering on a stone slab and the camera slowly panning on the priests who sit around the wall and wait in frozen postures. As soon as Herod's quivering comes to an end, four women silently emerge from a narrow door in the wall and bind his head with a rag. Injected with this glacial imagery, the adverbial phrase stops being a mere temporal marker and constitutes yet another indication that Christ's story is a matter of ruthless historical nemesis.

Another instance of how visual rendering and textual reordering exaggerate the wrathful tone of the original emerges in the scene of Christ's death. The frame is black, and Christ's off-screen voice quotes Isaiah's prophecy which, in Matthew's original, had appeared back in chapter 13: "You will listen and listen but not at all understand, you will look and look but never see at all." As listening and looking are the two actions involved in film consumption, *Il Vangelo* leaves off with a curse against all those who listen and look but are not driven by the will to understand and see. A visual reminder of "the blind leaders" who prompt the film's anger, the black frame forces us to listen without looking at anything, the implication being that we should look at ourselves, at how we interact with a text in which we are all implicated.

And once we use Pasolini's film in the light of the black invitation to self-awareness, *Il Vangelo* discloses yet another reality inside Christ's story: its phallocentrism. Although such an effect is not entirely deliberate—at least not in all of its ramifications—it is our task as viewers instructed by years of feminism to pick up this subtext in *Il Vangelo*. Whenever Christianity is at issue, one cannot overlook male dominance, for in a traditionally Christian light, history is His Story. Pasolini's cinematic translation of the Word enhances our recognition of this bias, perhaps without intending to do so. The angry intransigence with which Pasolini set out to respect Matthew's original and his own homosexuality created this powerful subtext in the film.

Pasolini did not develop the role of women in *Il Vangelo* as other films normally do. The character of Salome perhaps constitutes the most striking example of this lapse. Traditionally conceived with the sluggish sensuality of cinema's biblical royal courts, Salome has always represented an unquestionable sign of erotic appeal. Systematically played by glamorous, dancing nymphs in jewels and silks, she appears on the screen only to play with the imagination of the male spectator and impose/confirm a model of successful femininity. She is the woman who literally makes men lose their heads. Yet, the screen time dedicated to her and her provocative appearance engenders the feeling that women had some role in the making of the text, albeit within the limits of their status as sexual objects. The enticing fullness of her body on the screen conceals the void in and of her presence.

In Pasolini's *Il Vangelo*, Salome (Paola Tedesco) is a blank-eyed, virginal figure who performs an asexual dance with grace and levity. As she is practically a child, there is no attempt to make the audience complicitous with Herod's lustful gaze. It is as if the film suggests that Salome's dance is like an empty canvas onto which Herod projects his sexual desire. She is the predestined victim of an authoritarian gaze which forces her to be a signifier of pleasure regardless of her desire to be so. Thus, instead of following the traditional accounts of her dance, *Il Vangelo* makes Salome's episode a precursor of *Salò*, for Herod colonizes the woman's body just as will the sado-fascist libertines in the later film. The point is not that Pasolini's visual translation is more accurate than the others. In fact, it may be less so, because it desexualizes an episode which is likely to have had strong sexual connotations. But whereas the others enlarged the role of Salome and made the gap between male presence/female absence less noticeable, Pasolini's film does just the opposite.

Salome is not the only major example of desexualization of women in *Il Vangelo*. Another iconographic convention has always demanded that Mary Magdalene be the locus of loose sexuality on its way to repentance, with more or less explicit hints at a relationship with Christ. De Mille's highly praised *King of Kings* went so far as to begin the narration of Christ's story with shots of this holy whore's gilded abode,

Il Vangelo secondo Matteo: *Pasolini on the set with actress Paola Tedesco (on the right). Casting her in the role of Salome was the most blatant example of Pasolini's deheterosexualization of Christ's story.* Courtesy of the Museum of Modern Art/Film Stills Archive.

seen in prismatic colors. Such a portrayal, to be sure, entailed the eternal reproduction of the spectator as a maliciously inferring subject. Indeed, by at last giving a screen existence to Christ's desire for Magdalene, Scorsese's *The Last Temptation of Christ* was nothing but the inevitable conclusion of years of heterosexual logic. In some films, such as *Jesus Christ Superstar* (1972), the figure of Mary Magdalene merged with that of Mary of Bethany (actress/singer Yvonne Elliman), with the result that the latter too was made into a sexually appealing creature. Interestingly, Pasolini decided to dispense with Mary Magdalene altogether and gave the part of Mary of Bethany to writer Natalia Ginzburg, who was neither young nor sensuous. In addition, her role was minimal, a question of a few seconds, just enough to bring about the contrast between Judas and Christ.

The absence of sexual connotations in both Salome and Mary Magdalene, together with their minimal roles, exposes the extent to which we rely on the representation of woman as sex and just how much the founding text of Christianity is at a loss to provide her with another meaningful function. We are left, of course, with The Mother who, in *Il Vangelo*, is played by no less than Pasolini's own mother. Too old to be a credible Madonna, Susanna Pasolini ruthlessly exposes the film's autobiographical dimension and indirectly suggests that Christ's story is like an open matrix for the most personal and diverse appropriations. For example, the interminable shot of The Mother seen from the crucified Son's point of view suggests that this Catholic myth appeals to any guilt-ridden son who indulges in staring at his own mother's pain for which, to be sure, he feels responsible. Thus, at closer inspection, even the Mother's role appears derivative, an image of spiritual purity which is less a tribute to her own goodness than to the Son's need for a nostalgic last glance at incommensurable love. Prompted by Pasolini's Freudian understanding of the homosexual discourse (excessive love for/by the mother equals homosexuality), the portrayal of the mother and the desexualization of the other women show that only the mother myth can fill the void left by the temptress: once again *la maman et la putain*. But Pasolini's understanding somehow transcended the mother/ whore myth, showing that in either case it is an all-male affair. Beauty and visual dominance go to men, unquestioningly. Christ himself and some of the Apostles are indeed beautiful young men, and the camera often indulges in capturing their grace. Obversely, the shot which most recurs in the depiction of the Mother shows her emerging from the dark, silently appearing on the doorway as if imperiously summoned by the narrative. Like Mary of Bethany or the women binding Herod's head, she enters the stage only in response to the father's call. And just as silently, all the women slip back into the dark, where they represent the absence which allows His presence to shine.

11

Uccellacci uccellini

Totò and Ninetto, father and son, are walking on a road on the outskirts of Rome. They stop for coffee at a roadside café where Ninetto
joins a group of kids who are practicing the steps of a new dance.
Father and son resume their walk only to stop a little further on, where
Ninetto goes to visit a girlfriend while Totò watches an ambulance taking away two corpses. Totò and Ninetto are then joined by a talking
raven who says he comes from the land of ideology and is the son of
Father Doubt and Mother Consciousness. The raven repeatedly asks
them where they are going, without ever getting a clear answer. The
three walk together under the sun, and, to break the monotony, the
raven tells Totò and Ninetto a medieval fable. It is the story of Brother
Ciccillo and Brother Ninetto, two friars in the group led by Saint Francis. Francis orders them to preach love to the birds, in particular to the
hawks and the sparrows, which hate each other. Although Ciccillo and
Ninetto succeed in "talking" to both species, the war between hawks
and sparrows goes on. Hearing of this, Saint Francis tells Ciccillo and
Ninetto that they should persevere in their attempt at converting
hawks and sparrows. Back to the present, where Totò and Ninetto,
still followed by the raven, demand money from their distressed
tenants and ignore their pleas. Resuming their walk, they first encounter a group of street actors and then go to their landlord's house,
where Totò is treated as cruelly as he has treated his tenants. Outside
the landlord's house, the three encounter the funeral of Togliatti, the
former head of the Italian Communist party. Finally, after having sex
with a whore, Totò and Ninetto kill and eat the raven.

The conventionalist critique of realism depends in large part on the attribution to realism of extremely naive beliefs which very few theorists or practitioners of realism have actually held.

Terry Lovell

Two men, father (Totò) and son (Ninetto Davoli), are walking on a freeway under construction. The frontal medium shot with a telephoto lens makes their motion imperceptible and highlights their solitude in the dazzling light. In this rather metaphysical atmosphere à la De Chirico, they start talking about death (they had previously come across a house where two people had just died) and about how the poor, by dying, move from one death to another (the theme of *La ricotta*). Although their language suggests their place of origin—the father speaks Italian with a Neapolitan accent; the son with a Roman accent—we do not know where they are going or where they come from. A street sign informing us that Istanbul is 4,253 kilometers away prevents us from locating them realistically. Suddenly, we hear a voice saying, "Friends, where are you going?" They (and we) scan the horizon but see no one. Then the son bursts out laughing and joyously points to a raven perched on an iron rail. No sooner do we realize that the talking bird will accompany father and son on their road to nowhere than we perceive the presence of a perverted scheme: a black bird, the inversion of the white dove of the Holy Ghost, joins father and son to form an unholy trinity. As the basic structure of the film, this iconoclastic conceit illustrates the extent to which *Uccellacci uccellini* (Hawks and Sparrows, 1966) hinges on a double gesture: Something with which the audience is familiar, the ternary structure at the heart of both Christianity and Marxist dialectics, is at once offered and subverted, upheld and rejected.

In *Il cinema Italiano degli anni sessanta*, Miccichè argues that *Uccellacci uccellini* belongs, together with Taviani's *I sovversivi* (The Subversive Ones, 1967), Bertolucci's *Prima della rivoluzione* (Before the Revolution, 1966), Bellocchio's *I pugni in tasca* (Fists in the Pocket, 1967), and Vancini's *Le stagioni del nostro amore* (The Seasons of Our Love, 1966), to a group of films he calls "the films of crisis," that is, films characterized by "the double motif of a disappointed (or unfounded) past hope and the necessity (or impossibility) of refounding the future."[1] The year 1964 brought the evident crisis of Marxism, for which the death of party leader Togliatti set a convenient date as well as an incentive for revision. Inevitably, his death affected the Italian intelligentsia, whose postwar mandate had obviously expired and whose passion smoldered, as if waiting for the 1968 explosion. Western history was undergoing a crisis, faced with Vietnam, the Palestinian issue, and the emergence of the Third World. (Pontecorvo's realist masterpiece, *The Battle of Algiers*, was made in the same year as *Uccellacci uccellini*.) As noted by Pasolini in the preface to the filmscript *Uccellacci uccellini*, the words *individuo* (individual) and *il popolo* (the people) were losing their meanings.[2] Once the foundation of bourgeois philosophy, the individual was slowly being transformed into the programmed executor of a multinational will. And *il popolo* could no longer function as the recipient of populist ideals because it was becoming an undifferentiated mass.

The crisis made itself felt in the realist camp as well. According to Pasolini, realist narrative, after perfecting its capacity to portray problematic individuals in a complex society, had now to confront the disappearance of the former and the homogenization of the latter. The notion of realism lost ground and was about to face the long series of attacks that would brand it as illusionism and as virtually undistinguishable from naturalism. Behind all this, there lurked the crisis of the very concept of reality. Antonioni's landmark film *Blow-up* (1966) well epitomized the philosophical crisis facing reality and cinematic realism. By showing Thomas returning a nonexistent tennis ball to the mimes on the court, *Blow-up*'s final sequence sanctioned the disintegration of objective reality and the advent of unconditional subjectivism. One could no longer say "seeing is believing" (one of the cornerstones of cinematic realism), for the contrary was true: believing is seeing. If we believe there is a ball, then we see a ball.

Pasolini thus found himself in a quandary. If he was aware of the disintegration of the political and epistemological parameters that grounded his realism, he also refused to abandon the notions of meaning and reality. In Pasolini's 1966 essay, "The End of the Avant-garde," he stated his position unequivocally:

> It seems to me, in short, that in any case a "reality" to be evoked is not lacking and, on the contrary, that we are guilty if we do not do so. And since that reality speaks to us every day with its language, transcending our meanings—in an as yet undefined "sense" (it is only certain that it is desperation and furious confrontation)—it is well, it seems to me, to bend our meanings to it! (*HE*, 138)[3]

Pasolini wanted to preserve reality's central role. For him, meaning was in crisis because reality was in crisis. Perspective and representation had to be questioned because reality no longer tolerated a totalizing image. Instead of representing "this situation through analogy," that is, by narrating the crisis of one or more individuals in this historical moment, Pasolini chose "to take this situation as the very subject of the story." He decided to make three different short films unified by the fairy tale device of staging talking animals. Each of them was supposed to refer to contemporary reality by means of fragmentary, allegorical *tableaux*, punctuated by Brechtian intertitles and shot with the technique of the cinema of poetry. After viewing the rushes, however, Pasolini decided to eliminate the episode with Totò and the Eagle, and to make one film only. The result is a provocative anti-narrative sequel of panels, each of them having its own autonomy and yet cleverly dependent upon the rest. This stylistic pastiche and narrative anarchy allowed Pasolini to say what he wanted to say about the situation of crisis, while keeping at bay the dangers of naturalist fiction and of avant-garde opacity. Hence the perceptive judgment of Luigi Faccini, who hailed the film as "the first example, in Italy, of realistic cinema. That is of a cinema that does not represent society in a naturalistic way but is—realistically and stylistically—homologous to its concrete structures."

"A Stately Raven of the Saintly Days of Yore"

– Where is mankind headed?
– Bah!

> From the heart of an interview with Mao by E. Snow

These are the words superimposed on the first frame of the film, an image of Totò and Ninetto walking towards the camera. This shot cleverly inaugurates and defines the textual trajectory in all its complexity. In the first place, it states an initial enigma: "Where is mankind headed?" Conventionally, all narratives begin with a lack of some sort, or a problem, the solution of which is one of the duties of commercial cinema. *Uccellacci uccellini* will never solve the initial enigma, thereby implicitly declaring the end of teleological narratives, an end already foreshadowed in Mao's answer: "Bah!" Moreover, Mao's name and his ironic answer well encapsulate the film's desire to be ideological and comic at once.

In the second place, Totò and Ninetto are immediately called into question as individual characters and become mere examples of mankind in transition. More specifically, Totò and Ninetto represent "the innocent Italians who are around us, who are not involved in history, who are just acquiring the very first iota of consciousness."[4] By giving them such a malleable role, *Uccellacci uccellini* heralds the crisis of the well-rounded characters of classic cinema and suggests that we should not expect much consistency from them. The film claims its right to shape the characters differently and differentially in each of the situations in the film. To put it differently, Totò and Ninetto do not have psychological consistency, and their identity will always be defined by their contingent relationship to the other elements within each episode. In the first sequence, for example, they represent "innocent" mankind in the face of the mystery of death; later, when visiting their own property, they represent power; and when in the engineer's house, submission.

Third, this frame is an indirect tribute to the written text/image articulation of silent cinema—a tribute reiterated throughout the film by Chaplinesque references and Brechtian intertitles. But there is more. The written text/image relationship foreshadows and enriches the film's theme. By pitting the raven against Totò and Ninetto, *Uccellacci uccellini* also sets up at least three other oppositions: ideology versus innocence, mind versus body, and, above all, word versus image. The first element in these oppositions attempts to explain the second, but cannot. This is the crisis. Ideology can no longer claim to grasp the *telos* of history; the mind can no longer explain or contain the body; and the word cannot exhaust the image. Pasolini's theoretical reflections on the primacy of communication through images here find a visual translation.

Finally, Pasolini's ironic phrasing of Mao's answer, "Bah!," suggests that, in a sense, ideology's crisis derives less from its own inadequacy than from the kind of questions asked by Snow. This last point is to be kept in mind when assessing the role of the raven.[5]

As is suggested by an intertitle, the raven is "a leftist intellectual before party leader Togliatti's death"—indeed an autobiographical projection of Pasolini looking back nostalgically at the fifties. It is very likely that such an intellectual would have claimed to know the answer to Snow's question: Mankind is heading towards the catastrophic fall of capitalism and the subsequent dictatorship of the proletariat. *Uccellacci uccellini* thus stages the crisis of *this* particular kind of ideology and is the harbinger of a new type of ideological thinking that honestly admits to its own permanent crisis. Pasolini once said, "We want the crisis of Marxism to be perpetual, because it is only in this way that Marxism will stay in history and will avoid entering the museums as well as being smothered by the Party's conformity."[6] In an interview with Duflot, he remarked that "an ideology that is not in crisis is not an ideology." *Krisis*, in ancient Greek, meant "turning point," from *krinein*, "to separate, to decide." A permanent crisis ensures constant decision-making based on a critical evaluation of historical turning points. Ideology must be in crisis. Ideology *wants* to be in crisis as long as it is forced to answer foolish questions such as the one asked by Snow.

Ideology resigns its role as the bearded soothsayer reading the dissected bowels of history, but it does not disappear. Pasolini's own definition of the film as "ideo-comic" proves that ideology stays but no longer has the same power. It is assimilated into the comic register and thus incorporates irony and laughter. The idea of "the low" assimilating "the high" is most effectively communicated in the film by the last sequence when Totò and Ninetto eat the raven. It is the rebellion of the body that no longer tolerates the tyranny of the mind. It is, above all, the inversion of the relationship between word and image. Tired of being verbally explained and fed up with its ancillary status, the image eats the word. The wandering image of Totò and Ninetto does not want to be forced into *one* meaning by the word. Significantly, the last three shots of the film portray the leftovers of the raven. The dismemberment of the raven warns us against re-membering it as a unified image, an univocal answer to a single question. It reminds us that just as reality cannot suffer the same totalizing image for a long time, so ideology's main role is that of liberating humans from the slavery of noncontradictory certainties. Ideology is there to enhance and broach the crisis, not to foreclose it. The raven itself seems to be aware of this, for it recounts a religious fable and reveals its openness to change.

A tribute to Rossellini's *Francesco, giullare di Dio* (St. Francis, God's Juggler, 1950), the religious fable narrates the story of Brother Ciccillo and Brother Ninetto who are sent out to preach love to hawks and sparrows alike. They start with the hawks, and, after a year devoted to intense praying and thinking, Brother Ciccillo breaks the code of the hawks' language and gets them to acknowledge the Lord. His communication with these birds is verbal in that it consists of codified sounds emitted through the mouth.

In turning to the sparrows, the friar experiences a frustrating failure of his "scientific" method: the sparrows do not understand the sounds that he mouths. Just when he is ready to give up, he observes Ninetto playing hopscotch and notices a similarity between his hopping and the birds'. Enlightened, Ciccillo imitates Ninetto, and, hopping about, they both succeed in telling the sparrows about God's message of love. Both classes of birds have been redeemed: "love, LOVE!" But a little later, a hawk attacks a sparrow and kills it. Frustrated, the two brothers report their failure to Saint Francis, who tells them to persevere in their effort, quoting an encyclical by Pope Paul VI: "We know that justice is progressive and we know that, as society progresses, the awareness of its imperfect composition awakens, and the strident inequalities that afflict mankind come to the surface."[7]

This fable reveals the raven's awareness of three things. The first is Pasolini's old idea that Marxism is not "Christ's greatest enemy" but that it in fact "comprehends religion's highest moments." If it wants to survive, ideology must seek allies against "bourgeois materialism" which "opposes any religious instance as well as any movement aimed at knowing the real."[8] Ideological thinking should open up to the sacred and should enhance peace and love rather than just class struggle. Marxism, Pasolini noted while discussing ideology in *Uccellacci uccellini*, "is not over insofar as it is able to accept many new realities hinted at in the film (the scandal of the Third World, the Chinese, and, above all, the immensity of human history and the end of the world, with the religiosity which this implies—and which constitutes the *other* theme of the film)."[9]

Furthermore, the fable demonstrates the limits of verbal, rational language and reaffirms the existence of another kind of speech, a gestural speech which is closer to the language of reality. By acknowledging that rational discourse is a privilege of the ruling classes, the raven implicitly admits to Marxism's failure to fabricate a theory of the body. Pasolini is clearly testing his ideas about a language which comes before words. He also implicitly celebrates the power of cinema over literature, for it can speak like the sparrows do. In effect, the fable is a visual essay reaching the same conclusions as the article "A Cinema of Poetry" (included in the published screenplay), where Pasolini argues that cinema has a double nature: it is at once rational and irrational, word and image.

Finally, by acknowledging the need for two different languages suitable for two different kinds of public, the raven inaugurates a useful and pragmatic meditation on the existence of more than one public. The Left always knew that audiences are divided according to class (only recently have sex and race been added) but somehow never followed up on such a conviction. For the most part, leftist filmmakers of the sixties disregarded the tastes and pleasures of the sparrows and preferred, instead, to make their films in the language of the hawks. Pasolini himself embarked on such a road until *La trilogia della vita*. The fable told by the raven does not suggest that leftist filmmakers should speak the language of the sparrows only. Rather, it simply and warmly recommends an awareness, on the filmmakers' part, of the need to diversify one's language.

For all of these reasons, it would be inaccurate to argue that *Uccellacci uccellini* does away with ideology. Pasolini's film welcomes its crisis and probes the ways in which reality can be evoked—"we are guilty if we do not do so"—without flattening out its complexity. It is with *Uccellacci uccellini* that Pasolini tries to exemplify the kind of ideological labor that might be capable of "bending our meanings" to the language spoken by reality. I find the idea of an intellectual, ideological labor that "bends meanings" particularly apt in describing what *Uccellacci uccellini* proposes as a substitute for old-fashioned Marxism.

Bending the Meaning

Uccellacci uccellini "bends meaning" by using familiar images in a distorted way. It takes a signifier whose signified seems incontrovertibly fixed and shows that it can mean something unexpected. The film's very structure is patterned after this strategy. With its talking birds, unrealistic events, and expository intertitles, *Uccellacci uccellini* resembles a fairy tale: "Once upon a time there were two. . . ." Essentially, the story is an allegorical journey where the protagonists face trials and situations beaded together so as to engender a moral. Indeed, nothing could have been more familiar to the audience than this narrative structure. But the aroused expectations are never fulfilled: the narrative eschews linear development and dissipates; the recounted episodes are in fact merely juxtaposed panels whose sequence is irrelevant; and, most important, no single moral will result from the film, the final shot reiterating the image of a road to nowhere.

A similar strategy is at work in the choice of employing Totò, one of Italy's most popular actors, in that particular role. Throughout the postwar period, Totò had made some one hundred films. In most of them he was exploited for his extraordinary comic abilities in roles that had no depth. According to Pasolini, "the code through which one could interpret Totò" was that of "the petite bourgeoisie taken to its extreme expression of vulgarity, inertia, and cultural indifference."[10] With *Uccellacci uccellini*, Pasolini intended "to tear Totò away from the code." Accustomed to his almost exclusively clownesque dimension, Italian spectators "were a bit disappointed, mainly because they went to see Totò and have their usual laugh, which they gradually realized they would not be able to do."[11] In short, the expected image did come, but it did not bring the expected fulfillment.

This point clarifies Pasolini's stand on mainstream cinema. The vast majority of narrative films keeps its promises and feeds the audience images that fulfill their expectations. Unlike *Uccellacci uccellini*, classical narratives do not dissipate. Genre conventions set and respect the kind of pleasures and disappointments, foreplay and delays, that we may conceivably expect from the story. And actors usually play roles confirming the reasons for their fame. In sum, commercial cinema grants the pleasure of recognition which, Bill Nichols argues, "stands on a tautological principle": "it reconfirms our way of seeing" and "has the force of a mold shaping new information to expected meanings" so that "meaning appears to be already there as it does in the everyday world."[12] Recognition makes for a happy and unquestioned sequence: expected things come to the surface and our gaze is fulfilled. *In Uccellacci uccellini*, the cement binding together expected image and fulfilled gaze has come unfastened. The text produces a gaping space that pushes spectators to seek new relationships to suture the gap that has just been opened. Tainted with intellectualism as it is, such an operation exemplifies Pasolini's hope of "bending" new information to *unexpected* meanings.

It may be reasonably argued that the system of values sustained by the text, hinging as it does on a binary opposition (innocence vs. ideology), bestows clear-cut meanings on the film's signifiers. That is, father and son seem to keep the promise that *Uccellacci uccellini* makes at the outset, when they are set against reason. My contention is that the film "bends" even the image of Totò and Ninetto to accommodate its desire for contradictory meaning. Not surprisingly, the meaning which is "bent" to signify its opposite, the code which is at once offered and "decodified" is, in a sense, the most familiar of all: genital heterosexuality. In order to illustrate how this takes place, I will turn to a close reading of one of the film's central signifiers: the moon.

The credits are sung as a motet "against a freeze-frame with a white and lost daytime moon suspended among moving clouds." A little later, the father opens the film's spoken register by saying: "With the moon, one does not catch any!" He then proceeds to explain, in his comic language, how the gravitational pull of the moon controls the tides, thereby suggesting that by "any" he meant "any fish." Yet, the absence of an explicit object for the verb "to catch" immediately establishes the moon as a problematic signifier about which we are forced to wonder. During the course of the film, the image of the "lost daytime moon" returns as the background of the explanatory, Brechtian intertitles that punctuate the narrative. And in the final sequence, before eating the raven, Totò and Ninetto have sex with a prostitute named "Luna" (Italian for moon). In keeping with Pasolini's idea that here "the woman represents vitality," the raven suggests that their escapade is a symptom of nonproblematic sexuality.[13] In sum, the moon, with its extravagant appearances, signals a vital energy that belongs to Totò/Ninetto/woman, to the body and the image, and is somehow opposed to the raven/reason/ideology. This is, however, just the obvious meaning which seems always to have been there for us to recognize. As the crisis of ideology is also the crisis of any *one* meaning, *Uccellacci uccellini* constructs another reading for the signifier "moon," one that "bends" the moon's seemingly natural, obvious meaning and makes it signify something else. Differently put, the text liberates the moon from the meaning that it had itself created, so that bodily energy and genital sexuality come to signify their opposites as well, that is, respectively, intellectual laboring and anal sexuality.

The raven recounts the religious fable at the very moment in which Totò is looking for a place to defecate. It is as if the raven/mind sublimated Totò's bodily need into a religious vision, exemplifying the birth of ideology according to Marx: "The phantoms formed in the human brain are also, necessarily, sublimates of the human, material life-process which is empirically verifiable and bound to material premises." After the fable, Totò resolves to satisfy his urge and goes to a nearby field. He is immediately followed by his son, while the raven perches on a signpost saying "Private Property." The text then cross-cuts between the image of the straw screen behind which father and son are evacuating and that of a daytime moon. Meanwhile, we hear Ninetto asking his father whether or not he, too, can see the moon, for "it seems like a dream, like something I only see." By talking about the moon, they imitate the raven who a few minutes earlier had translated their urge to defecate into a religious fable. In other words, Totò and Ninetto sublimate their material life process and transform their feces into a symbolic product. *Uccellacci uccellini*, via the image of the moon, invites its intellectual spectators (the hawks in the theater) to consider the relationship between anality and symbolic production.

Discussing Jonathan Swift's "excremental vision," Norman O. Brown makes a rather long observation which, given the importance of anal imagery in Pasolini's films, deserves to be quoted in full:

> According to Freudian theory the human infant passes through a stage—the anal stage—as a result of which the libido, the life energy of the body, gets concentrated in the anal zone. This infantile stage of anal erotism takes the essential form of attaching symbolic meaning to the anal product. As a result of these symbolic equations the anal product acquires for the child the significance of being his own child or creation, which he may use either to obtain narcissistic pleasure in play, or to obtain love from another (feces as gift), or to assert independence from another (feces as property), or to commit aggression against another (feces as weapon).[14]

Whereas a society based on private property sustains the idea of "feces as property," or, more specifically, "feces as money," in this crucial moment of the film, father, son, and bird flaunt and valorize another use for the anal product. The raven illustrates the use of scatological material as a gift: he offers a story with a message of love. As if inspired by the raven's ideological stand, Totò decides to use his feces as weapon: he violates someone else's property and does publicly what is meant to be done in private. His son, in keeping with Pasolini's use of the actor Ninetto Davoli, exemplifies the act of playing with the feces by using it as dream material. Thus, temporarily abolishing their opposition, father, son, and raven participate in a joint effort that contradicts capitalism's tenets (feces as property) and glorifies symbolic production as the generous offering (feces as gift) of a creative (feces as play) Marxism (feces as weapon). It is of course significant that their triple transgression becomes clear through a close reading of the role played by the moon as sublimated feces. Indeed, on closer inspection, the moon turns out to be less a signifier of bodily vitality than the product/production of intellectual labor.

A detail in the prostitute sequence—the sequence that most seems to fix the moon as a signifier of "natural" sexual energy—confirms this hypothesis. Neither Totò nor Ninetto openly admits to his desire to have sex with Luna. Doubled over, they feign stomach cramps and ask to leave; that is, they openly relate the oncoming sexual intercourse to evacuation, so that their desire for Luna also carries the connotation of a desire for anal/intellectual production. The bodily vitality of the father and the son is also a vitality of the mind. The genital sex that they have with Luna is practically subverted by the connotations of anal eroticism carried by the moon.

To summarize: if the moon seems to constitute a paean to bodily instincts, it also signals a strong commitment to intellectual labor; if it appears as innocent nature, as something which is already there waiting for us by the roadside, it also reveals itself as a cultural product to be used and exchanged; if it gives the impression of representing the views of a society which values genitality and disqualifies infantile sexuality as regressive, it also subtly enforces a positive image of anal eroticism. Liberated by the slavery of its obvious meaning, the signifier "moon" exhibits a contradictory complexity that is emblematic of Pasolini's idea of "bending meanings" to an ambiguous reality.

Before examining the film's remaining panels, I want to clarify the theoretical implications of the idea that "we must bend our meanings." The corollary to this is the awareness that there is no "natural," single meaning waiting for us to stumble upon. What we find is a familiar image (Luna) which, as a result of social concretions, has been tagged with a certain meaning (heterosexuality). We cannot deny the existence of either the image or its meaning. Nor should we claim that, once stripped of its pseudo-natural meaning (heterosexuality), the familiar image (Luna) may mean just anything. Total closure (what the raven does) and total openness (the idea of an endlessly receding chain of signifiers) are both refused by Pasolini. What we can do is appropri-ate the existing meaning and bend it to our needs, thus showing the existence of other possible realities. Such an operation is dictated by bodily needs (Totò's urge), but is accomplished by means of an ideolog-ical laboring, a labor forging ideas as weapons to be used in the semi-otic warfare that, according to Pasolini, goes by the name of "reality." Ideological laboring, then, is the key offered by *Uccellacci uccellini*, a key which the ideal spectator (a hawk who loves the sparrows) will use more or less as I shall suggest in the next section.

Ideological Laboring

Between the first excremental vision and its final return, Totò and Ninetto face four important thematic situations. To interpret them re-quires an ideological key suggested by the text itself.

After fleeing from the owners of the field in which they defecated, Totò and Ninetto visit the tenants of a little country house that they own. Insofar as they do not have what is called a "realistically" consis-tent personality, they do not act in conformity with the symbolic aggression against private property that they have just perpetrated. They are realistic in accordance with Pasolini's contemporary notion of realism; that is, their behavior bends in accordance with the position that they occupy within the system of differences exhibited in each of the episodes. If, there in the field, they stood for gestural anarchy, here, they represent mankind in a position of dominance. They irre-sponsibly abuse their power without attempting to reconstruct the en-tire social field of which they are part. The raven does this, for it hints at the fact that Totò and Ninetto, qua petty bourgeois, are also domi-nated by their social superiors and should therefore take into account the affinities they share with the people they are oppressing.

The disenfranchised tenants are portrayed with stark, neorealistic tones and with constant references, both aural and visual, to China. The young man eating his swallow nest stares at the camera, at us, his eyes bespeaking angry brooding. The shot is held long enough to dis-rupt the narrative and force us to heed a question of which the young man is the iconic translation: What if Communist China had a solution for the miserable condition in which its people are forced to live? Such a question made sense in 1966.

A straight cut to the big eyes of a black child informs us that of all the possible connotations contained in the "Chinese" episode, the Third World theme is taken up and explored by the text. Totò and Ninetto meet a bizarre group of people (three blacks, a woman, and three southern Italians: all circus actors) who are pushing an old Cadillac. As minorities, they live in a void with precarious identities, trying to make the best out of a worn-out American product. Forced to perform "flying spectacles" on an itinerant stage, figures of and for our imagination, they are, like Stracci in *La ricotta*, extras in life. Visually, this wild bunch seems to have emerged from Fellini's imagination. The Felliniesque style of this episode, however, is not meant as an homage to a "great Italian director." In Pasolini's eyes, Fellini was a neodecadent director, someone too absorbed in his own fantastic imagination. Fellini "dances," as the director in *La ricotta* put it. The Felliniesque style, then, is a practical signal reminding us that we are in the face of distorted figures of our imagination.

This episode is nearly pedagogical in intent, for it elucidates the notion of positional awareness. On the one hand, it enforces the idea that we must deal with the problem of minorities and of the Third World. On the other, it denounces the inevitable risks that a Western eye encounters when confronted with such a task, namely, the risk of resembling Fellini, of "dancing" gracefully within one's own enlarged phantoms and projecting a private drama on a public screen. The Third World is constantly open to the self-indulgent speculations and appropriations of Western intellectuals who then become so engrossed in their own speculations that they forget the position from which they look. It is difficult to represent innocence, marginals, and the Third World without patronizing exoticism and ethnocentrism. By adopting the style of a heavily criticized director, Pasolini reminds us that his own way of seeing and portraying the disenfranchised is a product of his projections. He is aware of the position from which he looks and of the dangers it entails. Needless to say, such a positional awareness is absolutely indispensable for "a certain realism."

It is hardly coincidental that a few seconds later we get a shot suggesting that realism also consists of looking at oneself looking. It is a medium frontal shot of Totò and Ninetto sitting in the middle of the road and enjoying the "flying spectacle" put up by the street actors— a spectacle that we do not see but imagine taking place where the camera is, in front of the two. The upper edge of the frame, representing what goes on behind Totò's and Ninetto's backs, literally bristles with legs walking from left to right. From their cadenced pace, we can infer that it is a funeral (later we will understand that it is Togliatti's funeral). The music, the Communist anthem *Fischia il vento*, which had already haunted the narrative upon the raven's appearance, stresses the importance of what father and son are missing. They stare at the spectacle of their own imagination while behind them a reality unfolds, a reality to which they are oblivious. Given the absolutely frontal perspective of this shot, Totò and Ninetto are staring

Uccellacci uccellini: *Semihidden behind the father (Totò), the son's (Ninetto Davoli) gaze is yet another example of partially obscured vision.* Courtesy of the Museum of Modern Art/Film Stills Archive.

directly at us. We see what they do not see. But it is as if they saw what we would be missing if we failed to reckon with what was behind our backs: the reality of a consumption circuit that overdetermines the film as well as our viewing of it.

The next panel shows father and son in a position of subordination. The engineer, to whom they owe money, treats them in the same manner as they have treated their tenants, the only difference being that he has more style: "I am a businessman, I do only business, I care only for business!" he says, thus rejecting Totò's excuses for his insolvency. As the first true bourgeois ever to appear in a Pasolini film, the figure of the engineer lends itself to some interesting observations. His house is visually characterized by the copious display of paintings and statues, *objets d'art* meant to reveal the good taste of the owner as well as his economic power. This is the fate of high art for Pasolini, who, in a sense, strove to make artifacts which no bourgeois could ever fully enjoy. The engineer's specialized outlook finds a perfect resonance within the attitude of the intellectuals who gather at his house to celebrate the tenth annual meeting of the "Dantist dentists." Unlike the engineer, they cannot afford to buy works of art and therefore content themselves with parading their tasteful consumption (i.e., their cultural capital). Like the engineer, however, they care only for art and thus have a very narrow and specialized view of their position in the social text. By confining their intellectual labor to tracing literary genealogies, they concentrate on the object of vision and forget their positions as viewing subjects. They do not really acknowledge the engineer's house in which they are confined, by which they are defined, and which their presence refines. They do not take into consideration in whose interest they valorize aesthetic objects. At this point, the intensity of the film's ideo-comic anger is such that Ninetto even says that for the first time he understands the raven's preaching.

When Totò and Ninetto leave the engineer's house, *Uccellacci uccellini* quotes the documentary images of Togliatti's funeral. It is as if the temporary agreement among the father, the son, and the bird has opened to a sight of reality within fiction. We see a few moving, contradictory images: Communists making the sign of the cross like good Catholics in the face of death; Communist leaders solemnly embodying power's self-representation in public. Above all we see a few images of simple beauty: silent fists, ancient tears. For a few seconds father and son are given back to history, in accordance with the raven's Messianic project and promise. But it is only for a few seconds. Pasolini's Marxist Messiah, enmeshed in perennial crisis, comes to warn us that His light cannot shine continuously, that the light is intermittent: the Messiah as firefly.

12

La terra vista dalla luna and Che cosa sono le nuvole?

La terra vista dalla luna (The Earth Seen from the Moon, 1967). Ciancicato Miao (Totò) weeps on the grave of his deceased wife with his son Baciù (Ninetto). He decides to remarry, and, after trying a widow, a prostitute, and a mannequin, he finds his ideal wife: the deaf mute Assurdina Cai (Silvana Mangano). After a few months of happy but meager living, they wish to improve their condition and to buy the little house in front of the poor shack in which they have been living. They plan a scam: Assurdina is to fake a suicide attempt by pretending to throw herself from the top of the colosseum while Ciancicato and Baciù ask people for donations. But she slips on a banana peel and dies. Weeping, father and son return home only to find Assurdina, who says she is dead but can still do everything she did while alive.

Che cosa sono le nuvole? (What Are the Clouds?, 1967). In a country theater, life-sized puppets perform *Othello*. At the climax of the story—when Othello is about to kill Desdemona—the spectators rush on stage and tear Othello and Iago to death. Their bodies are tossed in the garbage, picked up by a truck, and thrown in a dump. There, they see the sky for the first time and are spellbound by the beauty of the clouds.

> *Painting is an essentially concrete art and can only consist of the representation of real and existing things. It is a completely physical language, the words of which consist of all visible objects.*
>
> Gustave Courbet

161

Although they were released one and a half years apart within two different compilation films (*Le Streghe* [The Witches, 1967] and *Capriccio all'Italiana* [Caprice Italian-Style, 1968]), *La terra vista dalla luna* (The Earth Seen from the Moon) and *Che cosa sono le nuvole?* (What Are the Clouds?) ought to be treated in the same chapter.[1] They were shot one after the other, employed the "picaresque" couple Totò and Ninetto, and, most important of all, were part of a unitary project in the wake of the theoretical conclusions reached by *Uccellacci uccellini*.

As I suggested in the previous chapter, *Uccellacci uccellini* set up an opposition between Totò/Ninetto and the raven which mirrored Pasolini's contemporary reflections on the image/word dichotomy. Totò and Ninetto were the wandering images whose meaning Mao's words could not explain. The raven was an embodiment of *logos*, the word that names and by naming aspires to bestow reality on the thing named. The conflict between the two found a symbolic conclusion in the film's ending, when Totò and Ninetto, tired of the raven's repeated attempts to explain them, ate the bird. The restless image devoured the word. Through this gesture, the image reclaimed autonomy from verbal discourse *and* incorporated the latter's signifying potential.

Given the assumption that words cannot totally explain images, Pasolini found himself in a rather difficult position. How could he come up with a written theory of the image when words were proving defective? It would certainly make more sense to abandon the world of *logos* and try to "write" essays in the language of images. After *Uccellacci uccellini*, then, Pasolini decided to let the image of Totò/Ninetto—for him the pair were an icon of raw, vital energy—wander a little longer and see what would happen after they had assimilated the word (raven). Hence his journey to the sources of cinema:

> For a long time I had been thinking about a full-length film made up of episodes, some long, others short, but all humorous. It should have been called *Che cos'è il cinema?* (What Is Cinema?) or maybe just *Smandolinate* (Serenades with a Mandolin). De Laurentiis offered me the chance to make two of the episodes: first *La terra vista dalla luna*, and now *Che cosa sono le nuvole?*[2]

Beneath the mask of two light comedic works, Pasolini explored the possibility of cinematically articulating a discourse on "the image" and strove to clarify such theoretical issues as the distinction between naturalism and realism. This is nowhere clearer than in his use of color. *La terra vista dalla luna* and *Che cosa sono le nuvole?* marked Pasolini's transition to color (after the brief experiment with the two *tableaux vivants* in *La ricotta*). In the steps, perhaps, of Antonioni's *Red Desert*, a film he briefly analyzed in the article "Il 'cinema di poesia,'" Pasolini used color in an expressionistic way. In *La terra vista dalla luna*, Totò and Ninetto have orange hair, houses are painted in fairy-tale hues. In *Che cosa sono le nuvole?*, Totò has a green face and the background colors are blue or bright gray.

What Is Cinema? A Pantomime in Two Acts

The continuity between *Uccellacci uccellini* and *La terra vista dalla luna* extends well beyond having the same two actors play father and son. The moon, as you will recall, was the richest signifier in the previous film, the multivalent emblem of contradiction. Not surprisingly, then, the title of Pasolini's new film explicitly refers to the vision of human reality obtained from or by the light of the moon, as if the author wanted to prolong his unmasking gaze at humanity. Furthermore, in *Uccellacci uccellini*, the raven made its bothersome appearance just after Totò had broached the subject of death. Ideology, qua symbolic activity, came to fill the gap opened by the quintessential mystery confronting mankind. As embodiment of an old-fashioned Marxism, however, the raven was not interested in the question of death and thus sidetracked the film towards other concerns. *La terra vista dalla luna* again raises the question of death. It opens with a shot of Totò and Ninetto crying on the tomb of their wife/mother and makes Assurdina's death its climax as well as its denouement. Finally, *Uccellacci uccellini* began by contrasting the image of the nowhere-bound Totò and Ninetto with the words of the Chinese Communist leader Mao. In *La terra vista dalla luna*, Totò and Ninetto's last name is "Miao" (Italian for "meow"). Not only does their new name encapsulate the passage from the political to the comic register, but it also indicates the incorporation of ideology into a bodily, animal-like reality.

La terra vista dalla luna exploits Totò's uncanny talent for mimic expression and gestural language by having him marry the deaf mute Assurdina. As a large part of the film hinges on Totò's efforts to communicate with Assurdina, *La terra vista dalla luna* emphasizes visual language and minimizes the verbal register. The gestures of the characters are stylized and excessive. The dialogue is largely inessential. And the narrative is punctuated with explanatory intertitles. In fact, *La terra vista dalla luna* inaugurates Pasolini's shift towards the increasingly silent cinema of his "aristocratic" period (*Edipo re*, *Teorema*, *Porcile*, and *Medea*). The first answer to the question "What Is cinema?" would then be: cinema is the prime vehicle for body language and can exist even without spoken words.

When Assurdina first enters Totò's miserable shack, she finds an abominable mess. But she is a good woman, an expert in the millennial art of housecleaning, and in a few minutes the mess is gone, the place shining with the touching humbleness of dignified poverty. While cleaning up, she comes across a few disparate objects which testify to Pasolini's surrealist intentions as well as to cinema's potential for assembling the most diverse visual material: an alarm clock inside a chamber pot, a bomb, a radio, a skull, a live Chinese servant, and a portrait of Charlie Chaplin. After the clean-up, Assurdina's new order retains only the picture of "the little tramp" and the chamber-pot (no longer housing the alarm clock but flowers, in that mixture of vulgarity and beauty which we found in *Accattone*).

This entire sequence is a simple and effective translation of an argument that Pasolini had developed two years earlier in the article "A Cinema of Poetry." Unlike writers, filmmakers do not take their signs from a dictionary, "from a shrine, a protective sheath, or from some baggage, but from chaos, where they are nothing more than possibilities or shadows of a mechanical, oneiric communication" (*HE*, 169). After taking the "im-sign [image-sign] from the meaningless jumble of possible expressions (chaos)," filmmakers must "make its individual existence possible, and conceive of it as placed in a dictionary of meaningful im-signs." What is cinema? It is what Assurdina has done by retrieving a few things from chaos and placing them in a meaningful context. It is a selection of images from the "infinite dictionary" of the world.

Assurdina's decision to keep the portrait of Chaplin is of course an indication of the kind of cinema that Pasolini thinks has best fulfilled the potential of the image. It may be useful to remind the reader of Pasolini's cinematic loves. As has often been repeated, he acknowledged three masters: Chaplin, Dreyer, and Mizoguchi. From a stylistic point of view, however, it is hard to imagine three directors further removed from him. Like Pasolini, Chaplin was reluctant to move the camera. But unlike Pasolini, he abhorred montage and used close-ups sparingly. As for Dreyer, the only film which may bear a resemblance to Pasolini's style is *La Passion de Jeanne d'Arc* (The Passion of Joan of Arc, 1927), almost entirely made up of close-ups. But Dreyer ended his career as a champion of long-takes, with films approaching the ideal of one shot per sequence. And Mizoguchi's style was more like Rossellini's, with the camera watching the events at a respectful distance. Pasolini, then, was not attracted to these directors for stylistic reasons. If anything, Pasolini admired their disrespect for stylistic rules. Dreyer, for example, was one of the few Western directors to systematically violate screen direction and the 180-degree rule, which is what Pasolini's films often do, albeit in a less intriguing way. What attracted Pasolini was *the feeling* that these directors created in their works. According to him, all three of them knew how to capture the epic and spiritual elements of life. Both Mizoguchi and Dreyer took their scenes as far as they could go. In Mizoguchi in particular, one finds the sublime and savage extremes that Pasolini saw lurking beneath the mask of everyday reality.

Pasolini's use of Chaplin and silent cinema is also an indication of the attempt to shun naturalism in the cinema. As he explained in four telling paragraphs written for *Bianco e Nero* in 1971, Chaplin's silent gags "convey the essential humanity of an action and of a character, presenting them in a brief, inspired moment which conveys its reality at its apex (and the context is therefore realistic, albeit without a touch of naturalism)" (*HE*, 254). This point is important for it further clarifies Pasolini's distinction between naturalism and realism. Realism is what conveys "the essential humanity of an action." A little later, Pasolini argues that with the advent of sound "physical presence and oral word are integrated and cannot avoid those 'touches of naturalism' which are incompatible with the *purely realistic* syntheses of the gags." Naturalism is thus inevitable when "physical presence" and "oral word" come together. If naturalism is the unavoidable curse inherent in cinema as audio-visual technology, it can be avoided in a film where one can cut and operate a selection in order to capture "the essential humanity." If Assurdina had kept everything she found in Totò's shack, she would have done what a long-take does, that is, she would not have selected the essential. Realism is Assurdina's choice of the essential: a portrait of the tramp and a chamber pot with a flower. Again, Pasolini's cinema defines itself as a mixture of vulgarity and beauty, low and high, all under the sign of "the tramp."

Totò, however, does not content himself with dignified poverty. Motivated by greed, he convinces Assurdina to fake the intention to commit suicide from the top of the colosseum. We see Assurdina miming her suicidal script under one of the colosseum's arches, which acts like a frame. A large crowd of people assembles in the street and tries to make out the meaning of her gestures. Totò, of course, monitors and guides the crowd's interpretive efforts, making sure that they "read" the image of Assurdina correctly. Except there is a banal accident: Assurdina slips, falls down, and dies. What is cinema? Cinema is a large number of people giving meaning to images, but no sooner does one claim to have the right answer than the image dies.

Pasolini, however, did not want a tragic ending for this comic fable. Upon their return home, Totò and Ninetto have the spooky surprise of finding Assurdina ready to resume her life as before, while a last in-

La terra vista dalla luna: *Ciancicato Miao (Totò) communicates with his deaf and mute wife through sign language.* Courtesy of the Museum of Modern Art/ Film Stills Archive.

tertitle offers the moral of the story: "To be dead or alive is the same thing." It is the first symptom of Pasolini's fascination with the Hindu notion that life is nothing but the illusory unfolding of Brahma, a dream within a dream, as Totò would say in *Che cosa sono le nuvole?* Furthermore, Assurdina's zombie-like existence remakes the point already made in *La ricotta* and in *Uccellacci uccellini*: for those who

La terra vista dalla luna: *Framed by one of the colosseum's arches, Assurdina Cai (Silvana Mangano) is the film image open to the public's interpretation.* Courtesy of the Museum of Modern Art/Film Stills Archive.

are outside dominant discourse, for those who have no voice in history, "to be dead or alive is the same thing." All possible interpretations for this ambiguous ending aside, Assurdina's fate confirms the central role of death in Pasolini's cinema—*Che cosa sono le nuvole?*, too, ends with the death of the two protagonists. Discussing these two films, Pasolini himself noted:

> What ideology is behind two farces? It is not very comical, to tell the truth. The basic ideology is picaresque, but, like most things where vitality is central, it masks a deeper ideology, that of death.[3]

For the first time, Pasolini explicitly recognized death as an ideology, a perspective, and a point of view. To be sure, he had already talked about the presence of death in his thought and works, but he had not been theoretical about it. At the time of *Accattone* and *Mamma Roma*, death "was the tragic idea that contradicts everything; the only thing that makes man great."[4] Two years later, in a interview on *Il Vangelo secondo Matteo*, death acquired a more substantial status as negative certainty and limit. You can demystify just about anything, argued Pasolini: God, nature, and reality, but you cannot demystify "the problem of death." Death is "the one problem I cannot demystify and therefore represents everything profoundly irrational, and somehow religious, in the mystery of the world."[5] One senses in these definitions Pasolini's struggle to find a theoretical explanation for the seeming paradox that death is a mystery and yet provides a certainty. By calling it, finally, an ideology, Pasolini took the important step towards regarding death as a discursive position, a perspective which affords a certain view.

As a point of fact, it was around the time of *La terra vista dalla luna* and *Che cosa sono le nuvole?* that Pasolini tried to weave death into his semiotics and film theory. In four 1967 articles, later collected in *Heretical Empiricism*, he argued that the life of an individual is made up of an infinite number of "signifying actions" (physical presence, words, deeds, etc.) which make up the meaning, the role, that an individual has in history. The question that Pasolini, as a "certain realist," asked himself was: How do we select the actions in someone's life so as to engender a realistic narration, one that captures what is essential, as Chaplin's films did? To answer this question, he thought he had found a powerful ally in the signifier death: "*Death effects an instantaneous montage of our lives*; that is, it chooses the truly meaningful moments . . . and puts them in a sequence" (*HE*, 236); "A life, with all its actions, can be completely and truly deciphered only after death; at that point its rhythm is compressed and the insignificant is eliminated" (*HE*, 246); "Death effects a rapid synthesis of a past life, and the retroactive light that it shines on that life highlights its essential moments, making of them actions which are mythical or moral outside of time. Well, this is the way in which *a life becomes a story*" (*HE*, 251). Pasolini's faith in the correctness of post-mortem judgment revealed his nostalgia for God's final judgment. Death does not eliminate what *is* insignificant but what a biographer, a historian, a society at a given time *deems* insignificant. What counts is that Pasolini searched for a position from which the inessential could be discarded. Death became a useful tool in his realism. I have already argued that, in *Accattone*, the protagonist's death put the spectator in the position of making a final, post-mortem judgment on *Accattone*, and as such it signified the film's will to realism. I am now in a position to reinforce that claim. According to Pasolini, both death and realism organize things into a perspective that discards the inessential and captures "the essential humanity." The result is a contradiction between the belief in an essential humanity and the awareness that no ultimate essence can ever be found. But we are by now familiar with such a double gesture in Pasolini; indeed it is *the essence* of "a certain realism."

Needless to say, Pasolini also probed the analogy between death and montage. Transposing this analogy into film theory, Pasolini argued that cinema is like life, a chaos of possibilities, an infinite long-take which would not have a completed meaning if it were not for editing. Editing selects what is essential and transforms cinema into a film: "Editing is thus very similar to the choice which death makes of the acts of life, placing them outside of time" (*HE*, 250). While hardly a rigorous theory of cutting, this statement obtains, as usual, an intuitive, almost pedagogical, validity. Cutting interrupts the flow of a shot and declares, as it were, its death, its termination. Each cut gives a temporal dimension to a shot and determines how long its life was. Each cut, then, demands that the spectator assess the meaning of a shot. Seen in this light, Pasolini's editing style inseminated his films with countless little deaths and thus acted as a constant invitation to "final judgments."

Che cosa sono le nuvole? is a more complex and interesting work that leaves us disappointed that Pasolini could not continue in his "What Is Cinema?" project (Totò died while Pasolini was in Morocco shooting *Edipo re*). The setting in a marionette theater and the inclusion in the cast of Franco Franchi (a popular B-movie actor with mimic skills à la Totò) indicate that Pasolini intended to insist on body language as the essence of cinematic representation. *Che cosa sono le nuvole?*, however, exhibits a marked self-reflexive dimension that is missing from *La terra vista dalla luna*. Pasolini's new short film portrays a stage performance of living marionettes orchestrated by a puppeteer. The presence of actors on a stage, an audience, and a puppeteer/director sustain the metacinematic self-referentiality which is splendidly announced in the initial sequence.

After a shot of the puppets aligned against the wall, we cut to a movie poster on the ground that says: "Yesterday—*La terra vista dalla luna*." The camera then tilts to frame a wall with three more posters on it, two of which announce coming attractions: *Mandolini* (Mandolins) and *Le avventure del re magio randagio* (The Adventures of the Stray Wise Man). The third announces the feature of the day: *Che cosa sono le nuvole?*. All four posters are reproductions of paintings by Velasquez. The one advertising *Che cosa sono le nuvole?* is nothing less than *Las Meninas*, the Spanish painter's enigmatic work so cleverly analyzed by Foucault in the first chapter of *Les Mots et les choses* (The Order of Things, 1966). In one stroke, Pasolini has thus made reference to a painting that is the epitome of self-referential ambiguity *and* to a book which examines the relationship between things and names. The contiguity of Foucault's and Pasolini's interests at this point in time is nowhere clearer than in this remark made by the French philosopher in *Les Mots et les choses*:

> The relation of language to painting is an infinite relation. It is not that words are imperfect, or that, when confronted by the visible, they prove insuperably inadequate. Neither can be reduced to the other's terms: it is in vain that we say what we see; what we see never resides in what we say.[6]

Pasolini accepted and appropriated Foucault's argument of an incommensurability between word and image. He rejected, however, the book's conclusion which, in a typically post-structuralist fashion, radically questioned all signs, be it verbal or iconic. *Che cosa sono le nuvole?* sets out to prove the primacy of images and to describe a Pasolinian "order of things." The curtain is raised, the performance begins: *Othello*.

The choice of having the live puppets perform *Othello* is meaningful in and of itself, for it is the story of man engaged in a double act of sign reading. Othello must decipher the threatening signs coming from an external reality: Is Desdemona actually betraying him? And he must also interpret his feelings, the signs rising from his inner self: Does the adamant certainty of his feelings correspond to any truth?

Che cosa sono le nuvole? addresses the question of Othello's (Ninetto Davoli's) problematic decoding of reality in a disarmingly simple, didactic way. It highlights and dramatizes the gesture of looking as Othello spies Iago from behind a wing. In effect, it is with this film that Pasolini finalizes the symbolic use of the furtive gaze that was introduced in *Accattone* (Balilla's peeping through the holes of an urinal grating) and *Mamma Roma* (similar shot of Ettore).

We are midway in the marionettes' performance. The audience, a northern Italian peasant crowd dressed up in their Sunday clothes, starts to inveigh against Iago's (Totò's) scheming. Suddenly, we cut to an empty frame, a most rare occurrence in Pasolini's cinema. It is a medium close-up of the back wall and a stage wing in front of it. The telephoto lens flattens the perspective to such a degree that we do not perceive any space between the wall and the wing. All we see is a frame divided in two different shades of gray. Slowly, Ninetto's curls emerge from behind the wing. We gradually see one eye, and then the other. It is the climax of the play, the beginning of Othello's doubts and torment, appropriately emphasized with a carefully constructed shot. The shot of Ninetto's furtive gaze will be repeated in *Edipo re* and *Teorema*. And other characters, too, will be defined by it. The ramifications of this type of vision will have to be postponed until later (see the section on the "partially obscured vision" in the next chapter). Here, suffice it to say that the furtive vision implies the character's observation of something essential, something which the narrative highlights as the focus of "a certain realism."

Assailed by doubts, Othello starts asking the questions which will allow *Che cosa sono le nuvole?* to argue its points most explicitly. Othello first indicates Iago and then asks the puppeteer (Francesco Leonetti), "Why do I have to believe him?" The puppeteer's reply— "Because in fact you want to kill Desdemona, and maybe Desdemona wants to be killed by you"—points out a truth existing behind rational explanations, the truth of psychoanalysis. But the "innocent" Othello/Ninetto finds this too difficult and, a little later, reformulates his question in a different way and asks Totò/Iago, "What is the truth? Is it what I think or what people think or what that guy up there thinks?" Totò's answer is exemplary: "What do you feel? Concentrate!" he says, while his long, crooked chin points to Ninetto's chest, where the heart is, "Concentrate!" And when Ninetto nods, "Yes! I feel something," Totò brings a finger to his lips and whispers: "But. . . shhhh! You must not name it, for no sooner do you name it than truth vanishes."

This scene constitutes the clearest formulation of the epistemological role of the body to be found in Pasolini's entire work, be it film or writing. Pasolini achieves such a degree of clarity through images. Only through cinema is he able to formulate an intuitive truth which my words here are already dissolving. It may be argued that Totò has used words to make his point, and that without words the whole conversation would not have taken place. Totò, however, denounces the harmful effect that words may have on truth: if they become too powerful, they make truth disappear. Words must be grounded in a body, in an image. What is cinema? Cinema is an audio-visual technique that utilizes words but harnesses them to the image. And the talking images of the cinema are the closest thing we have to "the language of reality."

The puppet show ends with a quotation from Rossellini's *Paisà* (Paisan, 1946), namely from the Neapolitan episode in which the black G.I. interrupts a marionette show by climbing on the stage and trying to help out the Moor in his struggle against the Christian. Outraged at Iago and Othello, the audience rushes on stage to prevent them from killing Desdemona (Laura Betti). Othello and Iago are thus killed by the spectators, who are so engrossed in the events portrayed on stage that they want to intervene, just as they would in the real world. What is cinema? Cinema is the system of signs which engenders such an impression of reality that the public is often mystified.

Pasolini does not want to demystify the impression of reality, so that the next sequence abandons theoretical analysis and replaces it with an embracing affirmation of reality as "cinema in nature." Killed by the audience, Othello and Iago are now two lifeless marionettes. The garbage collector throws them on his truck and takes them away, singing a song about love and the trouble that words have in expressing it. Totò and Ninetto end up in the dump. And there, on top of a pile of garbage, from the vantage point of death, they look up towards the sky:

> Until the camera, finally still, points upwards, fixing the immense blue sky, swept by fast-moving white clouds. The eyes in Othello's cleft and swollen face light up with ardent curiosity and irrepressible joy. And the eyes of Iago, likewise, stare at this never-before-seen sight of the sky and the world, in ecstasy and amazement.
>
> *Othello*: liiih, what are those?
> *Iago*: They are . . . they are . . . clouds . . .
> *Othello:* liiih, what are those?
> *Iago:* They are . . . they are . . . clouds . . .
> *Othello:* And what are clouds?
> *Iago:* Who knows?
> *Othello:* How beautiful they are! How beautiful they are!
> *Iago* (by now wholly in ecstasy): Oh, torturous, incredibly marvelous beauty of creation!
> And the clouds drift by, moving at speed over the great blue sky.

What is cinema? Who knows? But, how beautiful it is, how beautiful it is!

13

Edipo re

Edipo re is divided into four "movements," as Pasolini chose to define them.

1. In the 1920s, in a small northern Italian town, an infantry officer and his wife have their first son. The father openly shows his resentment towards the baby and, one night, grabs him by the ankles. . . .

2. A shepherd finds a newborn child amidst the rocks and takes him to Polybus, king of Corinth, who decides to adopt him. Some twenty years later, at the end of a discus-throwing competition that Oedipus wins by cheating, his outraged friends suggest that Oedipus is not who he thinks he is. Anguished, he turns to the Delphic oracle and finds out that he will eventually kill his father and make love to his mother. In order to outsmart Fate, Oedipus travels away from Corinth. He runs into a king on a cart with four guards. After a long fight, Oedipus kills three of the guards and slays the king. He then arrives in Thebes, where a young man, Anghelos, informs him that the city is devastated by a plague provoked by the Sphinx. Oedipus pushes the Sphinx off the top of a mountain and becomes king of Thebes as well as Jocasta's husband. But the happiness is short-lived, for a new plague strikes Thebes.

3. The third movement corresponds to Sophocles' tragedy. Leading a group of Thebans, a priest imperiously and yet respectfully demands that Oedipus take action to end the plague ravaging the

city. Oedipus starts an investigation but is met with the reticence of Tiresias, the blind seer, whom he mistreats badly. Finally, after a nerve-racking search for witnesses conducted with the help of the messenger Anghelos, Oedipus discovers the truth. Jocasta hangs herself and Oedipus puts out his own eyes.

4. We are back in the twentieth century. Accompanied by Anghelos, blind Oedipus plays the flute, first in Bologna, then in Milan, near a factory, and finally in the meadow where his mother used to take him as a child.

> *Our major Western tradition of thought devastated the psyche by insisting that big words were labels given by the mind, with only subjective reality. Invisibles, principles, generals, and universal powers—such as Truth, Terror, Time— were merely names, defined according to the operations we put them through, making sense only within mental word-games. They had no substance, said nominalism; they were not real. Thus, the soul came to distrust its speech of spiritual and imaginal realities. A counter-position, deriving mainly from Plato, held to the reality in and of these grand words and was called realism. But in the course of time nominalism even renamed realism, so that a "realist" today is one who points his finger at facts independent of ideas about them and looks with suspicion upon universal words with capital letters.*
>
> James Hillman

Edipo re (Oedipus Rex, 1967) marked a new phase in Pasolini's cinematography in more than one respect. It initiated Pasolini's explicit appropriation of Greek myth, which would produce two more films, *Medea* and *Appunti per un 'Orestiade Africana*. It was the first film he shot abroad, in beautiful, Third World settings, a habit which would eventually get out of hand and make him forget his own position as a Western eye. Above all, *Edipo re* was the first of four difficult, art-house films—what Pasolini would later define as "aristocratic" or "unpopular" cinema.

The three previous films with Totò and Ninetto had represented his final attempt to create a *cinema nazional-popolare*, and had thus signaled the end of a world, "the world as Gramsci knew it."[1] With *Edipo re*, Pasolini made no attempt to please the general public. Seeking to oppose mass culture, he wanted to make an "unconsumable" cinema "just like poetry, where each book is published in an edition with a limited number of copies, only a few thousand, because the readers are only a few thousand."[2] To bring about "the forced aristocracy of poetry," Pasolini envisaged two strategies: "either turn out silent films, or alternatively, films that are only spoken, exclusively spoken." In *Edipo re* and his "aristocratic films" to come, Pasolini tried both solutions, alternating between silence (the first, the second, and the fourth movement are virtually silent) and verbal excess (in the third movement), between poetry of the image and highly stylized, poetic dialogue.

These stylistic and ideological shifts, however, did not affect the way in which Pasolini looked at his own cinema. Shortly after the release of *Edipo re*, Marisa Rusconi interviewed him for the distinguished theater journal *Sipario*.[3] During the course of the interview, she remarked that Pasolini's filmography seemed to include different strands, "the realistic with *Accattone* and *Mamma Roma*, the historical with *Il Vangelo secondo Matteo* and *Edipo re*, and that of contemporary fables such as *La ricotta*, *Uccellacci uccellini*, and *La terra vista dalla luna*." Pasolini replied that instead of "different strands" one should talk of "minimal variations on a main theme which is realism," but, he hastened to add, "it is essential to keep in mind that for me reality is unnatural." Again, Pasolini positioned himself within realism, but with reservations: "a certain realism." By saying that "reality is unnatural," he clearly intended to warn critics that his latest film had completely abandoned the conventions of naturalism and yet had maintained a realist attitude. Critics, however, considered *Edipo re* as the proof of Pasolini's final rejection of realism, the beginning of his mythical phase. The question for us then becomes: How does a film like *Edipo re*, with its mythical dimension and its "aristocratic" reconditeness, continue the project of "a certain realism"?

On the most immediate level, it should be noted that *Edipo re* brings Pasolini's tendency to highlight physical, bodily presence to completion. Until this film, the body entered Pasolini's films conceptually rather than visually, by means of "oblique" signifiers of corporeality (Accattone's tears, Ettore's and Stracci's fever, Totò's urge to defecate). Only in *La ricotta* and *Il Vangelo* were the bodies of actors displayed in seminudity. In *Edipo re*, the human body makes its grandiose appearance, indicating the direction that Pasolini's subsequent films would take. The setting in a mythical past and the shooting in the Third World reflect a time and space characterized by a different relationship with the body; human flesh is now displayed in all of its physical immediacy. In fact, *Edipo re* is the first film by Pasolini to contain explicit sex scenes, those between Oedipus and Jocasta. In true Pasolinian form, however, it is the portrayal of the plague and of death that offer Pasolini the best opportunity to uncover human bodies.

Luxuriant and pathological, the images depicting the two plagues that ravaged Thebes are among Pasolini's most beautiful creations. The camera probes blistered limbs and sculpturesque torsoes, while the women's chants on the soundtrack bespeak a long tradition of enchanted and modulated observation of harsh reality. Sensuality and death, eros and pathology mix as never before, forcing the viewer to see beauty in death, the sublime in horror. It is in the midst of these passionate sequences that the answer to the question of *Edipo re*'s realism must be sought.

The sequences depicting Oedipus' lovemaking to Jocasta and its disastrous aftermath are the transition between the second and the third movement of the film. Oedipus has just made love to Jocasta in what is the first explicitly erotic scene in Pasolini's cinema. Abruptly, we cut from their naked bodies to a corpse with a child next to it. Cut to an image of ravens circling in the sky and then to a cut of another dead body. The camera slowly pans along its limbs, tilts to show the ground filled with corpses, and then cuts to the naked breast of a majestic, dead woman. With the point of view of death thus established, the camera briefly returns to Oedipus standing in front of his palace. No sooner do we hear a familiar voice uttering the lines of Sophocles' tragedy than we cut to a shot of *Pasolini himself* leading a group of Thebans.

> If these sons and I come here to beseech you, it is not because we look at you as a god. Weren't you the one who rid this city of the nightmare of the Sphinx as soon as you arrived in this city? This you did not do because you knew more than we do but because a god helped you. We beseech you. Find a remedy given to you by the gods or by a mortal like us.

Pasolini's decision to cast himself in this role undoubtedly enriches the meaning of this sequence. Clad in a black cape, with seashells around his face (a bit like the sacrificial victim in *Medea*), Pasolini plays the man who cannot keep silent any longer, the priest who urges Oedipus to take action in a stagnant situation. I would argue that Pasolini appears in the film as the author who wants to "find a remedy" to the stagnant situation of realism. To put it differently, Pasolini's presence in the film and the particular role he plays indicate that in *Edipo re* "a certain realism" has taken the road of autobiography.

Edipo is different from my other films because it is definitely autobiographical while others are not, or at least much less so, or, if they are, it is
unconsciously and indirectly. In *Edipo* I told the story of my Oedipus
complex. The boy in the prologue is myself, and his father, the infantry
officer, is my own father. The mother, a governess, is also my own
mother. I merely told the story of my life, mystified of course, and given
an epic style through the Oedipus legend.[4]

Through autobiography *Edipo re* intersects the discourse of realism,
modifying it. Conventionally, realism obeyed the tacit rule of impassive observation of external reality, and, odd as it may now seem, the
representation of inner experience was never part of the realist agenda. Leftist critics (e.g., Adelio Ferrero) always regarded Pasolini's "unconscious" and "indirect" autobiography suspiciously and reproached
him for what they considered an illicit exhibition of private obsessions.
The categorical imperative for leftist directors demanded that they
transcend their own private problems and delve deeply into the representation of objective reality. But Pasolini, faced with the crisis of realism, decided to make a "definitely autobiographical" film in which he
could reveal the truth about himself, "mystified of course."

The Autobiography of a Fly
in the Honey

With *Edipo re* Pasolini harnesses autobiography to realism for other
than narcissistic reasons. Pasolini's *autobiografismo* originates in two
major areas. The first is a direct consequence of Pasolini's reflections
on the idea of reality. As the idea of an objective "out there" crumbles, the subject comes to the fore, inextricably implicated in the making of the object. As I argued in the second chapter, the recognition of
the role of the subject is certainly one of Pasolini's greatest contributions to the history of realism, so that the critics who blame(d) him for
indulging in private obsessions miss(ed) the epistemological validity of
his practice.

Second, Pasolini's autobiographical impulse is also the result of his
inability to be self-effacing. Child Oedipus' raised hand (see below) is
symbolic of the vision that cannot forget itself. As is often the case
with women's writing, autobiography arises from a position of subordination, from a position in which the subject cannot forget him/
herself. People feel compelled to talk about themselves when their
identity is precarious, when they cannot efface their subjactivity from
the picture. In Pasolini's case, autobiography has its roots in the "land

of flies and honey." An anonymous graffito in a public toilet in New York, the expression "like flies in the honey. . ." has been used extensively enough within gay culture to have become an intriguing metaphor for a sociosexual condition.[5] It captures perfectly the double-edged, compelling quality of Pasolini's homosexual discourse. It would be unfair to stress always and only the traumatic aspects of such a discourse, for it was a purveyor of pleasure as well. Honey is sweet but sticky; and it must be at once sublime and atrocious—to use two of Pasolini's favorite adjectives—for the fly that cannot fly away and is condemned to pleasure. Think, for example, of Pasolini's description of *teta veleta* (see chapter 1) as "that terrible and anxious sweetness that seizes the viscera and consumes them, burns them, twists them, like a hot melting gust of wind in the presence of the love object." There is an aspect of intense pleasure, of honey, in this description, but there is also the tortured component of being stuck.

Edipo re is the autobiography of a fly in the honey, "mystified of course." There is no question that, among the discourses in his authorial intertext, Pasolini gave preference to homosexuality. Nowhere is this more evident than in his choice to convey his life's story through the Oedipus legend. It would be misleading to ask the question, Why does Pasolini turn *Edipo re* into an autobiographical film? Rather, one ought to ask, Why does Pasolini use "the Oedipus legend" to tell the story of his life? Pasolini chooses the Greek myth given primacy by Freud as the motor of human development because it is the myth which contains a "scientific" explanation for his homosexuality. It all comes from an excessive love for the mother. The mother as honey.

Although she is almost always frozen in a posture of impassive tenderness, Jocasta receives a great deal of visual attention.[6] We see her playing with her maids in what is the first group of women in Pasolini's cinema, after the brief shots of prostitutes in *Accattone* and *Mamma Roma*. In *Edipo re*, the women enjoy themselves and romp together—a running band is one of Pasolini's most recurrent and lyrical figures. On two occasions, Pasolini cuts away from the image of a tormented, enraged Oedipus to give us enigmatic, brief shots of Jocasta. It is a clever use of the cutaway figure, something which Pasolini uses only in this film. On the whole, however, *Edipo re* does not focus on the love between Oedipus and his mother. The center of the narrative is Oedipus, alone, in the desert.

Oedipus is not the intellectual figure of traditional accounts. The Sphinx does not pose any riddle for him to solve, but laconically states: "There is an abyss within you." Oedipus' answer, "I do not want to know," qualifies him as yet another Accattone or Stracci, yet another embodiment of innocent corporeality. The physical immediacy of

Franco Citti's body, his muscles and sweat highlighted by an attentive camera, make of him an icon of bodily reality. His is a blissful ignorance, an intellectual apathy which entails, however, a different kind of knowledge, the silent knowledge of and from the flesh. Adult Oedipus is visually defined by his two recurrent gestures: biting the back of his left hand and spinning around at a crossroads, with his eyes closed, the brim of his hat covering his face. The first suggests an impotent rage aimed at his own body and, more specifically, at the part of his body—the left hand—which, as a child, he raised to protect his eyes from the sight of a threatening father. The second aptly uses the visual metaphor of going in circles to suggest his attempt to ignore the knowledge arising from this deepest memory within.

In addition to Oedipus' body, the other visual lynchpin of the film is the Moroccan desert. *Edipo re* brings the symbolic use of the land of silence, discovered by Pasolini with *Sopraluoghi in Palestina*, to a climax. Together with slow, reverential panning shots of the desert, the most recurrent stylistic figure in the film is the alternation of long shots and close-ups. If the long shots pit Oedipus against a landscape of' lonely confrontation with the gods, the close-ups dramatically return to the face as the site where such a confrontation leaves its most visible traces. As *Edipo re*'s most striking feature is its insistence on the face and body of Franco Citti in the desert, a question inevitably arises: Why did Pasolini choose Citti as the iconic translation of his "mystified" self? The role that Citti played in *Accattone* was already an indication of his potential as a metonym for the author, but then, after a secondary role in *Mamma Roma*, Citti disappeared from Pasolini's filmography. He now returns as Oedipus, in the desert. After *Edipo re* and a secondary but revealing role in *Porcile*, Citti would be given two crucial roles in *La trilogia della vita*, respectively in *Il Decamerone* and *I racconti di Canterbury*. The significance of Citti's presence in *Edipo re* as well as in other Pasolini films cannot be gauged, however, without a concurrent consideration of his counterpart: Ninetto Davoli.

Pasolini's most significant change from Sophocles' original *Oedipus* is the replacement of Antigone with Anghelos, the messenger, played by Ninetto Davoli. Anghelos functions as *trait d'union* between Oedipus and Tiresias, takes care of blind Oedipus in the end, and, most important, observes Oedipus struggling with himself and the community. Oedipus acts and Anghelos observes. Ninetto's eyes are often the focus of Pasolini's attention, especially when they appear as a furtive gaze, a sort of peeking. In *Uccellacci uccellini* it was Totò who put his umbrella in front of Ninetto's eyes to keep him from watching a woman giving birth. In *Che cosa sono le nuvole?*, Ninetto/Othello spied on Totò/Iago. In *Edipo re*, he peeks at Oedipus and the Sphinx from behind a rock. His subsequent roles as the postman Angelino in *Teorema* and Marracchione in *Porcile* will confirm that his is the innocent gaze intent on observing the tragedy around him. When in the company of Totò, Ninetto's curiosity resulted in questions that called for his older companion's populist wisdom. Bereft of Totò, Ninetto no longer has anybody to turn to with his innocent questions. All he can do, now, is observe. Ninetto embodies Pasolini's ideal of an innocent look at life.[7]

Both Citti and Davoli are thus icons of corporeality, but their vital energies are different. Citti is the creature of the desert where a titanic fight against fate takes place. Davoli is the smiling body unaware of itself. As aptly observed by Georgia Brown, Citti's role in Pasolini's films is "to act out pathology."[8] Ninetto, instead, represents sentimental pathos. More than a recipient of erotic desires, Ninetto is, according to Gualtiero De Santis, "the natural icon of a homosexual man's sentimental attachment to another man." Together, Citti and Davoli give body to the image of the fly in the honey. Citti is the honey as stickiness, Davoli the honey as sweetness.

It comes as no surprise, then, that *Edipo re* ends with Oedipus and Anghelos together. An apt visual translation of Pasolini's divided self, they walk together through the important phases of Pasolini's life: the city of his student years, Bologna; the site of his Marxist commitment, a factory; and, finally, the symbol of his Freudian phase, the return to the world of his infancy. Oedipus has now lost his innocence and has sublimated his monstrous knowledge into art. Afflicted by a blindness that endows him, in fact, with better sight, Oedipus becomes like Tiresias. A visionary artist, he can see what others cannot see: He is Pasolini, a certain realist. With Oedipus, Anghelos runs after pigeons and plays soccer with other kids. He enjoys himself in playful physical activities without too much concern for his surroundings. He is subjected, however, to Oedipus' imperious calls, to the bitter reminder that honey is not only sweet but also sticky.

To complete my analysis of *Edipo re* as the autobiography of a homosexual, I should mention an important sequence made more so by the critics' systematic ignorance of it.[9] It is a short (nineteen shots), torturously beautiful scene inserted by Pasolini into the film's second movement, between two shots of Oedipus circling at a crossroads. After visiting the Delphic oracle, Oedipus tries to escape his fate, and, wandering about, he comes across a black-clad old man dancing in a circle, surrounded by young boys. The text, at this point, strives hard to convey a sense of loss and fear. Everything in the sound track (an obsessive crescendo of guttural cries) and in the visuals (the wrinkled face of the man who only has two teeth and strangely beckons to Oedipus) is geared to evoking nightmare. One shot of the sequence is

Edipo re: *Oedipus (Franco Citti) and Anghelos (Ninetto Davoli), the two faces of autobiographical representation.* Courtesy of the Museum of Modern Art/ Film Stills Archive.

practically lifted from the horror genre: the hallucinatory encounter with one's self, with the *doppelgänger*. After a twice-repeated shot/ countershot of Oedipus looking and the group he is looking at, we see Oedipus' large-brimmed leather hat from the back. The position assigned to this shot by the editing makes us believe that it is Oedipus turned around, but we soon discover that it is a tanned Moroccan boy who sneers at Oedipus (and at us, because we've been conned). We then cut to the young boys beckoning to Oedipus with their hands. "Come here, come here," their smiling, perturbing faces say, another classic shot in the iconography of paranoia. A cut to a close-up of the old man's wrinkled face finally clarifies that these mysterious people want Oedipus to enter a stone arch. As if in a dream, Oedipus complies, and, after a series of arches opening onto one another in what resembles a dusty labyrinth, he comes upon a naked girl at the end of a corridor. As the girl seems to have been waiting, we realize that the old man's invitation was nothing but pandering. Here, the camera does something unique in Pasolini's cinematography. The habitual reverse-figure shot (a frontal shot of the girl followed by one of Oedipus biting his hand) is briefer than usual and is immediately replaced by an over-the-shoulder shot of the girl, the frame partially taken up by Oedipus' back. The reason for this deviation from Pasolini's customary style becomes apparent when Oedipus averts his eyes from the girl and turns towards us. The over-the-shoulder shot allowed Pasolini to show both the girl's face and Oedipus' profile, his features contracted in a rigid spasm, one fixed eye clearly visible in the foreground. To be sure, the risk, here as in the rest of the film, is that of taking the images too literally, but it is hard to think of a better cinematic depiction of the nightmare of forced heterosexuality.

Edipo re is perhaps Pasolini's most realistic film in that it talks about what he regarded as his own deepest reality. I would like to stress "he regarded," however, because homosexuality, in and of itself, is not necessarily the deepest layer in one's psychic formation. Pasolini's adherence to Freudianism, together with the external imposition of invisibility, however, situated his homosexual discourse behind the scenes. "There is an abyss within you." The Sphinx's remark suggests that Oedipus/Pasolini lived his life by the metaphor of depth, *in* which things are hidden and *from* which they must arise. I am reminded of Murnau's superb metaphor of homosexuality as Nosferatu, the vampire. It is only by making love to your vampire in the daylight that you can get rid of him. Otherwise, what is repressed returns. And the more you deny it, the more it will come back and bite you.

I have argued that *Edipo re*, in spite of its flight into the world of myth, continues, if not perfects, the project of "a certain realism" in two respects: visually, with the overbearing presence of the body on the screen, and thematically, with the autobiographical narration of Pasolini's own history, "mystified of course." There is yet another level on which *Edipo re* intersects the discourse of realism: theory. At the end of the first movement, the father, after making love to his wife, gets up from the bed, resolutely walks up to the child, and grabs him by the feet. With a straight cut worthy of the memorable spaceship-into-a-bone shot in Kubrick's *2001, A Space Odyssey*, we move to the Moroccan desert. The camera pans slowly to the right, discovering a pinkish, lunar landscape whose breathtaking vastness gives the impression that the pan could last forever without exhausting its boundaries. It is something like the discovery of the cinematic screen, which, in this case, becomes the Freudian memory screen. The camera mimes Pasolini's effort to explore the memory screen on which the story of the Oedipus complex is represented. This ingenious parallel between memory and the cinematic screen signals Pasolini's attempt to continue (after his two previous, short films) making theory through cinema. *Edipo re* offers its intellectual, art-house public the opportunity to think about the relationship between the cinematic screen and reality.

Screen, Reality, and Partially Obscured Vision

In the second chapter of this book, I quoted a long passage from *Gennariello* in which Pasolini described his "first memories." Arguing that "in memory life becomes a silent film," he emphasized the recollection of "a white, transparent curtain" motionlessly hanging "from a window which looks out onto a somewhat sad and dark lane." I remarked, on that occasion, that Pasolini's recollection suggested the existence of a relation between the curtain and the cinematic screen. In fact, seven years before *Gennariello*, *Edipo re*'s first movement had already introduced the "white, transparent curtain" and had stressed its value. Seven of the eighty-four shots making up the first movement have the curtain in them. This is not an insignificant number, given that in this film Pasolini's narrative style is reduced to the utmost essentialism, each shot conveying necessary information without redundance. It is my contention that *Edipo re*'s first movement harbors a most explicit reflection on the curtain as cinematic screen.

We see the child waking up in the middle of the night and calling out for his mother. When she does not answer, he gets up and walks across a dark room at the end of which there is a window with a "white, transparent curtain." He moves it away and reaches the balcony. Across the "sad lane" there is another window curtain. And against the white transparency of this second curtain, we see the silhouettes of his parents dancing and hugging. Related to the child's frustrated desire for the mother, the curtain separates him from her and yet is transparent enough to permit him to catch a glimpse of what he should not be seeing. Thus, as he will later do in *Gennariello*, Pasolini suggests an analogy between the curtain and the screen which bears scrutiny.

Like the curtain, the film screen separates spectators from reality and frustrates them with the lure of an unreachable presence. The screen/curtain contains the promise of something important, of the obscure object of one's desire, but it never allows a true perception of the real, never a real contact. Cinema's illusionism is mercilessly exposed by this analogy. Classic realism's myth of the film screen as a window on reality is drastically redefined. Cinema can indeed be a window on the reality that matters most but—and it is an important "but"—there is a curtain stretched across the window so that our vision is partial, a mere guessing of shapes, a candlelight game of Chinese shadows. Still, Pasolini would argue, the screen, like the curtain, is transparent enough to give us an idea (*eidon* = image) of what is actually going on, a better idea than any other sign system.

In the introduction to *Edipo re*'s script, Pasolini compared the different images of Silvana Mangano that we may perceive from cinema and from Moravia's pen.[10] While conceding that some things such as her "scent of primroses" are hopelessly lost in both media, he concluded that we do get a better sense of who Mangano is from the cinematic image. Realistically speaking, then, it is better to relinquish all nostalgia for a vision of reality without the curtain. It is advisable to stop denouncing the partiality of the vision obtained through the curtain and make the best of the imperfect sight that we are lucky enough to get. In other words, we can either concentrate our attention on the screen as separation from a mythic real (which is what the antirealists have done) or, quite humbly, and perhaps naively, rejoice in the possibility of catching a glimpse of what the desired object is actually doing. Realist cinema would then be the kind of cinema that tries to take advantage of the humble resemblance between the shadows on the screen/curtain and the real. Instead of placing Hollywood fictions or modernist nightmares behind the curtain, Pasolini's cinema in this period strove to represent the thing that he knew best, his visual relationship with the curtain/screen.

As might be expected from a story concerned with blindness and insight, *Edipo re* lends itself to a fruitful examination of the gaze. Shots of eyes abound. Shortly before hearing the Delphic oracle's response, we get an extreme close-up of Oedipus taking his hand away from his eyes, and a close-up of his eyes will be repeated once again. *Edipo re* is the third and last film in which Pasolini uses such shots, the first two being *Accattone* and *Il Vangelo secondo Matteo*. *Edipo re* abounds in images of partial vision: child Oedipus looking through the fingers of his raised hand; eyes semicovered by the brims of hats; lovemaking framed so that one of Mangano's eyes is left visible; Anghelos peeking at the Sphinx from behind a rock; and the unfocused images from Oedipus' point of view as he walks away from the devastating prophecy of the Delphic oracle. The imposition of an obstacle to vision affects the audience as well, for there are some twenty shots against the light of the sun (a rare occurrence in Pasolini; only *Teorema* will use this technique in the portrayal of the god-like visitor). I have already indicated Pasolini's fascination with either monoscopic or obscured vision. A recurrent topos in his visual rhetoric, it has different roles in each film, but *Edipo re*'s use of obscured vision prompts a tentative mapping of its origin and meaning.

During the first movement, on three different occasions child Oedipus raises his left hand to his eyes, as if to protect them: twice before his father and once upon hearing and seeing the fireworks explode. The threat causing the child to raise his hand is external to him and signals an objective reality at work against the subject. Nevertheless, the child raises his hand because *he* has decided to do so. After all, he could just have shut his eyes or turned around. The child intends to keep looking, albeit behind the protection of his hand raised as a screen. The ensuing partially obscured vision is thus halfway between subjective intention and objective determination. The external imposition of controls on his vision (the father's ominous look) happens together with the subject's individual response to that imposition (the child raising his hand and returning the look).

Within *Edipo re*'s autobiographical context, the external imposition is the aggressive world of the father, the masculine aspiration to an all-knowing, total vision, in short the ethos of white, male, heterosexual certainties which admit no rejoinder. The child's subjective response is not pure and simple rejection; it is neither castration nor blindness, as the outcome of Sophocles' tragedy would seem to imply. Rather, it is child Oedipus' partial vision obtained through the screen of a bodily part, a simultaneous acceptance and subversion of the world of the father. As a consequence, the partially obscured vision so often depicted in Pasolini's films entails a tripartite figure: a) a subject of vision who is determined to observe and to function in a world that threatens him to the point of making it necessary for him to protect his eyes; b) a subject of vision who resents the external imposition and will spend his life in the attempt to unmask/denounce events bearing some kind of analogical resemblance with his own primal scene; c) a subject of vision who cannot overlook the screen put up by his own hand, that is, a subject who cannot forget his own body as a prime determinant of vision. It must be noted that the imposition of a screen obscuring vision is initially lived as a diminishment, a reduction of one's visual field, yet it results in ultimate freedom from the paranoid duty of objective vision. The subject cannot forget the screen that filters his perception and does not waste away in nostalgia for an objective vision that he never had. This is the source of Pasolini's idea that the empire of signs is the empire of passion, that the body acts as a subject of vision, in short, that subj*activity* is at the heart of the semiotic process.

These are three interrelated facets of a specific way of looking at the heart of Pasolini's "certain realism." The will to look from behind an imposed mask, the desire to unmask, and the awareness of oneself looking are the three aspects suggestively evoked in the figure of the partially obscured vision. It is hardly coincidental that the key to an understanding of such an intriguing and recurrent figure is provided by *Edipo re*, the film in which Pasolini told the story of his own life.[11] The autobiographical context allowed him to map the genesis of his own visual relationship with the world. Scanning the memory screen, he brought to the fore its analogy with the cinematic screen and gave his intellectual public a hermetic and yet clear explanation of what type of vision is required to capture a certain reality.

14

La sequenza del fiore di carta

Riccetto, a teenager with curly hair (*ricci* = curls), walks along Rome's *Via Nazionale*. Amidst the chaotic traffic, he projects a relaxed attitude and a carefree smile, engaging in small talk with passers-by. All of a sudden, disturbing black and white images (war, bombings, etc.) are superimposed on the screen. An off-screen voice, God's voice, calls Riccetto, but he pays no attention. Riccetto now carries a tall, red paper flower while God's voice becomes increasingly impatient. After repeated warnings that "innocence is a sin" and must be punished, God says that He must curse and destroy all those "who walk with a happy look amidst injustice and war, horror and blood." After a shot of the blue sky and a sepia-toned image of war casualties, the film ends with a shot of Riccetto's dead body, his arms spread out, the paper flower next to him.

> *For inside this cage, in which they had been born and in which they would die, the only tolerable framework of experience was the Real, which was simply an irresistible instinct to act so that things should have importance. Only if things had some importance could one breathe, and suffer.*
>
> Raoul Vaneigem

Pasolini's shortest film (only ten and a half minutes), *La sequenza del fiore di carta* (The Sequence of the Paper Flower) is the third episode in the compilation film *Amore e rabbia* (Love and Anger, 1969). When Pasolini shot his episode in the summer of 1967, the entire film was to be something quite different. Initially entitled *Vangelo '70* (Gospel '70), the compilation was to engage five different directors in the cinematic and political adaptation of parables from the Gospels: Lizzani was supposed to adapt "The Good Samaritan," Godard, "The Prodigal Son," Bertolucci, "The Barren Fig Tree," Zurlini, "The Passion and Crucifixion," and Pasolini, "The Innocent Fig Tree." Zurlini's episode, however, grew out of proportion and became a feature film, *Seduto alla sua destra* (Black Jesus, 1969), loosely based on the life and death of Patrice Lumumba. Meanwhile, the initial intent of the compilation had changed, veering towards the idea of expressing the European Left's rage against the Vietnam war. The remaining episode was entrusted to Bellocchio, who shot *Discutiamo, discutiamo* (Let's Talk, Let's Talk), an outrageously off-beat satire aimed at Communist intellectuals after the events of May 1968.

It is easy to detect Pasolini's *longa manus* behind the working idea of *Vangelo '70*, for it aimed at making the Gospels contemporary by means of analogies with the modern world, much like his *Il Vangelo secondo Matteo* had done. *La sequenza del fiore di carta* again utilized Matthew's text to represent the anger of an author who, evidently, had mixed feelings about innocence—Pasolini had just celebrated its value in the films with Totò and Ninetto. It may be useful to quote in full Matthew's verses, which, incidentally, had already been dramatized in *Il Vangelo secondo Matteo* with Judas in the foreground with Christ:

> In the early morning, as He returned to the city, He felt hungry and, noticing a single fig tree by the roadside, He walked to it and found on it nothing but leaves. He said to it, "let there be no fruit from you any more forever." And instantly, the fig tree withered. As the disciples observed it, they marveled and said, "how did the fig tree wither so quickly?" Jesus answered them, "I assure you, if you have faith and do not doubt, you will not only do what was done to the fig tree, but if you say to this mountain, "be lifted and thrown into the sea," it will happen. And everything you ask in prayer, you will obtain, if you have faith." (Matt. 21: 18–22)

In *La sequenza del fiore di carta*, Pasolini's reading of Matthew totally eschews the motif of the faith that moves mountains and concentrates instead on the fig tree as the symbol for a nature which is cursed because it does not bear the expected fruit. Inevitably, this reading exposes a seeming contradiction in Jesus' action: How can He blame the fig tree for not bearing fruit in March, when, after all, it is merely obeying its own nature? Pasolini explains: "This is an episode which has always been very mysterious to me and there are several contradictory interpretations of it. The way I have interpreted it goes like this: there are moments in history when one cannot be innocent, one must be aware; not to be aware is to be guilty."[1]

Needless to say, *La sequenza del fiore di carta* stars Ninetto Davoli in the role of Riccetto—a name which Pasolini had already used for the protagonist of his major novel, *Ragazzi di vita*. The visual and conceptual theme of joyous, thoughtless innocence on its road to nowhere is taken up again, but this time the setting changes and the chaotic inner city replaces the desolate Roman hinterland. We see Riccetto walking and hopping along Rome's Via Nazionale, carrying a tall red flower. He engages in casual, mindless conversations with some passers-by, flirts with a girl, gets a short ride on a truck, and then walks and hops again. Meanwhile, from the very beginning of his walk, the colors of Via Nazionale and Riccetto's hopping figure are intermittently haunted by the superimposition of black-and-white images: a world map, flags flapping in the wind, soldiers, Che Guevara's dead body, the earth, airplanes dropping bombs, President Johnson, and Queen Elizabeth.

Having thus established the contrast between innocence and history, the film uses the audial register to introduce its third element, namely, God's voice. God's first sentences are introduced by the same notes of Bach's *Matthäus Passion* that Pasolini used in *Accattone*: "Listen to me, Riccetto, it is God speaking to you, are you listening?" From this moment on, the sound track will consist of a sort of aural parallel montage that alternates between the noise of the traffic and God's ever more pressing demands for attention. In order to indicate the variety of means deployed by God in the attempt to reach Riccetto, God's voice changes in pitch and tone. An unnamed child, Graziella Chiarcossi, Aldo Puglisi, Bernardo Bertolucci, and Pasolini himself lent their voices to the invisible God of *La sequenza del fiore di carta*. Only once does Riccetto acknowledge His voice, with a barely audible "no" after God's first "are you listening?" For the rest of the film, he will proceed carelessly, hearing but not listening, thus corroborating Isaiah's prophecy with which Pasolini concluded *Il Vangelo secondo Matteo*: "You will hear but will not listen . . ." The film ends with the camera tilting upward, following the wires of the trolley-cars and then decisively framing the sky in a shot reminiscent of the end of *Che cosa sono le nuvole?*. Cut to a bird's-eye, or better yet, God's-eye shot of Riccetto's dead body lying on the asphalt, his arms spread in a crucified posture, his right hand still holding on to the red paper flower.

A most absolute indictment of innocence, *La sequenza del fiore di carta* owes much of its conceptual framing to the mixture of the Catholic and Marxist discourses in Pasolini's authorial intertext. Seen from an autobiographical point of view, the film's three protagonists (Riccetto, history, and God) create a vivid allegory of the ideal self according to Pasolini: passion, reason, and ideology. Riccetto is the life of the body, the pure vital energy which must achieve the historical awareness brought about by reason, the result being the voice of ideology, a plural yet clear-cut voice which enables one to judge, condemn, and "move the mountain." As such, *La sequenza del fiore di carta* clarifies the burden that ideological commitment represented for Pasolini. The voice of God seems almost like the voice of the Party, the same Party that expelled him from its ranks in 1949. In its typically Italian blend of Catholicism and Marxism, ideology is a source of guilt; it is the voice of a most exigent and exacting God that prevents the innocent body from being the way it wants to be. While providing a suggestive portrayal of the inner blackmail afflicting the "Catho-leftist" self, *La sequenza del fiore di carta* also explains why Pasolini would soon shrug ideology off his shoulders, efface historical awareness, and take refuge in his new God/ideology, the myth of sex and the body.

As I mentioned before, *La sequenza del fiore di carta* implicitly raises the doubt that Christ's demands on the fig tree may be unreasonable. God/ideology prevents Riccetto/body not only from being what it wants to be, but especially from being what it cannot but be. Like the fig tree in March, Riccetto *cannot* bear the fruits of historical reason. To understand the dilemma proposed by the film, it is worth detailing the last three sentences uttered by Pasolini as part of God's aural collage:

> – I want you to know and to will. It is contradictory, I know, perhaps it is even insoluble because you are innocent, you cannot help it, and since you are innocent, you can have neither conscience nor will.
> – Listen to me, Riccetto, listen to me. Just nod your head, look up once, it would be enough.
> – Innocence is a sin, innocence is a sin, do you understand? And the innocent ones will be condemned because they no longer have the right to be so.

Pasolini gave himself the role of uttering what in many ways is the conceptual pivot of the film, namely, God's awareness of the insoluble contradiction on which His demands are based. The innocent ones cannot be otherwise. Sinful bodies cannot but sin. Passion is a force which cannot be negotiated by Reason's unilateral demands. The ideal solution, then, would still be the one portrayed at the end of *Uccellacci uccellini*, where the innocent Totò and Ninetto ate the raven and thus assimilated rationality and bent it to their needs. In the portrayal of the untenable dilemma of a body that cannot but live in sin, it is possible to detect the point at which the Marxist and Catholic discourses intersect with the homosexual one. Given the intractable manner in which both the reason of Marxism and Catholicism treat homosexuality, the emergence of the other two discourses (psychoanalysis and humanism) seems not only necessary but inevitable. Hence, Pasolini's new mythical phase, where the allegory of the self is reframed within the slow emergence of metahistory against the images of history.

15

Appunti per un film sull'India

Appunti per un film sull'India documents Pasolini's preliminary research for a narrative film (that he never made) to be shot in India. It is the story of the hardships that a maharaja's family endures after the maharaja's decision to give his body to starving tiger cubs. Pasolini interviews potential actors, sounds out various groups of people (Hindi monks, writers, and an ex-maharaja and his wife) and shows the locations where the action would take place. Concurrently, Pasolini interviews workers, peasants, intellectuals, and casual bystanders on the most urgent problems facing India.

> *If I am to analyze this film properly I must not mistake it for reality; but if I do not mistake it for reality, I cannot analyze it properly.*
>
> Dai Vaughn

Pasolini's long-lasting affair with the Third World was actually coextensive with his cinematic career. In 1961, shortly after the filming of *Accattone*, Pasolini took a trip to India with Alberto Moravia and Elsa Morante. The period was that of the Christmas holidays, which Pasolini found unbearable in Italy. It was a path-breaking experience, a sudden illumination. He visited Sister Teresa and her leprosarium in Calcutta, had encounters with Nehru and the urban intelligentsia, got his first exposure to Eastern religion, and, above all, experienced firsthand the second largest subproletariat in the world. While in India, he recorded his first encounter with the Third World through written notes which first appeared in the newspaper *Il giorno* and were later published in a book, *L'odore dell'India* (The Scent of India, 1962).[1]

Betraying the archetypically Western reaction to the Orient with a combination of fascination and revulsion, *L'odore dell'India* sketches a poetic portrait of India. To be sure, Pasolini also analyzes social structures and dedicates vigorous pages to hunger and religion. But his prose is essentially aimed at recovering unnameable physical sensations and their effect on physiognomy. Significantly, his complex reactions to the Indian subcontinent are encapsulated in and by one of the five senses: "that smell of poor food and of corpses which in India is like a continuous, powerful air current that gives one a kind of fever."[2] As to physiognomy, he often uses writing to describe the signs that culture, in its anthropological sense, leaves on faces. For example, describing Sundar, one of the first boys he encountered in Bombay, he writes: "The Muslim religion gives an air of timid shrewdness to his sweet, delicate face."[3]

At the end of 1967, after filming *Edipo re*, Pasolini returned to India to shoot some visual notes about a film that he intended to make, a film whose "fundamental themes," he explains at the outset of *Appunti per un film sull'India* (Notes for an Indian Film, 1968), "are the fundamental themes of the Third World: hunger and religion." The film would never be made, leaving us to wonder just how convinced Pasolini was that he would actually make it.

Appunti per un film sull'India was broadcast on Italian television in 1968 and was presented the same year in the documentary section of the Venice Film Festival. But documentary it is not. It picks up the genre inaugurated by *Sopraluoghi in Palestina* and gives it a new, more intriguing identity, for it adds a fictional dimension. As it will again in *Appunti per un'Orestiade Africana*, Pasolini's voice explains what the story in the intended film will be and links it to places and faces observed by his camera. As a consequence of this, the images of these two films exist in a state of double motivation, as it were. Spectators cannot but respond to them on a documentary level, but they are also asked to project them into the fiction woven by Pasolini's voice. For example, when we see a beautiful young girl, at once embarrassed and proud before the camera, we enjoy the image in its documentary aspect, while we try to see her as Pasolini asks us to see her, as the ideal image for one of the daughters of the maharaja. There is a continual tension between a here and an elsewhere, between the text and the allusion to something else contained in it. Such a tension takes hold in the spectators' minds. We are invited to engage in a pendular motion between two poles, the first bearing the connotations of a documentary reality made more intriguing by the fictional promise, the second being like illustrated storytelling. For all of these reasons, *Appunti per un film sull'India* is not a documentary, although the camera most often behaves as if it were. It is not yet fiction, at least not in the conventional sense of the term. And it is not just a personal home movie, although it is because of such films that one gets the feeling that the raw beauty of the image/sound connection is something within everyone's reach. *Appunti per un film sull'India* belongs to a hybrid genre harkening back, interestingly enough, to another "Indian" film, Rossellini's *India* (1957).

The film that Pasolini asks us to visualize tells the story of a maharaja who lives with his family "in a place far removed from everyday common reality (a royal palace), and since he has been weaned on an ancient culture (lost and contaminated by the modern world), he is, in a way, outside history."[4] But "one winter's day," while "traveling through his domains," the maharaja catches a glimpse of some tiger cubs dying of hunger. "Overcome by pity," he begins to pray, and "at the end of his long prayer, he dismisses his small entourage, strips his clothes off and, still praying, he gives himself as food for the hungry tiger cubs and lets them devour him." The maharaja's children, two girls and two boys, grow up and "the family sets out on a journey," but "something has changed in the world." According to Pasolini's description, "in the early scenes the world seemed fabulous and unreal, a world where religion was everything, in perfect harmony with all the ups and downs of reality." Now, however, "as through a process of degeneration or a deep and general form of corruption, we are in the modern world." The widow and the children journey through this changed world and, "with a precise and obsessive rhythm," one by one they perish and die, "each death taking place in meaningful circumstances" and "capturing a moment of the reality of India."

With *Appunti per un film sull'India*, Pasolini starts verifying the hypothesis that will sustain his cinema to come: modernity is an evil against which a return to some kind of religious faith, some kind of spirituality, is necessary. The Third World, which makes its first appearance in Pasolini's work as itself (in *Edipo re* it served as a setting), attracts Pasolini as an immense archive of human behaviors that were hopelessly lost in 1968 Italy. Far from the Christian connotations that the sacred would take in an Italian situation (*Teorema*), Pasolini imagines the sacred at work and visualizes a pan-existentialism of sorts. The image of a rich man giving his body to hungry tigers permits us to see what Pasolini is doing with the signifier religion: he is liberating himself from Catholic discourse and visualizing a position from which religion is lived as a compulsive feeling of interconnectedness with all forms of reality.

As an audio-visual document, *Appunti per un film sull'India* is uneven. Like the book, it fails when Pasolini attempts broad generalizations about the subproletariat and the Indian intelligentsia. There are several interviews with workers, peasants, intellectuals, and Communist party members, but, as in *Comizi d'amore*, Pasolini is too enthusiastic an interviewer and lets people know what *he* thinks it would be correct to say. In *Comizi d'amore*, however, Pasolini shared language and cultural codes with both the interviewees and the film spectators, so that the former were less intimidated and the latter were in a better position to gauge and interpret the physiognomies on the screen (what Pasolini back then had called "psychological truth"). In *Appunti per un film sull'India*, instead, it is harder for a Western viewer to read an Indian face, especially when the first, most evident expression is one of intimidation in the face of both the white and the glass eyes. *Appunti per un film sull'India*, in this respect, is less a documentary of India than the document of a Western, liberal humanist who ultimately regards India as being backward and is tempted to give such backwardness a palingenetic meaning. This may be intriguing as far as *we* are concerned, that is, the white West may indeed profit by an exposure to the East. But it turns into ethnocentric paternalism when Pasolini tells *them* what is valuable in their culture and of what they should be proud. The same goes for the parable of the maharaja, which may sit well in the context of European reception, but where India is concerned, with *people*, not tigers, dying of hunger is a bit farfetched. On this subject, however, Pasolini's film contains its own deconstruction, in the form of interviews with writers and gurus from whom Pasolini asks advice for the maharaja story. When they do not seem too receptive to Pasolini's idea, the tale of a man who lets his body be devoured by tigers acquires another dimension: it becomes perfect material for the psychoanalyst's couch.

Literally. There is a wonderful autobiographical subtext contained in the image of the maharaja devoured by a tiger: In *I quaderni rossi* (the unpublished notebooks written in 1946) we read that, in 1927,

> on a Sunday night, my mother, my father, and I had just returned home from the movies. (I had seen a movie of which I remember an interminable chase with a man on a horse, a dog, and I do not know how many other animals, all running after each other as in a mad merry-go-round, always ending up in the water of a pond.) While waiting for supper, I was glancing through an illustrated booklet picked up at the theater. I remember only one illustration, but I remember it with such a precision

that, even now, I feel perturbed by it. How long did I look at it! How intimidated did I feel by it! I devoured it with my eyes, and all my senses were excited at the idea of relishing it. I felt then the same pangs that I now feel before images or thoughts that I feel unable to express. The illustration represented a man lying prostrate under the paws of a tiger. One could see only his head and his back. The rest of his body disappeared (one could imagine it) under the muzzle of the wild animal. But I believed that the rest of his body had been swallowed, just like a mouse in a cat's mouth. . . . The young man seemed to be still alive and aware of being semi-devoured by the stupendous tiger. He lay with his head thrown back, in a woman-like position, defenseless, naked. Meanwhile, the animal was swallowing him ferociously. Confronted with this image, I was taken by a feeling similar to that which I had felt seeing the youth in Belluno [that is, the *teta veleta* feeling, see chapter 1, *Psychoanalysis*] two years earlier, only this time it was murkier, more continuous. I was all shivering inside, with a feeling of surrender. Meanwhile I began to wish I was the explorer devoured alive by the wild animal. Since then, before falling asleep, I would fantasize about being in the middle of a forest and being attacked by the tiger. And I would let myself be devoured . . . and then of course, although it was absurd, I would also devise a way to free myself and kill her [in Italian *tigre* is feminine].[5]

Twenty-four-year-old Pasolini writes a Proustian remembrance of erotic feelings past. Forty-six-year-old Pasolini films the possibility of telling a story in which being devoured becomes a sublime, religious gesture of defiance against modernity. In the space between a masturbatory exercise in poetic prose and the attempt to give a personal fantasy a political and religious context lies all the progress made by Pasolini thanks to "a certain realism."

Appunti per un film sull'India has something to offer at the level of the image. The hand-held camera continuously looks out for faces which may express the cultural difference that attracts Pasolini. It pans until it finds two eyes which may speak to our Western imagination. It x-rays facial expressions trying to recover the minimal tracks left by the passage of a harsh and different social reality; it stares at the sun-drenched solitude of the fields or at the dignified poverty of the rural areas, discovering the profound humbleness that makes it so different from metropolitan misery. And there is also a marked curiosity for "repulsive" images, a desire to let us know India's pathology: deformed limbs, beggars, untouchables. To be sure, all this is part of India's reality, but a twice-repeated shot of a gangrenous foot and of a hand eaten away by leprosy reveals Pasolini's intent to fabricate meaning from the abject, from what is repulsive and negative, and again, from death. "Each death taking place in meaningful circumstances," writes Pasolini of the maharaja's wife and children. In the film, as in the book, the end—the depiction of a cremation—is intensely felt: a simple Bach melody played on the flute, shots of people preparing the corpse with the camera at a respectful distance, away from faces and concentrated on the enshrouded body. Then Pasolini's voice: "A Westerner visiting India has everything but in fact gives nothing. India, instead, has nothing and gives everything." There is a moment of silence, while the camera abandons the corpse and starts prowling in the dust covered with leaves and petals. "But what?" And the fire is set, Bach becomes elegy, and the camera, finally, pans on the assembled faces.

16

Teorema

After a telegram announcing a guest's arrival is delivered by an arm-flopping postman, a charming young man arrives to spend some time with a wealthy Milanese family. The first to show interest in the guest, the maid Emilia offers herself to him. Shortly thereafter, Pietro, the son, is drawn to the visitor's body and ends up in bed with him. It is then mother Lucia's turn to yield to her desire for the young man, while the father, Paolo, after discovering that his son and the guest have been sleeping together, becomes seriously ill. Forced to his bed, Paolo is lovingly attended by his daughter Odetta and the guest. Prompted by the young visitor's kindness toward her father, Odetta opens herself up to him and they too make love. Finally, even Paolo is "seduced" by the charismatic presence of the nameless young man, who is then called away by another telegram. The maid Emilia leaves the family (to be replaced by another maid also named Emilia) and goes back to the farm where she sits and fasts, surrounded by an ever larger number of peasants. Meanwhile the members of the family dissolve in despair over the guest's absence. Pietro tries to recapture the young man's presence through painting, then leaves home and reiterates his need for transgression with an anguished attack against art. Odetta falls prey to an attack of catatonia and must be hospitalized. Lucia picks up younger men in a spiral of anxiety and addiction, and ends up in the shade of a country church, where she searches for peace. Paolo donates his factory to the workers and, in a climactic scene, undresses in the middle of the train station. Back at the farm, Emilia, after healing a sick child and levitating above the roof, sets out on the road to Milan accompanied by an older woman (played by Susanna Pasolini). They stop at the outskirts of Milan near a housing project. Emilia asks to be buried and starts crying tears that, she says, are not of sorrow but of regeneration. The film ends with Paolo naked and screaming on a desert slope.

> *To say that there are no absolute grounds for the use of such words as truth, certainty, reality and so on is not to say that these words lack meaning or are ineffectual.*
>
> Terry Eagleton

In a 1966 interview, Pasolini, who had just started his short-lived career in film theory, expressed a grudge he held against all the critics who had used his writings only to interpret his films and had not treated them as valid additions to the contemporary theoretical debate:

> In fact, I will tell you to your face: I am deeply offended by the fact that everything I do and say is twisted around to explain my style. It is a way of exorcising me, and perhaps of calling me stupid, a stupid person in life, who is perhaps competent in his work. Therefore it is also a way of excluding me and of silencing me. Unconsciously, it's understood. (*HE*, 224)

Pasolini was not being paranoid. Variously dismissed, his theories mostly served the purpose of substantiating the critics' reading of his films.[1] Although most concerned with himself as an *auteur*, he wanted to be taken seriously as a film theorist. I intend to fulfill his wish by using *Teorema* (1968) as a theoretical offering which integrated, if not amplified, his writings. Dissatisfied with verbal discourse, he "wrote" a theoretical piece in the language of cinema, exploring a territory—film *as* theory—which also appealed to such directors as Godard, Straub, and the later Rossellini.

It is commonly understood that *Teorema* sets out to prove a theorem about bourgeois society: given the hypothesis of a messianic visitation, the story depicted in this film would be the result. The idea of geometric rigor suggested by the title "theorem" is evoked through plot, cinematic technique, and editing. Pasolini himself said that *Teorema*'s allegorical framework "excludes the possibility of both *excursus* and *excessus*, and does not tolerate redundance" because "every character is symbolic and every action signifies another action."[2] The theorem demonstrated by Pasolini is then an allegory, the terrain of postmodern theorizing. Every title, in an allegory, signifies another title. And it may be useful to remember that Pasolini had the keenest awareness of etimology and that the title has its roots in *theorema*, Greek for spectacle, intuition, theorem; from *theorein*, to look at, to observe; from *theoros*, spectator. Theory and spectatorship, the theory of looking, are thus implied. And so are the ideas of theory as spectacle and spectacle as theory.[3]

Teorema starts with a television crew interviewing a group of workers outside a factory. We learn that their boss donated the factory to them and that the traditional terms of class struggle were thus altered by an act which, as a worker says, "is not an isolated case but belongs to a general tendency of the modern world." The general tone of the interview is one of anxiety over the changes upsetting the socio-historical configuration as Pasolini, the Christological Marxist, knew it. The interview ends with the reporter's voice beseeching in the wind: "Can anyone answer these questions? . . . Can anyone answer these questions?" It is at this point that the title appears on the screen and the credits unfold over the undulating image of a dark red desert. The unanswered questions usher us into a narrative marked by the workers' hesitant Marxist reasoning when confronted with new, pressing questions. Since such fundamental signifiers as "bourgeoisie," "factory," and "class struggle" can no longer go unquestioned, the text postulates a crisis of signs following the disintegration of History as the ultimate signified. Thus, the film's first sequence positions the viewer within the uncertainty of postmodernity, the end of teleological master-narratives, the crisis of signs.

Eventually, viewers find out that *Teorema* narrates the events leading up to the donation of the factory, and that what precedes the credits is in fact the conclusion of the story. The discrepancy between the order of the narration and the narrated suggests Pasolini's will to offer a solution: if the unanswered questions appeared at the end, we would leave the theater with the impression that the film presented a dilemma we were not equipped to solve. Quite the contrary, the text offers itself as an exemplary working out of an initially opaque situation and encourages us to recognize that signs, slippery though they may have become, still lend themselves to interpretation. When the unanswered questions loom up again at the end of the film and project their disquieting shadows outside the theater, we may remember how the film forced signs-in-crisis to tell the truth about themselves.

We must remember that it was at this time that Pasolini coined the phrase "a certain realism" (in his 1968 interview with Oswald Stack). Coming at the peak of his theoretical fervor, *Teorema* exemplifies Pasolini's will to overcome the epistemological crisis besetting realism's foundations: How can we read signs? How can we know anything, after the traditional terms of knowledge have been upset? *Teorema*'s first section, shot in dark sepia tones and underscored by angst-ridden music, is reticent about the characters. Their actions are unclear. After the mysterious guest's arrival, "normal" colors are re-established and characters meet their fates, meanwhile revealing what they were all about. *Teorema* narrates the self-discovery of five allegorical characters and asks the viewer to watch them do it and to learn. In fact, it is with this controversial film, this allegorical essay, that Pasolini images and stages the combination of forces that make up "a certain realism."

"A Certain Realism"

Released during the period of euphoria in 1968, *Teorema* appealed to all the seekers of social flight; it pleased progressive Catholics, and was contemptuously criticized by Left and Right alike, albeit for different reasons.[4] Whereas the Right condemned the film as a hymn to sexual promiscuity, the Left considered it ambiguous and visionary. Although leftist critics were not entirely wrong in questioning the film's openness to the most diverse appropriations, they ended up paying less attention to the film than to its author. Pasolini was accused of the inability "to dialectize personal confession with his intentions of social demystification."[5] Yet the Left, engrossed in the "political" game of detecting who was being the most revisionist, failed to use the film for what it could offer.

Teorema needs adequate translation. The abundance of biblical references, for example, is a symptom of Pasolini's idiolectal use of religious material and must not lead one to the categorical conclusion that the mysterious visitor is either the God of the Old Testament or the Messiah of Christianity.[6] Similarly, that the five characters' encounters with the real takes the form of sexual intercourse is clearly a consequence of the "sex lib" spirit of the times. Sex in the film must be carried beyond its intrinsic meaning of bodies copulating. The sexual act does not mean that either Lucia or Pietro is interested in getting laid—they are not real people but allegorical signs. Sex in *Teorema* must be restored to its function as a sign that desire is more important than reason. More specifically, sex in *Teorema* signifies transgression against the Law that regulates physical and intellectual processes alike. On the one hand, sex violates bourgeois morals which insist that bodies keep a respectful distance from each other; on the other hand, sex is a metaphorical violation of Theory's demand that the knowing subject keep an aseptic distance from the object. Unless we change our ways of relating to signs, unless we let desire take charge, we will not solve the crisis of signs postulated at the beginning of the film. This, in a nutshell, is the theorem. Moreover, the combination of religious and sexual imagery fulfills that most Pasolinian intent to provoke in one and the same gesture both Right and Left. If sexuality provokes the old bourgeoisie, religious images constitute a deliberate attack upon the consumerist hedonism of the new bourgeoisie that is "liberating" itself.[7] With this in mind, I will now proceed to analyze the two images that illustrate the epistemological framework of "a certain realism": the visitor (Terence Stamp) and the desert.

As chief representative of the film's ambiguity, the visitor has given rise to several interpretations because, in effect, he is open to more than one reading. Each different reading, however, reveals less about him than it does about the viewer's point of view. In a sense, the visitor constitutes a sort of provocative mirror held up to the faces of the spectators in order to reflect the reality of their readings. The visitor does not have a univalent meaning because he creates the possibility for meaning to exist for us as well as for the other characters in the film. It is only after their encounter with him that the characters (the signs in the narrative) will cease being opaque and will act out their textual destiny. In his excellent study on Pasolini, Rinaldi points out that "after the visitor's departure, the characters will have to preserve the reality principle which they have been forced to acknowledge."[8] He also argues, however, that the visitor is "sort of a unique God," thereby implying that our interpretation of his role and presence should proceed to a *reductio ad unum*. In fact, the visitor is not one and the same for all the characters, for he simply makes the knowledge of their respective realities possible. The mysterious guest is like an acid test revealing the identity of the signs-in-crisis. He embodies an exceptional force capable of driving the signs in the text to a passionate (pathological) self-revelation. Hence, it is less a question of defining him than of understanding his effects.

The figure of the visitor is perhaps the best representation of passion to be found in Pasolini's entire work. In the allegorical context of the film, the visitor represents passion because he enforces a sense of subjective reality on the otherwise dull signs in the text, not because he makes love to them all. The rational composition of the frames, the abundance of wide-angle shots, and the stylized quality of the acting utterly eliminate any trace of traditionally conceived passion from the film. There is no sensual abandonment nor any "I did not know it could be so nice." In *Teorema*, moaning and screaming are the sounds of fury rather than lovemaking. Sexual relations per se lose importance and merely suggest that the guest can have an impact upon all the five characters. Indeed, paradoxical though it may sound, *Teorema* is the film by Pasolini in which homosexuality has the least amount of structural importance in the text. Homosexuality in *Teorema* is of course prominent, but I would like to argue that its prominence derives from the fact that for the first time it is visually present in the text. For the first time in Pasolini's cinema, we see a homosexual relationship (when Pietro slips into the visitor's bed). *Teorema*, however, does not depict the homosexual condition, which is what other films had done. For example, *Accattone*, *Mamma Roma*, and *La ricotta* portrayed, by means of their subtexts, homosexuality as a social position. In *Teorema*, homosexuality is not singled out, nor is it pitted against heterosexuality. Its importance is visual and *not* thematic.

As the visitor makes love to everyone in the family, homosexuality and heterosexuality are put on the same level by the text. This is not to say that the visitor's masculinity is indifferent. Of course it is not, and spectators reacted to the film in the way they did because the visitor is male. Similarly, the social consequences of Paolo and Pietro's sexual transgressions are different than those of Lucia, Odetta, and the maid. But *Teorema* is an allegory in which every sexual encounter signifies the encounter of a sign-in-crisis with passion. As a nonrational force, passion has similar effects on the signs in the text. It pushes them to find out who they are.

There is a sense in which the visitor, *qua* allegorical personification of passion in a visual essay, may be referred to as *it*, as the film itself obliquely suggests. *Teorema* quotes Tolstoy's *The Death of Ivan Ilych*, a novella that opens with Ivan's death and then goes back to recount his life. Seen from the point of view of his death, Ivan's life appears "most simple and most ordinary and therefore most terrible."[9] As with Paolo and Lucia in *Teorema*, ordinariness and stability blind Ivan to the reality of his position, to the fragility of his social and emotional relationships. Ivan's incurable disease, which manifests itself through a sharp pain in his side, becomes his purveyor of truth as it forces him to look at things from an estranged perspective. Tolstoy repeatedly stresses the apocalyptic (revelatory) role that the disease plays in Ivan's life by referring to his pain as *It*.[10] Although initially compared to Ivan's butler Gerasim (who performs that funny business of holding his master's legs on his shoulders), the guest is, in fact, like Ivan's pain: *it* affects the body of each family member and alters it accordingly. The head of the family, Paolo, recognizes this when he says to the guest: "You have come only to bring destruction." Like Ivan's pain, *Teorema*'s mysterious guest destroys his old, seemingly natural identity and exposes his positional truth, that is, the truth from and of his position in the social text at a given historical juncture.

When the visitor/*it* makes its first appearance in the film, Odetta is asked, in English, by a friend: "Who is that boy?" Also in English, she answers: "A boy." In addition to emphasizing the irrelevance of *its* name, the use of English, coupled with the shift to "real" colors at *its* entrance, indicates that *Teorema* wants to cluster signifiers of difference around *it*. The visitor/*it*, who reads Rimbaud—the poet of *l'énormité devenant norme*—is different from all other characters, and more important, brings out their differences from one another. After *its* arrival, Paolo, Lucia, Pietro, Odetta, and Emilia part with the code which has thus far regulated their lives and recognize the difference which is inscribed in their bodies. In fact, within the frame of *Teorema*'s allegorical argument, the visitor/*it* represents Pasolini's conviction that the reading of signs is relational: making love with signs means letting one's body relate to them.

Complementary and concomitant to the visitor is the desert, the other force making up "a certain realism." In addition to the credits sequence and the two scenes indicating respectively Paolo's seduction and his final despair, *Teorema* is literally punctuated by brief shots of a dark, red desert (actually the slopes of Mount Etna). Technically it is a flash forward, for it prefigures the space in which Paolo will end up and in which we can visualize the other three family members, at least metaphorically. (Even Emilia ends up in a desert of sorts, although she is not in despair, but cries tears of hope.) As the image of what exceeds, defines, and awaits the characters, the desert transposes the story into another, a nonrealistic dimension; it is the key to the allegory.

In the experimental novel *Teorema*, Pasolini suggested that the Jews conceived the idea of God's absolute nature after roaming in the desert, for everything in it appeared as *one*. In the last pages, Paolo, the father, says to himself, in a sort of inner scream:

> As already happened to the people of Israel, or to Paul, the Apostle, the desert confronts me as that which is indispensable. Or, better yet, as reality once it is stripped of everything but its essence, reality as represented by those who live and think of it, even if they are not philosophers.[11]

As the visual representation of a reality "stripped of everything but its essence," the desert is the desire for, and therefore the image of, an absolute reality, something which realism has been after for a long while—at least according to Pasolini (see chapter 12). To the destruction of bonds and common grounds, to the radical difference brought about by the guest, the desert opposes the image of a common horizon. Unlike the visitor, the desert does not adjust to the needs of the characters and their differences, but makes them all equally naked in the face of a natural landscape stripped of any diversity. The desert is a powerful image imposing itself on the characters and forcing them to come to terms with their cosmic reality between being and nothingness. Whenever the desert rushes in, the characters are confronted with their fundamental solitude, and they crystallize whatever they know about themselves into an absolute conclusion. Essence, the image of the absolute, appears in spurts, randomly yet regularly affecting the activity of the signs.[12] Thus, just as "God led his people through the desert" (Exodus 13:18, which is quoted in a subtitle over the first image of the desert), *Teorema* leads its signs-in-crisis through the awareness that they (we) cannot dispense with the longing for absolute knowledge. The point is important, for it clarifies why Pasolini was reluctant to dismiss God. He knew that God cannot be denied without enormous implications, for "the denial of God," as Adorno puts it, "contains an irremediable contradiction: it negates knowledge itself."[13] Although no longer a believer himself, Pasolini strove to maintain what God represents, the desire for absolutes which is a necessary stage in any committed discursive practice, like that in "a certain realism." Thus a paradoxical situation arises in which we must search for absolutes while simultaneously recognizing that, insofar as they fixate values in time and space, we must keep them at bay. Absolutes, *Salò o le 120 giornate di Sodoma* teaches, are tyrannical. Hence they must be there only as contingent desire and not as permanent essence: they must be mobilized only on condition that they efface themselves after producing the desired effect of making knowledge possible. The random shots of the desert in *Teorema* are therefore like insertions of the Absolute into a world otherwise fragmented by Difference.

The visitor and the desert are complementary images that Pasolini's film mobilizes against the crisis of signs postulated at the outset. The corporeal and the spiritual, difference and the absolute, the material and the immaterial work together in *Teorema*. Here, perhaps for the first and only time, Pasolini went beyond the binary oppositions that usually make up his films, so that the visitor and the desert constitute an oxymoronic couple that best illustrates the workings of "a certain realism." The visitor/*it* makes the signs in the text reveal their difference, and the desert places them within and against a common background. Difference and absoluteness, the reality of the fragment and the desire for totality, cannot exclude each other but must coexist. Such is the uneasy balance of a postmodern theory refusing to drown in pluralism while acknowledging plurality.

Teorema's most remarkable feature is that it is completely clear about what makes the signs readable while proving opaque about what they mean. Illustrating a process of theoretical knowledge, it offers a method and the means to practice it but refuses to effect closure on the signs. It offers realistic glasses to its viewers, but the reality it portrays is open to interpretation, to use, by the different passions of the spectators. In keeping with the film's abstraction and with my desire to use the film in a theoretical fashion (my passion), I will now examine the path, the itinerary, of each of the characters—the stuff of the theorem.

The Theorem

The promised land of survival will be the realm of peaceful death that the humanists are fighting for. But what about the impossibility of living, what about this stifling mediocrity and this absence of passion?

Raoul Vaneigem

Pasolini chose a reality that was on everyone's lips in 1968: the death of the bourgeois family and its replacement by a new order. Articulating the sexual and Oedipal moments of the nuclear family with their economic pre-condition, *Teorema* depicts the role played by traditional parents, Father and Mother, as well as the one played by the new generation, Son and Daughter. The question that the film sets out to answer is: What will happen after traditional roles are exposed as meaningless, after the code legitimizing the social contract (represented by the Father) has been destroyed? This destruction proves fatal to the bourgeoisie, while its replacement, here sketched in visionary, deliberately naive overtones through that "non-character" Emilia, survives.

The manner in which *Teorema* introduces Paolo (Massimo Girotti) exemplifies allegorical realism's clockwork precision in the production of meaning. *Qua pater familias*, Paolo is the first character to appear, and he does so as he leaves his factory in the back of a Mercedes. The camera merely frames his face, so that we do not see the chauffeur, the hands behind the wheel. Since the manual labor that permits his motion is excluded from sight, Paolo is presented as the signifier of that very repression, the owner of the means of production who has a stake in concealing the socioeconomical relations by virtue of which he enjoys his position. Furthermore, since Paolo's power extends to the reproductive sphere, we see him once more in the prologue, not in person, but as a photographic image in Odetta's album. His paternal smile controls the private sphere without having the appearance of doing so; his image is enough, a veritable reminder of the name of the father that holds the other members in their places.

Inured to seeing himself as an individual in the free market of equal opportunities, he then succumbs to passion and realizes that his identity, rather than natural, is social and is therefore defined by his particular position in the relations of re/production. This revelation shatters his confidence and threatens his life, so much so that he is taken seriously ill. As with Ivan Ilych, Paolo's disease takes on metaphysical connotations and enforces a confrontation with death and the absolute; as Ivan dies from his illness, so Paolo will never really recover and, in a sense, will experience death as the collapsing of his stable identity:

> You have utterly destroyed the image I have always had of myself. Now I am unable to conceive of anything that could make me regain my identity. What do you suggest? A form of social death? Total obliteration of myself? How could this be done by a man committed to the concepts of order, foresight, and above all possession?

Unable to continue signifying and guaranteeing a symbolic order in which he was an unquestioned authority, Paolo rids himself of the signifiers of his old identity (factory, Mercedes, and clothes) and heads towards the desert. While he had asked himself no questions in his former life, he is now "full of questions to which he has no answer" and he screams, his anguish reminding us of the conventionalist nostalgia for the lost absolute.[14]

Unlike the rest of the family, Lucia (Silvana Mangano) is first presented inside the villa, reading a book. Although she could afford a maid and thus dispense with domestic labor, her place is in the house, enclosed in the private sphere of which she is the appointed guardian angel. Freed from economic necessity and with a great deal of leisure time, she merely has a representative function: she is in charge of symbolizing the family status. Significantly, we cannot make out the title of the book that she reads, as if it were not important. The missing title indicates that her reading is a question of form rather than content, of signifying a cultivated way of spending time rather than using the words in the book. The book cover is empty because she is empty, or, rather, emptied by the surroundings which make her a blank, ready to be filled in with the assigned image.

The scene of her escalating interest in the guest clarifies the role that passion will play in her life. We first see a point-of-view close-up of the visitor's book, the Feltrinelli edition of Rimbaud's poems, and we are therefore invited to establish a connection between its clearly legible title and the unreadable cover of Lucia's book. We then cut to a close-up of Lucia followed by a careful pan over all of the visitor's clothes spread on the bed. To the extent that these clothes are *its* cover, Lucia's interest in them testifies to her growing awareness of the need to fill her own emptiness with a title. Insofar as the clothes are signifiers of *its* absence, of absence *tout court*, Lucia cannot escape seeing herself reflected in them. Illuminated by passion, she discovers that her "life was devoid of any interest" and "that her emptiness was filled with petty values and horrendous conventions." At last realizing that *she* is the missing title, she strives to remedy the lack but is still imprisoned in and by the world that conceived her. All of her attempts to recover an identity, a sense of her own presence, occur within the pre-emptied space of her social milieu: sex and religion, unfulfilling sexual encounters and churches; once again, *la maman et la putain*. At closer inspection, her entrapment in this binary fate is a corollary of what she is enjoined to signify within the patriarchal symbolic order. From first shot to last, Lucia is always perfectly made up, even in the most unlikely situations. Insofar as Lucia must be esthetically pleasing, her figure suggests the presence of someone expecting to be pleased: the beholder, the owner of the gaze. Beauty is in the eye of the beholder, says our culture, but when the beholder is always a man, then beauty is subjected to his imaginary, to his pendular motion between arousal and rejection, purity and abjection, desire and guilt. Lucia's sexual intercourse in a ditch is nothing but a visual definition of the mire into which fetishistically admired objects are at times forced to sink.

When we first see him coming out of a well-known Milanese high school, Pietro (Andrès-José Cruz) seems a cheerful flower of the bourgeoisie. The text, however, enables us to see what he cannot yet see. While walking among his peers, Pietro grabs the coat of a nicely built, bigger friend, puts it on, tries a few clownlike steps, and makes everybody laugh. A later scene, Pietro's pathetically shy disrobing in front of the visitor, will clarify the meaning of this seemingly irrelevant occurrence. Pietro, or, to be more precise, his body, is the tragic locus of a fracture, a tension between what he is and what he wants to/must be. On the one hand, he must signify power and potency, but on the other, he is very thin and pale, has stooped shoulders and freckles. As a consequence, the germ of a rebellion arises within him against the established order that expects him to fit a subjectively impossible image. Of course the homosexual/heterosexual opposition finds its expression in Pietro. Yet the dialectic between his real self and his ego-ideal is by no means restricted to that dialectic, for essentially Pietro is rejecting his duties as *the Son*.

The self-deception that Pietro exercises exacts too high a toll, and he will be the first in the family to fall prey to *it*. Pietro's attack of passion brings not only despair but also liberation, for he now dares to use his own cultural capital to symbolically negate his class. Fascinated with avant-garde painting, Pietro explores the avenues of modernist art and its dark alleys designed to *épater le bourgeois*. Modernist art is for Pietro the means to individuation, to a symbolic re-enactment of the coat episode. It is because he sees himself as a noble family's decayed son trying to live like his ancestors that Pietro opts for art. It is because modernism transgresses each and every rule *within* bourgeois art that Pietro first urinates on the canvas and then paints with his eyes covered. His highest achievement consists of transparent plastic sheets traversed by nervous color strokes and then juxtaposed in a multi-layered web of traces. We cannot see him full-figure because his creation lies between him and the camera. In this static long take are all the splendor and the misery of modernism, for while his art adequately renders the palimpsestic nature of signs, it also serves as his means for hiding. All the furious monologues accompanying his pictorial experiments reveal his lucid consciousness:

> I must try to devise new techniques that will be unrecognizable, unlike anything that has ever been done before, so as to avoid childish ridicule and build a world of my own, a world not comparable, a world that isn't subject to existing values. Values must be utterly new, as the technique. No one must realize that its author is worthless, that he is an inferior abnormal being, that like a worm he writhes in order merely to survive. No one must catch him guilty of naiveté. Everything must appear as perfect, based on unknown rules, rules that as a result cannot be judged.

The necessity for originality betrays the artist's paranoid need to demand autonomy from the past while he is unable to move beyond the complacence of intellectual negation. Pietro has indeed managed to sublimate his guilt about his own body, but he still does not love it, does not entrust it with the search for pleasure, so that everything is consumed in the mind.

As she aimlessly walks amidst parked cars, with her books guardedly held against her breast, Odetta (Anne Wiazemsky) is immediately defined as a wanderer who has something to protect. When she sees her boyfriend and resists his attempt to take away one of her books, we realize the reason for both of her gestures: she wanders in an attempt to escape the expropriation of what she needs to protect. But he is stronger than she is, and grabs the large photo album she keeps among her books. No sooner do we see that she carries around a visual journal than we catch a glimpse of a page-size portrait of Paolo, the father. If the blatant suggestion of an Electra conflict is but Pasolini's superficial tribute to his own Freudianism, the incident reveals that Odetta has no image of herself except through the eye of an overpowering male. To the extent that her relationship to the world is informed by patriarchal discourse, Odetta is doomed to circle aimlessly around the lack she is enjoined to represent. She seems to have no reality of her own, and we even feel she is attracted to the visitor because of what the guest/*it* did for her father. Her feeble identity is underscored by the frequent wide-angle close-ups making her features dilate to the outskirts of the frame. When the camera circles around Odetta, who is rotating in her own turn, we get the impression of someone very near the clinical limit of breakdown. And her clenched fist seems the ironic sign of her failure to grasp herself in any way.

Teorema prompts a radical interpretation of the character of Odetta. She is the only member of the family portrayed as the locus of the partially obscured vision which, in Pasolini, signifies the point of view of central characters. In *Teorema* there are three characters "blessed" with this vision: the postman Angelino (Ninetto Davoli, of course), the maid (Laura Betti), and Odetta, when she gazes at the street from behind the villa's black iron gate. A radical reading suggests that Odetta is the character who most breaks with the past, as if her quiet and seemingly vicarious existence hides a subterranean flow of uncompromising determination. In keeping with the findings of the antipsychiatry movement (Laing and Cooper in England, Szasz in the United States, Basaglia in Italy, all of whom were writing their major works during this period), a radical reading would construe Odetta's behavior as a sign of refusal rather than a mere psychotic attack.

After her encounter with passion, Odetta finds her will, the will to reject a text that did not let her have an image of her own. Odetta does not passively fall prey to a catatonic attack; she *chooses* the psychiatric ward, for she now prefers to embody madness rather than live as an appendage of the Father. Hence she makes herself absent, refusing to lend her body any further to a text that had no real place for her. Once we see her case as the outcome of a woman's impossible relation to patriarchy's petrifying gaze, Odetta's case arouses less pity than rage. In fact, it is the same rage we experience with Agnese's tantrums (*Sedotta e abbandonata*, Seduced and Abandoned, Pietro Germi, 1964), or with Juliet's monsters (*Giulietta degli spiriti*, Juliet of the Spirits, Federico Fellini, 1965). It is the same rage we sense lurking behind Anna's unresolved disappearance from the text in Antonioni's *L'avventura* (L'Avventura, 1960) or behind the neurotic laughter with which Gavino's mother protects herself from the law of the Father in Taviani's *Padre Padrone* (1977). Reacting against the historical duty of fitting into the symbolic order of phallocentrism, these women stray from the path and risk the dangers of radical difference. Odetta, the Deviant.

Teorema: *The last image of Emilia (Laura Betti) represents another example of partially obscured vision.* Courtesy of the Museum of Modern Art/Film Stills Archive.

Emilia's character is visually and narratively overrepresented and testifies to Pasolini's nonrational belief in the "complicity between the subproletariat and God."[15] Introduced in a frontal close-up, Emilia (Laura Betti) will be relentlessly portrayed with this kind of shot betraying Pasolini's reverential attitude toward the peasantry, his will to stare at them in order to transfigure them. Everything in Emilia's trajectory is designed to arouse the feeling of the sacred. She is the first one to hear the call of passion, offering herself to *it*, after an attempted suicide which can only be effectively explained in terms of the text's desire to cluster marks of exceptional behavior around her. The courtyard in which she sits and levitates enjoys the privilege of the only 360-degree slow pan in the film, and is thus charged to signify the curved space of the harmoniously cyclical life (civilization of the circle) that Pasolini opposed to the incessant forward movement of so-called progress (civilization of the line).

Although Emilia is clearly conceived as the anti-bourgeois character, she lacks human depth. She never talks (except at the end), she rarely changes expression, she is the most abstract of the five characters. Indeed, she is there as an allegorical representation of alterity to the status quo. No longer able to conceive such otherness within the terms of class struggle (the factory has been donated), Pasolini images, with Emilia, a byzantine icon to be contemplated with eyes full of emotion. Emilia's healing power and her levitating above the roof are symptomatic of a film that does not fear ridicule and strives to convey the exceptional with all the means in its power.[16] Her final self-burial, leaving her eyes uncovered, is an effective dramatization of the gaze "from the far edge of some buried age" described in the poem recited by Orson Welles in *La ricotta*. Emilia indicates the ideal gaze from an *ex*ternal position. As her ecstasy is *ex*orbitant and *ex*cessive, she is a an allegory of what exists outside the system.

Therefore

An essay about the crisis in signification, *Teorema* dramatizes what realism needs in order to keep using the word *reality*. By presenting the signs as unresolved at the beginning, and by showing them as progressively exploding/imploding after their encounter with passion, Pasolini *visually* enunciates the theory of "a certain realism" that he did not state in writing. According to such a theory, signs make sense only if they are met with passion, the force making necessary what seems arbitrary, the power inhabiting the flesh and therefore speaking with the strength of bodily humors. Passion for the life of the body is also the passion for the absolute, for the body has absolute demands. Pasolini's film, a theoretical piece in "the written language of reality," makes a statement on behalf of the epistemological role of the body, on behalf of *it*.

As *theorein* means observation, *Teorema* tackles the issue of spectatorship as well. The film sketches the prolegomena to a theory of realism as a mode of reading; this is a theory that Pasolini never developed, but it can be extrapolated from his various writings (see chapter 3). Such a theory could perhaps be best enunciated in the context of a visual essay. Through the exemplary relationship between the visitor (the realist viewer) and the other characters in the text, *Teorema* illustrates what will and should happen when we watch films. In the first place, sign reading (film viewing) is as much a physical operation as it is a mental one. The encounter between text and spectator "is a relationship between individuals which happens under the ambiguous sign of the instincts and under the religious (not confessional) sign of charity" (*HE*, 270). Instincts and *caritas* are the charismatic qualities of the visitor. The spectator's encounter with the text is like lovemaking, in that films address his/her body. Only an investigation of the ways images speak to and are read by the body will set off a reliable reception theory for the cinema. Second, it is precisely the bodily aspect of sign reading which grounds decoding operations that would otherwise spin in relativism. The spectator needs to let her/his body vent the "true" interpretation of a sign, even when the mind seems to flounder in uncertainty. The truth thus provided, however, will not have the universal character that traditional theory demands it to reveal at the end of its impartial path. It will be the truth of a contingent relationship, a truth revealing as much about the object as it does about the knowing subject. The subject should not, however, be intimidated by the lack of universality in her/his judgment: the spectator's truth unveils the reality of difference. That is why an excessively careful, rationally circumspect reading will not do, for it fails to let the truth of the subject come forward, thus muffling even the sound of the object.

17

Porcile

Porcile (Pigsty, 1969) consists of two stories told alternately.

(1) Julian Klotz, the son of a wealthy German industrialist, is a puzzle to both his parents and his girlfriend Ida. In a time of social unrest (1968), he sides neither with nor against his father, neither with nor against the student movement. There is a jealously guarded secret behind his ambivalence, and when he falls prey to a catatonic seizure (much like Odetta in *Teorema*) his mother and Ida wonder what the secret might be. Meanwhile Mr. Herdhitze, a businessman with a Nazi past and a rival of Klotz's, pays him a visit. During a heated yet ironic conversation/confrontation, Klotz threatens to make Herdhitze's Nazi past public, but Herdhitze has something worse to reveal. Herdhitze knows that Julian likes to have sex with pigs. Crushed by the revelation, Klotz accepts a merger with Herdhitze's companies. After Herdhitze's revelation, Julian comes back to life, bids farewell to Ida and, during the party celebrating the merger, goes to the pigsty where he is devoured by the pigs.

(2) A young man wanders in the wilderness of a volcanic landscape, eating butterflies and snakes. He then confronts a soldier lagging behind a search patrol (uniforms and weapons situate the action around the fifteenth century). After a long struggle, with no words exchanged, the young man kills the soldier, eats his body, and throws his head into a steaming crater. Suddenly, the nameless cannibal is no longer alone, but has a small group of men with him. They capture three women and kill the soldiers escorting them. Later, they capture another woman, but the man who was with her escapes unnoticed and reports the out-

laws' position to the local authorities. Using a couple of naked youths as bait, soldiers and villagers capture the outlaws, who are then condemned to the agony of a slow death. Shortly before the execution, the young man utters the only words in the narrative: "I killed my father, I ate human flesh, and I quiver with joy!"

> *Born in the wake of the progressive upheaval of 1848 and reaching maturity in the period of social cynicism and political disillusionment following after it—the period of the Second Empire—the French Realist movement in its dual character of protest against, yet expression of, a predominantly bourgeois society, was internally marked with the stamp of ambivalence.*
>
> Linda Nochlin

Being made of two intercut, seemingly separate stories, *Porcile* demands such a laborious reading on the viewer's part that to consider it a realist film might seem an act of cultural terrorism. One of the two stories, sometimes referred to as *Orgia* (Orgy), is set in a metahistorical desert and virtually dispenses with the spoken register altogether; the other, a cinematic adaptation of Pasolini's own play *Porcile* (Porcile), is shot in a minimalist style that could not be further away from the rendering of the everyday occurrences with which realism is commonly associated. Yet *Porcile* operates within a realist mode because it attempts, albeit in a cerebral way, to allude to a historical world outside of the text. Pasolini's film posits and sustains the notion of an external reality which is nothing less than the historical moment in which the film was made.

Porcile is an intriguing example of realism's growing pains, of that complex phenomenon whereby so many leftist directors sought to fabricate new modes of representation to better fulfill the demands of the changing times. Godard's *La Gai Savoir* (1968), Rocha's *Antonio das Mortes* (1969), Fassbinder's *Katzelmacher* (1969), Orsini's *I dannati della terra* (The Wretched of the Earth, 1968), and Taviani's *Sotto il segno dello scorpione* (Under the Sign of Scorpio, 1969) are but a few contemporary films made by directors whose engagement with social reality was beyond doubt and whose work ought to be rethought in light of a more supple notion of realism. Indeed, it would be absurd to retain the outmoded thematic, narrative, and stylistic parameters of lower-class life, straightforward narration, and invisible style. Realist signifying procedures change and have a history, because the people animated by a realist attitude change and are in history. And 1969 was no common historical conjuncture. In fact, in 1969, the way of thinking about social reality, rather than realism itself, had bouts of growing pains. Conveniently regarded as a watershed in all areas of cultural life, May 1968, did not leave cinema untouched. A brief digression may be useful in order to understand the ways in which *Porcile* is symptomatic of the vicissitudes of "a certain realism."

During the days between May 17 and June 5, 1968, amidst general strikes and factory occupations, an event took place which can be regarded as the first official and self-conscious attempt to revolutionize cinema's production and consumption alike. Initiated by the members of the film technicians' union and the editors of *Cahiers du cinéma*, a short-lived institution came into being, *Les étaux généraux du cinéma* (Estates General of the Cinema), which "reflected the new importance within an advanced capitalist society of the work of ideological opposition to existing social, political, and economic relations."[1] The general assemblies, which included the participation of leading film directors, critics, actors, and film technicians, issued a number of plans for the transformation of the film industry. All of the plans agreed upon spurning the production of "mere commodities" and recommended an effort to create films "with a more profound value." Spectators, it was thereby implied, did not enter theaters "to have fun but to think hard."[2] A politically committed avant-garde production was henceforth encouraged by such influential journals as *Cahiers du cinéma* and *Cinethique* in France, *Filmcritica* and *Cinema e film* in Italy, and (later) *Screen* in England.

Within such a global rethinking of every aspect of the cinematic apparatus, an attack was mounted on the relationship between reality and cinema. While the former was often reduced to "nothing but the expression of dominant ideology," the latter came to be increasingly regarded as the deceptive purveyor of "the impression of reality."[3] Leftist directors were put under the pressure of having to attempt an escape from what Pasolini called cinema's "fatally naturalistic vocation" (*HE*, 245). They were urged to make difficult films capable of implicating the audience in a rational process of self-distancing. Under the aegis of Brecht revisited—and often misinterpreted, for Brecht certainly did not recommend difficulty at the expense of popular accessibility—a modernist textuality came to be regarded as the only possible way out of the snares of the obvious. Conversely, everything that was not modernist came to be regarded as illusionist, that is, realist. What was being attacked was a mode of consumption which entailed the spectator's identification with the characters and which took the events on the screen for real, for realistic portrayals of "how things are." What was being forgotten, however, was that realism, besides entailing a concern with minute details, was first and foremost a matter of political attitude, a matter of desire for social impact. Pasolini never participated in making a scapegoat of the word *realism* and was always careful to employ the word *naturalism* to indicate cinema's "impression of reality." In fact, he even thought that filmmakers could harness cinema's inevitable "impression of reality" to a positive end and prompt the spectator to see that reality is like a film, that "reality is not natural." Concurrently, as we have seen for *Edipo re* and *Teorema*, he participated in the concerted attack against cinema as a commodity. "How can one be opposed to cinema as the medium of mass culture?" he asked himself. "By making an aristocratic cinema: an inconsumable one."[4]

Third in the series of his "aristocratic" films, *Porcile* is in my view the most effective. It perfectly expresses the balance between autobiographical information (the reality of the author) and social reality. *Porcile* offers an unsurpassed portrait of the dilemma between historical commitment and metahistorical oblivion. It certified Pasolini's interest in the student movement by starring the Godardian Jean-Pierre Leaud and Anne Wiazemski, and the rebels Pierre Clementi and Marco Ferreri, a director whose apocalyptic views on Italy are best illustrated by his choice to live and work in France. *Porcile* also offered a real treat to an intellectual public, for, as Marc Gervais aptly notes, "the intellect is defied, it must look for a meaning beyond the confusion, it must make an effort to arrive at a conclusion."[5] These "musts" are indeed reminiscent of Pasolini's idea of reality as a semiotic duty, an echoing "thou shalt interpret me" which the world throws in our faces daily. In sum, *Porcile* is the ideal work to analyze for anyone who wants to follow the trail of realism after the questioning of straightforward narration and the modernist challenge.

As mentioned earlier, *Porcile* consists of two stories that are imbricated in alternate montage. Most critics treat them separately, at best deriving a global sense from their juxtaposition as a whole. Yet there is only *one* story: the story of an ambivalent, divided unity. In order to prove my point, I will briefly describe the sequences as they appear in the film and insert my "suturing" reading in between. This strategy is also motivated by the fact that, to this day, *Porcile* is the only feature film by Pasolini that is not available on video in the United States. While it lies heavily, perhaps, on the reader who is not familiar with the film's beauty, my reading aims at restoring the film's complexity and at providing an example of a Barthesian, *S/Z*-like work about cinematic signifiers. Instead of reordering the text in accordance with its founding codes, as Barthes did, I will concentrate on *Porcile*'s lucid will to produce meaning through the images of each story *and* through the editing. This chapter will then consist of an elaborate, pendular motion between what is seen in the text and what can be visualized outside of it—all the while forcing the images to speak about the historical reality to which they point through the filter of a difficult cinema.

One Plus One Makes a Divided One

(1) We see a rectangular stone whose inscription is read to us by a male voice: "After having properly interrogated our conscience, we have decided to devour you on account of your disobedience." The camera pans to the right, framing another stone read by the same voice: "Wife, you and I are allies: you mother-father and I father-mother. Tenderness and toughness surround our son. West Germany is not Hitler's Germany! Here tenderness and toughness are mixed. We produce wool, beer, cheese, and buttons (cannons are only for export). On the other hand, Hitler, too, was partly female, as everyone knows, but he was a murderous female: our tradition has therefore improved. Why then did the murderous mother have obedient sons with blue eyes full of desperate love, while I, affectionate mother, I have this son who is neither obedient nor disobedient?"

On the first stone a father addresses a disobedient son in the name of a "we," a society that is so powerful that it is able to eliminate those who do not conform. "Devouring," however, bespeaks not only greedy consumption, but also assimilation. Thus the text suggests that, in addition to eliminating those who disobey, "we" also use them for our own metabolism and normal functioning. A society needs transgression to found its rule. The brutality of the verb "devour" stands in pointed contrast to "the interrogation of our conscience," which implies a civilized, democratic process. It is *homo hominis lupus* peeping through a humanistic veneer.

The second stone bestows historical concreteness upon the abstract father/son relationship evoked by the first: we are in post-Nazi Germany, a society in which soft persuasion ("tenderness") has infiltrated previous rigidity. That "cannons are only for export" indicates imperialism's new phase: wars are no longer directly fought among major powers, but in the Third World. The second inscription also expresses the bewilderment with which post-war parents looked at their sons and daughters (the sixties generation), who grew up in a better situation than their fathers and yet contested the parental order all the more vehemently. Finally, the second stone announces the presence of an ambivalent position which puzzles society's symbolic order. There is someone who is neither with "us" nor with "them." Such ambivalence is given strong sexual overtones by the reiterated play on gender roles and by the elliptical reference to Hitler's femininity.

Together the two stones have the weight of the Law, which, of course, speaks with the voice of the father.

> (2) Title and credits over the image of a modern and functional pigsty. The camera soon abandons the central perspective and follows snuffling and grunting pigs here and there. Over the entire sequence, the Nazi song *Horst Vessel Lied* delicately played on a harp.

Like all titles, the word *Porcile* posits a preliminary enigma. In this case, Which narrative and thematic links will the text establish for a pigsty to mean something beyond what we are being shown?

The juxtaposition of the music and the image suggests a relationship between Nazism and pigs. The first thing that comes to mind is "fascist pig," an insult quite popular among students in those days. But the rational design of the pigsty may also indicate that pigs are the victims of a perfected totalitarianism which organizes their lives in an absolute way. To the extent that they can be metaphors for oppressors and oppressed alike, pigs take up the ambivalence of the second stone.

> (3) A yellow butterfly flickering on black volcanic rocks. A long-haired young man (Pierre Clementi, hereafter referred to as PC) captures it and promptly puts it into his mouth. He then looks over his shoulder, as if afraid of being seen. By whom?

The butterfly's fragile, delicate beauty contrasts with the image of the pigs and makes PC's act all the more repulsive. Meanwhile, devouring is being reconfirmed as a central signifier. Although his clothes qualify him as a figure of the distant past, PC's long hair has a contemporary ring to it, for in 1969 the issue of the *capelloni* (literally, "the long-haired ones") was raging in Italy. Everything contributes to situating PC as a man living outside social norms. (The disobedient son of the first stone?) This puzzling scene ends with a shot that, in traditional cinema, would be followed by the countershot of what PC sees.

> (4) Brief, long-shot of a stately palace. In the mist, we see a large, rectangular pond whose still waters reflect the palace.

The visual precursor of *Salò*'s theater of cruelties, this palace epitomizes the grandeur with which power likes to represent itself in a civilized world. Its late Renaissance style conveys the idea of an order that seeks its visual legitimation in the past. In Pasolini's idiolect, *Il Palaz-*

zo (The Palace) is the symbol of a centralized and centralizing power.[6] The juxtaposition of scenes (3) and (4) suggests that PC sees, or is afraid of being seen by, this *Palazzo*. A center/margins dialectic is thus set in motion.

(5) Visibly sick, PC writhes and moans on the ground.

Was PC harmed by the ingestion of the butterfly? Or, more likely, by the sight of the *Palazzo*? Here, as in the rest of the film, the editing is so perfect that it produces a meaning that sutures the two stories.

(6) Very brief, medium-long shot of the *Palazzo*.

The fact that PC's convulsive pains are inserted between two shots of the *Palazzo* indicates that his sickness is not due to the butterfly. It is as if PC were able to scan history's horizons and catch a glimpse of the order that would condemn his life on the margins. The *Palazzo* looks at PC. Its impassive gaze frames his acts, even when it is not there. In fact, everything in the story must be visualized as being under the gaze of the *Palazzo*.

(7) In an alternation of long shots and medium close-ups, PC kills and eats a snake. Along the zig-zagging line of the horizon, where sharp-edged cliffs and morning sky meet, we see a long line of marching soldiers with helmets and pikes. Frightened, PC runs away and hides.

We are confronted with another of PC's repulsive acts of consumption. As with the butterfly, PC's action is not the result of "a proper interrogation of the conscience" which marked the devouring mentioned on the first stone. PC's actions spring from unbridled desire.

Replacing the countershot of the *Palazzo*, the marching soldiers are nothing but its extension, its pawns deployed to annex the margins.

PC's frantic movements and the ever-changing position of the camera (a novelty in Pasolini) convey the feeling of restlessly circulating energy.

(8) Brief shot of a young man (Jean-Pierre Leaud) inside the *Palazzo*. He whistles and stares at a wall covered with symmetrically arranged portraits.

The young man is Julian, the rich heir to a powerful German family. Although his immobility contrasts with PC's disorderly flight, a connection between the two is suggested by the object of their gazes. Both of them are looking at something which assigns them a position, defines them, holds them to their respective places.

Porcile: *The nameless rebel (Pierre Clementi) of "the other scene" eats a snake.*
Courtesy of the Museum of Modern Art/Film Stills Archive.

(9) PC wanders about in the blackish desert and comes upon a crater-
like space in which he finds skeletons and uniforms, guns and helmets.
He picks up a gun and inspects it.

What seemed aimless wandering becomes, retrospectively, a search
for weapons with which to defend himself. PC's inspection of the gun
forebodes an imminent confrontation.

(10) Profile medium shot of Julian standing in the middle of the room.
He is soon joined by a well-dressed young woman (Anne Wiazemsky)
who stops right in front of him. Cut to two frontal close-ups of, respectively, Julian and the woman.

The young woman is Ida, an heiress whose property, if it were
joined to that of Julian, would make them "the owners of half Ger-

Porcile: *Pasolini's camera often positioned itself to show only one of Pierre Clementi's eyes.* Courtesy of the Museum of Modern Art/Film Stills Archive.

many." Her decisive steps toward Julian reinforce the sense of imminent confrontation.

(11) PC tries a helmet on, takes it off, and then proceeds to lie on the ground, reclining his head as if under the weight of inner turmoil.

The helmet reaffirms PC's intention to appropriate the devices used by those controlling him. His doubts arise because he knows that, by accepting a confrontation with his enemies and using their weapons, he will be defined by them, he will play the *Palazzo*'s game. In other words, there is a strong desire to stay undefined, outside the history which guns and helmets represent.

(12) Frontal close-up of Ida, who breaks the silence and initiates a verbal "show-down" with Julian. The rigid alternation of close-ups is interrupted when Julian makes a stylized turn around himself and goes to the window, where the dialogue resumes in the same fashion.

Ida's initial words—"we are two bourgeois, Julian, and here we are analyzing ourselves, in accordance with our privilege"—inaugurate a discursive space imbued with rational self-consciousness. Words, acting, and camera style enhance the feeling of distance. The dialogue is poetic, with occasional rhymes. The actors do not attempt psychological realism, but merely speak their lines. The camera does not move, but stares at each of them separately, while the rhythmic editing gives the impression of a "lunatic tennis match."[7]

From their dialogue, we find out that Ida desires Julian, but he does not reciprocate. She urges him to explain "what on earth happened" to cause his "immobility." Julian first resorts to poetic images—a lost leaf . . . a squeaking door . . . a far distant grunt"—thus establishing an obscure connection with pigs. Then he proudly declares: "If you only could see me for what I really am, you would call an ambulance." The main narrative enigma thus takes shape: What does Julian want?

(13) Gun in his hands and helmet on his head, PC wanders about, stops to eat some weeds, and, standing at the left edge of the frame, looks outside of it. Pan to the left, towards the empty space.

It is as if Ida's pressing questions, her attempts to explain Julian, have convinced PC to take up gun and helmet and stay alert. Although eating weeds is much less disturbing than PC's previous acts, it emphasizes his desire to be outside conventions, acting out behaviors that would make a spectator "call an ambulance."

(14) Shot of a long corridor from the far end of which Mrs. Klotz (Margherita Lozano) pushes a wheelchair with Mr. Klotz (Alberto Lionello) in it. They join Julian and Ida and have a brief conversation with them, from which it emerges that the Klotzes would like to see Julian marry Ida.

Cut to another room, where fur-clad Ida confronts Julian, who is sunk in an old sedan chair. She urges him to join her and ten thousand other students in a demonstration against the Berlin wall. He mocks "the puritanical stupidity" of such a project, argues that their rebellion amounts to yet another instance of conformism, and confesses that he prefers staying home, enjoying "infinite repetitions of the same thing."

The Klotzes are in bed and they worry about Julian: "Is he with us or against us?"

Outside the *Palazzo*, Julian and Ida have one last long confrontation that ends with Julian's final rejection of her. "I will not kiss you nor will I kill you," says he, "because I love . . ." "Who?" Ida impatiently asks. "There is no who, there is only my love."

Mr. and Mrs. Klotz are the father and mother who, with the second stone at the beginning, wonder about a son who is neither obedient nor disobedient. Mr. Klotz has a moustache like Hitler's. The first words he says are in ancient Greek, a quotation from some old, dear, venerable text. Confined as he is to a wheelchair, he and his passive wife are allegorical embodiments of an old-fashioned capitalism and its humanistic culture. There is no room for contradiction in their world views. One is either "with us or against us."

Ida voices the ideals of the student movement, which also sees the world as the site of an either/or commitment. Ida and the Klotzes voice the kind of reasoning that sustains traditional Marxism, the idea of a social space fissured into two struggling classes. Are you here or there? Clearly, such a rationale is incapable of explaining Julian's ambiguity. Neither Ida nor the Klotzes can understand what Julian wants.

The main narrative enigma needs reformulation. We no longer ask "what does Julian want?" for we now know that he wants "infinite repetitions of the same thing." Rather, we should ask: What kind of rationality can explain Julian's love—a love whose object is unimportant, a love that counts as subjective desire?

The elements for a solution to this enigma are already there. Marxist rationality fails because it sticks only to one narrative, that of the surface and history. But we are privileged spectators of *another* narrative and are therefore in a position to see that Julian also lives in the atemporal black desert of the wildly free PC. The link that was merely suggested between Julian and PC is now revealed: beneath the historical positions which Julian is asked to take, PC is Julian's unconscious—an unconscious that is depicted rather conventionally as the seething space where the compulsion to repeat reigns supreme. The metahistorical desert is "the other scene" (*l'altra scena* is a common psychoanalytic term referring to the unconscious) which the text visualizes for us and in which Julian's desire can roam free, away from historical constraints. As Marxist reason fails to account for Julian's love, psychoanalysis enters the narrating as the rational discourse capable of explaining what Julian does.

We are now in a position to appreciate the stylistic differences between the two stories. Silence, the constant changes of focal length, the restless camera and characters, the setting in a volcanic desert (the slopes of Mount Etna) where the landscape's vastness overwhelms human forms and reduces them to mere particles in motion, all these are forceful visual underpinnings of "the other scene," of its uncathected energy, of its metahistorical depth. The German episode, by contrast, is shot in a compulsively frozen style. The camera never moves; it stares with a rigidity which parallels Julian's wish for immobility. The characters are always at the center of the frame, which is often filled with symmetrically arranged objects: doors, chairs, panels, paintings. As a result, the image is split in two halves and the depth cues are distributed on receding planes, as if successive layers were flaking off. It is the triumph of a central(ized) perspective, heralding a vanishing point that usually exists in the character's head.

(15) PC sees another orderly procession of marching soldiers. Terror is written on his face as he hides. After the column has gone by, he confronts a soldier who was lagging behind the rest, whistling. PC and the soldier engage in a long battle during which the soldier collapses to his knees, as if struck by a vision that prevents him from continuing the fight. PC kills him, cuts off his head, and throws it into a nearby smoking crater. He then proceeds to eat the soldier's body.

While cannibalism reinforces the feeling that psychoanalysis has entered the film, the attack on the head is emblematic of Julian's (and the text's) dissatisfaction with historical reason. It is a prehistoric ritual aimed at bringing about the advent of a new rationality. The importance of this moment is underscored by the repeated shots of PC's eyes semi-hidden by either rocks or his helmet, a clue to Pasolini's interest in the scene. (See "Partially Obscured Vision," in chapter 13.)

From the moment that Ida and the Klotzes multiplied their efforts to force Julian into a confrontation with history, Julian, in reaction, desires to disappear from it. The soldier, who lags behind and whistles as Julian did (see note 8), obliquely refers to Julian's refusal to march with the rest of the world. Hence the soldier's and Julian's ritualistic succumbing to PC.

(16) Frontal shot of Julian's head on a pillow. Cut to a frontal shot of him in bed, his fists clenched in *rigor mortis*. At the foot of his bed, Ida and his mother argue, each seeking to prove her superior knowledge of Julian's personality. Cut to a brief shot of Mr. Klotz playing the harp.

Cut to an inscribed stone read aloud by Klotz's voice off screen: "Oh, Mr. Herdhitze! Oh, Mr. Herdhitze! My mysterious rival! Great fathers are indeed cumbersome. They have filled our Köln with stately factories like churches. Smokestacks! Smokestacks! A real asphalt Athens!"

Cut to a brief frontal shot of Mr. Klotz playing the harp. Back to the stone: "They are the signs of the favor shown towards us by the great, old fathers, whereas nobody can see your factories, Mr. Herdhitze. Are they transparent? Oh, Mr. Herdhitze! Oh, Mr. Herdhitze! My mysterious rival coming up from nowhere!"

As the thematic link between the two episodes, the head reinforces the feeling that the text is exploring rationality. Like the soldier lagging behind, Julian has ceased interacting with his environment, and his body has vacated the scene. Ida and Mrs. Klotz give opposing explanations of Julian's catatonic state, but they are both bound to misinterpret him. Like Odetta in *Teorema*, Julian escapes a narrative which seems to have no place for him. It is as if he had entrusted his life to "the other scene" and was waiting for the text to produce a new kind of rationality that would integrate him back into life.

A new rationality is precisely what is announced by the two inscribed stones introducing a new character, Klotz's rival. However partial, the description of Herdhitze leaves no doubt: he represents a new social logic in opposition to Klotz's traditional sort of wealth and power. Klotz's capitalism is explicit about its mode of domination, for its "cumbersome" phallic "smokestacks" are everywhere to be seen. The visibility of Klotz's power has a double effect. It produces enemies who are just as visible (in the class struggle) and it forces the ruling class to devise an ideological justification to legitimize its position of dominance: an aristocratic humanism based upon reverence for "the great old fathers" and the desire to emulate Athens. In contrast, Herdhitze's power seems to come up "from nowhere." His factories cannot be seen because they are likely to be in some Third World country where labor is cheap. Herdhitze's power is almost invisible because it rests on the short-circuiting of space and time effected by the credit system. In short, Herdhitze represents what Pasolini called neo-capitalism, a new social logic producing a type of rationality that no longer demands an "either with me or against me" stand from Julian. Perhaps Herdhitze's world will tolerate, explain, and thus reabsorb Julian. This is what his name seems to suggest, for Herdhitze, in German, means "burning hearth" and is therefore related to the fiery crater into which the soldier's (Julian's) head ended up.

> (17) After a brief shot of the steaming crater, the camera picks up PC, who is still eating the soldier's body, and then pans to the left to reveal another man (Franco Citti, hereafter referred to as FC). A cart with three bound women and three soldiers makes its progress on the rocky terrain. PC and FC kill the soldiers and take possession of the women. Only FC, however, seems to be interested in them, as he rapes one under the gaze of the others.

Now that Julian has vacated the German episode, "the other scene" multiplies, as it were, and takes on the wild tones usually ascribed to it/id. Hence the exotic music—the first music in this episode—the murders, and the rape. Interestingly, PC does not participate in this last act, perhaps because he is the character with whom Pasolini admittedly identified. The camera is very careful in framing the rape in such a way that one of the woman's eyes is left visible (another example of "partially obscured vision").

(18) Klotz, with his harp, is joined by his assistant and informer Hans-Guenter (Marco Ferreri) who comes to report his findings about Herdhitze's identity. In the course of a highly stylized conversation, we find out that Herdhitze is none other than Mr. Hirt, an ex-Nazi who, during the war, delighted in collecting skulls of Bolshevik Jews, and after the war had a facelift.

Herdhitze's connection with the theme of the head is reinforced by the perverse reference to his macabre collection. Although the same age as Klotz, Herdhitze can embody a new social logic because of his chameleonic quality: his is the face of neo-capitalism which dispenses with its traditional identity. The ironic reference to Herdhitze's facelift done in Italy "because studies in plastic surgery are very advanced in that country" (a comment that will be repeated in a later scene) indicates that, behind the metaphor of the "bad Germans" lies Italy and its *trasformismo*.[8]

(19) A man and woman on a mule in the desert. When he disappears in the bushes, presumably to relieve himself, the mule wanders off and is captured by PC, FC, and their small band. They kill and behead the woman, while the man, who watched from the bushes, runs away unseen. PC throws the woman's head into the crater.

As Herdhitze's character gradually comes into focus, it is thus matched with the man witnessing PC's transgressions. The point is important, for it links Herdhitze to the man who will inform the community about PC's existence outside the law. Herdhitze will be the source of the kind of information that will lead to the "capture" of Julian's unconscious.

When we first see the woman on the mule and her man, we do not know who they are in relation to the story. The narration from "the other scene" relies on this expository strategy, withholding information and challenging the narrative conventions that give the audience the role of passive consumer of pre-existent articulations. Still, this is not gratuitous experimentation, for it is the content that dictates the form: "the other scene" is, by definition, the place in which connections must be sought out gropingly.

(20) Klotz's informer, Hans-Guenter, continues his report on Herdhitze's criminal activities. Planning to use this information to defeat his rival, Klotz rejoices. No sooner does Klotz exclaim "Very well, he is done for!" than the butler announces Herdhitze's unexpected visit.

The description of how Herdhitze's victims were murdered is portrayed perversely. Hans-Guenter delivers all the macabre details in seven short sentences that he spaces out as if reciting a poem. With each "line," the camera dollies in on his face and then cuts to a close-up of Klotz's hand playing a chord on his harp. A tribute to Eisenstein's *October* (Ten Days That Shook the World, 1928), this perverse montage signals the text's will to face the wreckage of history without emotional involvement, for what is under scrutiny here is *the present*, that is, Herdhitze's new face.

The text builds strong expectations for Herdhitze's appearance and at the end of this sequence brings them to a climax: Herdhitze's name is first announced by the butler, then chimed out three times by Guenter and Klotz, until, finally, we cut to "the other scene."

> (21) A festive tune accompanies the images of a curly-haired young man (Ninetto Davoli, hereafter referred to as ND) dancing around the bell atop a campanile. He soon stops and looks down at the street where a group of people gather around the man who witnessed the beheading of the woman. We then intercut between ND and the man, but we never hear the latter's words. In an intentionally hypercomposed frame, we see ND against a lush background of green leaves and purple flowers, his face turned into an icon of sad puzzlement.
>
> Cut to the desert, where soldiers hide in the bushes. We then see a girl and a boy, both naked, standing in the middle of a barren valley.

ND's smiling grace and merry dancing not only are at odds with the gruesome tone of "the other scene," but they also seem a gratuitous detour from the story. The shot of ND's head among flowers—a shot that has caused an astute critic like Noel Purdon to speak of a "delirious homage by Pasolini to Ninetto Davoli"[9]—indeed seems a frame disengaged from the demands of contextual meaning. As we see him wondering about the villagers' commotion, we are forced to wonder ourselves: Why do we see this scene through his eyes? Why does the camera abandon its objective point of view and anchor our gaze to ND's? Who is he? It is not until later that we can answer these questions and find out the relevance of ND's seemingly gratuitous gaze.

Similarly, we are forced to wonder about the naked girl and boy. What are they doing there?

> (22) Very brief shot of Julian lying in bed.

The cut to Julian's still body establishes a relationship between him and the naked bodies. It reconfirms that his catatonic state depends on "the other scene" and, indeed, expects something from it.

(23) Shot of the naked youths as masses of light and shadow in the desert night. On top of a cliff, very far from them, PC, FC, and the others are watching what, from a distance, looks like two faraway dots. We then have a spectacular half-mile zoom which enlarges the size of the "two dots" without resolving, however, their problematic image completely.

The two naked bodies now have a narrative function: they are the bait dangled in front of PC (Julian's unconscious). The villagers, whose appearance coincided with the appearance of Herdhitze, offer naked flesh in order to pin down PC's transgressions. If PC "bites," Julian's unconscious will be captured, rationalized, explained away in terms of sexuality.

PC hesitates, as if he wanted to ensure that these two naked youths are indeed a sign of a new rationality. The half-mile zoom translates Julian's wish to ascertain whether or not the text has produced a different logic from that of Ida and his parents. Only after a new rationality appears will Julian be able to enjoy his "infinite repetitions of the same thing" without being asked to take a political stand.

(24) Frontal close-up of Herdhitze, who initiates the confrontation with Klotz. The camera then frames the two rivals in a medium shot and retreats before them as they advance through the *Palazzo*'s interminable corridors (Klotz's wheelchair is pushed by Hans-Guenter).

Not surprisingly, PC's attempt to see clearly and understand the bait ends in Herdhitze's head, the new rationality behind the staging of the nudes. As the dialogue between Klotz and Herdhitze unfolds, it emerges that Herdhitze represents a social order in which moral values are replaced by pragmatism and efficiency: *technè* replaces *sophia*. Lamenting the decline of his humanistic values, Klotz alludes to Herdhitze's "scientific culture," but Herdhitze corrects him by replacing "scientific" with "technical," and prophesies a day "when mankind will no longer have problems of conscience." Unlike Klotz, who, as the father whose words appear on the initial tablet (scene 1), devoured his disobedient son (after having "properly interrogated his conscience"), Herdhitze does not directly eliminate his opposition. He offers bait, the promise of liberation and hedonism. If not for psychoanalysis itself, Herdhitze is the spokesman for a society in which sexuality is the most marketable commodity and psychoanalysis is institutionalized as the maintenance/repair service of such a commodity.

(25) Brief long shot of the naked youths from PC's point of view.

Everyone waits. PC hesitates. The fate of PC/Julian's unconscious depends on the outcome of the confrontation between Klotz and Herdhitze. He will not move until he knows who wins.

(26) The confrontation continues in a large room decorated with wall-size paintings of amorous scenes. Klotz tries to corner Herdhitze by broaching the subject of the Jews.

As in scene 24, the conversation between Klotz and Herdhitze illustrates the extent to which *Porcile* strives to make its intellectual public think of the contemporary, historical reality in those countries caught in the transition between old capitalism and consumer society. Klotz confirms his dependence on ideological thinking, whereas Herdhitze aspires to be the executioner of all ideologies. Klotz tries to blackmail Herdhitze by reminding him of the Jews, that is, by seeking to prove that the possession of historical information is valid and can affect reality. But no sooner does Klotz coyly mention the Jews than Herdhitze changes the subject. He wants to talk about pigs instead. "Pigs or Jews?" asks Klotz. "Pigs, pigs," replies Herdhitze.

(27) Brief medium shot of the naked youths.

Although PC has not moved any closer, the naked bodies are now larger than before. It is as if the half-mile zoom had continued. This unrealistic point of view highlights Herdhitze's counterattack.

(28) Slowly but implacably, Herdhitze reveals the truth about Julian's desire. We find out that Julian has a passion for "pastoral strolls" which always end in the pigsty, where he indulges in: "ehm . . . ehm . . . ," concludes Herdhitze, sparing Klotz the details.

As mentioned earlier, pigs are a signifier of ambivalence, for they can refer to oppressors and oppressed alike. Politically, Julian's compulsive copulation with pigs suggests his desire to remain ambivalent, loving and hating his father and the students at once. Sexually, it is yet another metaphor for a sexuality consumed under the aegis of ambiguous feelings (Pasolini's homosexual discourse). What counts is that Herdhitze has the kind of information that unravels Julian's mystery and therefore annexes all those who, like Julian, are neither against nor for the system. Herdhitze is willing to tolerate Julian's ambivalence and his transgressions ("poor Julian, God knows how much he must have suffered") and thus reintegrates him within the social order. For, as Pasolini once put it, "in a society in which everything is forbidden, you can actually do everything. But in a society where only some things are permitted, you can only do those things."[10]

(29) PC and the rest descend on the prey/bait and the soldiers capture them. The naked youths are covered with blankets. FC resists capture fiercely, while PC undresses and lets the soldiers tie his hands.

At the exact moment when Julian's desire is acknowledged and tolerated in the historical episode, PC stops being free. He is tied up, that is, explained. From now on the *Palazzo* will codify his transgressions.

The portrayal of the capture adds interesting connotations. The self-consuming intellectual, PC, does not oppose resistance but mimes Gandhi's passive yet stubborn protest. The heavily built, proletarian FC wages a losing battle.

(30) The *Horst Vessel Lied* played on the harp accompanies the image of Julian eating an abundant breakfast. He is visited by Ida, who congratulates him for his recovery, informs him of the merger between his father and Herdhitze, and bids him farewell: she loves another man, Pubi Jannings, a liberal-minded young man "whose shoulders are twice as broad as his waist." Julian, in return, speaks about his "love" and recounts a dream: a little pig with which he was playing bit off four fingers of his right hand: "The fingers, however, remain attached and do not bleed, as if made of rubber. So I wander with my fingers hanging loose, distraught by that bite. A bid for martyrdom? Who knows what the truth of dreams is, in addition to their making us anxious for the truth."

Everything falls into place with clockwork precision. No sooner is his unconscious "captured" than Julian returns to life. Instructed by Herdhitze, Klotz has learned how to accept his son's wish to confine himself in an erotic pigsty. Indeed, this sequence marks the triumph of psychoanalysis. Not only is the word "truth" now associated with dreams, but Julian's own dream resembles a hallucination of the Wolf-Man, one of Freud's most notorious cases:

When I was five years old I was playing in the garden near my nurse and I was carving with a pocket knife in the bark of one of the walnut trees that also come into my dream. Suddenly, to my unspeakable terror, I noticed that I had cut through the little finger of my (right or left?) hand, so that it was only hanging on by its skin. I felt no pain, but great fear.[11]

It is, at this point, worth recalling that the "Wolf-Man" once "was running after a beautiful big butterfly, with striped yellow wings" (see scene 3); that, among "the blasphemous thoughts which used to come into his head like an inspiration from the devil," there was "God-swine"; that "his governess, who was inclined to disordered fancies, pronounced that some colored sugar-sticks were pieces of chopped up snakes" (see scene 7); and that Freud, in the last pages of his account, noted:

> I have been driven to regard as the earliest recognizable sexual organization the so-called "cannibalistic" or "oral" phase, during which the original attachment of sexual excitation to the nutritional instinct still dominates the scene. . . . In this phase, the sexual aim could only be cannibalism—eating; it makes its appearance with our present patient by means of a regression from a higher stage, in the form of fear of "being eaten by the wolf." We were, indeed, obliged to translate this into a fear of being copulated with by his father.[12]

Julian's dream is therefore the last in a series of references to and borrowings from the story of the "Wolf-Man" with which *Porcile* legitimizes its dramatization of "the other scene." In fact, it is tempting to regard Pasolini's film as the cinematic case history of the pig-man, the man who is "neither obedient nor disobedient," the man who wants to beg out of history and enjoy "infinite repetitions of the same thing."

Ida disappears in a cloud of irony. While it is perhaps too cynical a dismissal of the hopes that she embodied at an earlier stage, her avowal of love for the athletic Pubi is one of those uncannily prophetic images that Pasolini had from time to time. In 1969, there was no indication that rebellion would subside into a generic liberalism obsessed with body-building.

> (31) The camera tilts upward following the vertical shape of a castle in whose courtyard PC and the rest are tried. Amidst red flowers, ND watches the entire scene. Although we cannot hear the judge's voice (the bells are too loud), we can infer the harshness of the sentence by the defendants' devastated faces, who, with the exception of PC, seek religious comfort.

Following Julian's question about dreams and truth, the camera's upward movement reinforces the notion that truth is a matter of coming up, of surfacing from "the other scene."

ND returns as the interested observer with whom we are made to share our vision. Again, his gaze seems gratuitous and makes us wonder. The repetition of the shot of him amidst the flowers confirms that he is somehow outside of the gruesome events—the flowers are the only bright color in the entire episode. The bells that prevent us from

Porcile: *Herdhitze (Ugo Tognazzi) and Klotz (Alberto Lionello) celebrate the merger of their industries.* Courtesy of the Museum of Modern Art/Film Stills Archive.

hearing the judge's sentence are visually related to ND (see scene 21), whose presence is thereby imposed as a filter that mediates our experience of the film.

> (32) During the party celebrating the merger, Julian leaves the *Palazzo* and heads toward the pigsty. While on his way, he is hailed by a smiling peasant named Marracchione (Ninetto Davoli).

Playing both ND and Marracchione, Ninetto Davoli sutures the two stories and reveals their substantial unity. In Pasolini's visual idiolect, Ninetto Davoli represents an uncomplicated *joie de vivre* which Pasolini at once desires and condemns. *Porcile* is not the first case in which Pasolini gives Davoli the role of the innocent observer (see chapter 13, on *Edipo re*). Just as Davoli is the living sign of a life lived outside rational discourse, ND and Marracchione are, in a sense, outside both episodes. They are spectators to the events. If we remember that *Por-*

cile is a difficult film directed toward an intellectual public, the key role played by Ninetto Davoli is more than just a "delirious homage" to Pasolini's aesthetic ideal. It is a wishful attempt to relocate the subject of vision outside the difficult rational discourse which is the dominant mode of the film.

(33) A crowd of people gathers on the slopes of the volcano to attend the execution.

Given the explicit cruelty of some previous scenes and the look on the faces of the condemned, we expect a final horror.

(34) Julian enters the pigsty.

Needless to say, the pigsty is overlaid with the credits sequence. Far from indiscrete eyes, Julian sets out to do the one thing that he is now allowed to do.

(35) The execution requires a rather elaborate preparation. Big poles are inserted into the ground. While FC screams, PC impassively and meditatively repeats four times: "I killed my father, I ate human flesh, and I quiver with joy." Meanwhile, ND approaches him and listens to his words carefully. Only when the crowd leaves the execution site do we understand that the culprits, tied down to the poles, will be devoured by famished dogs.

The execution betrays the expectations built up by the long preparation. We are just given a single long shot of the staked bodies, while the dogs can hardly be seen.

PC's words, the only ones in the entire episode, confirm what we have long known: PC is a visual dramatization of Julian's unconscious. Slaying the father, cannibalism, and pleasure sum up "the other scene" as the exclusive locus of Freudian discourse.[13] Moreover, the image of PC staked to the ground cleverly illustrates Herdhitze's success: he has pinned down the transgressive potential of Julian's unconscious. PC/Julian's transgressions are now codified in sexual terms exclusively; they are, to use Deleuze and Guattari's terminology, territorialized.[14]

The last image of PC is an over-the-shoulder shot (rare in Pasolini) from the point of view of ND, who thereby rises to the role of privileged observer. While PC repeats his final statements, half of the frame is taken by the back of ND's head. He watches closely, attentively, and . . .

(36) A delegation of peasants interrupts the party in order to speak with "the stronger member" in the new alliance, Herdhitze. Speaking in the

name of the whole community, Marracchione, in tears, reports that Julian has been devoured by the pigs. Herdhitze inquires whether there are any traces of Julian's presence left in the pigsty. Marracchione replies that nothing, "not even a button, has survived the pigs' fury." The last image of the film is a frontal close- up of Herdhitze with his finger to his lips: "Shhh! Do not mention this to anyone."

ND/Marracchione's eyes now represent an entire social group: the fourth estate. The peasants make their appearance in the *Palazzo*, reporting a death that they neither judge nor understand. Will they comply with Herdhitze's request of silence? In the last image, Herdhitze is looking at us as well, demanding our silence and complicity. Will we comply?

In fact, the film's rhetorical strategy aims at making us want to denounce Herdhitze. *Porcile* is a compelling and clever attempt to recast realist filmmaking in the mode of a difficult cinema. *Teorema*, too, used this technique, taking as its subject matter the role of passion as the necessary complement to reason. *Porcile* now celebrates rational discourse as the powerful weapon that explains social and individual history. Pasolini's film tries to make the viewer work at piecing together the fragments of a picture, that is, it tries to foster what I called "the realist attitude." *Porcile* argues, visually, that there is an "other scene" with which we must reckon if we are to understand the ambiguities of the real. In addition, it offers a sharp, if allegorical, explanation of the wider historical context that contained the student movement and its new social logic. Finally, *Porcile* draws a symbolic picture of an intellect precariously situated at the intersection of history and metahistory. More than *Edipo re*, *Porcile* dramatizes Pasolini's recourse to both a Marxist and a Freudian grid to explain historical and personal events. Through the portrayal of Julian as someone who wants out of ideological commitment, Pasolini created a powerful autobiographical subtext and signals that he wants to enjoy his own "infinite repetitions of the same thing," disengaged from historical responsibilities. For all of these reasons—fostering a realist attitude in the viewer, attempting a non-naturalistic portrayal of reality, and revealing the reality of the author—*Porcile* represents the absolute zenith of "a certain realism."

After *Porcile*, "the infinite repetitions of the same thing" will predominate and "a certain realism" will fade away.

18

Medea

The young Jason is brought up by a wise centaur, Chiron, who tells him about his mythical lineage and the loss of the Golden Fleece to the inhabitant of Colchis. As a young man, Jason returns to his native Iolchos, in Tessaly, to reclaim the throne illegally usurped by his uncle Pelias. Pelias promises Jason the throne on condition that he bring back the Golden Fleece. Together with his Argonauts, Jason goes to the savage land of Colchis. Meanwhile, the barbaric people of Colchis perform a fertility ritual, sacrificing a young man and sprinkling the earth with his blood. Colchis' high priestess and the king's daughter, Medea, falls in love with Jason, helps him to steal the Fleece, and elopes with him, taking her brother Absyrtus with her. As they are followed by her father and his soldiers, she kills and dismembers Absyrtus, scattering his body along the way, so as to delay the pursuers. When Pelias refuses to keep his promise and give Jason back the throne, Jason goes to Corinth with Medea, where she has two sons by him. After a few years, Jason grows unhappy with the barbaric Medea and arranges to marry Glauce, Creon of Corinth's daughter. Deeply wounded, Medea yearns for revenge and sees in a vision how she can obtain it by using her magical powers. She thus executes her plan, the film virtually reshowing what she (and we) saw in her vision. She tricks Jason into believing that she is about to leave, makes love to him for the last time, and sends her two sons to her rival Glauce with a wedding dress as a gift. Glauce puts it on, is immediately seized by a strange fit, and dies in flames, soon followed by her father Creon. Finally, Medea kills her children, burns down the house, and even denies Jason the children's bodies, shouting amidst the flames: "Nothing is possible anymore!"

> *Both neurosis and psychosis are thus the expression of a rebellion on the part of the id against the external world, of its unwillingness—or, if one prefers, its incapacity—to adapt itself to exigencies of reality, to* Ananke *(Necessity).*
>
> Sigmund Freud

Pasolini's phase of "unpopular" and "aristocratic" experimentation ended in 1970 with *Medea* and *Appunti per un'Orestiade Africana* (next chapter). *Edipo re* joined autobiography, history, and myth in a very original way. *Teorema* dealt with the crisis of realism/reality by means of an allegorical tale of passion as the force which can make absolute what the subject knows to be relative. *Porcile* depicted the dilemma of a subject caught between historical consciousness and the temptation of escaping into metahistory. With *Medea*, Pasolini took a final leap into the depths of myth and forsook his capacity to evoke/provoke contemporary reality as he had in the previous three films. Everything in *Medea* is static, as if frozen in a hieratic gesture. Everything must be static, because *Medea* is the work of a man who has lost faith in history and finds shelter in the Manichaean myth of a timeless conflict between irreconcilable opposites. Such a decisive flight from history is hardly the ideal terrain for "a certain realism." But Pasolini's realist desire is so compelling that *Medea* contains a most explicit, if wishful, reference to its own realism.

The opening sequence in *Medea* depicts the education of Jason by the centaur. The first three lessons are imparted by a fabulous being, half man, half horse. By the time Jason reaches the age of reason, the centaur loses his fabulous double nature and becomes a man. Shortly before letting Jason go into the real world, the centaur predicts his journey in search of the Golden Fleece:

> You will go to a distant land across the sea. You will find a world whose use of reason is far different from our own. Life there is very realistic, for only those who are mythical are realistic; and only those who are realistic are mythical. That is what is foreseen by our divine reason. What it cannot foresee, unfortunately, are all the mistakes it will lead you to. And they will be many!

From the standpoint of the diegesis, the centaur's speech does not need to define Medea's world as "realistic." "Mythical" is enough. The association of "realistic" and "mythical" does not enhance Jason's understanding of what he will find. Such an association, instead, functions as a prescription for the viewer. Pasolini wants his "aristocratic" public to know that he regards his mythical phase as yet another turn on the road to "a certain realism."[1] As "myth" is probably the word most often associated with Pasolini's cinema, it may be useful to elucidate what role that myth may have played in his work at this particular stage in his life.

Pasolini had already associated myth and realism in 1965, when he suggested that Bertolucci's style "is derived from Rossellinian neorealism and the mythic realism of some younger master" such as himself (*HE*, 180). As Marcus points out, such a definition makes sense only in the light of Pasolini's stance against naturalism.[2] Images, whether in reality or in a film, are intrinsically mythical because they are outside *logos*, because their mode of communication exceeds rationality. Whereas films in the language of prose (commercial cinema, neorealism, classic realism) tend to eliminate that element of irrationality and fix the meaning of images, Pasolini's own style is "mythical" in that it seeks to enhance the nonrational aspect of the visible. Mythical realism, opposing as it does naturalism, eschews superficial details and accurate description in order to seek what is essential.

In *Medea*, however, the centaur's statement is no mere allusion to a nonnaturalist style. It is the epigrammatic enunciation of Pasolini's idea that realism must now go against the philosophy of the Enlightenment, that it must stop the advance of rationality at the expense of mythical thinking. During his third lesson, the centaur voices the idea that Pasolini himself kept repeating in all of his contemporary articles and interviews: "There is nothing natural in nature, my boy, keep that clearly in mind. When nature begins to seem natural, it will be all over, and something else will begin. Farewell sky, farewell sea!" It was the Enlightenment that stripped the world of its mythical halo and reduced the entire realm of non-human reality to a state of nature to be scientifically studied and technologically mastered. In Pasolini's terms, the philosophy of the Enlightenment could be defined as reason severed from passion: pure reason. It must be noted that Pasolini does not reject reason per se, but a specific, mutant form of rationality which, in Adorno and Horkheimer's seminal assessment of the dialectic of the Enlightenment, goes by the name of *ratio*.[3] Ratio is rational activity deprived of any moral goal and transformed into a pure instrument of domination. The distinction between reason and ratio is important, because many critics assume that Pasolini's mythical phase implied a wholesale rejection of rationality. In fact, Pasolini's emphasis on myth is itself a product of his own reasoning, of his ideological labors, of his own musings on the state of things. By harnessing "a certain realism" to myth, Pasolini is fighting his old battle to broaden rational activity to include states of awe and nonreason.

Pasolini's involvement with mythical thinking had other, more personal motivations as well. The following statements taken from three separate interviews indicate that a most definite shift was taking place in his life: "My future has frighteningly and suddenly become reduced"; "There is a real psychological change in my personality due to my older age"; "I no longer have any kind of hope, be it practical or ideological."[4] Unfortunately, age does not normally get the same epistemological attention as the triad class/gender/race, and it is therefore hard to speculate on its effects. Nevertheless, we are faced with a man approaching fifty who can no longer believe in historical change, a man who perceives a pattern of recourses in history. While personal in its specific phenomenology, what happens to Pasolini is inscribed in a general state that makes people see or want to see things from a different, "wiser" perspective. It is yet another confirmation that truth is positional and is lived in the body. Pasolini's need for a new vision found occasional complicity in Freud's Eros vs. Thanatos, in the metahistorical elements of the Christian God, and in Levi-Strauss's idea of unvariable structures of the Mind. But his humanist formation, his being "a force of the past," led him towards a valorization of Greek myth. As many before him (Nietzsche, Heidegger, Freud, to name but a few) had done, Pasolini returned to Greece, to what Western culture considers the beginning of it all. He came to the conclusion that we, in the modern world, subsist on the remnants of images by which the Greek world had tried to explain the world. In other words, he strove to prove that historical change can be understood in terms of Greek myths. At this point Jung came to his rescue, for Pasolini's encounter with Jung's works facilitated his synthesis of myth, realism, and cinema.

At the end of the infinite regression of a mind capable of disproving just about anything, Pasolini found a resting place in Jungian myth. Reading Jung offered Pasolini a theory of the archetypes that would satisfy his need for a static vision of history. After the intense allegories of passion *within* history (*Edipo re, Teorema, Porcile*), Pasolini longed for an absolute metahistorical reality behind the surface, for a static universe crystallized into a formula. The God of Catholicism was of no help, because Pasolini had rejected what Jung called "the monotheism of consciousness."[5] Pasolini needed to find an ultimate principle ambiguous enough to generate multiple differences, endless variations, and play. And Jungian myth is just that, the return to Greek polytheism, the fantasy of different gods. One day you sacrifice on the altar of Apollonian beauty, another day you get lost in the Dionysian wilderness.

Moreover, Jungian myth satisfied Pasolini's anticapitalist stance because mythical thinking is not practical thinking. Mythical explanations are not etiologies, causal explanations, name tags. Rather, they are metaphors, and as such they rest on a permanent ambiguity. But, more important, myths, in a Jungian perspective, are ways of seeing, of imaging. More than Freud, Jung maintained that "the psyche consists essentially of images" and that "psyche creates reality every day."[6] There is sense in which, for Jung, not even a psychosis engenders a loss of reality. Rather, it creates another reality. For Jung, reality is made up of the images that our psyche creates, images that speak a mythic language because they elude literalism. Pasolini's theory of the cinematic image could not have found a better ally, for Jungian myth challenged him to find the appropriate images to express the mythical forces at work behind everyday reality.

And behind one's own bodily reality. From a mythical perspective, the body stops being the locus of scientific explanations and becomes a citadel of metaphoric images. Oedipus and Medea, Tiresias and Jason were also, in Pasolini as well as in Greek mythology, ways of giving images to instincts and drives. In this respect, too, the reading of Jung had the effect of confirming Pasolini's ideas about cinema. In the essay "The Spiritual Problem of Modern Man," Jung even discusses cinema within the context of the "rediscovery of the body after its long depreciation in the name of the spirit."[7] A film, he argues, "makes it possible to experience without danger all the excitement, the passion and desirousness which must be repressed in a humanitarian ordering of life." In sum, not only did myth provide a sense that there is an archetypal reality, but it also suggested that such a reality was best expressed through images and not words.

Unfortunately, however, the potentially fertile incorporation of mythical thinking into "a certain realism" did not always produce the desired effect, at least not in *Medea*.

The Slow Demise of "a Certain Realism"

Loosely based on Euripides' and Seneca's tragedies, *Medea* is a film about conflict, about opposites which never coincide except when in love or at war. The idea of duality is immediately established in the half-man, half-horse figure of the centaur. It is then taken up by the transformation of the centaur into a man, the former signifying the world of myth, the latter a universe flatly explained by *ratio*. *Ratio triumphans*, however, does not succeed in effacing its mythical past and the fabulous is not totally superseded, but we find out midway in the film that it coexists beside the human form. The conflict implicit in the figure of the centaur finds full expression in the figures of Jason and Medea.

Jason is the hero of the moment (the *mens momentanea*) who not only has lost his sense of the metaphysical, but doesn't even ask himself questions of this sort. He is the resolute technician whose search is aimed towards success.[8] Interestingly, Pasolini did not choose an intellectual for the role of Jason, but opted for Giuseppe Gentile, an athlete who had won Italy two gold medals during the 1968 Olympic Games. The casting of Gentile as Jason indicates that Pasolini considered the "new bourgeoisie" (yuppies) the contemporary embodiment of the spirit of the Enlightenment. Gentile's tanned skin and muscles indicate vigor, exertion, and power, a life spent out in the sun. Throughout the film, the camera concentrates on his body more than on his head, so that medium shots replace the habitual close-ups. Young and beautiful, with no sign of existential anguish on his face, Jason is an iconic translation of the "fitness and fun" ideology, of the hedonism so rabidly attacked in Pasolini's essays on cultural criticism.

Medea (Maria Callas) represents, instead, "the archaic, hieratic, religious universe," the barbaric and prehistoric elements of civilization.[9] Considering that this is the world whose disappearance Pasolini regretted, he failed to create a powerful and compelling Medea. He chose Callas because of her "barbaric features" and it was, in my opinion, the biggest casting error in his career.[10] Callas brought to the character of Medea all the glamour of her public image—something which Pasolini, aware as he was of what actors are in real life, should have taken into account. To be sure, Medea/Callas fulfilled Pasolini's desire to paint a strong image of Jason's opposite. Unlike Jason, she was pale, middle-aged, frozen in a blank stupor which was meant to signify a life spent inside, literally and metaphorically. The obsessive close-ups of her expressionless face (for the first time Pasolini indulges in profile shots) and the stiffness of her movements, encumbered by heavy costumes, evoke the immobility of someone asking herself one question too many. The problem, however, is that Medea is not meant to signify intellectual life, but primitive existence in touch with a "nature that is not natural." With the exception of the scene in which she paces up and down the room followed by a chorus of women, the character of Medea suggests more rigidity than primitive vitality. And Callas fails to convey the sense of passion that, after all, Medea had to signify, especially in view of her opposition to Jason.

As a film, *Medea* fails because Pasolini was trying too hard to make an intellectual film "based on a theoretical foundation, on the history of religion."[11] Derived mostly from the reading of Mircea Eliade, the theoretical foundation of the film is the contrast between the line and the circle as metaphors for historical development. Jason is visually symbolized by perspective, as emphasized by the linear disposition of his men along the beach. He stands for what Eliade calls civilization of the line, a world view which regards history as straighforward progress: Western teleology. Medea, instead, is defined by the wheel that she spins and by her woeful remark that the Argonauts' camp has not been built on a proper center: she is the civilization of the circle, a culture characterized by cyclical motions, the eternal return of the seasons. The circle and the line, *Medea* suggests, face each other *ab aeterno*, so that the result is an archetypal conflict, a "hieratic vision of an immobile reality."

In spite of this intriguing theoretical foundation, *Medea* does not succeed in providing analogical links between its diegetic world and contemporary social reality. Pasolini intended to use the past as "a metaphor for the present," but there is nothing in the film which prompts the viewer to pursue this metaphorical lead.[12] Only intellectual abstraction and familiarity with his intentions allow the viewer to see in Jason and Medea two metaphors for the present. Similarly, only a public familiar with all the aspects of the myth can follow the chain of events. In *Teorema* and *Porcile* the public was certainly asked to make an intellectual effort and to work at piecing together the story, but everyone was, so to speak, on an equal footing. No previous knowledge was required; all that was needed was intellectual desire. Here, even the most well-intentioned spectator flounders in the film's excess of elliptical narration. For example, the characters of Glauce (Margareth Clementi) and Creon (Massimo Girotti) are not given any substantive existence: they come out of the blue with their funny costumes and rigid expressions, so that we cannot understand what they stand for unless we already know the story.[13] Pasolini is no longer demanding of his public a pendular motion between text and reality. In perfect keeping with the art for art's sake spirit of this film (a long way from his other productions!), he does not address intellectuals here, but erudites.

Medea is also the least autobiographical of Pasolini's films. To be sure, his favorite themes are here. But one does not feel the presence of a problematic author confronting himself with and within the material. For the first time, Pasolini has attempted to efface himself: "I was an objective author, telling a story in an objective manner."[14] The question then becomes, Is the film successful in its own terms, as an "objective" portrayal of an archetypal conflict?

The answer is no. For one thing the conceptual message is muddled. On the one hand, *Medea* attempts to evoke a timeless, eternal conflict and the persistence of old forms of being (the centaur, Medea) juxtaposed to the new ones. On the other hand, the film suggests that Jason's world is slowly destroying Medea's, so that the line triumphs over the circle after all. As often happens with myth and archetypes, the signifiers are so open and all-encompassing that the possibile permutations are endless and contradictions efface one another. *Medea*'s mythical gaze seeks to distill the essence, to find the absolute, to capture those gestures that belong to "a certain realism" if, and only if, they are captured with the awareness that they are not final. *Medea* fails to unearth the mythical Ur-code of historical progression because there is no such thing. Myths are metaphors people live by. In this respect *Edipo re* was successful because it illustrated the myth by which Pasolini lived his own life. When it comes to an entire culture, we certainly may attempt to capture its spirit, its myth, but then we had better be careful in delineating its historical contours so that *some* historical specificity is preserved. And, most of all, we ought to take the visual distortion caused by our own myths into consideration. We must look at ourselves looking. Self-consciousness and positional awareness are a must when we try to make generalizations about cultures. *Medea* fails as a realist project because Pasolini failed to include himself in the picture, as he did in the contemporary *Appunti per un'Orestiade Africana* which, instead, is a small realist masterpiece.

Medea signals its author's abandonment of the ideological attitude and historical awareness without which, Pasolini once argued, there can be no realism. Pasolini did not ask himself whether or not the idea of a Greek myth explaining universal history and the life of primitive civilization was not in fact an act of cultural imperialism. After all, the idea of the "circle" can be a convenient Western projection onto other cultures, an offshoot of the paternalistic notion that the Third World has not gone through historical evolution. In *Medea* Pasolini's own myth (innocence vs. history) got loose, free from the duties of ideological and positional awareness.

Medea begins and ends with a freeze-frame of the rising sun on a marine landscape. The prosaic image encapsulates the film's search for a National Geographic beauty and signals that any splendid remake of Greek myth is like a postcard for erudite tourists. Ironically, Pasolini himself, in one of the poems written during the shooting of the film, denounced and condemned the effect that tourism and Western money were having on Turkey. Of course, he meant "vulgar" tourists with Polaroids or Nikons. And he presumed that his own case, with a movie camera loaded with Kodak Eastmancolor, was different. In fact,

Medea, with its alleged ethnographic accuracy and its use of real Third World natives portraying themselves as an endangered species to be nostalgically contemplated, evokes the Other only to subsume it. In this respect, *Medea* is the precursor of Herzog's *Fitzcarraldo* (1981), a film in which an immense amount of German capital enlists Peruvian Indians and forces them to work (and die, literally) in fulfillment of the director's exotic wish. Only a relatively limited budget prevented Pasolini from being excessively burdened with *his* dreams (*A Burden of Dreams* is the documentary that Les Blank shot on the set of *Fitzcarraldo*).

Pathological Reflections

Once the failure of *Medea* as a "mythical realist" film has been established, it is possible to recognize that the film is not without its intense moments. They all occur prior to the telling of the classic tragedy and are Pasolini's own invention, proving the hypothesis that Greek myth enabled him to vent his own preoccupations. For all of its exoticism, the scene of the human sacrifice is compelling, especially in light of Pasolini's likely identification with the victim of ritualistic violence. There are no words spoken. The editing is fast-paced and alternates medium-long shots with close-ups of the participants. We do not know why or how the victim has been chosen. Coming as it does right after the equation of myth with realism, the sacrifice begs to be taken as essence, a visual reflection upon the inescapable violence with which a society chooses to purify itself. It is highly doubtful that Jason's society will be much different in this respect, for every society has its human sacrifices, its ritualistic scapegoats; Pasolini clearly perceived himself to be one.

The film's most emotionally intense sequence, however, is found elsewhere. It is not, as one might expect, Medea's murder of her two children which, due to Callas's lack of expression and the little interest Pasolini showed in the event, turns out to be a letdown. Rather, it is Aeetes' (Medea's father's) sudden discovery of his son Absyrtus, dead and dismembered. Pasolini fleshes out what in Euripides is merely a grievous recollection of Medea without any reference to the father. In fact Pasolini even alters the original myth, according to which Aeetes deceived Jason and violently opposed his quest for the Golden Fleece. In *Medea*, instead, Aeetes seems to be the peaceful leader of an archaic peasant community.

After Medea and Jason abduct the Fleece, we see Aeetes' pursuit in the magnificent desert of the Cappadocian highlands. By means of a few long shots, the film establishes the idea of the chase and then cuts

to Jason's cart. We see Medea grabbing an ax and killing her own
brother. The camera does not show any blood, but it indulges in a
close-up of Medea hitting him several times. She then picks up her
brother's head and throws it on the road to delay the pursuit of Aeetes
and his party. At this point, Pasolini abandons Medea and her fellow
fugitives to dedicate several minutes to the portrayal of what happens
on Aeetes' side. We see the king and his men stopping and pausing in
front of the head. However exotic, the music sustains the intense emotion of this moment, for we hear a slow lament rising through a few
simple chords played on an Indian sitar.

The camera concentrates on Aeetes, who wears typically Pasolinian
headgear that practically covers his eyes and makes him the locus of
the partially obstructed vision so often encountered in his films—a
vision which always has positive, albeit slightly tragic, connotations.
It is a vision that always indicates the observation of something important. Pasolini's interest in Aeetes' vision is confirmed by the rest of
the sequence, in which Aeetes' soldiers tenderly pick up his son's dismembered body. On three different occasions, we get a POV shot of
a dismembered limb and then a close-up of the king's face. The second time that this combination occurs, Aeetes lifts the leather patch
that is dangling in front of his eyes to get a better look. And the third
time, we see him raising his hand to cover his eyes, the despairing
gesture of child Oedipus.

Pasolini then cuts briefly to Jason and his group setting their boat to
sea, as if to continue the narrative as quickly as possible, and we immediately return to Aeetes, who is coming back home. The horsemen
dismount and Aeetes slowly walks toward his wife with their son's
head in his hands. After a low-angle close-up of Aeetes' wife reminiscent of the Mother in *Il Vangelo secondo Matteo*, the camera zooms in
the king's face to his semi-covered eyes. Collective grief then erupts,
with black-clad women crying in ritualistic mourning. This two-minute
sequence ends with a medium shot of the king at the center of the
frame, his eyes peeking through the visor.

Pasolini's compassionate interest in the father's point of view bears
scrutiny. It can be partially explained by the figure of his son, Medea's
brother, whom the narrative had already singled out as a beautiful and
effeminate man. He smiled at Jason when he first met him; he helped
Medea steal the Fleece without asking any questions. His curly hair
and his disarmingly naive look made him a Ninetto-type, an icon of innocent proximity to nature, but with more of an androgynous physiognomy. His warm, smiling presence during the initial sacrifice, his
physiognomic difference from the rest of the crowd, and his exchange
of glances with the victim all contribute to transforming the human

sacrifice into an allegory of legalized violence against socially designated victims such as homosexuals.

Another explanation for Pasolini's interest in Aeetes' grief might be
the shift in perspective provoked by older age. Pasolini now feels that
he belongs to the generation of the fathers. Whereas *Edipo re* touched
upon the slaying of the father, Pasolini is now concerned with the killing of the sons—in connection, perhaps, with his contemporary love/
hate declarations for the younger generation. But there is more. In
addition to these contingent motives, one finds Pasolini's usual fascination with images of dismemberment. It is often in relation to ritualistic
or excessive violence that Pasolini reaches some of his most intense
moments. The attention given to Aeetes' grief, the repeated use of the
figure with partially obscured vision, and the passion of these moments
(as opposed to the coldness with which Medea's grief is portrayed) are
also the consequence of Pasolini's interest in violations of the body.
The mythical context of this film makes it the ideal terrain for an examination of the recurrent figure of abject imagery in his films.

In addition to contributing to the sexual liberation of the screen,
Pasolini was also the director of the graphic portrayal of violence and
horror. He started with the beating of Maddalena by the Neapolitan
pimps in *Accattone*, an episode which, if not graphic, is nonetheless
controversial because of the Bach sound track. And it ended, of course,
in the visual holocaust of *Salò*, where violence takes cinematic form
in a matter-of-fact way, without epic overtones. Dismemberment, decapitation, and crucifixion are common enough in his films to beg for
an explanation. I shall call the horror-provoking image in Pasolini's
films "the pathological image." The recurrence of the pathological
image can best be analyzed through its three areas of impact: (1) the
spectator, (2) the text, and (3) the author.

(1) Pathological images in Pasolini's films do not have the same sensationalist, crowd-attracting function as they do in much commercial
cinema. The violence in his films is often of the kind that spectators
find repulsive, the kind that we find in "splatter" films, with the substantial difference that Pasolini does not attract horror fans. There certainly is a desire to *épater le bourgeois* behind the pathological image.
Pasolini wants to provoke the audience, he wants to force it to sit
through a few minutes of his "horrendous universe." The pathological
image on the screen, however, also has a "pedagogical" function. There
is a dark side to our culture that emerges every day in the images
of televised horror, wars, torture, and crime. But when going to the
movies, most viewers shun pathological imagery unless it is the highly
spectacular "FX" type that exorcises pathology by giving it a comic-

strip quality. By forcing spectators to acknowledge the existence of a certain type of visual imagery, Pasolini's films attempt to cure them of the tyranny of "good taste." Pasolini believes that behind the surface of every Jason, that is, of every enlightened, modern person, there lurks a repressed Medea where violence and transgression reign supreme. The public projection of such repression would then act as an invitation to dance in the dark, to accept the encounter with darkness instead of shutting one's eyes.

(2) From the standpoint of the text, images of mutilation have an obvious realistic value. They show what is prohibited, what the censors want to cut, what many people do not want to see. In this respect, the pathological is part of a constellation of images to be unmasked, like the lower classes and sexuality. At the same time, decapitation and dismemberment, wounds and blisters, act as reminders of the body or, better yet, of corporeal vulnerability. By emphasizing what can happen to the body, Pasolini's cinema inevitably teaches that punishment and suffering result in bodily mutilation and that all intense communication stems from images of corporeality. And by suggesting that the sight of physical violence can be a valuable, if not necessary, experience, his films evoke the ghost of an unpleasant reality.

(3) The pathological image becomes even more interesting when considered from the point of view of the author. What do we make of Pasolini's use of sick imagery? Can we use the pathological image in our turn? Pasolini's fascination with pathology is most readily explained by the meaning that passion (pathos) has in Catholic culture, where it is first and foremost the image of a suffering Christ. As the tremendous image of a crucified Christ dominates the Catholic imagination, there is a sense in which Pasolini is not doing anything new, but is simply bringing out a certain pathology already present in our culture. From the fifth century on, religious art indulged in the portrayal of Christ on the cross, wounded, nails through His flesh, pierced by lance and thorns; of martyred saints and women's *pietas*. Such images were meant to have a curative, energizing effect on those exposed to them. Such art was meant to cure believers' souls by exposing them to the inevitability of suffering and its redemptive potential, by encouraging them to regard pain as a noble means to achieve a superior state. At once open wound and cure, Catholicism has been the most prolific purveyor of psychopathological imagery in Western history.

Once connected with Catholic mythology, the pathological image acquires an intriguing dimension. It is meant as a cure; it offers a healthy, spiritual suffering. Christ, however, is but one of many possible pathological images. His is the one with which we are most familiar and which we most easily accept. But mythology, too, is an inexhaustible source of pathological imagery which can have curative powers, as in Jungian psychotherapy. It is no accident that Pasolini's pathological imagery increased at a time when he started reading Jung. My recourse to Jungian archetypal theory as re-elaborated by James Hillman in his impressive *tour de force* on "soul-making," *Re-visioning Psychology*, will clarify the subjective importance of the pathological image.

Specifying that by the word "soul" he means "a perspective rather than a substance, a viewpoint towards things rather than a thing itself," Hillman concerns himself with the various paths to "soul-making."[15] Human beings are not born with a soul, but they may or may not choose to construct psychic depths by making flesh and body into soul. Hillman distinguishes four major ways in which "soul-making" can take place. There is "personifying," the act of giving a bodily image to instincts, desires, and feelings, so that one's inner life becomes a mythical battlefield; "psychologizing," the act of seeing through phenomena in order to capture their essence; and "de-humanizing," as the practical realization that our psychological afflictions do not depend on us alone, but rather are positional. The fourth way is "pathologizing," "the psyche's autonomous ability to create illness, morbidity, disorder, abnormality, and suffering in any aspect of its behavior and to experience and imagine life through this deformed and afflicted perspective."[16] According to Hillman, all this is medically pathological only in the eyes of traditional psychiatry. In fact, he argues, "pathologizing is itself a way of seeing"; "the pathological experience gives an indelible sense of soul, unlike those we may get through love or beauty, through nature, community, or religion."[17] Only when they fall apart do things open up into new meanings: "While pathologizing, the psyche is going through a reversion into a mythical style of consciousness" which many condemn "as regression to magical, primitive levels," thereby forgetting that "the psyche reverts not only to escape reality but to find another reality."[18]

> The crazy artist, the daft poet, and the mad professor are neither romantic clichés nor antibourgeois postures. They are metaphors for the intimate relation between pathologizing and imagination. Pathologizing processes are a source of imaginative work, and the work provides a container for the pathologizing process.[19]

Pasolini's fascination with ancient mythology makes new sense, and so does the recurrence of the pathological image. Sophocles and Euripides spoke the same pathological language, for "only in mythology does pathology receive an adequate mirror since myths speak the same distorted language."[20] Greek myth, or the Christian myth for that matter, provided Pasolini with a culturally legitimate outlet for his "pedagogical" desire to pathologize the cinema as a private and public experience of soul-making.

19

Appunti per un'Orestiade Africana

Like *Appunti per un film sull'India*, *Appunti per un'Orestiade Africana* (Notes for an African Orestes, 1970) consists of audio-visual notes for a proposed film that would never be made. It skillfully combines three different types of filmic material: (1) Documentary footage shot in Tanzania, with Pasolini's voice-over either commenting upon the images in an ethnographic mode or explaining his intentions to adapt Aeschylus' *Orestes* into a contemporary African setting. These two themes blend in the search for faces and places that would fit his purpose. (2) An interview with some African students at the university of Rome. Pasolini sounds them out on the pertinence of the comparison he established between the institution of Greek democracy in Athens and the newly acquired independence of many African states. (3) A twelve-minute jazz session in which the musicians who composed (Gato Barbieri) and performed (Gato Barbieri, sax; Donald Moye, drums; and Marcello Melio, bass) Cassandra's prophetic dream from the *Orestes* accompany the singers Yvonne Murray and Archie Savage.

> *Ecology is validating the reality of all things being linked together. It's showing us that the human reality and the other realities of the Earth are really inseparable.*
>
> Dean James Parks Morton

After the credits have unfolded on a map of Africa on the right, and a copy of Aeschylus' *Orestes* appears on the left, we see Pasolini's unmistakable features reflected in a shop window.[1] He wears dark glasses and holds a camera to his eyes: "Here I am with the camera reflected in the glass window of a shop in an African city." We cut to a medium shot of the entire window obscured by Pasolini's shadow: "I have obviously come here to film, but to film what? Not a documentary. Not a feature picture. I have come to shoot some notes for a film on Aeschylus' *Orestes*."

A most unusual and beautiful film, *Appunti per un'Orestiade Africana* thus opens with an air of uncertainty and self-reflexiveness, indeed the ideal mode for a white director shooting in the Third World. Shot in the same period as *Medea*, *Appunti per un'Orestiade Africana* is equally concerned with the idea of proving the universal validity of Greek myth. Unlike *Medea*, however, *Appunti per un'Orestiade Africana* deconstructs such a project by means of a self-awareness which marks a peak in Pasolini's "certain realism." Whereas *Medea* preached its message from an erudite pedestal, *Appunti per un'Orestiade Africana* engages the viewer in being a witness to Pasolini's reasoning. In the first ten minutes of the film, he briefly summarizes Aeschylus' *Orestes* and states his intentions. He then provides an indirect critique of his own project by means of an interview with African students. From this moment on, the film's images are no longer completely bound to the story. They are just images that may or may not remind us of Agamemnon. The judgment is ours.

The *Orestes* narrates how Orestes decides to kill his own mother Clytemnestra, who murdered his father Agamemnon after he returned from Troy. After the matricide, Orestes is tormented by the Erinyes, infernal deities charged with punishing crimes against the family. Athena, the goddess of Reason, intercedes in favor of Orestes by having him judged in a regular trial by, as Pasolini says, "the first tribunal in history." Defended by Athena herself, Orestes is acquitted of the crime, but the Erinyes, although defeated, do not disappear. Instead they are transformed into the Eumenides, who represent the survival of the dark and irrational underworld in the new world of Reason. According to Pasolini:

> *Orestes* synthesizes African history over the last hundred years: the sudden and almost divine passing from a "savage" state to a civil and democratic one. The series of kings, who dominated the African lands (and who in their turn were dominated by the dark Erinyes) in the atrocious and century-old stagnation of a tribal and prehistoric culture, have suddenly been swept away. And Reason, almost *motu proprio*, has established democratic institutions. We must add that now, in the sixties, the years of the "Third World," the years of "negritude," the burning problem and question is the transformation of the Erinyes into Eumenides.

Aeschylus' genius foreshadowed all of this. All advanced people today agree that archaic civilizations—superficially referred to in terms of folklore—must not be forgotten, despised, or betrayed. Rather, they ought to be absorbed within the new civilization, integrating it, making it specific, concrete, historical. The terrifying and fantastic divinities of African prehistory should undergo the same process as the Erinyes, they should become Eumenides.[2]

However ethnocentric, the idea of black Africa as an external force capable of injecting a different world view into the pale veins of Western rationalism bears scrutiny. Concerned with the fast-paced modernization of the newly born African states, Pasolini asked himself the question: Will the consumer syndrome destroy their way of life and corrupt the Africans? Or will *we* learn something from them? As a film in which there is not one single white face (except two musicians and Pasolini), *Appunti per un'Orestiade Africana* makes no bones about where we should stand. Pasolini's farsightedness epitomizes the commitment of a director who obsessively raised the issue of racial difference in his films beginning with *La rabbia*. Today, the massive African immigration to Italy and the rise in racism reveals the timeliness of Pasolini's desire to know more about black Africa.[3]

The problem, of course, is whether or not "Aeschylus' genius foreshadowed all this." With this statement, Pasolini's humanistic formation betrays its potential for ethnocentrism, for he was imposing Greek myth on the Other's history—indeed performing a sort of cultural colonialism. *Appunti per un'Orestiade Africana*, however, has an antidote to this: Pasolini's discussion of his own project with the African students in Rome. Visually, the students' pensive faces are introduced when we as yet do not know who they are, in what seems a cutaway shot just after Pasolini finishes summarizing the *Orestes*. It is as if their presence were haunting Pasolini's storytelling. A few minutes later, we understand who they are and what their role in the film is. "Now you have seen my notes," says Pasolini, "and I would like to ask you a few questions on this project." Although only some of the students reply, the camera mercilessly explores all of their faces and we can read on them the shadow of many doubts.

Most of the students' answers diplomatically say that, yes, they see a remote connection between African development and *Orestes*, but that Pasolini should not push the analogy too far and should also be careful in handling the discourse on tribalism. An Ethiopian student soon exposes Pasolini's Eurocentric myopia by remarking that Africa is not a nation but an immense continent with different histories and cultures. It is an embarrassing moment, for, along with Pasolini, white viewers must confront their own habit of lumping the many African realities into one convenient password. A little later, the same student will find the courage to say that he sees no relation betwen Orestes' experience and theirs.

After hearing another student, who softens the tone of his colleague's denial but basically expresses the same reservations, we go back to Africa, with Pasolini illustrating the role his images would have had in his adapation of the *Orestes*. The students, however, soon reappear for a second round of interviews that furthers the gap between their conception and his misconception. A student who had previously expressed a mild approval of Pasolini's project remarks that "one cannot say that Europeans have brought democracy to Africa in the same way that Athena in the *Orestes* gave democracy to the Athenians." Recognizing the truth of such an observation, Pasolini replies: "When I say democracy, I mean formal democracy," an answer that unwittingly encapsulates the problems contained in his unconditional faith in Greek myth. Pasolini's mythical perspective is only concerned with *forms*, and it therefore establishes similarities between events and cultures on a purely abstract, quasi-structuralist basis. The students' criticism suggests that historical specificity matters and that one has to find the right balance between metahistorical and historical perspectives, in order to avoid the opposite dangers of teleology and relativism.

Mythology must meet ideology, an encounter at the heart of *Appunti per un'Orestiade Africana*. Held in check by the self-criticism implicit in the interview with the students, the rest of the film merits both aesthetic and ideological appreciation. Using high-contrast black and white film, Pasolini exhibits his usual skill in the choice of faces: his reflections on the black physiognomy of Greek myth are captivating. The visual translation of the Erinyes, a sequence of thirteen shots of trees and plants bent by the wind, is also shown with great aesthetic effect. The images of laborers in the fields and of objects such as utensils and boats lying in the solitude of a black sun are torturously elegiac. There is a home-movie quality to *Appunti per un'Orestiade Africana*, a sense of enthusiasm at the rediscovery of what a good image with the right sound track can do. When we cut from the face of a student to the ominous silhouette of a baobab, and Gato Barbieri's saxophone weaves an air of Latin jazz around it, then we are brought back to the essence of cinema. Seen from the standpoint of the present time, when video cameras are becoming increasingly accessible to middle-class pockets, *Appunti per un'Orestiade Africana* suggests that we can all create beautiful collages of images and sounds, just as we can all take audio-visual notes on our trips.

Appunti per un'Orestiade Africana deserves a unique place in Pasoli-

ni's filmography for its candor and honesty. Take, for example, the
Ethiopian student who denies the validity of the project. After he
states his case, the camera does not ignore him, but repeatedly brings
his features back to us, as if to remind us of his dissent. As Pasolini's
authorial voice thus becomes more vulnerable, the film wanders and
takes risks. A twelve-minute sequence of music and singing is a
courageous attempt to bestow a diegetic status on the sound track,
something vaguely reminiscent of what Godard had done two years
earlier in *One Plus One* (1968). Similarly, the passages from Aeschylus' *Orestes* read aloud signal less erudition than experimentation and
are gracefully integrated in the film by virtue of its freewheeling structure. Pasolini experiments with both content and form, giving the
whole an unusual freshness which is all the more surprising if we consider that at the same time he was also packaging the unbearable
Medea.

In the context of *Appunti per un'Orestiade Africana*, Pasolini's habitual use of the words "real" and "realistic" cannot bother us, not even
the sophisticated antirealists among us, for we know just what they
mean. For example, at one point Pasolini says: "My film wants to have
a folk quality and I want to spread the chorus to real, realistic situations." Meanwhile, the camera is intent on showing us tools and huts
and the faraway silhouette of a man who does not want to be photographed. Reality resists becoming an image, but it's there. No one
would feel like quibbling over the meaning of "real" here, for we
know, or, better yet, we feel what Pasolini is attempting to do: he does
not want to have Eddie Murphy playing an African king. The same
holds true for the breathtaking newsreel sequences from the Biafran
war, which Pasolini thought he would include as a visual translation of
the Trojan war. We see the execution of a "rebel" by a firing squad,
the last tremors on a blindfolded face and a bound body. This is a real
execution. The heaped-up bodies are real. My body sees it, feels goose
bumps, has a lump in its throat. To argue that Pasolini mistook the
code of cinema for the code of reality would be intellectualist bravado.

Black Is Green

With *Appunti per un'Orestiade Africana*, Pasolini again takes up
his favorite theme—the dualism between the rational and the
nonrational—and situates it in a self-conscious, mythical perspective.
If we lift the film from the context of Pasolini's filmography and graft it
onto the intertextual space constituted by New Age philosophy and
feminist theology, we come upon something of great moment: the

Erinyes as symbol of what ought to be preserved from the ancient world and incorporated into the new.

Called by Aeschylus "children of Eternal Night" and by Sophocles "Daughters of the Earth and Shadows," the Erinyes were born to Gaea, the Earth Goddess, who had been fertilized by the blood of Uranus, the Sky.[4] They were symbolic stand-ins for an ancestral feminine spirit which countered the masculine powers of aseptic reasoning (Athena, the goddess of reason, was only nominally feminine, for she was born of Zeus's head). Pasolini's film then advocates the return of feminine nocturnal deities linked with the cult of the Earth. My contention is that *Appunti per un'Orestiade Africana*, with its tentative integration of mythology and politics, reveals the extent to which Pasolini's work was before its time. Historically, the counterculture had not yet produced the discourse of the Earth Goddess within which to articulate his passionate defense of past values.[5] Above all, the Green Movement, which would have made Pasolini feel that his concerns were indeed political, had yet to appear.

Seeing *Appunti per un'Orestiade Africana* today, after so many things have changed or happened (the dissolution of the capitalism-communism constellation, the feminist rewriting of "his-story," and the mobilization of social antagonism around issues concerning the Earth), one cannot help feeling that Pasolini was indeed searching for a new myth, and that he looked for it where his humanistic background told him to look: Greece. He was attacked by the guardians of political discourse, who were at that point fixated with the color red. Black was fine too, of course, provided that it mixed with red hope, as in Cuba, or in the socialist African states that Pasolini chose for *Appunti per un'Orestiade Africana*. In this political climate, Pasolini had the ability to see and the courage to say that

> in all Third World countries, the choice between neocapitalism and socialism is indifferent and interchangeable. Both models belong to worlds equally advanced which, from the heights of modernity, send out their technicians who are, in the end, equally repressive.[6]

For him, Africa's problems lay elsewhere, outside the East-West power struggle. Pasolini's love for peasant subcultures, for myth and the sacred, for the barbaric and prehistoric, may indeed have been somewhat self-serving and paternalistic, but certainly it bespoke a nostalgia for a time and place in which (we think) humans respected and feared nature. In a recent article entitled "The Meaning of Gaea," David Spengler offers us a brief definition of the sacred which ought to be kept in mind when dealing with Pasolini:

> If something is sacred, it is assumed to have value beyond its form, use-
> fulness, duration, and products. It is valuable; it is precious. It is worthy
> of respect and honor, love and compassion; it is worth entering in com-
> munion with. Its very being is its only justification; it needs no other.[7]

The "pirate" Pasolini was coming to these conclusions, but the cultural milieu around him put him in the impossible position of having to choose between mythology and ideology. Frustrated by the arrogance of the ultra-Left and the blindness of orthodox Marxists, he chose mythology, without being able to fully articulate the explosive political potential contained in the fusion of the two.[8]

Appunti per un'Orestiade Africana is the closest thing we have to such a fusion, and it thus contains precious intuitions. Pasolini's view of the Erinyes as the force to be recuperated from our past may act as a corrective to much New Age spirituality. The contemporary philoso-phy of Gaea tends to regard spirituality and the Earth myth as a matter of holistic healing, light, and radiance—forgetting, once again, that the night is as indispensable to the Earth as the day. On a microcosmic level, Pasolini's plea for the black, feminine deities of the Earth sug-gests that we ought to accept darkness as inevitable. On a macrocosmic level, it advocates a polytheism that includes honoring and cherishing the gods of conflict and death, the deities of the underworld.

Seen in this light or, rather, in this darkness, *Appunti per un'Ores-tiade Africana* begins to yield its fruits. With this film Pasolini perfects his myth of blackness by enhancing its metaphorical dimension. Not only is black beautiful, but it also points to everything that Western culture must learn or, better yet, unlearn, if it is to survive. Equally suggestive is the ideologization of black peasants. On four occasions (including the final sequence) we see black laborers in the sunburnt fields and we hear a revolutionary Soviet song in the background. If in 1970 this could be read as a sign of Pasolini's wish for a socialist Africa, today it becomes an emblem of his intuition that myth must be ideologized and ideology must be mythologized.

Finally, the most striking feature in *Appunti per un'Orestiade Afri-cana*, that which sets it apart from all the other films by Pasolini, is its visual interest in women: women dancing, laughing, coming out of factories. For the first time Pasolini's camera refrains from searching out male beauty and focuses on women instead, so much so that *this*, rather than *Il fiore delle mille e una notte* (Arabian Nights), is Pasolini's true "feminist" film. To be sure, the equation of femininity with irra-tionality is rooted in a millennial stereotype. But once it is freed from the inevitable by-products of humanist ideology, *Appunti per un'Ores-*

tiade Africana, qua celebration of the Other, is not without its powerful feminist subtext. If the mythical subtext of the Erinyes offers a cure for Western, male rationality, the tribute to black women satisfies the need to give visual attention to nonsexual images of women, to femininity.

20

Le mura di Sana'a

While in North Yemen, then a pro-Chinese, socialist country, Pasolini had the opportunity to further his reflections on modernity's impact on the Third World. *Le mura di Sana'a* (The Walls of Sana'a, 1974) is a fourteen-minute documentary shot by Pasolini on Sunday, October 18, 1970, with some film left over after shooting the episode of Alibech in *The Decameron* (which, incidentally, was not included in the final print). Pasolini's voice-over comments upon the images. Stunned by the medieval beauty of Sana'a, North Yemen's capital, Pasolini was "hurt by the defacement invading the city like leprosy, with a pain, an anger, a feeling of powerlessness, and at the same time I had a feverish desire to do something."

> *The modern world, both in its capitalistic and socialistic forms, has created the pervasive sense that the physical, material world is the fundamental reality. So, if we do have this desire to be in harmony with that which we believe to be most real, and we believe* matter *to be that fundamental reality, then our desire will be to be in harmony with matter.*
>
> David Ray Griffin

Le mura di Sana'a begins with a long shot of a man on a stool in the middle of a field. Periodically, he whips the ground with a long, thin, flexuous rope. Dubbed in the studio with a loud, whip-like noise, this opening shot is at once visually haunting and aurally compelling. Soon, an intertitle explains: "Documentary in the form of an appeal to UNESCO dedicated to this Yemenite scarecrow." No sooner do we realize what the man is doing than we feel we must examine the image more closely, and longer. The idea of a man whipping the air to keep birds away from the field is so far removed from our world that we almost need to verify it, to see more and better. But Pasolini cuts abruptly and lets this image seep into our memory. There, in our memory, this shot will remind us of the double-edged quality of Pasolini's nostalgia: Is it possible to regret a world in which people spend their days whipping invisible birds?

With the shot of a stone commemorating the arrival of Chinese troops, Pasolini's voice begins the spoken commentary, never leaving the images but seldom providing the kind of logical matching to which we are accustomed in documentary. Pasolini does not illustrate the images, he does not explain what they are. He lets them speak for themselves while he articulates a verbal text designed to achieve a maximum of factual information and rhetorical exhortation:

> Until ten years ago, Yemen was a medieval country . . . but, at this time, we find, at least in Sana'a, its capital, an indiscriminate desire for modernity and progress, in the very sense that these words have for us. We cannot, however, pretend to ignore that such a desire was imported in Yemen, it was not born there.

While Pasolini argues that the Chinese have brought modernity along with the revolution that overthrew the old Mutawakkite dynasty, the images switch from the rural, desert landscape to the city of Sana'a. At this point, the shots become longer and more uniform. They are all slow pans from right to left on the palaces and narrow alleys which give Sana'a an exclusive beauty "much like Venice or Urbino or Prague or Amsterdam." But,

> the Yemenite ruling class, ashamed of it because it is dirty and poor, has certainly decided upon its destruction. On the other hand, the destruction of the ancient world, that is, of the real world, is taking place everywhere. Unreality is spreading everywhere through neocapitalist policies of property razing.

Spurred by the realist "desire to do something," Pasolini did not resist the temptation to drive his point home, and he inserted a brief sequence that he shot at a later time, in Italy. We see him standing amidst a small group of people in a meadow near the medieval town of Orte, in central Italy. We then get a countershot of the town itself, photographed in such a way as to include the view of a tall, modern building that Pasolini describes caustically: "To call it ugly would be an understatement." He asks the people around him for their opinions. As usual, his style of formulating the questions suggests what the answers ought to be, and the majority of townspeople agree with him. Only one old man says that "Orte is my town; I have always lived here and I like everything they do"—indeed not the most sagacious reply, in spite of the old man's courage in disagreeing with a question that has so blatantly set up the right and wrong answers. Within the context of Pasolini's filmography, this short sequence deserves attention because it is the first one that Pasolini ever shot in the rain. It is as if he wanted to express his feelings about what had happened to the Italy he loved by filling the frame with black umbrellas and gray, melancholy hues.

We then cut back to the walls surrounding Sana'a, and while the camera slowly pans from right to left thirteen times, giving us thirteen different perspectives of the endangered walls, his voice concludes with the impressive crescendo of *ars retorica*:

> For Italy, it is all over. But Yemen can still be saved entirely.
> We appeal to UNESCO—Help Yemen save itself from destruction, begun with the destruction of the walls of Sana'a.
> We appeal to UNESCO—Help Yemen to become aware of its identity and of what a precious country it is.
> We appeal to UNESCO—Help stop this pitiful destruction of national patrimony in a country where no one denounces it.
> We appeal to UNESCO—Find the possibility of giving this nation the awareness of being a common good for mankind, one which must protect itself to remain so.
> We appeal to UNESCO—Intervene, while there is still time, to convince an ingenuous ruling class that Yemen's only wealth is its beauty, and that preserving that beauty means possessing an economic resource that costs nothing. Yemen is still in time to avoid the errors of other countries.
> We appeal to UNESCO—In the name of the true, unexpressed wish of the Yemenite people, in the name of the simple men whom poverty has kept pure, in the name of the grace of obscure centuries, in the name of the scandalous, revolutionary force of the past.

Pasolini voices explicitly what his last few films have suggested by means of images: "the scandalous revolutionary force of the past." Seen from our vantage point twenty years later, his argument, although couched within the rhetoric of the good subproletariat, is an index of a precociously postmodern spirituality.[1] Pasolini's attack upon

Yemen's indiscriminate desire for modernity, his passionate plea for the inherent and objective beauty of Sana'a, his idea that good and truth lie not in material gains but in a feeling of harmony, his implicit argument against both socialism and capitalism, and, above all, his notion that the past is revolutionary, all are symptoms of a mode of feeling which had no name then, which could not but be labeled as right-wing within the existing rigid binary oppositions of the political spectrum. Today, we would not hesitate to ascribe Pasolini's position to a new type of ecological conscience that is concerned with the emergence of postmodern spiritual energies, that is, energies that do not feel obligated to support "the indiscriminate desire for modernity."

Within the mosaic of Pasolini's filmography, *Le mura di Sana'a* is an important little piece for its explicit treatment of the issue of reality. In the first place, *Le mura di Sana'a* defines Pasolini's ardent desire for a concrete intervention in and on behalf of the real, his will to use cinema as a weapon. Pasolini's documentary did have an impact, albeit belatedly. In 1988 an international convention—with heavy Italian participation—provided funding for the restoration of old Sana'a, to be accomplished within the next fifteen years.[2] Not that Pasolini would be happy with this project, which came too late and has the suspicious look of yet another financial enterprise. Still, as an attempt to recover from the wrong steps taken years ago, it is better than nothing, perhaps even a symptom of a new hope.

In addition, *Le mura di Sana'a* contains a clear indication of the wrong turn Pasolini took in his concept of reality. Until this time, he seemed to oscillate between the idea of reality as that which lies beneath the mask imposed by dominant ideology, and the ontological fallacy that ascribes a surplus of authenticity to some privileged signifier. Coupled with his left-wing populism, the latter approach reproduced the myth of the poor as the locus of the real. This documentary gives evidence of Pasolini's progressive slippage towards the ontological fallacy: the idea that the ancient world is the real world in opposition to the unreality of the rest. I do not intend to hold Pasolini responsible for a metaphysical argument, for that is certainly not the discursive level on which his words sought to operate. And, indeed, I can understand why he says what he says. I, too, feel, at times, that our consumer's paradise is in fact unreal. But the idea that reality is all on one side, and that modern life is less real, is bound, sooner or later, to engender confusion. And we must take issue with the privileged position that Pasolini gives himself as the interpreter of the "true, inexpressed will of the Yemenite people." Pasolini is tagging the backs of the "innocent ones" with the burden of signifying a truth and a reality that he, as an inspired intellectual, can detect, while they cannot. If we consider *Le mura di Sana'a* from the point of view of Pasolini's notion of what reality is, we can see the underlying ideological and conceptual errors in his contemporaneous project, *La trilogia della vita*, the subject of the next chapter.

21

La trilogia della vita

Il Decamerone (The Decameron, 1971) narrates nine tales from Boccaccio's *Decamerone*. Two of them (*Ciappelletto* and *Giotto*) are interspersed between the others, serving as a frame for the rest. (1) *Ciappelletto*: A notorious crook and homosexual, Ciappelletto is sent by his father on a business trip to Northern Europe. There he falls fatally ill and arranges a lengthy, false confession on his deathbed. The priest is so impressed with his "holiness" that after his death Ciappelletto is honored as a saint. (2) *Andreuccio da Perugia*: After being robbed by a woman who pretended to be his long-lost sister, Andreuccio joins two thieves who are raiding a dead bishop's tomb in search of a precious ring. After helping Andreuccio into the sarcophagus, they become angry at Andreuccio's reluctance to hand them the ring, so they close the lid on him. The next day, another thief tries to enter the sarcophagus but is bitten by Andreuccio and runs away in terror, leaving him free with the ring. (3) *Masetto*: Pretending to be deaf and mute, Masetto is hired as a gardener in a nuns' convent. One by one, the nuns make love to him until he is exhausted and tells everything to the Mother Superior who, instead of being angry, celebrates the "miracle" of his recovered speech and begs him to stay in the convent. (4) *Peronella*: Startled by her husband's unexpected arrival, Peronella hides her lover in a large jar. She then convinces her husband that the man inside the jar is inspecting it and wants to buy it, provided that it is thoroughly cleaned. While the husband happily gets into the jar to clean, the two lovers resume their lovemaking. (5) *Giotto*: Pasolini changed the original story with Giotto and re-created it with Giotto's pupil instead of Giotto himself. The pupil and a friend are traveling through the countryside when a storm breaks out. All wet and dirty, they seek refuge in a shack, where they are helped by a peasant who gives them burlap cloaks. As they leave, they laugh at the thought of how nobody would ever guess that such a poor appearance concealed a painter of genius. Pasolini then imagines that Giotto's pupil (played by Pasolini himself) goes to Naples to paint a fresco on the walls of the Santa Chiara church. (6) *Caterina*: Caterina secretly arranges to spend the night with her lover Riccardo on the terrace of her house. Her father discovers them in the morning, but since Riccardo is a wealthy young man, he accepts their deed and makes sure that they will get married. (7) *Isabetta and Lorenzo*: Three Sicilian brothers kill their sister's low-born lover. In a dream, the girl finds out where he is buried, uncovers his body, chops his head off, and buries it in a pot of basil which she nurtures with the utmost love and grace. (8) *Don Gianni*: A priest convinces a peasant that he can turn his young wife into a mare (an animal the peasant needs) and then back into a woman. With his consent he asks the woman to undress and starts penetrating her, with the excuse that he is giving the mare a tail. (9) *Tingoccio and Meuccio*: Two young rakes are afraid of hell, but when one of them dies, he appears to the other in a dream and reassures him that sex is not a sin. The latter then rushes to a girlfriend to indulge in sexual excess.

I racconti di Canterbury (Canterbury Tales, 1972). A group of pilgrims journeying to Canterbury tell stories to one another. (1) *The Merchant's Tale*: Thanks to a spell cast by the gods of love, old Sir January loses his sight shortly after marrying the young and beautiful May, who thus can make love to the equally beautiful Damian. Eventually, the gods restore the old man's sight in time to see his wife with the lover, but she manages to make him believe that what he saw was not true. (2) *The Miller's Tale*: In order to distract a gullible husband from his wife, a young student preaches that the second Flood is coming. While he is enjoying the fruit of his cunning, two rivals treacherously poke a red-hot poker up the student's ass. (3) *The Friar's Tale*: The Devil takes the soul of a summoner who has the habit of spying upon homosexual couples in order to blackmail them. (4) *The Cook's Tale*: A Chaplinesque young urchin is seen enjoying life and playing tricks on everyone. After getting fired from a job at the local market, he eventually ends up in the gallows, without, however, losing his zest for life. (5) *The Reeve's Tale*: Two Cambridge students avenge themselves on a miller who was cheating them by sleeping with his more than willing wife and daughter. (6) *The Pardoner's Tale*: Three young rogues in search of Death discover a treasure chest beneath a tree; instead of sharing the treasure, they plot to eliminate one another and encounter death amidst horrible torments. (7) *The Wife of Bath's Tale*: She recounts the story of her past as an insatiable lover. (8) *The Summoner's Tale*: After relating a practical joke at the expense of an avid friar, the summoner depicts an image of Hell in which all the wicked friars are gorged and excreted by Satan. Interspersed throughout the film is the image of Geoffrey Chaucer (played by Pasolini) conceiving or writing the tales.

Il fiore delle mille e una notte (Arabian Nights, 1974). Sold as a slave in an auction, the black girl Zumurrud chooses the inexperienced Nur ed Din as her master and enjoys initiating him sexually. She then tells him the tale of a wager between Harun el Rashid and Queen Zobeida, who put a boy and a girl together to verify which of the sexes is more prone to desire. The contest, however, ends in a tie. Next morning, the evil Bassun drugs the gullible Nur ed Din and kidnaps Zumurrud. A friendly woman helps Nur ed Din to retrieve Zumurrud but he falls asleep and thus lets one of the Forty Thieves carry her away. She succeeds in escaping, and, dressed as a man, she arrives in a city that was waiting to enthrone the first male newcomer as its king. Zumurrud is thus married to Hiyat, the high priest's daughter, to whom she eventually confides her secret. The two women become friends.

Elsewhere, the huntsman Taji meets Aziz and listens to his story. On the very day of his wedding with Aziza, Aziz fell in love with Budur, a woman who attracted him in a web of sign language. The altruistic Aziza helped Aziz decode Budur's signs and consummate his passion, but she eventually committed suicide. As Aziz was unfaithful to Budur as well, the latter had him castrated. Aziz concludes his tale by telling Taji about Princess Dunia, who hates men because she thinks they are all unfaithful. Taji sets out to make Dunia fall in love with him, and to this end he hires two men to help him restore a mosaic that had influenced Princess Dunia's anti-male beliefs. The two men tell Taji the story of how they chose to live a life of poverty. The elder, Shazaman, tells how a jealous demon changed him into a monkey and how a king's daughter broke the spell at the expense of her own life. The younger, Yunan, tells how he was shipwrecked and cast ashore on a possessed island, and how he toppled the island's idol and ended up fulfilling a prophecy of murder by killing a boy with whom he had slept. After the mosaic is restored, Princess Dunia accepts Taji's offer of love.

Meanwhile, Nur ed Din has been held captive by three girls who pamper him. He soon grows tired of this and runs off into the desert where he meets a lion that leads him to Zumurrud's city. Dressed as a king, she summons Nur ed Din to her room, teases him by making him believe that she is indeed a man who is about to force him into homosexual acts, and in the end reveals her identity to him. "What a night! God has created none like this before. Its beginning was bitter, but how sweet the end!"

> *Alone I came into the world*
> *All alone I'll leave it again*
> *And there's nothing in between.*
> *I chase the wind, but she's too fast*
> *And reality I won't grasp*
> *All is left to do is dream*
>
> *The Thought*

After *Medea* and *Appunti per un'Orestiade Africana*, Pasolini abandoned the idea of revisiting Greek myth for realist purposes and rejected the idea of "aristocratic" cinema. From a theoretical standpoint, his most important essay indicating this last transformation is "The Unpopular Cinema" (*HE*, 267–275). Here he attacks Godard, Straub, and Rocha on the grounds that they have locked themselves in an art-house ghetto where they enjoy "the applause of the few." Conceived under the blackmail of leftist avant-gardism, their films represent "an excessive transgression of the code" which "ends by creating a sort of nostalgia for it." Their transgressions "do not take place on the barricades" but "within a concentration camp where *everything is transgression*, and the enemy has disappeared: he is fighting elsewhere." A film director, says Pasolini, should then forestall the modernist impulse towards permanent and systematic violations of the code and "go continuously backwards, to the firing line," where the real danger is, where one is exposed to the many rather than to the few. While reductive with respect to Godard and Rocha, Pasolini's argument has undeniable merits that could not have been appreciated then (leftist blackmail was "in") but that have been confirmed by subsequent trends in political filmmaking. Unfortunately, however, if the idea of making more accessible films was good, Pasolini's execution was inadequate, at least from the standpoint of "a certain realism."

La trilogia della vita (The Trilogy of Life) is made up of three distinct films, *Il Decamerone*, *I racconti di Canterbury*, and *Il fiore delle mille e una notte*, which are analyzed separately by critics. While certainly legitimate, such an approach, in the context of the present book, would risk overlooking the deep unity underlying these three films. From the point of view of "a certain realism," they are all products of an author so totally engrossed in himself that he loses the precarious balance which has thus far supported him. A series of circumstances, personal (age), contextual (his diatribe with/in the Left), and historical (the so-called sexual liberation), led him to forsake the principles of ideological and positional awareness that he had strenuously defended until the late sixties. Of course Pasolini still explained these three films in terms of realism and reality. My contention, however, is that, from the standpoint of "a certain realism," *La trilogia della vita* was a failure.

A Realism That Failed

Since *La trilogia della vita* exhibits a few interesting features even from the standpoint of realism, I shall first consider its strong points and then move on to its flaws.

La trilogia della vita originates in a rather lucid vision of contemporary reality. However self-serving the motives behind it, the idea of an unstoppable homogenization of Italy's traditional socioanthropological differences is sound, for the transformation of all Italians into petty-bourgeois consumers has indeed occurred. This is not necessarily a bad thing, nor was it any better before, but Pasolini thought it was, and just when the student movement and the radical intelligentsia entertained revolutionary dreams, he realized that something else was in fact happening. The conviction that subproletarian and peasant bodies were an endangered species, along with the attendant belief in "the scandalous, revolutionary force of the past," led him to make films exalting the by-gone days when, he assumed, the people had not yet been colonized by the center.

La trilogia della vita is the ultimate cinematic translation of theoretical and stylistic reflections dating as far back as *Comizi d'amore*, when Pasolini discovered the existence of a "psychological truth" somehow more important than "logical truth." Rudimentary though this statement was, it signaled his growing interest in people's faces and, more generally, in the language of reality as the system of signs contained in physiognomic traits and bodily gestures. In 1969, he declared that, thanks to the cinema, he had discovered a reality which had nothing to do with traditionally conceived realism, a reality that was expressed by wrinkles and lines, teeth and scars, ways of growing and aging.[1]

Concerned with what I previously called "the language of presence" (see chapter 2), *La trilogia della vita* earned points in its war against the omnipresent television set. Television, Pasolini argued, was succeeding where Hitler and Mussolini had failed. If the aim of all fascism is the imposition of *one* model of behavior on the people, then the media has perfected a form of totalitarianism, all the more insidious because it falls under the guise of freedom and entertainment. "TV has so codified a kind of 'unreality' that its unique human model is more and more the hypocritical, conformist, petit bourgeois."[2] Hence Pasolini's "ambition to make films which are political in that they are deeply 'real' in the choice of the characters, in what they say and do." According to Pasolini, *La trilogia della vita* founded a new kind of "physiognomic realism" because he "chose actors who are real people so that their physical presence on the screen gives a feeling of reality," and thereby constitutes "an imposition of reality" on the spectators.[3]

Finally, another potentially positive aspect of *La trilogia della vita* was its open treatment of sexuality. In his 1974 article entitled "Tetis" (the Greek mnemonic behind *teta veleta*), Pasolini argued that the filmmaker's freedom in the representation of sexual acts had enormously increased since the fifties. Concurrently, he stressed that he had greatly contributed (paying the personal price of repeated trials) "to enlarging the expressive space granted by society."[4] Pasolini's struggle against censorship "prepared the terrain for reforms and tolerance on the part of Italian bourgeois society." His interest in doing this, he claimed, was not pornographic but had its origin in realism, because "the only reality left is that of the body." Forced by his left-wing critics to discuss *La trilogia della vita* on the terrain of ideology, he accused them of not seeing that in his last films "ideology was there, indeed, in that big penis on the screen, above their heads unwilling to understand." Pasolini was not entirely wrong. After eighty years of cinematography bent on the fetishization and progressive undressing of the female body, the sudden appearance of the male organ had its ideological implications—it had the typical realist effect of unmasking what lies concealed under a mask. The fetishization of sexual organs, however, contained inevitable risks.

Blaming his own skepticism on older age and becoming irritated with "leftist blackmail," Pasolini "could no longer believe in a progressive reality, a reality that one ought to try to affect through one's work."[5] Seeking freedom from ideological duties, he involved himself in a formalism which he had contemptuously criticized all of his life:

> *La trilogia della vita* has been my most ambitious project, requiring from me the most intense formal attention and stylistic commitment. A political-ideological film is easy. But it is rather more difficult to make a pure film, attempting to create a pure act of narration as the classics did, keeping oneself outside of ideologies while at the same time avoiding escapism.[6]

The twice repeated word "pure" brings the poem *In morte del realismo* ("On the Death of Realism," see chapter 3) to mind, in which Pasolini so vigorously attacked the enemies of realism and labeled them "neo-purists." At that stage, in 1961, he had claimed that realism was a matter of ideological awareness. Ten years later, he celebrated the worth of "keeping outside of ideologies." But there is no "outside" of ideology. All one can do is pass from one ideology to another. It is not a matter of moralistically accusing Pasolini for doing what nearly every director does. It is, however, necessary to denounce the extent to which his new ideology of "formal attention and stylistic commitment" led him to overlook one of the basic principles of "a certain realism": you should be aware of the impact that your work has.

By breaking with Pasolini's previously held beliefs, *La trilogia della vita* harmed not only realism but reality itself—something that Pasolini was to regret publicly in his notorious repudiation of the three films. Take the issue of sexuality and his idea of "an ontology of reality whose symbol is naked sex." For all the urgency that the project of "liberating" the screen might have had, it was perhaps more important to avoid feeding the ongoing commercialization of sexuality. *La trilogia della vita*'s tremendous box-office turnout revealed that these films were not popular in the Gramscian *nazional popolare* sense, but rather as blockbusters that enticed spectators with their *non-ideologized* display of flesh on the screen. If his earlier films had used sexuality within the context of an astute politics of the body, here both body and sexuality were for sale. It is as if all of Pasolini's past mythologies, once held in check by his political awareness, had suddenly coalesced into the sexual knot.

If there is a "hidden ideology" in these films, it is the idea of an "authentic" sexuality preceding social conditioning: Freud married to Rousseau.[7] Our Western imagination has been fed the notion of "the animal within," and we have been urged to get in perfect tune with it so that we can listen to the authentic voice of the flesh. The body becomes an FM station: turn the knob, carefully play with it, and you'll find it. In fact, Stephen Heath argues,

> sexuality is without the importance ascribed to it in our contemporary society (Western capitalist); it is without that importance because it does not exist as such, because there is no such a thing as sexuality; what we are experiencing is the fabrication of a "sexuality," the construction of something called "sexuality" through a set of representations—images, discourses, ways of picturing and describing—that propose and confirm, that make up this sexuality to which we are often referred and held in our lives, a whole sexual fix precisely.[8]

By offering its public a "fix," *La trilogia della vita* contributed to the diffusion of what Bourdieu aptly defined as *le devoir d'orgasme* (the duty of orgasm) and thus to that very process of homogenization denounced by Pasolini himself.[9] Exploiting the success of *La trilogia della vita*, the film industry inundated the market with sequels and imitations. As critic Morandini pointed out, only for the first of these three films could Pasolini be acquitted of any responsibility in this phenomenon.[10] But when films like *Decameroticus*, *The Hot Nights of the Decameron*, and *Put Your Devil in My Hell* were excreted, he *should* have realized what he was doing.

Moreover, with *La trilogia della vita*, the idea of the lower classes/ Third World as the locus of unbridled sexual energy also got out of hand, and, as James Roy McBean wrote, "one cannot help feeling that is all more than a bit self-serving."[11] *La trilogia della vita* operated as if its author did not know that the search for a "savage" adolescent by a cultivated older man was a *topos* of homosexual literature and practice. Steeped in what has been called "the prince and the pauper syndrome," these films reinforced such a syndrome, leaving us with the sour aftertaste of having been relentlessly exposed to an unchecked personal mania: the intellectual colonizes the disenfranchised Other to fulfill his own dreams.[12] I do not judge Pasolini's habit of mercenary sex with "innocent bodies"; in fact, I even admire his persistence in a behavior for which middle-class hypocrisy chastised him. But I do condemn his preposterous notion that lower class/Arab sexuality is "the real sexuality," and I denounce his use of the money made available to him by a system that he nominally condemned so that he could make irresponsible films.

Pasolini's exoticism, which he expressed in *Edipo re* and *Medea*, is intolerably overblown in *Il fiore delle mille e una notte*. The myriad of Arab children running towards the camera in a postcard setting can only remind us of the superficial experience of every Western tourist vacationing in the Third World. Shot in Eritrea, Ethiopia, Iran, Yemen, and Nepal, this film belongs to the widespread cultural appropriation of the exotic Other by middle-class pockets. Because Pasolini forgets the lesson imparted to him by the African students in Rome, *Il fiore delle mille e una notte* flounders in ethnocentrism. To be a European filming in the Middle and Far East is by no means an innocent deed to be taken lightly, for, as Edward Said argues, "one belongs to a power with definite interests in the Orient, and, more important, one belongs to a part of the earth with a definite history of involvement in the Orient since the time of Homer."[13] It does not matter if *Medea* and *Il fiore delle mille e una notte* do not purport to offer an ideologically sensitive view of the Orient, for the Orient appears on the screen.

Third World faces and places are enlisted in what seems yet another version of old colonialist projections. Only by dissociating himself from the context and by maintaining a patronizing relationship with the Orient can Pasolini exploit it artistically, enhance the mythology of Arab sexuality, and give us shots worthy of a travel brochure.

From the standpoint of "a certain realism," *La trilogia della vita* is a disheartening failure. It may be argued that Pasolini had repudiated ideology and was no longer interested in realism. Nevertheless, since he persisted in using the word "realism" to describe his work and the word "reality" to legitimize the motivations behind it, we must make a judgment as to which period of his career produced the best realism. Is the cause of reality/realism better served by *Accattone* or *Il Decamerone*? To be sure, the realism of *Accattone* would not have made any sense in 1970. *Teorema* and *Porcile*, however, acknowledged the need to revise and change old realist parameters in accordance with sociocultural changes. The kind of problematic realism of these two films was, in my view, Pasolini's most effective contribution to realism. He saw *La trilogia della vita* in the same light as *Teorema*, as yet another turn on the same road. In fact, he suddenly changed roads altogether.

From a thematic and conceptual point of view, *La trilogia della vita* did not contain anything that was not in Pasolini before. If we watch the films immediately preceding *La trilogia della vita*, we might even say that we saw it coming. *La trilogia della vita*, however, suddenly precipitated what was previously held in problematic suspension. As I suggested above, Pasolini lost control of his private mythologies of sex and innocence. And he even allowed his two most interesting contributions to realist representation to get out of hand: the autobiographical dimension and the language of physical presence.

The inclusion of the author's reality in the film was a necessary step for a realism that strove to avoid the snares of objective representation. Pasolini's films always enabled the viewer to judge the position from which reality was being approached. In *La trilogia della vita*, the author took over as an absolute tyrant, all the while forgetting to verify his position vis-à-vis the material. This is not to say that there was an excess of autobiography. *Edipo re* was admittedly autobiographical and, to some degree, succeeded in giving a cinematic self-portrait in the mode of the problematic realism explored after *Uccellacci uccellini*. What one finds in *La trilogia della vita* is an author so engrossed in himself that he did not respect the signs in the text. Like *Salò*'s Sadean libertines, Pasolini wanted absolute control over the bodies in the film, forcing smiles that looked false, demanding passion where there was none, reaching the bottom of the already dubious practice of dubbing. And all in the name of pure creation!

It is of course hardly coincidental that in two of these films Pasolini himself appeared in the role of the artist. It has been argued that his appearance was metacinematic and "asserts his own awareness of the reflexive nature of his film."[14] In light of the astounding lack of self-reflexiveness discussed above, it is highly dubious that *La trilogia della vita* had Brechtian intentions. Pasolini's presence in these films did not reinforce an intentional undermining of illusionism as, say, Coppola did in *Apocalypse Now* (1979). Nor was it a subtle reminder that the author is a cog in the productive wheel, as Godard's presence was in *Le mépris* (Contempt, 1962). Instead, it was a peremptory statement of authorship, the overwhelming presence of a "pure" creator intimidating what was being created. His was a dream of absolute art, where the author pulls the signs out of chaos, rapes them (instead of loving them), and enjoys poetic license.

Another symptom indicating that Pasolini had lost control of his subjectivity was the escalation of his anti-naturalist style. In each of his films there are elements that endanger narrative illusionism, such as actors looking into the camera, frontal close-up shots without their "natural" countershots to give narrative purpose to the characters' gaze, and, above all, hesitations on the non-professional actors' part, revealing their awe in front of the camera. All this, Mancini and Perella argued, "bears witness to something seen, heard, and desired by the director's *body*."[15] Indeed, this was one of Pasolini's greatest innovations against naturalism (what critics usually call classic realism). In *La trilogia della vita*, though, this strategy, too, got out of hand, and Pasolini's camera produced unpleasant results. Aesthetically, it made for an excess of sloppy editing. Ideologically, it reinforced our irritation at the sight of "innocent" faces enjoined to give pleasure to the director.

And, of course, when the subject isolates himself in an absolute position, the object gets out of hand as well. The myth of absolute subjectivity and the myth of absolute objectivity go hand in hand, for both fail to acknowledge the relational nature of the semiotic process. Blinded by a passion no longer restrained by reason, Pasolini imposed his absolute desire on the object and did not see that he was re-creating the fiction of an "authentic" reality that speaks in and of itself to all. In *La trilogia della vita*, innocent bodies and broken rows of teeth were entrusted with the task of signifying "the real," as if it were an exclusive property of some images. Hence, he had in effect returned to "ontological realism," to the neorealist fallacy of the absolute power of images. *Accattone* exposed the ambivalence of the image; *Uccellacci uccellini* celebrated the effort of "bending our meanings" to make them fit an ambiguous, contradictory reality. *La trilogia della vita*, instead, surrendered to the faith in ontological plenitude. Whereas Pasolini's film theory of reality as language strove to make cultural what was natural, *La trilogia della vita* made natural what was cultural. And it was precisely because of the countless declarations made to defend these films that Pasolini somehow deserved the reputation of being a naive believer in reality as full presence.

I have argued that Pasolini made *La trilogia della vita* while undergoing a "sexual fix." Also, as society was becoming more tolerant and nudes were invading the cinematic screen, Pasolini's homosexual discourse was suddenly offered more freedom. These three films, then, are the ideal ground to verify Pasolini's homosexual gaze, the visual position and regime of a man who was persecuted all his life for his sexual deviance and yet would not accept the idea of a gay liberation movement. In fact, Pasolini's homosexual discourse constituted the main frame, the central gaze, and the lens through which the dream of sexual liberation was conjured. As I attempt a realist reading of nonrealist films, I will now use *Il Decamerone*, *I racconti di Canterbury*, and *Il fiore delle mille e una notte* to explore this frame, gaze, and lens. My discussion will *not* do justice to whatever "artistic merit" they may have. Some good studies on this aspect of *La trilogia della vita* already exist and the reader may refer to these.[16]

The Homosexual Frame

Il Decamerone rests on "the Neapolitan fallacy" to which Pasolini was increasingly prey. According to this fallacy, "Naples, where I shot most of the film, is the city of innocent reality," its population living "in a kind of prehistoric limbo" that has made them "become a pure reality, an ontological reality."[17] While faulty, this idea would not necessarily entail the failure of the film, at least not if the text took pains to make the viewer aware of the logic behind it. As it is, however, *Il Decamerone* is a gallery of Neapolitan faces, songs, and gestures without analogical reference to contemporary reality for the viewer to appreciate. I am not arguing that Pasolini misreads Boccaccio by transposing into a Neapolitan context tales that in the book take place elsewhere. *Il Decamerone* fails as a realist project because it assumes that the viewers would all be struck by Neapolitan images as by epiphanies of the real.

As a Boccaccio-based film hinging predominantly on formal concerns and the portrayal of sex, *Il Decamerone* roused the interest of humanist scholars and pleased the general public. While the public was not in a position to evaluate Pasolini's formal manipulation of the original, scholars were divided. Some denounced an alleged betrayal of Boccaccio, as if fidelity had been Pasolini's intention. Others, more convincingly, set out to capture the sense of Pasolini's operation, be it the implications of the use of dialect or the subproletarianization of the screen. For the most part, *Il Decamerone* was praised for the way it re-elaborated Boccaccio's frame-story by making two tales (Ciappelletto and Giotto) the continuum into which the other seven are inserted. In effect, it is in the film's framing structure that Pasolini's inventiveness can be appreciated. Here, however, I shall analyze Pasolini's frame in the light of his repeated declarations that the ideology in *La trilogia della vita* is "deeply hidden."

Il Decamerone begins with an image of Franco Citti beating to death someone wrapped in a burlap sack—we only hear a faint sound coming from the sack and all we know is that it contains a human body. As it is not until much later in the film that we find out that Citti is Ciappelletto, such a beginning emphasizes the connotations normally brought by Citti the actor: struggle against the body, passion, and violence. The casting of Pasolini's "pathological self" in this role is not surprising, for Ciappelletto is one of the two homosexual characters in Boccaccio's *Decameron*. It must be noted, however, that Boccaccio is not at all interested in Ciappelletto's homosexuality. It is only because he wants to make Ciappelletto the living symbol of all possible evils that Boccaccio succinctly mentions that "he liked women in the same way dogs like the stick."[18]

After this initial sequence of violence against an unseen body, the film moves on to the tale of Andreuccio, a visual tribute to Ninetto Davoli's poor acting as well as an aural "imposition of reality" in the form of unembellished Neapolitan dialect. Andreuccio is conned by the mysterious woman's words, and his misfortunes remind the viewer that narrative can always be used to serve someone's dirty schemes. In the wake of such a memento, *Il Decamerone* returns to Franco Citti, still without letting the viewer know that he is Ciappelletto.

A small crowd is gathered around an old storyteller who boasts of his Neapolitan—that is, of his highly gestural—style of telling a tale of Boccaccio's (the tale of the prioress and the breeches). Since it is Pasolini's invention, this brief scene is indeed the ideal spot for reading with a magnifying lens. The camera frames a largely built, bald man completely enraptured in the tale of the lascivious nuns; it then cuts to a shot of his enormous crotch, and cuts back to a medium shot where we see Citti standing next to him and stealing a coin from his purse. Citti then walks around the man's back, approaches a boy, and offers him the money that he just stole. Citti's face alludes to a sexual encounter to be consummated elsewhere. The boy smiles, coyly. Not only does this scene qualify Citti's character as homosexual, but it makes him into a perfect metaphor for the director of *Il Decamerone*.

Pasolini, too, "steals" money from a public absorbed in the consumption of sexual tales, and then uses it to buy an Alfa Romeo with which to cruise in Rome's blasted outskirts.

After such a confession, the text predictably moves on to two tales of lust and cunning, those of Masetto and Peronella, which are among the worst things Pasolini ever did. The stereotypical imagery in the nun's episodes and the forced laughter in the second are good examples of what I defined as "the author's tyrannical will" over the profilmic material. We then go back to the frame-story, find out who Citti is, and see Ciappelletto's visit to the "northern countries." Not surprisingly, no sooner does the theme of death enter the text than the film's visual inventiveness picks up, offering us splendid pictorial quotations from Brueghel's *The Combat of Lent and Carnival* and *The Triumph of Death.*[19]

In the midst of another tribute to Neapolitan singing (a maudlin song about sentiments and death which will be taken up, albeit with a very different accent, by the first character to appear in *I racconti di Canterbury*), Ciappelletto takes ill, delivers his false confession, and dies. The first of the two framing tales thus ends, with the camera looking down from a distance at the crowd gathered around Ciappelletto's enshrouded body, honoring him for what he was *not*. Besides reiterating Pasolini's fascination with images of death, the visual attention dedicated to this scene short-circuits one of his favorite theoretical motifs: death provides a montage of our lives, causes the inessential to disappear, and lets the truth of a person shine forward (see *Accattone*). Well, this was theory. In practice, death provides a montage of our lives, but what stays in people's memories is not necessarily the essential. It can also be a bunch of lies.

The tripartite telling of Ciappelletto's tale thus consists of (a) violent disposal of some body; (b) mercenary sex with kids; (c) death and misinterpretation. If the first portion of the frame is autobiographical in Pasolini's usual roundabout way, the second is iconically so, for Giotto's best pupil is played by Pasolini himself. The connection between Ciappelletto and Giotto's pupil, that is, between Citti and Pasolini, is ensured by a straight cut from Ciappelletto's deathbed to Giotto's tale. In addition to the obvious painter/filmmaker equation, Boccaccio's tale offered something else to Pasolini: the quintessential realist theme of the discrepancy between reality and appearance. "Nature," says the narrator in Boccaccio, "has frequently planted astonishing genius in men of monstrously ugly appearance," the implication being that we should not stop at the monstrous surface, but rather reach for the sublime behind it.[20]

Giotto's pupil arrives in Naples, sets up his working environment, and goes to the market to look for faces to be reproduced through his "physiognomical realism." Here we get a shot (which will be repeated twice) of Pasolini framing his object of vision within a square constructed by placing the index and middle fingers of the left hand against the index and middle fingers of the right. While a standard gesture for apprentice filmmakers learning how to think in terms of framing, this is yet another variation of the partially obscured vision that recurs in his films. In *Il Decamerone*, this shot acquires a significance of its own in that the observer is no less than Pasolini. Having thus far been associated in his filmography with the thief, child-Oedipus, Ninetto, Odetta and the servant in *Teorema*, and Aeetes in *Medea*, this image finally takes on the explicit autobiographical connotation that was merely implied all along.

The tale of Caterina and Riccardo follows, the first in the film to portray sex and humor in a graceful way. We cut back to the frame-story which now depicts the working style of Pasolini/the artist. By means of a series of frontal shots of the painter frozen in the act of seizing the sparks of inspiration, the text informs us of its author's self-perception. Far from being the self-conscious artist capable of meta-cinematic reflections, Pasolini/Giotto's pupil is "the genius rapt with inspiration who takes his models from life but must be motivated by some transcendent creative impulse."[21] Tainted by a commonplace romanticism, this self-representation reveals the extent to which Pasolini stopped making "aristocratic" films only to slip into the mythology of the "aristocratic" artist.

But it also serves as adequate introduction to Pasolini's most inspired appropriation of the original, the tragic story of Isabetta and Lorenzo. Pasolini takes Boccaccio's image of the three brothers who, "talking and laughing, and pretending to leave the city, took Lorenzo with them"[22] and blows it up into a full sequence modeled on the *ragazzi*'s world: a frantic race through the woods, the sweat of an all-male brigade, and the epic, tragic element looming up from behind ritualistic laughter. This is clearly the tale which gave space to Pasolini's uncanny ability to use the cinematic screen for "pathologizing" (see *Medea*). In this haunting visual translation of a tale of murder and decapitation, Pasolini succeeds in confronting the viewer with the inevitable, intimate connection existing between passion and pathology. And wishing, perhaps, to emphasize the vitality contained in such a connection, Pasolini alters Boccaccio's ending. In the film, Isabetta does not die, but jealously guards and intensely stares at the pot of basil in which she has hidden her lover's head.

After a few shots of the painter gazing at his next characters in the market, the text moves on to the stories of Gemmata and Tingoccio/

Il Decamerone: *Pasolini in the role of Giotto's pupil reinforces the myth of the inspired artist.* Courtesy of the Museum of Modern Art/Film Stills Archive.

Il Decamerone: *Shocked to discover their daughter naked with a man, Caterina's mother (Eleonora Carina) and father (unidentified) epitomize the reaction Pasolini expected from the public.* Courtesy of the Museum of Modern Art/ Film Stills Archive.

Meuccio, which revert, unfortunately, to the Neapolitan fallacy: sex and dialect, all in the name of ontology. The rough-sounding, highly improbable Neapolitan carnival is interrupted shortly before the end of the story of Tingoccio and Meuccio by a frontal shot of the painter lying on his bunk. Pasolini/Giotto's pupil suddenly wakes up as if in the grip of a nightmare and looks into the camera. We then cut to a brief, visionary dream of his: a Madonna with child (played by *mamma* Mangano) supervises a scene where some reprobate sex offenders are being pushed down a hill by demons, while four nuns hide their eyes.

It is a Catholic vision of guilt and fear under the benevolent aegis of the great Mother. Is Hell the outcome of sexual sins?

Of course not, the story of Tingoccio and Meuccio concludes. After reassuring the viewer (but maybe not Pasolini) that sex is not a mortal sin, *Il Decamerone* returns to the church where Pasolini/the artist has completed the second of the three panels that he was supposed to paint. Looking at his own incomplete work (thus announcing a sequel), Pasolini/the artist utters his by now famous last remark: "Why realize a work of art when it is so beautiful just to dream about it?" I am aware that this last sentence has sent aesthetic *frissons* down the spines of many cultivated spectators, but I must confess my utter incapacity to find it either deep or redeeming. Whereas many artists are forced "just to dream about it," a few are given the possibility "to realize" it by the film industry, which keeps funding "dreams" so long as they have the box-office turnout of *Il Decamerone*.

Il Decamerone's frame-story is thus closely knit around homosexuality sublimated into the dream of pure art. Ciappelletto is forced to lie about himself and, in order to be given the last sacraments, must pass for straight. When the painter borrows a cloak from a peasant in a hut, the motif of the self-disguise turns into self-denial. Ascetically oblivious to the needs of his own body (he first forgets to eat and then gulps down his food), Pasolini/the artist corrects Ciappelletto's tendencies and takes refuge in art. Taking refuge in art is a paradigm in the homosexual discourse (e.g., Oscar Wilde) and *Il Decamerone* enunciates it explicitly. Art, like homosexuality, is an *opus contra naturam*.

As the meaning of an image is determined by the frame in which it appears, it emerges that the film's frame (controverting nature) contradicts the film's purported message (the ideology of finding natural sex). A sinful homosexuality casts a dark shadow on the joy of sex so often associated with *Il Decamerone*. Running counter to Pasolini's intention to celebrate the beauty of innocent bodies copulating under a Mediterranean sun, the frame evokes the somber tones of deception. At this point, I cannot help noticing—and disliking, although my dislike may indeed be rooted in my heterosexual apperception—Pasolini's systematically bad portrayal of actual lovemaking. He seems incapable of evoking tenderness and affection, except perhaps with Isabetta's and Caterina's stories, but here too the affection is mostly rendered by means of smiling close-ups. A most definite drawback for someone declaring the intention of liberating the screen, Pasolini's image of sexual encounters is framed by and within the gesture of compulsive sexuality consummated quickly. The characters in *Il Decamerone* rush to do it, with a heaviness which symbolizes the dead weight of male bodies throwing themselves on stereotypically lustful females. In *Teorema*, this was an acceptable strategy, because allegory required that the images be immediately recognizable and translated into another level of meaning. But in a film which boasts its celebration of the reality of the body, the one-sided portrayal of the flesh is profoundly unrealistic.

The Homosexual Gaze

If *Medea* was a lofty bore, *I racconti di Canterbury* was a "popular" disaster, in many ways a bad copy of *Il Decamerone* and probably Pasolini's most uninteresting film. Clearly less at ease with the English author, Pasolini was less creative with the frame and vacillated between preserving Chaucer's idea of different social types telling a story and having the author function as *trait d'union* for the tales in the film. He thus opted for a compromise. After an initial reference to the pilgrims meeting on their way to Canterbury, he entrusted the rest of the frame-story into the hands of the Chaucer character, played, of course, by Pasolini himself. While sparing us the mythology of pure and inspired art, he gave us the image of a more detached, immobile author, sitting at his desk, reading Boccaccio (a detail far from being ascertained by scholars), playing with a cat, getting scolded by his wife, and finally signing *The Canterbury Tales* with a telling remark: "Here end the Canterbury Tales told for the sheer pleasure of telling them." As if wishing to conclude with a polemical note aimed at his leftist critics, Pasolini thus reiterated his right to the pleasure of dreaming and his intention to stay away from commitment. At the same time, he offered a smiling image of himself as a man who has reached the serene wisdom of old storytellers.

The film, however, contradicts such an image in the most absolute fashion. As critics have unanimously remarked, *I racconti di Canterbury* darkens the picture of joyous, spontaneous sexuality to the point that there is little joy left. Sex is the source of physical suffering (the Miller's tale), restless longing (the Merchant's tale), and in the case of the Pardoner's tale it even adds images of masochism to Chaucer's text. As with *Il Decamerone*, *I racconti di Canterbury* exposes the corruption of Pasolini's idea that meaning proceeds from the body. What in his theories was a much needed blow to the supremacy of the mind, here becomes a joke for drunk students. Of course, there are a few beautiful sequences that deserve to be remembered, but they all derive from the pathological Shadow, rather than from the wise celebrant of pure vitality. Again, one gets the impression that Pasolini felt obliged to sing joys that he did not feel. As a result, he forced the signs in the text into the position of *having to* signify something which was, in fact, contradicted by the film's major concerns, namely, anality and a degraded perspective on heterosexuality. It may be argued that such things as flatulence and sexual corruption are plentiful in Chaucer's original, and indeed they are. Nevertheless, Pasolini focused only on these aspects and blew them out of proportion.

A brief look at the film's progression will substantiate my point. In the Merchant's tale we see the old, repulsive January choosing his young wife May on the basis of a quick glimpse of her behind. And the adulterous romance between May and Demian is essentially the portrait of sexual frustration, so that we are left with visions of exaggerated crotch shots—a far distant cry from the haunting ways in which the body entered his previous films. In *Teorema* the guest's crotch was idealized by Rimbaud's book lying on his lap. Here, it is the ideology of the phallus as "the real."

The Friar's tale is a visual masterpiece, a superb mixture of Chaucerian text and Pasolinian insertions, and will be examined below. Suffice it to say, for the time being, that it emphasizes the theme of anality by portraying homosexual lovemaking where Chaucer does not. The Cook's tale, a matter of a few fragments in Chaucer, is here blown up into a tribute to Chaplin/Ninetto which is, in my view, unfunny and proves that his favorite male actor (along with Citti) was best employed when either a support to a lead (Totò) or relegated to secondary parts (*Edipo re*, *Teorema*, *Porcile*). The Miller's tale depicts Nicholas's elaborate, ingenious scheming to achieve adulterous gratification with Alyson, but his success is marred by the ending, with a burning rod in his own behind. In the tale of the Wife of Bath (Laura Betti), Pasolini develops the image of the nymphomaniac to grotesque proportions, while stressing the attendant stereotype of men dying from too much sexual exertion. The Reeve's tale, the most faithful to the original, is perhaps the only one in which cunning and spontaneous sex live up to Pasolini's declared intentions. Here too, however, the first sight that the students have of the miller's wife and daughter is that of their buttocks idiotically hanging out of two holes in their house, in what is meant to be, perhaps, a medieval toilet. The Pardoner's tale starts out with the most lurid images of sexual exchange in a brothel, but it then turns into a mythical parable of punished greed. Narrated with Pasolini's elliptical style at its best, the story confirms Pasolini's talent for epic tales of death and retribution. Finally, the Summoner's tale, the film's last, is the triumph of anality in all respects, first in the practical joke at the friar's expense and then in the wild scenes from Hell revisited by Pasolini, with the devil's anus expelling friars and with demons sodomizing reprobates.

It is not the presence of anal imagery per se that is bad. Rather, it is its degradation into jokes worthy of B-movies. Indeed, we are far from the symbolic exuberance evoked by the complex figures of anality in *Uccellacci uccellini*. Contempt for the flesh and truculent anality dominate, instead of the famed reality of the body. It may be argued that innocent sexuality is hard to depict for a man whose body lingered in the limbo of homosexual (self-) contempt. But then why succumb to the ideology of the joy of sex? The only way to redeem *I racconti di Canterbury*, perhaps, is to consider it as a Pasolinian version of camp. According to Jack Babuscio's pointed assessment, camp entails four basic elements, all of them present in varying degrees in *I racconti di Canterbury*: irony, aestheticism, theatricality, and humor.[23] While the last three are easy to detect in the film, irony is harder to find in a film which seems to contradict the author's intention without his knowing it. And yet a twisted and tragic form of irony is there, in the Friar's tale.

Situated after the Merchant's tale, which ends with January regaining his sight, Pasolini's captivating version of the Friar's tale offers, intentionally or not, a detached explanation of why anality leads to despair. Interpreted by Citti (who else?) in the role of the Devil, the Friar's tale shows a corrupt summoner who spies upon two homosexuals and then proceeds to blackmail them. Whereas one is rich enough to bail himself out, the other one is sentenced to death. We see him burning at the stake under the impressive and impassive gaze of bishops and aristocrats, Power intent upon representing itself. With four shots (long to medium to two close-ups) of still soldiers and notables attending the ceremonial sacrifice, Pasolini evokes the hieratic nature of publicly represented capital punishment. A clever scenographic invention, all the banners are rigidly stretched horizontally, as if starched, thus contributing to a feeling of airless timelessness.

The striking part of this first half of the tale is that spectators are forced to see things from the perspective of the Devil. We first see him spying on the summoner spying on the homosexuals and then observing the man burning at the stake. The day after—and here is where Chaucer's story virtually begins in the book—the Devil rides up to the summoner, who is on his way to collect the rent from an insolvent woman. The two talk about their respective jobs and discover that they both collect "payments" from people. Thinking that he has gained the Devil's friendship and wanting to impress him with a display of brutal heartlessness, the summoner mistreats the woman who cannot pay. In an atmosphere reminiscent of Dreyer's *Vredens Dag* (Day of Wrath, 1944), the woman begs, implores, and finally curses the summoner, "may the Devil take you!" At this point Citti asks, "Woman, do you

I racconti di Canterbury: *As the complement to Sergio Citti, Ninetto Davoli, here in the role of Peterkin, is the icon of the joy of living.* Courtesy of the Museum of Modern Art/Film Stills Archive.

really mean that?" Naturally she does, and we are left with the satisfaction of seeing the summoner pay for his sleaziness.

Pasolini bent Chaucer's original considerably. As it is, the Friar's tale does not mention homosexuality at all, nor does it include any description of the summoner's actual spying on couples. The Friar merely recounts the story of a corrupt man who supervises a blackmail organization and who is an unsurpassed "expert at knowing a wounded deer from one unhurt."[24] The entire section on spying, then, is all Pasolini's. His inclusion of homosexuals as the spied-upon couples suggests that, for him, homosexuality entails a state of permanent visibility (the thief in *Accattone*), a visual fragility subjected to the whims of power. As a deviant, you are forced to live in the constant worry of being seen, so you try to become invisible. But your attempts at concealing your real self from the eyes of power make your identity precarious, generating the autobiographical desire of defining and finding yourself. Hence Pasolini's autobiographical realism, the urge of settling accounts with a reality that cannot be seen.

I racconti di Canterbury: *Public punishment of unrepentant homosexuality.*
Courtesy of the Museum of Modern Art/Film Stills Archive.

If it would be reductive to ascribe Pasolini's pursuit of an elusive
reality (with its corollary of an ongoing experimentation in the field of
realism) to homosexuality, I feel that the role played by the way he
lived his homosexuality cannot be ignored. In fact, it can hardly be
overestimated, for there exists a point where realism, autobiography,
and homosexuality coalesce in the haunting image of the partially
obscured vision which, to no one's surprise, is at the very heart of his
Friar's tale. Nowhere in Pasolini is the association between this shot
and homosexuality more evident. We either see what the Devil sees
through a hole or cracks in doors, or we look at one of his eyes looking. I have argued in other parts of this book that this image of partial
vision can be conveniently assumed to be a visual metaphor for Pasolini's realist and autobiographical gaze. I now add homosexuality, because such a shot visualizes a subject's position and his visual regime at
the intersection between his desire for free vision and the existence of
objective obstacles. This is not to say that Pasolini intended this recurrent image to carry the connotation of his own visual regime. Yet,
given the way in which Pasolini lived his own homosexuality, the many
shots of partially obscured vision in his films capture, with the nonver-

bal power of an image, the drama of a gaze forced into fear and self-denial: a gaze that is self-reflective and realist because it seeks to see, to find out, to know.

The Friar's tale is a source of precious information on another level as well. Throughout the whole episode, but especially in the first section, we see what the Devil sees. At the end of the story, we rejoice at the summoner's punishment brought about by the Devil. The homosexual gaze is forced into an alliance with the Lord of Darkness, who seems to be the only hope for any kind of justice. Such an alliance implies a proximity to all the other signifiers of negation, opposition, and negativity, the ultimate of which is death. The Devil in the tale is a bearer of death. Seeing things through the Devil's eyes entails having one's eyes filled with images of death. One cannot but remember, at this point, the central role that death has had in Pasolini's films, the kind of precious perspective that it always seemed to disclose. Think of Accattone dying: "Now I'm fine!" Think of Othello and Iago discovering the beauty of creation only after death, on a pile of garbage. The Friar's tale suggests that the perspective from the point of view of death is related to the homosexual gaze.

Pasolini was tormented by critics because of what Miccichè called *l'ideologia della morte* (the ideology of death).[25] From Right to Left, his frequent use of the signifier death has been regarded as some morbid residue of a decadent outlook. Our culture is so obsessed with the individual and the personal that we choose to mobilize psychoanalytic explanations, the notorious death instinct, as if this were something that one catches, like a virus. And we have not had enough common sense to explore homosexual narrative paradigms.

The history of what Vito Russo calls "the celluloid closet" went through three phases.[26] The first was invisibility: homosexuality could not be represented. It was the time when Murnau appropriated the figure of Nosferatu to his homosexual sensibility: a vampire, the undead who has no reflection in the mirror. It is also the time when James Whale, the first director ever to come out of the closet (and be fired for it), brought to the screen H. G. Wells's *The Invisible Man*. The second phase was that of the psycho-pathologization of the few homosexuals that made it to the screen. The case of Sebastian Venable in Mankiewicz's *Suddenly Last Summer* (1959) is emblematic. We do not see Sebastian for practically the entire film, and yet he is there, as the monster behind the screen. And when we do see him, he slinks along the streets in pursuit of boys ("famished for the dark ones") and is eventually devoured by his grimy victims. Death, usually violent, seems to be waiting at the end of the textual trajectories in which homosexuality appears.

The third phase was the slow emergence from the closet. It was here that death established itself as a homosexual narrative paradigm. As reported by Russo, "in twenty-two of twenty-eight films dealing with gay subjects from 1962 to 1978, major gay characters on screen ended in suicide or violent death."[27] Twenty-two out of twenty-eight! Can we still be surprised at Accattone's death? Pasolini's *ideologia della morte* may have had other determinants (Catholicism, for example), but it finds its most logical explanation in his homosexual discourse, qua discourse of suppression. Suppression entails a feeling of nonbeing which, upon one's entrance into discursive practices, is translated into the signifier death.

Hom(m)osexual Anamorphosis

Il fiore delle mille e una notte is the sunniest film in *La trilogia della vita*, the one most approaching the ideal representation of a "particularly deep-rooted, violent, and happy Eros, where there is not a single man, not even the most miserable of beggars, who does not have a profound sense of his own dignity."[28] The sex scenes are more relaxed and often bespeak a tenderness that was absent in the other two. The dominant trait of virtually all characters is their smiling faces. They smile making love, saying their lines, upon meeting in the markets, or in the sands of the desert. Most critics saluted this ubiquitous smile as a successful, if fabulous, symbol of the book and its world. Moravia, equally enthusiastic, relates it to the "unexpected, incredible, and wondrous homosexual adventure," the smile of someone operating "within the utopia of an unreachable happiness."[29] For my part, I must agree with Carlo Laurenzi, who found it "irritating and somewhat preposterous, just like the dubbing" (mostly in southern Italian).[30] I cannot help feeling an unnaturalness in the characters' smiles, the trace of too overt an imposition of the author on his material. This is not to say that smiling and laughing must always be motivated, nor must they be natural. But in *Il fiore delle mille e una notte*, the characters' smiles often have the ersatz quality of natives posing for a tourist's snapshot.

As the most ubiquitous sign in the film, smiling substantiates Pasolini's recently developed idea of reality as *gioco* (play), as a suprahuman Being at play with the universe. This conceptual turn may be monitored in the progression of the essays in *Heretical Empiricism*. Pasolini first elaborated a notion of cinema (not film) as the imaginary long-take following the life of a person all the time. He then postulated a Language of Reality as the plural system of signs (words, gestures, physiognomy) forcing us into an endless interpretation of our sur-

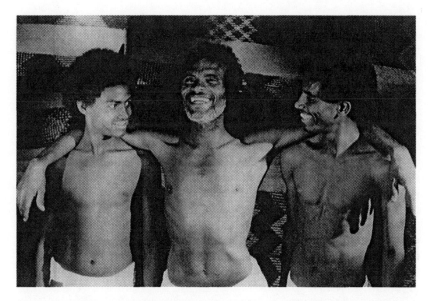

Il fiore delle mille e una notte: Snapshot laughter in front of a Western camera.
Courtesy of the Museum of Modern Art/Film Stills Archive.

roundings. Finally, he attributed a mystical immanence to such a Reality: as the centaur in *Medea* said, everything is sacred. The Language of Reality is nothing but the constant soliloquy that a Brahman-like divinity has with itself, and we are fragments of that speech.[31]

Two observations. Pasolini was closer to the ferments of the sixties generation than most of his contemporaries, and certainly more than he thought. The lasting legacy of that generation is less the perfunctory Maoism of marching students than the massive opening up to Eastern culture. Take New Age philosophy, Yoga, acupuncture, and Yin-and-Yang: today they are such ubiquitous presences in our lives that one cannot help feeling that we are living on the cusp of a movement of cultural fusion with/appropriation of the East begun with Schopenhauer, continued by Nietzsche, Hesse, and others, and slowly reaching mass proportions. The Italian intelligentsia was not ready for that, however. In the sixties, the most comprehensive Italian attempt to date to incorporate Eastern philosophy was still that of the Fascist thinker Julius Evola. Unbelievable though it now sounds, to say that reality is an illusion, during Pasolini's times, was considered a Right-wing statement, so that Pasolini, with his typical *spirito di contraddizione*, insisted on it even more. As with myth, he did not have the appropriate cultural milieu in which to develop a sound integration of ideology and the East, a problem which remains at the heart of much intellectual controversy to this day.[32]

Second, the use of the word "illusion" partially corrects and qualifies the irritating notion of Reality with a capital "R" and of "ontological realism." What we see is not the metaphysical "thing-in-itself" but an illusion, in a film as in reality. Those who criticize Pasolini for collapsing cinematic representation with unmediated reality ought to, at least, situate his ideas where they belong and understand his "extravagant" attempt to merge semiotics with religious pantheism. Again, one cannot help feeling that he came before his time and did not have the appropriate conceptual tools to express what he saw.

Since it is an illusion, reality is hardly worth being taken too seriously: hence the notion of *gioco* (play) which, Pasolini argues, does not exclude realism, for "strange though it may sound, 'to play' in the cinema means to be a professional and. . . to be realist."[33] By this, Pasolini meant that the *gioco* in cinematic narration is a reflection of the *gioco* which is at the heart of reality's unfolding. In other words, if a director wants to portray reality's *gioco*, s/he must obey reality's rules and narrate in accordance with its movements. Conscious of its "Reality Eater" role, *Il fiore delle mille e una notte* tries to mime reality's *gioco* in its very structure: "The journeys of *Il fiore delle mille e una notte* are always the outcome of an initial anomaly of Fate. Everything is normal, Fate is normality. And then the unexpected happens: Fate manifests itself in an abnormal manner." Then, "with the appearance of the first anomaly, another one immediately follows and a whole chain comes into being, and arranges itself, in a narrative form, according to the outline of a journey."[34]

Il fiore delle mille e una notte celebrates the workings of Fate as the underlying principle of reality's *gioco*. In a sense, then, Pasolini reverts to his old realist fantasy of finding an essence beyond the reality of appearances. It is no longer the Marxist economic base, nor is it some Greek myth. It is a new myth: Fate. Once they are viewed through the lens of Fate, the chance occurrences scattered through one's lifetime come together and show an order in depth. What kind of vision is required to perceive the underlying order behind *il gioco*?

It is hardly coincidental that Schopenhauer, the first Western philosopher to assimilate the Eastern notion of Fate, conceived of the best way for us to think of the kind of vision at work in *Il fiore delle mille e una notte*. Arguing that, as a rule, we dislike giving Fate too large a role and prefer "empirical interpretations," Schopenhauer wrote that, in fact, just as in the cases of those pictures called anamorphoses, which to the naked eye are only broken, fragmentary deformities but when reflected in a conic mirror show normal human forms—so the purely empirical interpretation of the course of the world resembles the seeing of those pictures with naked eyes, while the recognition of the intention of Fate resembles the reflection in the conic mirror, which binds together and organizes the disjointed, scattered fragments.[35]

To a reality increasingly perceived as an anamorphic picture with "fragmentary deformities," Pasolini applies his own "conic mirror," his cinema of "realism and fantasy," in order to catch a glimpse of what "organizes the disjointed, scattered fragments." The "conic mirror" is the last variant of Pasolini's realist gaze.

Il fiore delle mille e una notte tries to distill *il gioco*'s order by linking the tales with one another in a way similar to the way in which Fate "binds together and organizes" the chance occurrences in life. As is to be expected, Pasolini harnesses the notion of Fate to that of normality or, better yet, heterosexuality, so that deviancy becomes the underlying principle of its order. Enjoying an unprecedented expressive freedom, Pasolini is at last in a position to make his first film where homosexuality explicitly "organizes" and "binds" the text. Instead of hiding it in subtexts or using metaphors for it, he finally succeeds in presenting homosexuality as the "conic mirror" through which anamorphic reality can make sense. "Homosexuality, together with magic, is the antagonistic element of *Il fiore delle mille e una notte*. The protagonist element, let me say once more, is destiny, which, nevertheless, would not become aware of itself if it were not contradicted by the very thing that it cannot recover."[36] With the notion of reality as *gioco*, Pasolini is finally able to think of homosexuality in positive terms. Granted, it is "an anomaly of fate," but homosexuality has the sublime role of the violation making the larger order possible.

The larger order is heterosexuality, and, as I mentioned above, Pasolini seems to have found the serenity to want to portray it with a smile. It has even been suggested that *Il fiore delle mille e una notte* sings a paean to femininity and contains elements of a feminist critique to the male world—as one would also expect from Dacia Maraini's participation in the filmscript. Undoubtedly, men are often negatively compared to women. The tale providing the frame for the film sets Nur ed Din's dimwittedness against Zumurrud's genial capacity for making the best of any situation. Aziz (Ninetto Davoli) exploits Aziza's interpretive powers to his own ends. The film's finale, with the king who is in fact a queen, is an indictment of a male-dominated society obsessed with phallic symbols of power, and is an index of the actual superiority

290 La trilogia della vita

of women who deserve leading roles, albeit in disguise. But it is not all gold that glitters. A brief digression on Pasolini's relation to Woman/women may be useful here.[37]

Pasolini's explicit opinions on women varied in accordance with the context. Reported by his biographer Siciliano to have said that "they have no soul," he also often remarked that he saw them as victims. Occasionally, Pasolini exalted the nonrational principle needed to correct the course of Western history as being feminine (the Erinyes-Eumenides). He did not understand, however, the neo-feminist movement which by the early seventies was zeroing in on all the various aspects of the oppression of women in a society like Italy's. His stand on abortion and his irritation at the increasing freedom obtained by Italian girls prove that, here as elsewhere, his ideas were self-serving. All things considered, Pasolini did not think and act consistently with his strenuous belief in the importance of the private sphere. In one and the same gesture, he denied the legitimacy of feminism and the possibility of solidarity among homosexuals.

Turning to his films, one finds an occasionally genuine attempt at letting women speak, as in *Comizi d'amore*, where he ruthlessly probes the double standards in Italian culture. But that was a documentary. In his fiction films one finds a general inability on his part to portray complex female characters beyond the mother/whore scheme. Most women in his films are either sublime examples of meek, self-sacrificing femininity (e.g., Stella and Nannina in *Accattone*, Emilia and Odetta in *Teorema*) or sexual bait eagerly waiting on the margins of a male world (Bruna in *Mamma Roma*). Framed by a window in a building under construction, the winged girl whom Ninetto Innocenti goes to see in *Uccellacci uccellini* encapsulates both tendencies in one image. Ninetto is attracted to the angel and distracted by the sexual desire she represents. In sum, women are either de- or over-sexualized, without a clear attempt to probe the fact that their sexuality may indeed lie outside our (male) binary scheme.

On the subject of "physiognomic realism," Georgia Brown aptly remarked that "if men are photographed for reality, women can be immensely artificial."[38] Defined by Pasolini himself as his "tendency to 'Raphaelize' women,"[39] this artificiality is best exemplified by how he selected makeup, lighting, and framing for one of his favorite actresses: Silvana Mangano. Playing the high-coiffured mannequin in *Teorema* or the lip-biting Giocasta, she is always pale and somewhat eerie. The characters played by Mangano are perhaps his most vivid tribute to his beloved Mizoguchi, whose film *Ugetsu*, declaredly one of Pasolini's favorites, contains an unforgettable kabuki-like ghost-woman who waylays the protagonist.

When sexualized, Pasolini's women are framed in and by the tritest commonplace, which insists that their desire hinges on the penis. This is nowhere clearer than in *La trilogia della vita*, where shots of male organs juxtaposed to countershots of coveting females abound. Obviously a projection of how we (males) live our sexuality, this regime of representation has a conventionally Freudian underpinning: penis envy. Zumurrud's travesty as a man is in a sense just a cinematic translation of Lacan's idea that "it is in order to be the phallus, that is to say, the signifier of the desire of the Other, that the woman will reject an essential part of her femininity, notably all its attributes through masquerade."[40] The phallus is all there is. The shot of the nuns reaching out for Masetto's body encapsulates women's desire to possess it, while Aziz's vaginal penetration by means of a bronze phallus mounted on the tip of an arrow ritualizes Woman's desire to be filled at any cost. Absent in the original tale, this visual detail evokes pain and rage in the female spectators and testifies to Pasolini's entrapment in a phallocentric imagination.

Pasolini's tendency to "Raphaelize" women, however, also produces positive results that counter mainstream cinema. The beauty of the males, the shots emphasizing their organs, the aestheticized shot composition privileging male figures are all fragments of an imaginary archive of images opposing the dominant system of visual pleasure. Not that they are shot with women's pleasure in mind. But they are there, on the screen, and they create a ricochet effect: they remind us of the extent to which we are inured to seeing the opposite: tits and ass.

With one brief exception in *Salò*, Pasolini's films never allude to the possibility of female homosexuality. A symptom of his estrangement from the rising gay/lesbian movement, this omission also confirms that he saw the world from the masculine perspective alone. By definition subversive in a heterosexist country, his homosexuality also had a conservative element to it: the nostalgia for an all-male world, the refusal to see women. In short, Pasolini was a hom(m)osexual, that is, someone who inherits and brings to an extreme the misogynist tendencies in our culture, its wish for an all-male world.

Hom(m)osexuality runs through *Il fiore delle mille e una notte* practically from beginning to end. It starts with the old poet Ramsun picking up three beautiful Erithrean boys, an autobiographical confession invented by Pasolini, who thus establishes the connection between verbal creativity and homosexuality. The film contains dozens of instances in which a character quoting a few lines of poetry begins with the formula: "As the poet says." Although it is not men alone who use poetry (Zumurrud does too), the quotes always celebrate male beauty.

The stories of Yunan and Shazaman, the two artists helping Taji to make the mosaic for the queen Dunya, provide a cogent example of the conic mirror making events fall into place. In the book they are separate tales and there is no indication that Yunan and Shazaman work together in a crypto-homosexual bond. Contoured by the signifiers of Pasolini's homo-pathological vision (death and dismemberment), these two tales contain many visual allusions to male homoeroticism, so as to engender the feeling that the struggle against destiny is, more precisely, a struggle against heterosexuality lived as manifest destiny. Quite ingeniously, Pasolini narrates their stories in such a way that they form a curvilinear movement. We start in a underground bedroom with Shazaman making love to a girl therein kept prisoner by a demon (Franco Citti!). Yunan's tale, after portraying all the possible ways by which he attempts to escape his destiny, ends in another underground room where he first enjoys the company of a boy and then murders him in his sleep. Both Yunan and Shazaman will be sad artists, their eyes closed in the rapture of a vision.

A detail in the story of Taji and Dunya neatly summarizes the hom(m)osexual deception at the heart of *Il fiore delle mille e una notte*. Dunya is the beautiful princess who did not want to have anything to do with men because of a dream that she had. In this dream she saw a male dove selfishly abandon its female companion in a hunters' net. Men are all alike, she concludes. Faced with her refusal of men, Taji succeeds in creating another dream for her. With the help of Shazaman and Yunan, he makes a mosaic explaining why the male dove did not return to help the female. The male had been killed by the hunters and thus he could not return. Convinced by his claim that "the truth does not lie in one dream but in many dreams," Dunya will change her mind about men and will marry Taji.

Dunya, however, does not know the whole truth about Taji. When he first found out about Dunya's existence, Taji slew a dove in order to make it bleed on his jacket and cause his father to believe that he is dead. Taji, in other words, obtained his freedom from family ties by killing a dove. Dunya, of course, does not know this. Their union thus rests on Taji's unseen violence against the very object of her worries. Art lies, or, at least, it omits the truth. As in the Ciappelletto episode, art befuddles people so as to allow the artist to reach his goals. Deception through art can change fate by making people visualize other dreams, as *Il fiore delle mille e una notte* in a sense did.

Pasolini's idea of an anamorphic reality which people live as their manifest destiny is artistically fruitful. And so is his suggestion that we need transgression as the conic mirror that makes us perceive the underlying patterns behind the chaos of appearance. Pasolini's film, however, did not go far enough in his use of the conic mirror, for he was entrapped in his hom(m)osexuality. Spectators must appropriate the conic mirror for themselves and use it to "organize" the film's muddled message. And we must organize it by using the sentence with which Taji convinces Dunya to forsake her bad dream, and with which the film most appropriately begins: the truth is not in one dream but in several dreams. Taken out of context, this sentence is a splendid celebration of difference, an implicit indictment of a monotheistic perspective. The implicit celebration of Difference, however, cannot be exempt from the questions that ideological awareness would raise. Who are the dreamers? Do the dreams of famous filmmakers have more power than others? And, above all, why are we dreaming what we are dreaming?

22

Salò o le 120 giornate di Sodoma

The action takes place in 1944 during the *Repubblica di Salò*, that is the Nazi-controlled, northern Italian state which tried to oppose the Allies' progress (a small town on the Garda Lake, Salò was the seat of the government). After marrying each other's daughters, four dignitaries—a Duke, a Bishop, an *Eccellenza* (Chief Magistrate), and a President—organize mass arrests of youths in order to select sixteen perfect specimens and take them, together with guards, servants, and *fouteurs* (studs with enormous organs), into a palace near the town of Marzabotto (although not near Salò, Marzabotto was chosen because its population was massacred by the Nazis). In addition, there are four middle-aged women: three will recount arousing stories; the fourth will accompany their narration on the piano. The narrative is subsequently divided into three parts whose titles recall Dante's/De Sade's Hell: the Circle of Manias, the Circle of Shit, and the Circle of Blood. During the first, Signora Vaccari tells stories of her past encounters with sex maniacs, and the four libertines often interrupt her to act out their fantasies or make philosophical comments. Signora Maggi then continues the narration in the second circle. The theme of coprophagy comes to a climax with a dinner of excrement celebrating the President's marriage to a boy in drag. The final circle, centering around Signora Castelli's stories, is a prelude to the final horror, in which all the boys and girls who did not comply with the libertines' desires are tortured. The night before the "judgment day," the libertines catch a guard making love to a black servant—the only example of "normal" sex in the film.

They shoot both of them, while the guard raises his fist in a Communist salute. On the final day, the pianist commits suicide by throwing herself out of a window. The tortures then begin. Each of the libertines takes his turn as a voyeur, watching through binoculars as the other three perform the most horrible mutilations. The film ends with the image of two soldiers dancing together to a soft tune coming from the radio.

> *The thrill of a "more realistic" film always comes when we sense, at some level, that an already accepted (and thus tamed) realism is being pushed beyond, toward the real itself, and thus, as in life, screen events are "out of control" and we cannot predict what will happen.*
>
> Peter Brunette

Fate turned *Salò o le 120 giornate di Sodoma* (Salò, 1975, hereafter referred to as *Salò*) into Pasolini's last film. This is a large responsibility for a text, especially in view of Pasolini's fascination with how the little tear that Buonconte shed before dying altered the perspective of everything that had occurred in his life (see chapter 4, *Accattone*). How does *Salò* reflect back on Pasolini's filmography, which started, it will be remembered, with a quotation from Dante's account of that very tear? At the risk of sounding perversely snobbish, I would like to argue that, cinematically speaking, Pasolini's career could not have found a better ending. To be sure, *Salò* is a cry of despair, and its images are often unbearable. Nevertheless, it does not contain anything that we have not seen before. And unlike his other films, *Salò* cannot be pruned, trimmed, or reformed.

Salò radicalizes, and thus purifies, Pasolini's vocation as a Nietzschean, or, better, a "black" filmmaker (see *La rabbia*). In their discussion of Sade's novels in *The Dialectic of the Enlightenment*, Adorno and Horkheimer argued that Sade and Nietzsche were "two black writers" who exposed the dark side of reason:

Unlike its apologists, the black writers of the bourgeoisie have not tried to ward off the consequences of the Enlightenment by harmonizing theories. They have not postulated that formalistic reason is more closely allied to morality than to immorality. Whereas the optimistic writers merely disavowed and denied in order to protect the indissoluble union of reason and crime, civil society and domination, the dark chroniclers mercilessly declared the shocking truth.[1]

Pasolini was the black filmmaker of the bourgeoisie, and *Salò* retrospectively confirms it. When Sergio Citti (Franco's brother and Pasolini's life-long collaborator as well as director of "Pasolinian" films such as *Ostia* [1971] and *Storie Scellerate* [Wicked Stories, 1973]) asked his help for the screenplay of a film on Sade's *Les cent-vingts journées de Sodome* (The Hundred and Twenty Days of Sodom), Pasolini first accepted, then grew enthusiastic, and finally claimed the project all for himself.[2] And as if to prove that aesthetic success rewards those who work at what is congenial to them, *Salò* turned out to be Pasolini's most perfect film, a stylistic revelation for those who had given up on him after *La trilogia della vita*'s touristic beauty and cinematic sloppiness.[3]

Salò corrects the errors of *La trilogia della vita*, where Pasolini thought he could celebrate a joy that was not his. In a now famous article, Pasolini publicly repudiated the films which had made him one of Italy's most popular (and richest) filmmakers.[4] Three, he argued, were the reasons that had prompted him to make *La trilogia della vita*: (1) his struggle against censorship, on behalf of the sexual liberation of the screen; (2) his conviction that "the last bulwark of reality seemed to lie in those 'innocent' bodies with the archaic, dark, vital violence of their sexual organs"; (3) his personal fascination with "the representation of Eros in a human environment which has not been quite overtaken by history (in Naples, in the Middle East)."

> Now all that has been turned upside down.
> First: the progressive struggle for democratization of expression and for sexual liberation has been brutally superseded and cancelled out by the decision of consumerist power to grant a tolerance as vast as it is false.
> Second: even the "reality" of innocent bodies has been violated, manipulated, enslaved by consumerist power—indeed, such violence to human bodies has become the most typical feature of our time.
> Thirdly: private sexual lives (like my own) have suffered the trauma both of false tolerance and of physical degradation, and what used to be the joy and pain of sexual fantasies, is now suicidal disappointment or utter apathy.

Although still relying on the self-serving fallacy that reduced reality to sex, Pasolini left behind, at last, the dream of an innocent enclave outside history. Everybody is the same in the face of consumerist power, of the "new Power": "I write Power with the capital 'P' because I do not know what this new Power is. I simply acknowledge its existence."[5] Hearkening back to the rational lucidity evinced in *Porcile*, Pasolini returned to the investigation of the new social logic that shaped and framed contemporary reality.

Let us not be misunderstood. By his own admission, Pasolini was still confused about what this "Power" was doing and how to represent it. More than that, he confessed to having very "private" reasons determining his idea of a Power that changed the bodies of people. As with the vitriolic essays in *Scritti corsari*, his vision must be taken *cum grano salis*. What concerns me here is that Pasolini felt the need to relocate his focus on contemporary reality after the vacation taken with *La trilogia della vita*. With *Salò*, Pasolini returned to the representation of contemporary reality, not in a naturalistic fashion but by analogy, in the allegorical mode which constituted the peak of his "certain realism" (*Teorema, Porcile*). As the last tear shed by Pasolini before dying, *Salò* confirmed that his cinema had one obsessive concern: reality.

And realism. Paradoxically, however, *Salò* was the only film that Pasolini did not describe by mobilizing the term "realism." After his confused declarations about the realism of *Medea* and *La trilogia della vita*, the term had perhaps reached a nadir of meaning and could no longer serve his purposes. *Salò* nevertheless marked his most definite return to the portrayal of contemporary reality. Pasolini's many interviews on the film (unfortunately all before its showing) leave no doubt: he wanted to represent the new Power, the new reality, allegorically. And within the space of allegory, *Salò* harbored a powerful argument in favor of realism.

Let us take a close look at Pasolini's basic argument. He saw a "new Power" that tolerated no outside and therefore coopted "the last bulwark of reality." For Pasolini, reality was what lay outside the dominant logic, which produced "unreality" instead. In other words, the omnivorous postindustrial state was killing the outside and was thus disposing of reality. Let us now lift this argument from the context of Pasolini's obsessive concerns and graft it onto the critical discourse on/against realism that was flourishing in those years. For the most part, contemporary film theory was intent on demolishing the premises of mimetic realism, that is, the notion that a text can represent an outside reality. The argument against realism took the recurrent form of a critique of referentiality; in this view, there could no longer be any possibility for a text to represent an outside. Indeed, many of the essays that appeared in *Screen*, *Filmcritica*, and *Cahiers du cinéma* were re-elaborations and variations of Derrida's famous epigram "the outside is the inside." Discourse is all there is, discourse is all there ought to be: there is no outside.

Thus, on one side, Pasolini, in his furious isolation, was pouring at his contempt for a social text which left no outside. On the other, "anti-realists" were criticizing the dream of an outside. A most intriguing parallel existed between these two positions, as if they were both describing the same thing, albeit with very different connotations. Pasolini nostalgically missed what the antirealists attacked. To be sure, they were addressing two different types of text, respectively the social and the cinematic. But the terms with which they visualized the problems were the same.

My contention is that Pasolini, by lamenting the disappearance of "the last bulwark of reality," was lamenting the disappearance of referentiality. It does not really matter if for him the ultimate referent was sex or the innocent bodies. That was the debt he paid to his private obsessions. What counts is that he was regretting the disappearance of an outside reality and the reduction of everything to one discourse: the discourse of whoever makes the rules in the social text. Pasolini was left with a signifying system that had totally lost its referential dimension, its capacity to represent an outside. As a consequence of this, he could no longer conceive of reality. He was forced to dispense with this, his dearest concept, the idea that had accompanied him throughout his artistic trajectory. It is in the light of this observation that I shall propose a reading of *Salò* as the desperate, allegorical portrayal of the enemies of "a certain realism." Before pursuing my reading, however, it may be useful to dispel possible misconceptions about what *Salò* is.

What Is *Salò o le 120 giornate di Sodoma*?

Salò is "irredeemable"; *Salò* is "the reign of perversion"; *Salò* is "the most powerfully upsetting movie ever made."[6]

Why should I even attempt to prescribe an intellectual use of what for many is an unbearable spectacle? Is it good to become so inured to its images that one perceives them as aesthetic objects? I cannot forget the comment made by a woman friend of mine upon our first (and, for her, last) viewing of the film: "Only a man could have made this!" She was the only woman in the theater. Since then, I have seen the film a few more times in such different places as Paris, Cambridge, and Rome, and, again, I have remarked that the public was virtually all male. The more I watched the film, however, the less I was taken by its images of degradation. Once I saw it in San Francisco, where a predominantly (male) gay audience taught me something about film reception. As they had obviously watched *Salò* a few times, they were able to see ketchup and chocolate instead of blood and excrement. They knew some of its infamous lines by heart (the *Presidente*'s jokes) and they laughed. I felt like I was watching another rerun of the *Rocky*

Horror Picture Show. Recently, while analyzing *Salò* sequence by sequence on the VCR, I heard myself laughing at some scenes. I began to see its camp humor and theatricality, and a desperate beauty. On two or three occasions, I even felt that "surge of vitality" (*aumento di vitalità*) that Pasolini, quoting Berenson, said lies at the heart of an authentic artistic experience.[7] I admit to my own inability to derive theoretical insight from these scattered observations, but I sense that they deserve a place in this chapter, together with my intellectual somersaults.

The critical reception to the film varied considerably. Unduly yet understandably connected with the violent death of its author, *Salò* received enormous press attention. On the one hand, this stimulated the voyeuristic curiosity of many, and, on the other, it "forced" intellectuals to see the film and make statements about it. Some complained that *Salò* betrays Sade. Some regretted its playing with fascism. Some felt that *Salò* proved that now Pasolini had contempt for homosexuality and the flesh.[8] Others used it as a tool to understand contemporary reality. In most cases, perceptive and enriching articles were written—indeed some of the best pieces on Pasolini have been stimulated by *Salò*. But, what is *Salò*?

Salò is not a historical film about the puppet republic that saw the agony of the fascist idols in 1943–1945. Nor is it a film that sheds light on the historical phenomenon of fascism. Although a preliminary title informs us that the narrated events take place in 1944 in northern Italy, the libertines' quotations from Barthes and Klossowsky betray the text's utter disrespect for historical realism and chronological consistency. As with the road sign indicating Marzabotto (the Tuscan village destroyed by the Nazis), the fascist uniforms worn by the guards, and the Führer's speech on the radio, the name "Salò" is a mere device which the text uses to connote and enrich its allegory. All the reminders of fascism create an atmosphere and warn us that the film demands a political reading. "Fascism" was a central signifier for any political narration in Europe, and Pasolini did not use it solely to indicate the 1922–1945 dictatorship. In his review of Naldini's documentary, *Fascista* (1974), he thus described the difference between Mussolini's regime and the new Power:

> In Naldini's film we have seen youth regimented, in uniforms. Once out of uniform, however, the young would head to their native villages and fields, and would return to being the Italians of one hundred, one hundred fifty years before. Fascism had transformed them into clowns and serfs, and perhaps had even partially indoctrinated them, but did not touch their soul, their real identity. On the contrary, consumer society, i.e., this new fascism, has deeply changed this youth, has touched them

intimately and has given them other ways of thinking and living, in short other cultural models. It is no longer a question, as with Mussolini's regime, of a picturesque and superficial regimentation, but of a real regimentation which steals their soul from them.[9]

Pasolini did not have the slightest interest in portraying the days of historical fascism. His heart and mind were concentrated on the "real regimentation" which was stealing the people's "soul from them." Hence, *Salò*'s unrigorous use of fascist material did not seek to describe the past but to enlighten the present.

    Salò is not a rigorous cinematic adaptation of the Sadean text. Nor does it intend to establish a link between fascism and sexual perversion, as did, say, Cavani's *Portiere di notte* (The Night Porter, 1974) or Brass's *Salon Kitty* (1976). As with fascism, *Salò* quotes Sade, extensively, from beginning to end. It quotes his words, it gives image to some of the episodes narrated in *Les 120 journées de Sodome*, and it borrows its ferocious and claustrophobic storyline. If Pasolini needed a fascist iconography to ensure a political reading of his film, he also needed Sade to enforce the sense of violence perpetrated against the body. More important, Pasolini found in Sade a black writer, "a marvelous desecrator who used the Reason of the Enlightenment to desecrate not only what the Enlightenment desecrated but also the Enlightenment itself, through the monstrous use of its rationality."[10]

    Salò is not a film rejecting, denying, and denouncing homosexuality, nor is it the film in which Pasolini's own guilt would emerge in all of its force. The fact that the four libertines prohibit heterosexual behavior and declare their passion for sodomy does not imply a negative judgment on homosexuality, which, in any case, is not sodomy. In fact, one finds in *Salò* the first and only example of female homosexuality in Pasolini's films, and it has positive connotations. *Salò* does not deal with homosexuality per se. As with fascism and Sade, *Salò* quotes images of sodomitic behavior, partly because Pasolini is obviously intrigued by the opportunity of its portrayal, partly because it is in Sade's original, and partly because it is a metaphor for bodies forced to do what they "normally" do not like doing. Pasolini could not make heterosexuality the norm, for there would have been the risk of the victims enjoying it. Hence, with objective rigor, *Salò* quotes fragments of sodomitic discourse as it is found in Sade and in the studies on him.

    Beyond fascism, Sade, and sodomy, *Salò* quotes, albeit to a much lesser degree, Dante's *Inferno*, Barthes, Pound, Klossowsky, Nietzsche, Hitler, Proust, Orff, and Gassendi. During a coffee break, the *Eccellenza* (the writer Paolo Uberto Quintavalle) recites a passage from *The Genealogy of Morals*, but he ascribes it to Baudelaire. Upon the *Presidente*'s (Aldo Valletti) remark that it is Nietzsche, the *Eccellenza* replies that "it is neither; nor is it St. Paul's Epistle to the Romans: it is Dada." Names are thrown together because quotations do not signify creative appropriations of different texts but the mere weight of authority, the *ipse dixit*. It does not really matter who said what and when. What counts is that there is a space ritually dedicated to quotations proving that power is in the right hands. As an instrument of domination, culture can dispense with content and exist as mere form. In this respect, *Salò*'s cultural cauldron is a mimetic parody of *forced equivalence* in which all signs end up meaning the same thing.

It is worth paying closer attention to the film's full title: *Salò or the 120 days of Sodom*. Herein, we note that "or" does not serve its most usual disjunctive function, as in "love or hate." Likewise, it does not introduce an alternative as in "soup or salad." Nor does it express approximation as in "two or three." Rather, it suggests an equivalence, a "that is," *un'omologazione* (homogenization, the key word in Pasolini's *Scritti corsari*). The film's content is practically preannounced by the title. In other words, the "or" in the title indicates that the subject of the film will be an arbitrary equivalence imposed from above, whereby different texts and realities are all forced to signify *one* thing. Perhaps the film should have been entitled *Salò or the 120 Days of Sodom or Dante's Inferno or. . . .* This would have prevented the outrage of all fascism experts and Sade specialists who criticized the film for distorting history and/or *Les 120 journées de Sodome*.

Salò is thus an allegory of the annihilation of differences in the name of one principle. It is an allegory of equivalence turning into equiviolence. As an allegory, however, *Salò* constantly runs the risk of failing because of the nature of its images. If an allegory is meant to deliver another set of meanings to the literal, *Salò*'s images are too brutal, too horrifying, to let the viewer move from one level to the other. When viewers see a shocking image on the screen for the first time, they find it hard to climb allegory's fabulous pyramid. Thus Pasolini's film forces viewers to stick to the literal meaning.

At the end of his repudiation of *La trilogia della vita*, Pasolini wrote: "I readjust my commitment to greater legibility (*Salò?*)." With such a statement he captured the essence of his new film: its images are almost too legible so that, upon a first viewing, everybody has the same reaction. In this respect, *Salò* represents the victory of referentiality. Its images are not ambiguous, but have a meaning that the viewers cannot escape. While this ought to be seen in the light of Pasolini's critique of the fashionable postmodern illegibility of the sign,

Salò's excessive legibility is an obstacle to its allegorical intentions. Again, it takes repeated viewings for one to go beyond the literal and appreciate this film's tremendous allegory of the present.

As an allegorical indictment of contemporary reality, *Salò* has left its mark. Together with *Scritti corsari* and *Lettere Luterane*, Pasolini's last film offered a set of images and metaphors which many Italian intellectuals have since used to apprehend the cultural degradation of the last fifteen years. In itself, this constitutes a proof of Pasolini's return to the realist scene. His decision not to portray the new Power in a naturalistic fashion gives *Salò* an endurance, a capacity to last as a source of metaphors to be used when thinking and speaking of the present reality. This dimension of the film is sufficiently well known, however, and Pasolini's ideas on contemporary Italy have already been examined in this book. I will thus use *Salò* in a different way. Starting from the assumption that Pasolini's last film is a violent outcry against the enemies of reality, I shall treat *Salò* as a bitter, extreme parody of the enemies of realism.

In 1974, crowning a series of articles that demolished the notions of "reality" and "realism," *Screen* published MacCabe's article, "Notes on Some Brechtian Theses," which elaborated the category of the "classic realist text."[11] Although distinguishing between progressive, subversive, and reactionary realist texts, MacCabe argued that virtually all narrative films evince the realist fallacy typical of the nineteenth-century novel: the narrative produces a dominant discourse which indicates whether or not what the characters do and say is true. There is a master discourse that provides the viewer with a sense of where reality and truth lie. To put it in MacCabe's own words: "The narrative of events—the knowledge which the film provides of how things really are—is the metalanguage in which we can talk of the various characters in the film." Caught in the rhetoric of a radical equality at all costs, MacCabe used the word "realism" to indicate a text in which all the signs are subordinated to one principle. It is as if MacCabe and Pasolini were addressing the same kind of operation, the former in filmic texts, the latter in social texts.

The formal resemblance between the two arguments became even more striking two years later when, in the article "Theory and Film: Principles of Realism and Pleasure," MacCabe referred to "classical realism" as "the homogenization of different discourses by their relation to one dominant discourse—assured of its domination by the security and transparence of the image."[12] If we replace "image" with "new Power," we could very well be talking about how *Salò* describes the *omologazione* of reality affected by the new social logic. Pasolini accuses the enemies of reality of doing the same thing that MacCabe blames on realism. I am struck by this coincidence; suspicious of Mac-Cabe's use of the nineteenth-century novel as the basis of realism; annoyed by MacCabe's idea of calling "realist" a film like *American Graffiti*, whose director and public were certainly far from the ideological horizon of the historical forms of realism; and critical of Mac-Cabe's ignoring Pasolini's intention to lay a base for "a certain realism" (indeed, for him, Pasolini was probably a "naive" realist). I also suspect that Pasolini would not have called "realism" the homogenization of the discourses in the text, because for him realism and reality somehow went together, the former being the constant struggle to chase the latter, however elusive such a chase may turn out to be. Prompted by these reflections, and encouraged by the demand for an allegorical reading contained in the "or" of *Salò or the 120 Days of Sodom*, I shall read Pasolini's indictment of the enemies of reality as a parody of what the enemies of realism do.

Salò or the Classic Nonrealist Text

Four sado-fascists kidnap twenty-two boys and girls and force them not only to forget who they were in the real world but also to acquire another identity as instruments of their pleasure. The four libertines abusing their victims are like a film director who chooses the signs, that is, the characters of a story, and masterminds their interaction in a textual system. To the extent that the victims become captive signs and are locked in a space in which any communication with the outside world is prohibited, the resulting text will be nonrealist. Here, I shall call the imaginary director of a nonrealist text "the libertine author." And I shall call the signs employed in such a text "the captive signs."

Salò gives the nonrealist text an architectural metaphor: the *Palazzo*. Once inside the *Palazzo*, the captive signs can only hear far distant rumbles, cannons, bombers. Aural communication with the outside is blurred. The decor inside the *Palazzo* is that "of the Italian Bauhaus": "We have paintings by Feininger, Severini, and Duchamps."[13] The association with modernism is carried further by the abundance of art-deco mirrors, lamps, and various other objects. Interestingly, Pasolini had always resisted the temptation of creating intriguing images with mirrors in his films. Here, they become an essential part of the film, as if to indicate that, in the classic nonrealist text, signs can only signify themselves. Each of the circles begins with images of mirrors, images in front of mirrors. We even get a protracted shot of one of the favorite modernist metaphors, the text as *mise-en-abîme*, when the pianist (Sonia Saviange) and *signora Vaccari* (Hélène Surgère) perform a vaudeville number between two endlessly reflecting mirrors.

A crucial operation in the making of a nonrealist text is the preliminary enlistment of the signs which will be granted access into the *Palazzo*. *Salò* calls this important operation *antinferno* and uses two distinct sets of images: fascist dragnets and the three sequences in which the victims are rigorously examined by the libertines. The fascist dragnets are shot from afar, in a neorealist style. As a metaphor, they well convey the sense of the violence with which a nonrealist text enlists the captive signs and forces them to wear a uniform, to enter *one* form. In the three sequences depicting the physical scrutiny of the captive signs, Pasolini returns to his favorite figure, the reverse field made of frontal close-ups. This time, however, the exploration of faces is conducted from the point of view of the Sadean libertines, who do not tolerate the irregular features that so much intrigued Pasolini, the physiognomical realist. The choice of the bodies and faces follows criteria of beauty and perfection, à la Hollywood.

A detail in the third of the three sequences dedicated to the selection of the captive signs illustrates the extent to which *Salò* makes use of Sade's original while adding material that best parodies the making of a nonrealist text. In the book, we read that "a girl, beautiful as the daylight, was excluded because she had a tooth that had come in a little above the others."[14] In the film, this incident is given great emphasis. The four libertines sit on a couch and scrutinize the girl attentively, sipping their wine, while *signora Maggi* (Elsa De Giorgi) boasts of her beauty. Asked to undress, the girl smiles, revealing a gap in her teeth. Horrified at this sight, the *Duca* (Paolo Bonacelli) orders her immediate removal. Such a modification of the Sadean text is all the more interesting in view of Pasolini's idiolectal use of the mouth. Not only is *Salò* the only film in which there are no broken rows of teeth, but it also dramatizes the exclusion of the irregular mouth from the *Palazzo*, an apt metaphor for the principles of a nonrealist casting.

After the enlistment, the Duca announces the rules and regulations to the victims assembled in the yard, which is to say, the libertine author sets the rules by which the captive signs will interact in the text. All forms of interaction are allowed, except "normal" intercourse. The exclusion of heterosexual intercourse cuts any remaining link with the world of nature. The nonrealist text is afraid of natural bonds, of anything remotely reminiscent of methods of signification other than those imposed by the libertine author. Pasolini always attacked naturalism, and *Salò* did not represent a change of mind on his part. He was, however, also suspicious of the modernists' compulsively repeated rejection of naturalism. In an article entitled "The Fear of Naturalism," Pasolini asked himself: "But why, why such a fear of naturalism? What does this fear hide? Does it perhaps hide the fear of reality?" (*HE*, 245). The prohibition of "natural" sexuality is thus a symptom of the libertine author's fear of reality and realism.

Salò exaggerates this point by inserting deliberate attacks upon the most natural bonds par excellence: motherhood and the family. The attacks start from the very outset, when a boy captured by the fascists abruptly rejects the scarf that his mother hands him: "Go away!" Then there is the systematic violence perpetrated against the daughters of the libertines. During the narrations of the three *signore*, the four guards in fascist uniform literally sit on the libertines' daughters, suggesting visually the attempt to block natural ties. The marriages between the guards and the libertines are instances of the systematic creation of an autonomous system where meaning is subverted, as in a modernist text. But the most striking example of violence against the family is found in the cruel persecution of the girl who lost her mother and in the attendant story, told by the *Duca*, of how much he enjoyed killing his own mother.

After the *Antinferno* and the establishment of the rules, the three circles (Manias, Shit, and Blood) portray the actual, slow process whereby the equivalence among the captive signs is brought about. The captive signs are not aware of the general plan but nonetheless comply with the establishment of a system of equivalence whereby no discourse *inside the text* is granted any privilege (as happens, instead, in a realist text). The three *signore* all have the same status and so have their narratives. No single discourse produced by the text can be the principle of equivalence, for it can only be imposed by the libertine-author's will. In other words, *Salò* makes it clear that the homogenization is not carried out by a dominant discourse *in* the text, as is the case with the realist text according to MacCabe. In the nonrealist text parodied by *Salò*, the equivalence is enforced by an external principle, by the libertine author.

Under a system of equivalence there is a criterion—the Unique— that effaces the actual differences among signs.[15] For example, the new consumerist Power subsumes society under the unique principle of consumption, whereby all citizens are measured against the criterion of just how much they can buy. In a nonrealist text, the Unique is a principle that the libertine author imposes on the captive signs. The Unique cannot be God, as the libertines' explicit prohibition to even mention his name testifies. God would be outside of the system and thus would threaten its autonomy. Moreover, God is *causa prima*, and the libertines in *Salò* denounce external causality with the same violence as they oppose natural signification and commitment to origins (family). The Unique in *Salò* does not have an image, except perhaps negatively, in the black book where the masters record the non-conforming gestures of the captives. Yet the Unique is there as an imposition to collaborate, to participate in the search for pleasure.

In a classic nonrealist text, the captive signs are supposed to efface themselves and be ready to mean anything that the libertine author tells them to mean. The libertine author demands the strictest collaboration of the captive signs, and those who do not comply will be tortured in the final horror. What does the libertine author want? He wants pleasure. The captive signs must always be ready to give pleasure—the *Duca* will praise a boy who has an erection while viewing the tortures: "Good! You were ready!"

Let us look at this pleasure a little more closely. The libertines do not want to be tied down to conventions and rules. As the captive signs must be ready to signify pleasure when and how the masters want, we can say that the libertines use the signs in total disregard of their referential meaning. Their ideal is a sign capable of multiple permutations in accordance with their erotic fantasies. The nonrealist text is thus conceived as an erotic experience where signs can be used (by author and viewer) in an absolutely open way. In this respect, *Salò* can be seen as parodying the constitution of what Barthes, in *Le plaisir du texte* (The Pleasure of the Text), called "the text of bliss," that is "the text that imposes a state of loss, the text that discomforts (perhaps to the point of a certain boredom), unsettles the reader's historical, cultural, psychological assumptions, the consistency of his tastes, values, memories, brings to a crisis his relation with language."[16] *Salò* shows that such a crisis, once it is taken to its extreme, imprisons the signs in a web of refractions; that any text which unsettles values and tastes without indicating the road to a resettling achieves only a masturbatory pleasure inside the *Palazzo* of discourse; and that the state of loss, the bliss of the author and the reader, is achieved by forcing the signs to forget their history and above all by preventing them to mean anything outside of the pleasure system.

Enclosed in the pleasure palace, the captive signs cannot refer to an outside. A girl caught with a picture under her pillow is punished by the libertines, for the photographic image poses the threat of referential representation. The captive signs can only refer to one another, as is sadly indicated by the sequence in which they squeal on one another's secret activities. But the sequence which most clearly parodies the textual system where signs must not refer to an outside is the scatological eating ritual, which is Pasolini's own invention. *Salò* has taken the numerous instances of coprophilia and coprophagia in Sade,

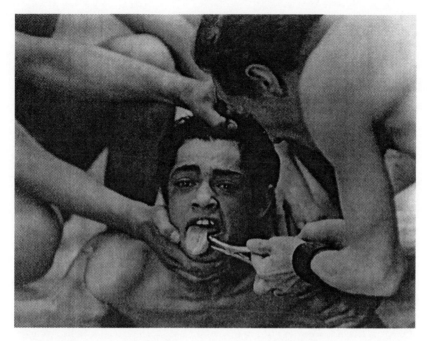

Salò o le 120 giornate di Sodoma: *The libertines' final solution aims at preventing the youth from communicating.* Courtesy of the Museum of Modern Art/ Film Stills Archive.

and has organized them into a provocative climax: a meal of excrement. In *Uccellacci uccellini*, defecation was a joyous act and the anal product was sublimated into symbolic production. In *Salò*, the captive signs are forbidden to defecate individually; their feces are taken away from them, examined, thrown into a common collector, and finally cooked all together. As with the mirrors, the act of eating what has already been consumed signals the vicious circle of a text in which the signs are condemned never to get out of themselves.

Equivalence; prohibition to refer to an outside; a textual system turned into an erotic playground; and an exaggerated attack upon natural signification: all these practices coalesce into a nonrealist gaze. When the time of the final bliss comes, after manias and violence have escalated, the four libertines initiate what is meant to be the ultimate proof of their ability to derive pleasure from the captive bodies. It is the climax of their erotic search: torture. At this point, Pasolini gives us an image which is so similar to and yet so different from the partially obscured vision discussed in his other films that a comparison is unavoidable.

Salò o le 120 giornate di Sodoma: *Partially obscured vision during the selection of the best behind.* Courtesy of the Museum of Modern Art/Film Stills Archive.

The libertines never participate in the torture as a group, but divide and take turns. While three of them unleash their hideous and campy brutality on the victims, the fourth, comfortably seated in a chair by a window, watches through a pair of binoculars. A dark ellipse surrounds the frame, the image is divided in two halves, and a thick, transparent glass is interposed between the observer and the observed. The resulting gaze, however, is a far cry from the partially obscured vision. The libertines' vision is magnified rather than obscured, enhanced rather than fragmented. Celebrating *ratio triumphans*, technical means enlarge or reduce—at one point the *Duca* inverts the binoculars—the image at will. It is the total triumph of the subject over the object. The last image seen through the binoculars is of three libertines alone, dancing a grotesque can-can. The nonrealist gaze sees its own replica everywhere.

The classic nonrealist text entails a claustrophobic enclosure within the walls of the *Palazzo*. In order to better elaborate the outside/inside dialectic, *Salò* makes a significant change from Sade's book and reduces the number of the narrators from four to three, assigning to the fourth *signora* the role of the pianist. While the narrators totally comply with the master plan, the pianist seems reluctant to participate.

Salò o le 120 giornate di Sodoma: *The Duke (Paolo Bonacelli) and production in consumer society.* Courtesy of the Museum of Modern Art/Film Stills Archive.

Throughout the entire film, her face is devoid of expression. From time to time, she stops playing the piano and turns around, usually when something outrageous is being said and done. The audience, searching for a positive character with whom to identify, cannot but see in the blank, pale features of the pianist a potentially "good" character, someone who seems to resist the imposition of pleasure. Our sympathy for her is bound to increase when she improvises a vaudeville number with *signora* Vaccari in order to pacify the libertines. Her potential for action and revealed feelings suggests that her previous silent behavior was due less to shyness than to a conscious choice, the choice of being different through indifference. She is, in other words, the only sign which consistently refuses to play in the text of bliss. To be sure, other signs before her have violated the norms: Ezio, by sleeping with a black servant and dying for it; the boy gunned down for his attempted escape from the truck; the girl who killed herself next to the altar of the Holy Mother; and the few gestures of solidarity and reciprocal comfort exchanged by two of the girls. But all of these violations have not had enough screen time to evoke a sense of identification in the viewer, who can, instead, attach his/her feelings to the pianist.

Salò o le 120 giornate di Sodoma: *The Duke enforces consumption.* Courtesy of the Museum of Modern Art/Film Stills Archive.

At the beginning of the torture sequence, we hear the piano in the background, its tone definitely more somber than before. After a shot of the *Duca* looking through his binoculars, we cut to the pianist getting up and leaving the piano. The camera follows her up the stairs to the last floor, and we then see her sitting on a window sill. We get a close-up of her looking out the window and bringing her right hand to her mouth. In all the copies of the film that I have seen, this last gesture of hers is puzzling. It is as if Pasolini had suddenly reverted to the hasty shooting of *La trilogia della vita,* and the scene stands out in the general formal accuracy of *Salò.* What does the pianist's hand to her mouth mean? Does she suddenly realize or see something that she had overlooked? Is she apologizing? Yawning? Pasolini must have had so clearly in mind what this simple gesture should evoke that he merely hinted at it, in the haste of a shot imperfectly spliced with the rest.

We then cut to a medium shot of the window from inside the room and we see the pianist jumping out. We hear a thudding sound and then cut to her body lying on the concrete. By committing suicide, the pianist finalizes her silent rebellion and indicates the road to an antagonism born of nonparticipation in the game. Needless to say, from the standpoint of realism, the pianist's suicide is a violation of the nonrealist rule. The silent pianist seeks to establish a connection with the outside that she evidently misses, and she makes this connection literally by throwing herself outside. In fact, if we remember how cinematic realism was being accused of conceiving itself as a window on the world, then the pianist becomes a sort of realist agent in the enemy's camp. She embodies the desperate will to search for a referent.

Finale Andante Con Moto

The reader may have noticed occasional similarities between Pasolini's and MacCabe's arguments, especially in what concerns homogenization and equivalence. In effect, *Salò* at once attacks, accepts, and corrects MacCabe's ideas. By associating the libertines with modernism, *Salò* attacks MacCabe's ideal of a text that eschews the naiveté of realism. Such a text, *Salò* argues, is so obsessed with the negation of naturalism, causality, and referentiality, that it creates an omnivorous textual enclosure with no bearing on or tie to the outside world of history. *Salò* accepts MacCabe's argument against the homogenization of discourses and his plea for difference. The system of equivalence is bad news for both Pasolini and MacCabe. But *Salò* also corrects Mac-Cabe's argument in one essential respect. MacCabe criticizes the realist text for harboring a single dominant discourse which homogenizes the signs and indicates their truth or lack thereof. *Salò*, however, shows that even a nonrealist text has a dominant discourse that homogenizes the signs and forces them *not* to point at truth and reality. It seems that some kind of dominant discourse is inevitable.

The realist dominant discourse worked like old fascism: it imposed the discourse of reality, although nearly everyone was aware that there is no such thing as Reality. In the case of Pasolini, moreover, the pursuit of reality was a textual goal, but it was constantly kept in check by his awareness that a perfect realism is impossible: hence, "a certain realism." The nonrealist dominant discourse, instead, is like new fascism: it imposes a dominant discourse under the pretense of the pleasure of the text, of freedom. The denial of hierarchy becomes a hierarchy itself. As such, it is more dangerous, because it is not subjected to constant verifications. In the impossibility of a total absence of dominant discourses, one has to choose for the lesser evil: Do you prefer chasing after "a certain reality," or would you rather play in the pleasure palace?

Coda

And the voice which I heard from heaven spoke to me again, and said, Go *and* take this little book which is open in the hand of the angel which stands upon the sea and upon the earth. And I went unto the angel, and said to him, Give me the little book. And he said to me, Take *it*, and eat it up; and it shall make thy belly bitter, but it shall be in thy mouth sweet as honey. And I took the little book out of the angel's hand, and ate it up; and it was in my mouth sweet as honey: and as soon as I had eaten it, my belly was bitter.

Revelations, 7–9

They go, no sound track,
cars and trucks under the arches,
along the asphalt, against the gasometer
in the golden hour of Hiroshima,
twenty years later, deeper and deeper
in their gesticulating death: and I,
late for death, early
for real life, drink the nightmare
of light like dazzling wine.
Nation without hope! The Apocalypse
which has exploded outside conscience
in the melancholy of Mannerist Italy,
has killed everyone—look at them—shadows
trickling gold in the gold of their agony.

P. P. Pasolini

Notes

Notes to Preface

1. Peter Carravetta, "Lines of Canonical Protest: Pasolini's Unfinished Revolution," *Art & Text*, Winter 1989: 55.
2. Jean Baudrillard, *The Evil Demon of Images* (Sidney: Power Institute of Fine Arts, 1987).
3. Umberto Eco, *Lector in fabula* (Milano: Bompiani, 1979), 59–60. Eco's book has not been translated into English. Only parts of it, along with parts from other books of his, went into *The Role of the Reader* (Bloomington: Indiana University Press, 1979), in which Eco does not tackle the interpretation vs. use distinction.
4. Robin Wood, "Responsibilities of a Gay Film Critic," *Movies and Methods*, vol. 2, ed. Bill Nichols (Berkeley, Los Angeles, London: University of California Press, 1985), 649–660.
5. Pier Paolo Pasolini, *Scritti Corsari* (Milano: Garzanti, 1975), 123–131.
6. Naomi Greene, *Pier Paolo Pasolini: Cinema as Heresy* (Princeton: Princeton University Press, 1990).
7. There are two biographies of Pasolini, one of which is available in English: Enzo Siciliano, *Vita di Pasolini* (Milano: Rizzoli, 1978), trans. by John Shepley as *Pasolini: A Biography* (New York: Random House, 1982); and Nico Naldini, *Pasolini: una vita* (Torino: Einaudi, 1989). Although extremely informative, Siciliano's biography is often too wrapped up in its author's artistic prose and relies too much on traditional psychoanalysis. Naldini (Pasolini's cousin), on the contrary, refrains from indulging in his literary talent and lets the protagonists speak as much as possible. His biography is made up almost entirely of quotes blended together with factual information. Moreover, for the part of Pasolini's life until 1946, Naldini extensively quotes, and therefore

uncovers, the unpublished *Quaderni rossi* (Red Notebooks), a journal that in-
fused the posthumously published, autobiographical novels *Amado mio* and
Atti impuri (Impure Acts). Throughout the present Essential Biography I refer
to Naldini's book in the text. In the rest of the book, however, references to
Naldini's biography will appear in the endnotes as *Naldini*.

8. Enzo Golino, *Pasolini: il sogno di una cosa* (Bologna: Il Mulino, 1985),
exhaustively investigates Pasolini's pedagogical vocation.

9. Published in *Cinecritica* 13 (April/June 1989): 35–53.

Notes to Chapter One

1. See "Entretien avec Jean-André Fieschi," *Cahiers du cinema* 195
(November 1967): 13.

2. *Naldini*, 20.

3. Pasolini, *L'odore dell'India* (Milano: Longanesi, 1974), 17–18.

4. *Naldini*, 94.

5. *Naldini*, 57.

6. *Naldini*, 194.

7. Franco Fortini, *Saggi Italiani* (Bari: De Donato, 1964), 122.

8. Pierre Bourdieu, *La Distinction* (Paris: Minuit, 1979), trans. by Richard
Nice as *Distinction* (Cambridge: Harvard University Press, 1984). This book is
essential to reframe the discourse on social classes beyond vulgar Marxism.
Bourdieu shows the extent to which any given social class is fragmented into
many class fractions that fight the war for "distinction" among one another.
Hereafter I will refer to the English edition.

9. *HE* will hereafter stand for *Heretical Empiricism* (Bloomington: Indiana
University Press, 1988), Ben Lawton and Louise K. Barnett's translation of
Pier Paolo Pasolini's major collection of theoretical essays, *Empirismo Eretico*
(Milano: Garzanti, 1972). References to this book will appear in the main text.

10. The first is in *Naldini*, 8–9, the second in "E tu chi eri?," interview with
Dacia Maraini, *Vogue Italia* (May 1971): 131–140.

11. See Henneth Lewes, *The Psychoanalytic Theory of Male Homosexuality*
(New York: Simon & Schuster, 1988), 24–47.

12. Giuseppe Zigaina, *Pasolini e la morte* (Bari: Marsilio, 1987).

13. *Naldini*, 29.

14. *Naldini*, 121.

15. *Naldini*, 126–127.

16. David Halperin, *One Hundred Years of Homosexuality* (New York:
Routledge, 1990). On the essentialism vs. constructionism debate, see also Di-
ana Fuss, *Essentially Speaking* (New York: Routledge, 1989) which contains a
most interesting assessment of the question of "identity politics."

17. Dario Bellezza, *Morte di Pasolini* (Milano: Mondadori, 1981).

18. Richard Dyer, "Pasolini and Homosexuality," in Paul Willemen, ed.,
Pasolini (London: British Film Institute, 1977), 58–59. See also Stefano Casi,
ed., *Desiderio di Pasolini* (Bologna: Sonda, 1990).

19. See Laura Betti, ed., *Pasolini: cronaca giudiziaria, persecuzione, morte*
(Milano: Garzanti, 1977).

20. *Naldini*, 18.
21. "Pier Paolo Pasolini par Lui-Même," *Avant-Scène* 97 (November 1969): 41.

Notes to Chapter Two

1. Richard Rorty, *Philosophy and the Mirror of Nature* (Princeton: Princeton University Press, 1979), 317.
2. Richard Rorty, "Pragmatism and Philosophy," in Kenneth Baynes, James Bohman, and Thomas McCarthy, eds., *After Philosophy* (Cambridge: MIT Press, 1987), 28.
3. Feminist thought is changing the foundations of our intellectual practice by asking the questions that Western culture traditionally repressed, first and foremost that of sexual difference: What does it mean to think as a man or as a woman? Does truth have a sex? Indeed, it is a question which must be addressed right away, for everything else depends on it. In fact, "the crisis of reason" which underlies much postmodernism is also a consequence of the questions raised by feminism and, more generally, by the irruption of the Other, of the Colonized, into History. On the relationship between feminism and postmodernism, see Linda Nicholson, ed., *Feminism/Postmodernism* (London: Routledge, 1990).
4. Antonio Gramsci, *Quaderni dal carcere* (Torino: Einaudi, 1975), 1517. A master of interdisciplinary extravagance, Gramsci inspired Pasolini to keep a realistic, that is, down to earth, level of discourse and never to lose sight of popular culture. The "lowering" of theoretical discourse and the attempt to make its language less difficult are among the first political objectives for anyone currently involved in college teaching. To the extent that our society is shunning theoretical reflection as impractical, our students need theory, perhaps to resist the silent indoctrination of contemporary, velvet-gloved totalitarianism. They are, however, afraid of theory, and often rightly so, because it comes as totally disengaged from their everyday experiences. Indeed, following Gramsci and Pasolini, we could start by convincing them that everybody does theory, that only a few do it as a profession and that such a professionalization often entails a loss of use-value without a correlative gain in truth-value.
5. In France, the country which probably has been the most attentive to Pasolini's work, a comprehensive anthology of the articles not published in *HE* is available with an excellent introduction by H. Joubert-Laurencin, ed., *Ecrits sur le cinema* (Lyon: Institut Lumière, 1987).
6. *Film Criticism* 11, nos. 1–2 (Fall-Winter 1986–87): 190–200.
7. In addition to the critiques/assessments mentioned in the text, others have written on Pasolini's theory: G. P. Brunetta, "Gli scritti cinematografici di Pier Paolo Pasolini," *La Battana*, Fiume, 11, no. 32 (March 1974): 127–135 (short and intelligent, argues in favor of Pasolini's non-scientific "extravagance"); Antonio Costa, "The Semiological Heresy of Pier Paolo Pasolini," in Paul Willemen, ed., *Pier Paolo Pasolini* (London: British Film Institute, 1977), 32–42 (very critical); Roberto Turigliatto, "La tecnica e il mito," in Fernaldo

Giammatteo, ed., *Lo scandalo Pasolini* (Roma: Bianco e Nero, 1976), 113–155 (mildly critical and for the most part explanatory); Christopher Wagstaff, "Reality into Poetry," *The Italianist* 5 (1985): 107–132 (very critical: a return to the early misreadings).

8. Umberto Eco, *La struttura assente* (Milano: Bompiani, 1968), 150–160. Eco misunderstands Pasolini on the subject of human action. Whereas the latter had the Marxist notion of practice in mind—what counts in one's life is the example given by one's actions—Eco thought that he was referring to actions as gestures; hence, his reference to proxemics.

9. Umberto Eco, *Segno* (Milano: Mondadori, 1973), 95–96. Eco was right, of course, in detecting in Pasolini a pansemiotic thrust tinted with mysticism, but he was wrong in using the word "metaphysics." Pasolini's mystical bent did not attempt to found a metaphysics. It merely intended to valorize poetic intuitions and metaphorical language in view of a nonrational epistemology.

10. Emilio Garroni, *Progetto di semiotica* (Bari: Laterza, 1972), 62–66. See also "Popolarità e comunicazione nel cinema," *Filmcritica* 175 (1967), now in Edoardo Bruno, ed., *Film segno* (Roma: Bulzoni, 1983), 27–56, where Garroni accuses Pasolini of surreptitiously proposing a return to neorealist populism.

11. See "Un'intervista con Christian Metz," *Film icona* 3 (1989): 10–16. Metz concludes his comments on Pasolini by praising the notion of the "free indirect subjective" which appeared in *HE*, "The Cinema of Poetry," a notion on which he himself is working right now, albeit "in a more scientific and less poetic way." Although a wonderful example of a theorist who often engages in self-criticism, Metz has never changed his mind with respect to Pasolini's excessive "poeticity." Again, we find that the adjective "poetic" is paradoxically used as a means to neutralize Pasolini. The fact is that Metz is perhaps one of the most stubborn believers in the scientific vocation of film criticism. It would be interesting to confront Metz with the possibility that perhaps he still finds Pasolini's essays genial and valid *because* (and not despite the fact that) they were "poetic."

12. In *Cinema: lingua e scrittura* (Milano: Bompiani, 1968), Bettetini briefly presents the terms of Pasolini's polemics with Eco and Metz without really taking a stand (pp. 72–75). In *L'indice del realismo* (Milano: Bompiani, 1971), a well-informed and interesting book dedicated to realism, he *never* uses Pasolini. It is in *Produzione del senso e messa in scena* (Milano: Bompiani, 1974) that Bettetini dismissively hints at Pasolini as Kracauer's double (p. 182).

13. Stephen Heath, "Film, Text, Cinetext," *Screen* 14, no. 3: 109–110.

14. Teresa De Lauretis, *Alice Doesn't* (Bloomington: University of Indiana Press, 1984), 48. Although not discussing Pasolini directly, the last chapter in this book is crucial in understanding where Eco's semiotics fell short and where (my reading of) Pasolini comes in.

15. Gilles Deleuze, *Cinema 1* (Minneapolis: University of Minnesota Press, 1986).

16. Naomi Greene, *Pier Paolo Pasolini*, op. cit., 92–126.

17. Giuliana Bruno, "Heresies: The Body of Pasolini's Semiotics," *Cinema Journal* 3 (Spring 1991): 29–42.

18. Ibid., 34.

19. Ibid., 33.

20. Interspersed with repetitions and misguided semiotic endeavors, there are statements on this entire subject in *HE* which have a typically Pasolinian voice: the uncanny ability to say things in such a way that they will stay with you forever. For example, explaining the effect that cinema has on our perception of reality, he evokes "someone who sees himself for the first time in a mirror and realizes that he is *always* an image and not only in the mirror—not a signified signifying "man," but a signifier himself" (296). Cinema, then, helps our realization that we are nothing but images. As such, it ought to prompt us to seek out who and what is directing our roles, our performance. Hence, no more ontology but only ideology:

> One fact is certain, in any case; that it is necessary to work on these problems, together or alone, with competence or with anger, but it is necessary to work on them. It is necessary to be ideological instead of ontological. Audiovisual techniques are in large measure already a part, that is, of the world of technical neocapitalism, which moves ahead, and whose tendency is to make its techniques ontological instead of ideological; to make them silent and unrelated; to make them habits; to make them religious forms (222).

21. Peter Brunette and David Willis, *Screen/play: Derrida and Film Theory* (Princeton: Princeton University Press, 1989).

22. Giuliana Bruno, "Heresies: The Body of Pasolini's Semiotics," op. cit., 32.

23. Pier Paolo Pasolini, *Lettere Luterane* (Torino: Einaudi, 1976), trans. by Stuart Hood as *Lutheran Letters* (Manchester: Carcanet, 1983), 26. My page numbers refer to the English version. At the end of the preliminary chapters, on page 28, Pasolini chooses "the scornful shadow of Sade," instead of "the monstrous shadow of Rousseau," as the muse to whom his pedagogical treatise will be dedicated. The change is significant, for it seals Pasolini's affinities with De Sade and confirms that, as I argued in the introduction, Pasolini belongs to Adorno's list of "the black writers of the bourgeoisie." *The Lutheran Letters'* indictment of television and compulsory schooling stands out as the most vitriolic criticism ever leveled at post-economic-miracle Italy.

24. *Lutheran Letters*, 28–29.

25. A residue of the "passive periphrastic" in modern English is contained in the word "propaganda": something which must be propagated.

26. *Lutheran Letters*, 30. Given the wonderful clarity of Pasolini's prose, it may be worth quoting the entire paragraph—the third in this chapter—from which I took these last words:

> Other "discourses of things" intervened a little later and then throughout my whole infancy and youth. Often such new "discourses of things"—especially after earliest infancy—contradicted the initial ones. I saw rustic objects in the courtyards of poor houses; I saw furnishings and furniture which were proletarian and sub-proletarian; I saw landscapes which were not city ones but suburban or poorly rural, etc. But how long it was, my dear Gennariello, before those first statements had doubts cast on them and were explicitly contradicted by later ones. For many

years their repressive power and their authoritarian spirit were invincible; it is true that I quickly understood that as well as my petty bourgeois world—so cosmically absolute—there was another world, indeed that there were other worlds. But for a long time it always seemed to me that the only true valid world, taught me by objects, by physical reality, was my world; whereas the others seemed to me to be extraneous, anomalous, disquieting, and devoid of truth.

In these first lessons, Pasolini seeks to substantiate the generation gap between himself and Gennariello by showing that what has changed is the language of things. His views may be too pessimistic—the following chapter (sixth lesson) will bear the significant title: "Our impotence in the face of the pedagogic language of things"—but they certainly enable us to think of and talk about ideology's interpellation (Althusser) and the Gaze (Lacan) in less abstract ways.

27. While rejecting the metaphysical implications of the traditional epistemological privilege granted to the eye, I find that the radical dethroning of sight may have gone a bit too far. Indeed, our knowledge feels more complete whenever we get to see something, whether in real life or on a screen. An example: I recently watched Ruttman's *Berlin, the Symphony of a Great City* (1927), a poetic documentary inspired by the theory of Dziga Vertov. Although I would not claim that I really know what Berlin was like—nor do I think that such was Ruttman's purpose—the mere sight of what, say, a shop would look like back then added something to my sense of historical knowledge that no description would have given me. It would be possible, of course, to have different epistemological parameters, as blind people do, but I regard the excessive attention devoted to the deconstruction of sight a moot point, the result of too many hours spent at our desks.

28. Since 1882, when William James's *Will to Believe* identified the category of "naive realism," the adjective "naive" has become the epithet most commonly employed by compulsive academics to disqualify anybody who shuns the airless heights of rational abstraction. A counter-deconstruction of the ideological implications contained in the accusations of "naiveté" would lead to extremely interesting results. In his response to Eco, who had accused his theories of being "naive," Pasolini thus replied: "That I am naive, there is no doubt, and in fact, because I am not a petty bourgeois—with all the violence of a maniac also in not wanting to be such—I am not afraid of naiveté; I am happy to be naive and also perhaps sometimes ridiculous" (278).

29. *Lutheran Letters*, 30.

30. The shadow of Merleau-Ponty, of course, looms large in Pasolini's argument of the bodiliness of sight. A reappraisal of the role of the body and of the corporeal situatedness of the knowing subject is, however, an essential component of feminist/gay/postmodern theory. For an outstanding discussion of the body as the site of an ultimate ambivalence which overruns the mind's attempts at univocal clarity, see Umberto Galimberti, *Il corpo* (Milano: Feltrinelli, 1987). For a stimulating if slightly fashionable postmodern perspective on the body see *Canadian Journal of Political and Social Theory* 11, nos. 1–2 (1987), entirely dedicated to the body.

31. Although unfaithful to the Italian original, the French title of the

book—*L'Experience hérétique*—has the merit of stressing the role of experience in Pasolini's theory.

32. *Le ceneri di Gramsci* (Milano: Garzanti, 1957), 49.

33. A. Costa, "The Semiological Heresy of P. P. Pasolini," in Paul Willemen, ed., *Pier Paolo Pasolini*, 32.

34. Antonio Gramsci, *Quaderni dal carcere*, op. cit., 1505. Interestingly, the other thinker who most influenced Italian thought during Pasolini's life, Benedetto Croce, highlighted the role of passion in a way similar to Gramsci's. Passion, in Croce's eyes, shapes the manner in which individuals respond to historical situations and allows the translation of philosophy into deed, of thought into action. See *Ciò che è morto e ciò che è vivo nella filosofia di Hegel* (Bari: La Terza, 1907), 50–79, and *Philosophy of the Practical* (London: Macmillan, 1913), 215–246.

35. For a telling example of the reappraisal of passion, see Aram Veeser's introduction to *The New Historicism*, ed. Aram Veeser (London: Routledge, 1989), in which it becomes clear that even such a discipline as history finds it necessary to abandon "the norm of disembodied objectivity." As to feminism, see *Diotima: il pensiero della differenza sessuale* (Milano: La Tartaruga, 1987), a collection of essays by leading Italian feminists. See also the work of Lea Melandri who, inspired by the writer Sibilla Aleramo, has sought to found "an ethics of passion."

36. Needless to say, "passion" is the most frequently recurring word in Leopold Von Sacher-Masoch's notorious novel.

37. Linda Williams, "Body Genres: Melodrama, Horror, Porn," *Film Quarterly* 4 (Summer 1991): 2–13.

38. See, for example, Jonathan Crary, "Modernizing Vision" in *Vision and Visuality* (Seattle: Bay Press, 1988), 29–51.

39. Teresa De Lauretis, "Oedipus Interruptus," *Wide Angle* 7, nos. 1–2 (1985): 36.

40. Pierre Bourdieu, *La Distinction*, op. cit., 80.

41. Teresa De Lauretis, *Alice Doesn't*, op. cit., 51.

Notes to Chapter Three

1. Oswald Stack, *Pasolini* (Bloomington: Indiana University Press, 1969), 29.

2. "Intellectualism . . . and the Teds," *Films and Filming* (January 1961): 17.

3. *Stack*, 29.

4. *Greene*, 20.

5. In Bourdieu's terminology, Pasolini found in cinema the perfect position from which he could express himself as sincerely and effectively as possible:

"Sincerity" (which is one of the preconditions of symbolic efficacy) is only possible—and real—in the case of perfect, immediate harmony between the expectations inscribed in the positions occupied (in a less consecrated area, one would say "job-description") and the dispositions of the occupant; it is the privilege of those who, guided by "their sense of their place," have found their natural site in the field of production. (Bourdieu, *Distinction*, 240)

6. Peter Wollen, *Signs and Meaning in the Cinema* (Bloomington: University of Indiana Press, 1972), 77.

7. Lino Miccichè, *Il cinema Italiano degli anni '60* (Bari: Marsilio, 1975), 45.

8. *Uccellacci uccellini* (Milano: Garzanti, 1966), 227.

9. Peter Bondanella aptly entitles the chapter dedicated to Italian cinema in the 1960s "a decisive decade." See *Italian Cinema from Neorealism to the Present* (New York: Continuum, 1990), 142–195.

10. Lino Miccichè, *Il cinema Italiano degli anni '60*, 45.

11. In his book *The Italian Political Filmmakers* (Cranbury: Associated University Presses, 1986), John Michalczyk quite aptly treats Pasolini as a political director together with Rosi, Bertolucci, Bellocchio, Pontecorvo, Petri, and Wertmuller.

12. *Stack*, 129.

13. See, for example, Carlo Lizzani, *Storia del cinema Italiano* (Roma: Editori Riuniti, 1973), chapters 24–27.

14. *La quinzaine littéraire*, March 1–15, 1969: 24.

15. Millicent Marcus, *Italian Cinema in the Light of Neorealism* (Princeton: Princeton University Press, 1986), 245–262.

16. See, for example, the controversy on Visconti's *Senso* (1954), to which *Cinema nuovo* dedicated a special issue entitled "Dal neorealismo al realismo" (vol. 4, no. 53, February 25, 1955). The participants were, among others, Aristarco, Chiarini, Calvino, Visconti, Bazin, and Taviani.

17. I derived the idea of a *mimetic* vs. *semiotic* realism from Gianni Scalia's outstanding article "Poiché realismo c'è . . . ," Lino Miccichè ed., *Il neorealismo cinematografico italiano* (Venezia: Marsilio, 1975), 141–162. The book contains an interesting section on the relationship between realism and neorealism. To this date, there is no in-depth study of the realist tradition in the cinema. Of course, all the surveys of film theory speak of Bazin and Kracauer as representatives of the realist school (e.g., Dudley Andrew, *The Major Film Theories* [London: Oxford, 1976]), and the various histories of the cinema all speak of the different directors and movements that I mentioned. But no book has attempted to gather all the directors, works, and ideas which have gravitated around the idea of reality. It is my conviction that such an enterprise would significantly alter our perception of realism, for we would come to acknowledge all the extravagant contributions counter to realism but in the name of reality—much in the tradition of Baudelaire's famous short piece *Puis que realisme il y a*. A useful, if short and by necessity superficial, historical survey of realism in the cinema is Roy Armes, *Film and Reality* (Baltimore: Penguin, 1974). There are also two very good anthologies illustrating both the *mimetic* and the *semiotic* kinds of realism: Edoardo Bruno, ed., *Teorie del realismo* (Roma: Bulzoni, 1977), and Cristopher Williams, *Realism and the Cinema* (London: British Film Institute, 1980).

18. Colin MacCabe, "Realism and the Cinema: Notes on Some Brechtian

Theses," *Screen* 15, no. 2 (Summer 1974): 7–17. By the same author, see also "Theory and Film: Principles of Realism and Pleasure," *Screen* 17, no. 3 (Autumn 1976): 25–41. These two articles were later collected in *Tracking the Signifier* (Minneapolis: University of Minnesota Press, 1985). For a further discussion of MacCabe's ideas in relationship to Pasolini, see the last chapter of this book, on *Salò*.

19. P. P. Pasolini, "In morte del realismo," *La religione del mio tempo* (Milano: Garzanti, 1961), 139–145. Pasolini read the poem out loud to a dumbfounded audience assembled at the Open Gate Theater in Rome for the annual ceremony of the Premio Strega. He thereby intended to protest the contemporary trend of Italian literature away from realism and dialects in favor of a return to the standard literary language. As it is, however, the poem settles the score with the realist heritage of which Pasolini himself had been critical in *Passione e ideologia*.

20. John Ellis, *Visible Fictions* (London: Routledge, 1982), 6.

21. Bertrand Philbert, *L'homosexualité à l'écran* (Paris: Veyrier, 1984), 50, and Vito Russo, *The Celluloid Closet* (New York: Harper, 1981), 78.

22. P. P. Pasolini, *Le belle bandiere* (Roma: Editori Riuniti, 1978), 60–61.

23. Bertolt Brecht, "The Popular and the Realistic," in *Brecht on Theatre* (London: Methuen, 1964), 109. It is a crucial article for anybody interested in reconsidering realism. In it Brecht makes it clear that "realism is not a pure question of form" and therefore "we must not abstract the one and only realism from certain given works, but shall make use of all means, old and new, tried and untried, deriving from art and deriving from other sources, in order to put living reality in the hands of living people in such a way that it can be mastered." Often used as an anti-Lukacsian argument, it could be turned against MacCabe himself who is abstracting "the one and only realism from certain given works."

24. Bertolt Brecht, ibid. As to Bazin's contrary statement, "realism, let me repeat, is to be defined not in terms of ends but of means, and neorealism by a specific kind of relationship of means to ends," see "Cabiria," *What Is Cinema?* 2: 87.

25. Roy Armes, *Patterns of Realism* (New York: Barnes, 1971), 17. By "realism of attitude" Armes contends that all the works which were produced before realism became a "specific historical development having its origins in the work of such men as Fielding in literature and Courbet in painting," that is a "realism of method." It is not clear whether or not he would agree to labeling as "realism of attitude" those works coming after the inception of realism of method. Personally, I find the distinction very useful. In fact, the demise of the idea of method should prompt us to resurrect "attitude" as the only viable tool indicating, with some approximation, the realism of a text.

26. Paul Ricoeur, *Freud and Philosophy* (New Haven: Yale University Press, 1970), 32–36.

27. Ibid., 28–32.

28. James Hillman, *Re-Visioning Psychology* (New York: Harper, 1975), 161–162. Hillman uses these words to describe an archetypal figure of the soul which opposes the Hero's straight journey and opts for errancy and wandering,

"picking up insights by the way": the knight errant. The words Hillman uses to describe such intellectual errancy are uncannily reminiscent of Pasolini's "extravagance" and piracy. Hillman is Pasolinian in that he stresses the importance of pathologizing, the soul's journey through negativity which "is present most profoundly in the individual sense of death, which he carries everywhere he goes" and "in each person's inward feeling of his peculiar 'differentness'" (70). Being a Jungian, Hillman stresses the image-making and mythical dimensions of the soul. The latter is not a given, but a construct, something that is progressively made up through various psychic activities, one of which is pathologizing. Pasolini's images of death and mythical horror, then, would be the result of a journey aimed at soul-making.

29. "L'inutile sforzo di Moravia per dimostrare l'inesistenza della realtà," *Il tempo illustrato*, 28 October 1973: 15.

Notes to Chapter Four

1. "Intellectualism . . . and the Teds," *Films and Filming* (January 1961): 17. The title signals the duality of which *Accattone* will be the bearer.

2. The expression is Bazin's, "In Defense of Rossellini," *What Is Cinema?* (Berkeley, Los Angeles, London: University of California Press, 1971), vol. 2, 94. An example of interesting thematic insight is Fabien Girard's *Pasolini ou le mythe de la barbarie* (Bruxelles: Editions de l'Université, 1981), which shows the extent to which Pasolini's films can all be grouped around and explained by his fondness for "barbarism." An example of wishful projection is Stephen Snyder's *Pier Paolo Pasolini* (Boston: Twayne, 1980), which is too obsessed with "defending" Pasolini from the charge of being a Marxist. In spite of some good intuitions on the Jungian subtext in Pasolini's films, Snyder forces a linear development onto Pasolini's oeuvre, from division to holism, from despair to harmony. As a consequence of his stand, *Salò* becomes a disturbing, illicit presence that perturbed the harmony of the *Arabian Nights*, something to be first excused and then excised.

3. The contrast with the marble angel is evoked by this phrase in the scenario, *Accattone* (Roma: 11 Cinematografo, 1961). As would be customary with most of his films, Pasolini published the scenario, with production notes and articles. Here, for example, one finds "Cinema and Literature: Notes after *Accattone*" in which Pasolini makes the distinction "lexicon"/"syntax" pertinent for film criticism. The "lexical choices" would involve settings, casting, and mise-en-scène, whereas the "syntax" would supervise shot composition, editing, and narrative structure. Seen in these terms, *Accattone*'s "lexical choices" follow neorealism but its "syntax" does not.

4. See, for example, Vittorio Spinazzola, *Cinema e pubblico* (Bompiani: Milano, 1974), 278–280. Although seemingly validated by Pasolini's comments at the time of *Accattone*'s release, such a view loses strength when confronted with the text's workings. In fact, Pasolini himself once remarked that the ideology of his films became clear to him a long time after their release.

5. Accused by his leftist critics of entertaining a spiritualistic and decadent

idea of death, Pasolini once replied that, quite the contrary, "his idea of death was a behavioral and moral idea; it was not concerned with the aftermath of death, but with the premise of it—not with the beyond, but with life" (HE, 249).

6. The spatial metaphors "high" (alto) and "low" (basso) are most common in Pasolini's descriptions of the different strata and positions in literature, language, and society. Interchangeable though they often are with the "legitimate"/"illegitimate" dichotomy— which would often sound better to our ears—I will often use "high" and "low" to respect Pasolini's sense of vertical polarity.

7. Enrico Magrelli, ed., Con Pier Paolo Pasolini (Roma: Bulzoni, 1977), 36, hereafter cited as Magrelli.

8. Insofar as it attempts to make aesthetic what has not yet entered the realm of legitimate representation, all realism can be seen as marked by this ambivalence. It is for this reason that in the poem "On the Death of Realism" Pasolini says that realism is a "mixed" style, both "difficult" and "vulgar," where "difficulty" connotes high culture and "vulgarity" is the sign of illegitimacy.

9. In addition to referring to "victory," "Vittorio" was the name of the Italian king and was traditionally appropriated by the social groups more inclined to monarchic beliefs, such as the declining aristocracy, the land-owning bourgeoisie, and the Catholic peasantry.

10. "As if in a dream" is one of the most recurrent expressions in Pasolini's screenplays. It well fits Accattone in this scene for it anticipates the dream he will have. But it is also appropriate for Accattone in general, for he often moves about the narrative in a dazzled state, between life and death, as it were.

11. Michel Foucault, Discipline and Punish (New York: Pantheon, 1977), 201. Pages 195–228 are dedicated to panopticism.

12. For the notion of gaze as "being seen" see Jacques Lacan, The Four Fundamental Concepts of Psychoanalysis (New York: Norton, 1978), 67–123. Lacan notes that "in the scopic field the gaze is outside, I am looked at, that is to say, I am a picture" (106), and "man, in effect, knows how to play with the mask as that beyond which there is the gaze" (107). The gaze therefore entails the presence of external forces which constitute us as objects of vision, which make us visible. It is Pasolini's notion of life as "double representation." Here I wish to capitalize the word "Gaze" in order to make it clear that I am referring to a supra-individual entity. For a brief and useful summary of the notion of "gaze" as elaborated by Sartre and Lacan, see Norman Bryson, "The Gaze in the Expanded Field," Vision and Visuality, op. cit., 87–108.

13. Pasolini's use of the expression "lifting the mask from Italy's face" to describe realism is certainly part of the realist ideology but acquires a wider significance in the light of the importance that wearing a mask has had for homosexuals. There is another reason why Accattone must be seen as a metaphor for homosexuality. In a short piece accompanying the script of Mamma Roma (Milano: Rizzoli, 1962), Pasolini makes it clear that the actor Franco Citti was perfect for the part because he is like Accattone: "His enormous vital

energy forces him to wage an endless struggle against himself, to live a kind of exceptional life, outside of all norms—which, incidentally, I understand very well" (142). Pasolini thus established an indirect autobiographical connection with Accattone via Franco Citti.

14. Thieves and criminals have been common narrative paradigms in the portrayal of homosexuality. One need only think of Genet and Fassbinder.

15. Bertolt Brecht, "The Popular and the Realistic," 110.

16. These examples from *HE* reveal how, six years after *Accattone*, the same example from Buonconte's story surfaced again and was grafted into theoretical discourse. On page 248, Pasolini sustained his discourse on death by bringing the example of Stalin: "Wouldn't Marxism, which made a virtually absolute public example of his image, still be ambiguously suspended in a lie which was unmasked only with the end of Stalin?"

Notes to Chapter Five

1. Pasolini, *La religione del mio tempo* (Milano: Garzanti, 1960), 47–48.

2. Now in *Ecrits sur le cinéma*, op. cit., 100–102.

3. Andre Bazin, *What Is Cinema?*, op. cit., vol. 2, p. 6.

4. Cesare Zavattini, "A Thesis on Neo-Realism," in David Overbey, *Springtime in Italy* (Hamden: Archon Books, 1978), 67–78. This book also contains an article by Rossellini, "A Few Words about Neo-Realism," which illustrates the extent to which Rossellini's humility towards life did not imply stylistic restriction but was, precisely, an attitude. As to De Sica's aphorism, it is quoted in *Kolker*, page 47.

5. "What I have in my head like a vision, like a visual field, are the frescoes by Masaccio and Giotto—the painters I like best, together with some of the Mannerists (for instance, Pontormo). And I am unable to visualize images, landscape, or figure compositions in any form other than through my initial passion for fourteenth-century painting, which has man at the center of every perspective." *Mamma Roma* (Milano: Rizzoli, 1962), 20.

6. For an excellent discussion of Rome in *Open City*, see Peter Brunette, *Roberto Rossellini* (New York: Oxford University Press, 1987), 51. See also page 221 for further discussion of the Rome theme in *It Was Night in Rome*.

7. Edward Branigan, "The Point-of-View Shot," in Bill Nichols, ed., *Movies and Methods* (Berkeley, Los Angeles, London: University of California Press, 1985), 672–691.

8. "Un'intervista con Christian Metz," op. cit., 12.

9. Gilles Deleuze, op. cit., 72–76. All the quotes from this book are from these four pages.

10. V. N. Volosinov, *Marxism and the Philosophy of Language* (New York: Seminar Press, 1973), 138. Although Bakhtin's name does not appear as co-author of the book, scholars have ascertained his participation in the project.

11. Ibid., 143–144.

12. Ibid., 144.

13. Snyder, *Pier Paolo Pasolini*, 53.

Notes to Chapter Six

1. *La ricotta* is a forty-minute episode in *RoGoPaG*, a film also including Rossellini's *Illibatezza* (Chastity), Godard's *Le Nouveau Monde* (The New World), and Gregoretti's *Polli d'allevamento* (The Scratching Chicken). *RoGoPaG* was banned soon after its release for an alleged offense to religion contained in Pasolini's episode. It was rereleased the following year under the title *Laviamoci il cervello* (Let's Brainwash Ourselves). At the time of its first release, Pasolini already knew that the film was going to run into trouble. He thus prefaced his episode with his off-screen voice:

> It is not difficult to predict—for this story of mine—biased, ambiguous, and scandalized judgments. In any case, I want to state here and now that, however *La ricotta* is taken, the story of the Passion, which *La ricotta* indirectly recalls, is for me the greatest event that ever happened and the books that recount it are the most sublime that have ever been written.

Pasolini was given four months suspended sentence. See *Pasolini: cronaca giudiziaria, persecuzione, morte,* op. cit., 154–164.

2. "*La ricotta*," *Cahiers du cinema* 174 (January 1966): 27–29.

3. "10 Giugno 1962," *Mamma Roma*, 159–160. Later, the poem was published in the section "Poesie mondane" (Worldly Poems), *Poesia in forma di rosa* (Poetry in the Form of a Rose) (Milano: Garzanti, 1964), 26.

4. "The Return of Diogenes as Postmodern Intellectual," foreword to Peter Sloterdijk, *Critique of Cynical Reason*, xi.

5. I used the word "weak" because of the name that the most vocal current of Italian postmodern philosophy has chosen for itself: *pensiero debole* (weak thought). According to these philosophers (Gianni Vattimo, Pier Aldo Rovatti, Umberto Eco, etc.), Western thought must renounce the strength with which it used to produce "truths" and ought to become "weak."

6. Giuliano Briganti, *Italian Mannerism*, trans. Margaret Kunzle (Leipzig: VEB Edition, 1962), 26.

7. Arnold Hauser, *Mannerism*, trans. Erich Mosbacher (New York: Knopf, 1965), 15.

8. Ibid., 4.

Notes to Chapter Seven

1. All the quotations in this paragraph are from "Gli anni della rabbia," *Vie nuove* (September 20, 1962): 11. See also Antonio Bertini, *Teoria e tecnica del film in Pasolini* (Roma: Bulzoni, 1979), 147–149, for Carlo di Carlo's recollection of his contribution to the editing of *La rabbia*.

2. Reading the newspapers of that period, one gets the impression that Pasolini was almost "forced" to withdraw his signature by his Marxist guilt magnified by the Left around him. Moravia, for example, entitled his brief review of *La rabbia*: "Pasolini nella trappola di Guareschi" (Pasolini in Guareschi's Trap), *Espresso*, April 21, 1963, and thus contributed to the general feeling that Pasolini *should not* have accepted collaboration with a fascist. I

think that it was, rather, Guareschi who fell into Pasolini's trap. Interestingly, the recent efforts made by the New Right to appropriate Pasolini have used his section of *La rabbia* to validate their claim that Pasolini was expressing right-wing beliefs (antimodernism; the idea that the revolution must save the past, etc.). Perhaps, the leftists who "blackmailed" Pasolini into withdrawing his signature from the film were unwittingly reacting against the "right-wing" elements in Pasolini's part more than against his collaboration with Guareschi.

3. From Greek *martus*, "witness, witness of Christ." It will be remembered that in the poem recited by Orson Welles in *La ricotta*, Pasolini uses the image of his witnessing "the first acts of post-history" to indicate the "monstrous" condition of postmodern awareness and *kynicism*. In the essay "The Unpopular Cinema" (*HE*, 267–275), Pasolini talks about the activity of a cinematographic author worthy of this name as *martyrdom*. It is the courage of seeing and saying things which must be seen and said, that is, "a certain realism."

4. "Pasolini e Guareschi: c'è rabbia e rabbia," *Paese sera*, April 14, 1963.

5. *20 disegni di Renato Guttuso presentati da Pier Paolo Pasolini* (Roma: Editori Riuniti, 1962). There are no page numbers. All the quotations in this paragraph are taken from the second and third pages.

6. See the chapter on *Salò* for references and further elaboration of the point. The notion of *Ratio* as reason which has lost its moral goals and subsists as form will be discussed in the context of Pasolini's antinaturalist stand in the chapter on *Medea*.

7. See, for example, *Magrelli*, page 100.

Notes to Chapter Eight

1. For a stimulating group of essays on documentary from the sixties onward, see Alan Rosenthal, *New Challenges for Documentary* (Berkeley, Los Angeles, London: University of California Press, 1988).

2. The directors were Antonioni, Fellini, Lattuada, Dino Risi, and Maselli-Zavattini. *Amore in città* began with the image of a woman buying a magazine entitled "*Amore in città*," while an off-screen voice explained:

> Each day throughout the world millions of people go to news-stands to buy magazines, drawn by an insatiable curiosity to learn more about the lives of others, hoping to find some connection or reflection on their own. In this film, we have created a new kind of magazine, "the film spectator," using film and sound instead of paper and ink. The first issue of our magazine is called: "*Amore in città*." It is devoted to searching the patterns of love peculiar to a great city, without fear, without taboos, seeking an intimacy with life, a closeness to reality, that celebrates life itself.

The idea of an investigation of love "without fear, without taboos" will be most definitely taken up by *Comizi d'amore* and, more generally, by all the documentaries on love.

3. "Les gris matins de la tolerance" appeared in *Le Monde*, March 23, 1977, and is now available in English, "Grey Mornings of Tolerance," in Beverly Allen, ed., *The Poetics of Heresy* (Saratoga: ANMA, 1982), 72–74.

4. Luciano De Giusti, ed., *Il cinema in forma di poesia* (Pordenone: Edizioni Cinemazero, 1979), 123–127.

5. I am thinking, of course, of the *teta veleta* episode, discussed in the first chapter of this book. As to Pasolini's political reflections on "physical presence" as a language, see chapter 2.

6. Pasolini did not include some of the observations Musatti made about the etiology of homosexuality. I have not been able to trace exactly what the omitted part was. According to Musatti, Pasolini cut the part in which he (Musatti) suggested that homosexuality implied immaturity and regression to a preadolescent state. Musatti was also convinced that for Pasolini homosexuality was something innate. See Cesare Musatti, "Quella volta che andò dallo psicanalista" (That Time He Went to See a Shrink), *Espresso* (November 16, 1975): 31. At the risk of contradicting "the father of Italian psychoanalysis," I would like to suggest that Pasolini accepted—at least for a few, crucial years in the sixties—the Freudian theory of an imperfectly solved Oedipus complex, *but* he did not tolerate the attendant implication of immaturity and regression.

7. Cited in Luciano De Giusti, *I film di Pier Paolo Pasolini* (Roma: Gremese, 1980), 64.

8. Luciano De Giusti, *Il cinema in forma di poesia*, op. cit., 126.

Notes to Chapter Nine

1. *Stack*, 73. See also *Sopraluoghi in Palestina* (Milano: Il Barcone-Documenti, 1967). On page 11 we read:

> In order to cover the budget for *Il Vangelo secondo Matteo* (distribution, minimal guarantee, etc.), Bini suddenly had to show some material to a group of people in order to document the work done so far and its possible development.
> During the Palestine trip I had left everything in the hands of Martelli, a cameraman who had followed me and Father Andrea Carraro from Italy. I only gave him instructions, once in a while, to take some particular shots of the landscape and the local people, which might be useful later, while creating sets and costumes. . . . When I got back to Rome, I forgot all about it until suddenly Bini had to have this showing. The material hadn't even been edited; it was just spliced together, almost haphazardly, by some assistant editor whose name I can't remember. I took the spliced material and since I did not have time to edit it, I left it just the way it was (except for a few cuts to make it fit within the time limits of the documentary). I did not even have time to write a commentary. We went into the dubbing studio and as the material gradually passed before my eyes, I improvised the commentary and I transformed myself into the narrator.

2. I am indebted, for this intuition, to Gian Piero Brunetta, *Forma e parola nel cinema* (Padova: Liviana, 1970), 108.

3. *Naldini*, 99. The same year, in *I quaderni rossi*, he writes: "Now I am like a desert that has been all explored: there is no way I can be saved. I have become all consciousness" (*Naldini*, 108). Or: "I am like a traveler who got stranded in the desert, finished up his supplies, and is now left to covet statues of porphyry and alabaster" (*Naldini*, 114).

4. *L'usignolo della chiesa cattolica* (Milano: Garzanti, 1958), 98.

5. The desert plays an important role in two of the most spiritual directors in Italian cinema: Rossellini (*Stromboli*, 1949; and *Il Messia* [The Messiah], 1975) and Antonioni (*Zabriskie Point*, 1970; and *Professione reporter* [The Passenger], 1975; *Deserto rosso* [Red Desert], 1964, does not have any actual desert scenes, but it alludes to the inner desert referred to by Pasolini perhaps more than the other two). Such a fascination is all the more intriguing in view of the fact that the Italian landscape has no desert.

6. After the New Testament itself, the Christian tradition of the Desert Fathers has been the most far-reaching influence on the spiritual development of both Eastern and Western forms of Christianity. It had its center in the desert regions between Cairo and Alexandria, in the fourth century. Pasolini's knowledge of the Desert Fathers is not proved. Nevertheless, the way in which he used the desert in *Teorema* (novel and film) and his enthusiastic judgment on Bunuel's *Simon del desierto* (Simon of the Desert, 1968) suggest that he was aware of it. Given the exorbitant nature of his Catholic discourse, it is only logical that he was attracted to the more spiritual, radical currents of Christianity. To have an idea of the extent to which the desert tradition offered a spiritual anchor to Pasolini's use of the signifier death, see Benedicta Ward, *The Desert Christian: Sayings of the Desert Fathers* (New York: Macmillan, 1975).

Notes to Chapter Ten

1. *Naldini*, 256.
2. "Marxismo e Cristianesimo," *L'eco di Brescia*, December 12, 1964: ii.
3. *Stack*, 79.
4. In *Mimesis* (Princeton: Princeton University Press, 1953), a book that Pasolini practically knew by heart, Erich Auerbach argues that the story of Christ had done literary realism a service in countering what was then the absolute rule of the "separation of styles." According to the writers of Classical antiquity, the narration of "everything commonly realistic, everything pertinent to everyday life" had to be kept "on the lowest level of style both in diction and in treatment," that is, on the level of *sermo humilis*; conversely, "everything problematic, everything psychologically or sociologically suggestive of serious, let alone tragic, complications" had to be dramatized in an elevated style, or *sermo sublimis* (31). Historically, the mixture of styles came about as a consequence of the fact that Christ's story was the dominant theme of medieval literature:

> That the King of Kings was treated as a low criminal, that he was mocked, spat upon, whipped, and nailed to the cross—that story no sooner comes to dominate the consciousness of the people than it completely destroys the aesthetics of the separation of styles; it engenders a new elevated style, which does not scorn everyday life and which is ready to absorb the sensorily realist, even the ugly, the undignified, the physically base (72).

I have already argued that the ambivalent images in *Accattone* can be seen as modern-day versions of a mixture between high and low styles. In fact, Pasolini's entire cinema hinges on this mixture, a sort of vertical oxymoron, whereby he uses Classical culture as a vehicle for his "undignified" and "physically base" characters.

5. See, for example, the paradigmatic reaction of many French intellectuals when *Il Vangelo* premiered in Paris; Antonietta Macciocchi, "Cristo e il Marxismo," *L'unità*, December 22, 1964: 12–13. Apparently, the only leftist intellectual to sympathize with Pasolini was Jean-Paul Sartre.

6. "L'Evangile de Pasolini," *Cahiers du cinema* 159 (October 1964): 24–27.

7. See *Stack*, 82, and *Magrelli*, 65.

8. *Duflot*, 27.

9. "Direct Sound: An Interview with Straub and Huillet," in Elizabeth Weis and John Belton, eds., *Theory and Practice of Film Sound* (New York: Co-
lumbia, 1985), 150.

10. On the change of style that took place with *Il Vangelo*, see *Stack*, 83–85; "Una discussione del '64," a self-interview in *Pier Paolo Pasolini nel dibattito culturale contemporaneo* (Alessandria: Amministrazione provinciale di Pavia, 1977), 118–122.

11. To give the reader an idea of the film's fidelity to the original, I have transcribed the correspondences between Matthew's and Pasolini's texts. The ordinal numbers on the left column refer to the sequences in the film (44), whereas the numbers on the right indicate chapters and verses from Matthew's *Gospel*.

Sequence	Matthew
1st	1:18–21
v.o.(voice over)	1:23 (prophecy)
2nd	2:1–8
3d	2:9–12
4th	2:13–15
v.o.	2:15 (prophecy)
5th	2:16–17
v.o.	2:18 (Jeremiah's prophecy)
6th	2:19 (But upon Herod's death)
7th	2:19–20
8th	3:1–16
v.o.	3:17 (voice from heaven)
9th	4:1–11
10th v.o.	4:16 (Isaiah's prophecy)
11th	4:17–22
12th	10:1–4
	10:16–20
	10:22
	10:28–31
	10:34–37 (Do not suppose I . . .)
	10:39
13th	8:2–4

Sequence	Matthew
14th	5:3–12
	7:9–12
	5:17
	5:13–15
	6:19–20
	6:24
	6:3
	5:38–39
	5:43–45
	7:1–3
	6:7–13
	6:25–34
	7:13–14
	11:25–28
15th	11:28–30
	12:1–8
	12:10–13
	12:18–21
	12:14
16th	14:15–21
17th	14:22–31
18th	11:2–6 (Baptist in jail)
19th	11:7–23½
	12:23–24
20th	12:30–31
	12:38–42
	12:46–47
	12:43–45
	12:46–47
	12:48–50
21st	No words/Pasolini's addition.
22nd	13:54–57
23d	19:16–24
24th	14:6–10
25th	14:10–12
	8:21–22
	8:19–20
26th	16:13–24
	17:22–23
	18:1–14
	18:21–22
	20:18–19
27th	21:1–3
28th	21:11–13
	21:15–17
29th	21:18–22

Sequence	Matthew
30th	21:23–44
	22:14
	22:16–39
31st	23, all verses except 14
	24:1–2
32nd	26:3–5
33d	26:6–13
34th	26:14–15
35th	26:20–35
36th	26:36–42
	26:51–56
	26:49–50
37th	26:58–66
	26:69–74
38th/39th	27:3–8
40th	27:11–17
	27:21–26
41st	27:27–34
42nd	27:45–49
v.o./black frame	13:14–15 (Isaiah's prophecy)
43d	28:5–8
44th	28:18–20
	27:45–49

12. *Stack*, 95–98.

13. For the relationship between Matthew and the Law, see John P. Meier, *Law and History in Matthew's Gospel* (Rome: Biblical Institute Press, 1976), 22–42.

Notes to Chapter Eleven

1. Lino Miccichè, *Il cinema Italiano degli anni sessanta*, op. cit., 164.

2. *Uccellacci uccellini* (Milano: Garzanti, 1966), ii.

3. I have slightly altered the English translation which has the word *signifieds* instead of *meanings*. Both are legitimate translations of the Italian *significati*. The former has more of a semiotic connotation. For the purpose of what I will be doing, I prefer to maintain the level of generality contained in *meanings*.

4. *Stack*, 107.

5. Why a raven, of all possible animals? Traditionally associated with death, ravens can be seen as embodying a desperate will to live and be everywhere: they inhabit five continents, are not limited to a single ecological habitat, and, in fact, derive life from the dead. In *The Folk-Lore of Birds* (London: Collins, 1958), 71, Edward Armstrong reports that "although the raven is predominantly an ominous bird, it has an ambivalent character" and that the historical roots of "the raven's ambivalence can be traced to two conflicting

334 Notes to Pages 150–162

strands of tradition, heathen and Christian." Whereas in the Christian tradition its image as a bird of doom is indeed predominant, pagan cults endow the raven with the role of messenger, divine guide, go-between for gods and men. The raven is also charged with meaning in light of the perverted trinitarian scheme underlying the film. According to *Genesis* 8, 7–11, Noah, after the flood, "sent forth a raven" to see whether or not the waters had subsided. The raven, however, did not return, but restlessly "went to and fro, until the waters were dried up." Noah then "sent forth a dove" which, upon her second mission, "came into him in the evening; and, lo, in her mouth was an olive leaf pluckt off: so Noah knew that the waters were abated from off the earth." Thus, whereas the dove returned with a symbol of peace, the raven refused ever to come back. Perhaps, in the raven's eyes, there was no peace to announce.

6. *Le belle bandiere* (Roma: Editori Riuniti, 1977), 349.

7. The ambivalence of such a quotation caused more than one commentator to search Marxist texts for its source. It is yet another example of how *Uccellacci uccellini* "bends meanings."

8. *Le belle bandiere*, op. cit., 259. The entire passage reads:

> Christ's greatest enemy is not Communist materialism but bourgeois materialism. The former is theoretical, philosophical, speculative, and therefore it *comprehends* religion's highest moments; the latter is totally pragmatic, empirical, instrumental; it opposes any sincerely religious instance as well as any movement aimed at knowing the real; or, better, it accepts them only if they are filtered through the canons of an old hypocrisy. The atheism of a Communist militant is extremely religious when compared to the cynicism of a capitalist: in the former you can always find the kind of idealism, despair, psychological violence, will to knowledge and faith which are elements, however dismembered, of a religion; in the latter you find nothing more than Big Mother (*Mammona*).

9. *Magrelli*, 80.

10. "Lettera di Pasolini ai critici milanesi," in *Comunicato stampa*, n.131.

11. *Stack*, 107.

12. Bill Nichols, *Ideology and the Image* (Bloomington: University of Indiana Press, 1981), 36–40.

13. *Stack*, 106.

14. Norman O. Brown, *Life Against Death* (Middletown: Wesleyan University Press, 1959), 191.

Notes to Chapter Twelve

1. The other episodes in *Le Streghe* are Francesco Rosi's *La siciliana* (The Sicilian Woman); Mauro Bolognini's *Senso civico* (Civic Duty); Luchino Visconti's *La strega bruciata viva* (The Witch Burnt Alive); and Vittorio De Sica's *Una serata come le altre* (An Evening Like Any Other). The film was conceived as a tribute by producer De Laurentiis to his wife Silvana Mangano, who stars in all of the episodes. The other episodes in *Capriccio all'italiana* are: Steno's *Il mostro della domenica* (The Sunday Monster); Mauro Bolognini's

Perchè (Why) and *La gelosa* (The Jealous Woman); and Pino Zac's *Viaggio di lavoro* (Business Trip).

2. From a TV interview, December 10, 1967, included in a program significantly entitled "Per conoscere la realtà" (To Know Reality).

3. Ibid.

4. *Magrelli*, 59.

5. Ibid., 70.

6. *The Order of Things* (New York: Vintage, 1970), 9.

Notes to Chapter Thirteen

1. "Incontro con P. P. Pasolini," *Controcampo* 10 (April 1969): 88: "The world as Gramsci knew it, and as I knew it until a short time ago, has changed. In the days when Gramsci was still theoretically valid, there was a clear distinction between the people (*popolo*) and the bourgeoisie. There was a clear distinction between the culture of the dominated class and that of the ruling class. But in recent years, in Italy, this distinction has disappeared, because the *popolo* has become 'bourgeoisified.'"

2. "La parola orale meravigliosa possibilità del cinema" (The Oral Word as a Marvelous Possibility of Cinema), *Cinema Nuovo* 201 (Sept.–Oct. 1969).

3. "Pasolini e l'autobiografia" (Pasolini and Autobiography), *Sipario* 258 (October 1967): 26–27.

4. "Rencontre avec P. P. Pasolini," *Cahiers du cinema* 192 (July–August 1967): 31.

5. The Italian painter Roberto Perpignani entitled an exhibit of paintings on Pasolini "Come le mosche nel miele" (Like Flies in the Honey). The image of flies in the honey is also the main visual element of the video *Tainted Love* by the gay British "noise" band, Coil. Interestingly, and not surprisingly, the 1967 album *Horse Rotorvator* (Relativity Records) by Coil dedicates "Ostia," a splendid five-minute song, to "the death of Pier Paolo Pasolini."

6. On the resemblance between Silvana Mangano and Susanna Pasolini, see "La Mangano mi ricorda mia madre" (Mangano Reminds Me of My Mother), *Tempo*, April 16, 1968: 32–33.

7. For an assessment of Ninetto Davoli in Pasolini's cinema, see Ben Lawton, "The Evolving Rejection of Homosexuality, the Sub-Proletariat, and the Third World in the Films of Pier Paolo Pasolini," *Italian Quarterly* 82–83 (Fall '80–Winter '91): 167–175.

8. "A Violent Life," *Village Voice*, May 1, 1990: 71.

9. To my knowledge, the only critic who paid attention to this sequence is Stephen Snyder, *Pasolini*, op. cit., 89–90. Unfortunately, Snyder misreads this sequence in a way that proves the disastrous effects of the critics' ignorance of the homosexual subtexts in Pasolini's films. According to Snyder, this sequence "implies that his [Oedipus'] failure to act more self-reliantly is merely prostitution."

10. *Edipo re* (Milano: Garzanti, 1967), 15–17.

11. As I hope to prove later in the book, the partially obscured vision is related to more than Pasolini's realism and autobiography: it has to do with his homosexual gaze (see the section on *I racconti di Canterbury* in chapter 21).

Note to Chapter Fourteen

1. *Stack*, 131.

Notes to Chapter Fifteen

1. *L'odore dell'India* (Milano: Longanesi, 1962) and *The Scent of India*, trans. David Price (London: Olive Press, 1984).

2. *L'odore dell'India*, 55, *The Scent of India*, 51. The entire paragraph in which this sentence appears is a perfect example of Pasolini's poetic prose as well as his ethnocentric love, and it deserves to be quoted in full. The reader should keep in mind that the English translator has used different words where Pasolini obsessively employed one: *odore*.

> He was covered with the usual white rags: while around him, along that street on the periphery (if periphery and center have any meaning for Indian cities), the usual lugubrious misery, the usual shops little more than boxes, the usual little houses (*casupole*) in ruins, the usual stores worn down by the breath of the monsoons, the usual high stench which smothers breathing. That smell of poor food and of corpses which in India is like a continuous powerful air current that gives one a kind of fever. And that odor which, little by little, becomes an almost living, physical entity, seems to interrupt the normal course of life in the body of the Indians. Its breath, attacking those little bodies, covered in their light and filthy linen, seems to corrode them, preventing them from growing, from reaching a human embodiment (*compiutezza umana*). (I slightly altered Price's translation of the last sentence, for it was wrong.)

The image of "little bodies" prevented from reaching *compiutezza umana* bespeaks a preconceived notion of what human is. If in the context of this paragraph such an expression is justifiable by the poetic context, I would argue that it is no accident that Pasolini's quasi-racist slips occur around the word *umano* (human). Again, it is the price of the humanist discourse.

3. *L'odore dell'India*, 12. *The Scent of India*, 17.

4. Pasolini's "Indian Story" was never published. Excerpts of it now exist, in English, in the catalog of the retrospective of his films that took place in New York, May–June 1990. All the quotations in this paragraph are taken from this source, pages 93–95.

5. *Naldini*, 12.

Notes to Chapter Sixteen

1. Even the most extensive essay dealing with Pasolini's film theory to date, Turigliatto's "La tecnica e il mito," in *Lo scandalo Pasolini, Bianco e Nero*, gennaio/aprile 1976: 113–156, is overtly concerned with inserting his words into his *oeuvre*. Two most notable exceptions are Teresa De Lauretis's "Language, Representation, Practice: Re-reading Pasolini's Essays on Cinema," *Italian Quarterly* 21–22 (Fall 1980-Winter 1981): 159–166, where she voices the need to recontextualize his essays, and by Giuliana Bruno's "Heresies: The Body of Pasolini's Semiotics," op. cit.

2. *Magrelli*, 92–93.

3. Perhaps it is no accident that the word "theorem" served the purpose of another open, multivalent title in Mehdi Charef's *Thé au Harem* (Tea in the Harem, 1985) where the protagonist, an Algerian boy in France, hears his teacher saying the word "théorème" and writes "thé au harem."

4. Like *Il Vangelo secondo Matteo*, *Teorema* was awarded a prize by the O.C.I.C., the *Office Catholique International du Cinema*, a decision that was fiercely contested by the Vatican press.

5. Maurizio Del Ministro, "Teorema," *Cinema Nuovo* 198 (March 1969): 133.

6. In fact, on one occasion, Pasolini himself referred to the visitor as "a blue-eyed student" who, in the film's allegorical context, signifies "ingham," the old Indian word for penis. *Magrelli*, 93.

7. Pasolini had a precocious sense of the birth of a "new bourgeoisie" and a "new petit bourgeoisie" as these were later to be theorized by Bourdieu's *Distinction*, 354–372. From duty to fun: this is what we can read between the lines of Pasolini's argument, *à propos Teorema*, that the film's

> condemnation of the bourgeoisie, which at an earlier stage prior to 1967 was precise and obvious, is "suspended" here, because the bourgeoisie is actually changing. The indignation and the rage against the classic bourgeoisie, as it has always been understood, no longer has a reason to exist, since the bourgeoisie is changing itself in a revolutionary way, i.e., it is identifying all mankind with the petit bourgeois.

See "Incontro con Pier Paolo Pasolini," interview with Lino Peroni, *Inquadratura* 15–16 (Fall 1968): 35–36.

8. Rinaldo Rinaldi, *Pier Paolo Pasolini* (Milano: Mursia, 1982), 258.

9. Leo Tolstoy, "The Death of Ivan Ilych," trans. Louise and Aylmer Maude in *Great Short Works of Leo Tolstoi* (New York: Harper and Row, 1967), 255.

10. For example: "*It* would come and stand before him and look at him, and he would be petrified and the light would die out of his eyes, and he would again begin asking himself whether *It* alone was true," 281.

11. *Teorema* (Milano: Garzanti, 1968), 197.

12. Millicent Marcus has emphasized the desert as a metaphor for realism by arguing that "the realist filmmaker must remain in the desert, ever seeking, but never achieving, the promised land of stylistic and ideological certainty." *Italian Cinema in the Light of Neorealism*, op. cit., 262.

13. M. Horkheimer and T. W. Adorno, *Dialectic of Enlightenment*, trans. John Cumming (New York: Seabury Press, 1972), 115.

14. As a radical denial of any foundation to philosophical discourse, conventionalism is naturalism's specular opposite and it can only be Paolo's destiny: the despairing rejection of all certainties (skepticism) is the next stage inevitably following the illusion of mastering reality. For an outstanding discussion of conventionalism, naturalism, and realism, see Terry Lovell, *Pictures of Reality* (London: British Film Institute, 1980).

15. *Complicità tra il sottoproletariato e Dio* is the title of one of the chapters in the novel *Teorema*, 106–111.

16. Interestingly, *Dark Forces* (1984), which can be considered Holly-

wood's remake of *Teorema*, is similarly unrestrained about the portrayal of the exceptional befalling a bourgeois milieu: the visitor effecting the disintegration of the family is a magician endowed with the most amazing powers of his craft. A comparison between these two films elicits extremely interesting conclusions about Hollywood vs. Italian "art" films, the sixties vs. the eighties.

Notes to Chapter Seventeen

1. Silvia Harvey, *May '68 and Film Culture* (London: British Film Institute, 1980), 17. Harvey's book is an intelligent and informative study of the positions that emerged from that heated conjuncture, seen in the light of its Russian Formalist antecedents.

2. Silvia Harvey, op. cit., 22.

3. Cfr. Jean-Paul Fargier, "Parenthesis or Indirect Route," *Cinethique* 5 (Sept.–Oct. 1969), trans. Susan Bennett in *Screen* 12, no. 1 (Summer 1971), and "Cinema, Ideology, Criticism," *Cahiers du cinema* 216–217 (Oct.–Nov. 1969), trans. Susan Bennett in the same issue of *Screen*.

4. "La Parola orale meravigliosa possibilità del cinema," op. cit.

5. Marc Gervais, *Pier Paolo Pasolini* (Paris: Seghers, 1973), 97. Gervais's book offers a very perceptive examination of Pasolini's films up through *Il Decamerone*.

6. See *Lettere Luterane*, op. cit., where Pasolini extensively used the metaphor of *Il Palazzo* to indicate the invisible yet real place in which Italian political decisions are made. His metaphor was so effective in describing the feeling that many Italians have of the ruling class that *Il Palazzo* has become common currency in journalistic writing.

7. This felicitous expression is Noel Purdon's in "Pasolini: The Films of Alienation," *Willemen*, op. cit., 53, perhaps the most interesting article written on *Porcile*.

8. Historically, the term *trasformismo* designated the strategy espoused by the *Sinistra storica* (Historical Left) in power in Italy between 1876–1887, when the Left's leader De Pretis formed his cabinet with ministers from the Right. In so doing, De Pretis aimed at entrusting the office to "experts" (Herdhitze's technicians), regardless of their ideological beliefs. In today's usage, *trasformismo* denotes the average Italian politician's uncanny ability of shifting sides with the most shameless opportunism. The most recent example of Italian *trasformismo* is Bettino Craxi and the Italian Socialist party.

9. "The Films of Alienation," op. cit., 45.

10. "Cuore" (Heart), *Scritti Corsari*, 154.

11. Sigmund Freud, *Three Case Histories* (New York: Collier, 1963), 276.

12. Ibid., 300. As to the other references, it is worth quoting the full passages to have a better sense of the extent to which Pasolini adapted the story of the Wolf-Man to his needs.

(*a*) "Once he was running after a beautiful big butterfly, with striped yellow wings which ended in points in the hope of catching it. (It was no doubt a "swallow-tail.") He was suddenly seized with a terrible fear of the creature, and, screaming, gave up the chase" (198).

(*b*) "In the evening, too, he used to make the round of all the holy pictures that hung in the room, taking a chair with him, upon which he climbed, and used to kiss each one of them devoutly. There was another fact that was utterly inconsistent with this pious ceremonial—but perhaps it was, nevertheless, quite consistent with it—for he recollected some blasphemous thoughts which used to come into his head like an inspiration from the devil. He was obliged to think 'God-swine' or 'God-shit'" (199).

(*c*) "Once, when the children were given some colored sugar sticks, the governess, who was inclined to disordered fancies, pronounced that they were pieces of chopped up snakes. He remembered afterwards that his father had once met a snake while he was walking along a footpath, and had beaten it to pieces with a stick" (208).

13. During the same period in which he shot *Porcile*, Pasolini said to Duflot:

Cannibalism is a semiological system. We must restore its allegorical value as a symbol of a rebellion taken to its extreme consequences. It is a form of extremism pushed to the limit of scandal, rebellion, and horror. It is also a system of exchange, or, if you prefer, a system of total refusal, and therefore a form of language, a monstrous refusal of the communication as practiced by men (*Duflot*, p. 95).

14. Gilles Deleuze and Félix Guattari, *The Anti-Oedipus*, trans. Robert Hurley, Mark Seem, and Helen R. Lane (New York: Viking, 1977), 25–28.

Notes to Chapter Eighteen

1. In the course of his book-length interview, Jean Duflot, *Entretiens avec Pasolini* (Paris: Belfond, 1970), 64, asked Pasolini: "Doesn't your choice of mythology over a commitment with the historical present keep you from engaging in realism?" Pasolini's answer confirmed the point made by the centaur: "My precise idea on this subject is that only those who believe in myths are *realistic*, and vice versa. The 'mythical' is nothing but the other side of realism." Hereafter, Duflot's book will be cited as *Duflot*.

2. Millicent Marcus, *Italian Cinema in the Light of Neorealism*, op. cit., 245–249.

3. *The Dialectic of the Enlightenment*, op. cit., 81–120.

4. *Magrelli*, 99; *Il Mondo*, May 31, 1973: 77; *Magrelli*, 101. Indeed, in nearly every interview of the time between 1970 and 1973, Pasolini makes more or less explicit remarks about his older age and its consequences. In 1971, he even went to Romania for a "Gerovital" cure—"Gerovital" was, at the time, supposed to slow the aging process. In sum, there are many indications that Pasolini was not aging "gracefully."

5. Cited in James Hillman, *Re-Visioning Psychology* (New York: Harper, 1975), 27. (Hereafter referred to as *Hillman*.)

6. *Hillman*, 23.

7. C. G. Jung, *Modern Man in Search of a Soul* (New York: Harvest, 1955), 219.

8. *Duflot*, 111–112.

9. P. P. Pasolini, *Medea* (Milano: Garzanti, 1970), 92.

10. "Médée, Notre Contemporaine," *Jeune cinema* 45 (March 1970).

11. *Duflot*, 112.

12. "Il sentimento della storia" (The Sentiment of History), *Cinema nuovo* 205 (May–June 1970): 172–173.

13. As to the costumes, Pasolini prided himself on having achieved a "visionary" mixture by using Turkish, Andalusian, and Mexican elements. See *Jeune cinema*, op. cit., 20.

14. "Pasolini ne Triche pas avec le Public" (Pasolini Does Not Cheat with the Public), *Jeune cinema* 74 (November 1973): 11.

15. *Hillman*, X.

16. Ibid., 57.

17. Ibid., 105–107.

18. Ibid., 99–100.

19. Ibid., 107.

20. Ibid., 99.

Notes to Chapter Nineteen

1. Ten years earlier, Pasolini had translated Aeschylus' *Orestes* into Italian: *Orestiade* (Torino: Einaudi, 1960).

2. "Nota per l'ambientazione dell'*Orestiade* in Africa," *La città futura* 23 (June 7, 1978): 9.

3. A small sector of the Italian population is fascinated by what the *extracomunitari* (literally, "those belonging outside the European community) may bring along. But there are many who resist this process. And racism raises its ugly head in a country which had thus far prided itself on being immune from it.

4. See *New Larousse Encyclopedia of Mythology* (New York: Crescent, 1959), 166–167.

5. It is enough to look at the most politicized of the New Age publications to realize the contemporary currency of Pasolini's intuitions. For example, *In Context: A Quarterly of Humane Sustainable Culture* 24 (Late Winter 1990) recently dedicated an issue to "postmodern spirituality" entitled "Earth and Spirit: Redefining the Sacred for the Planetary Era." In JoAnn McAlister's article, "Choosing Wonder," p. 36, we read:

> We have always told stories—whether magical, redemptive, or mechanistic—to decipher the world and describe our place within it. We can therefore assume that we *will* tell ourselves a new story of reality. Whether it will fulfill the function of *myth*—restoring harmony between the human enterprise and the Earth—is the question. And since myth is not a conscious creation, we know not where the human imagination will take us, nor when we will wake up with the dream that will sustain us. But a story is already emerging from contemporary science which reveals the lineaments of the evolving universe, and the interrelatedness of all

aspects of the Earth's functioning. Thomas Berry, the preeminent teller of this tale, even titles his recent book *The Dream of the Earth*. This new story of the unfolding of the universe can be the source of both a perceptual shift in our views about the nature of reality and a spiritual path that unfolds organically from the deeper dimensions of the universe itself.

Pasolini's obsessive concern with myth thus acquires a new sense. And so does his use of the word "reality," which McAlister uses with equal force. In the context of a discourse where words have a political weight, there is no room for semantic hairsplitting or poststructuralist *finesse*. Once again, Pasolini chose to be "naive," in order to be able to say certain things.

6. Cited in Tomaso Anzoino, *Pasolini* (Firenze: La Nuova Italia, 1974), 8–9.

7. *In Context*, op. cit., 46.

8. Pasolini had already used *Orestes* and the Erinyes against Marxist blindness in 1960, at the time of his translation. In the article "Pasternak e l'irrazionalità" (Pasternak and Irrationality," *Le belle bandiere*, op. cit., 52–54), he argued that neither the Italian nor the Soviet Marxists have faced the problem of human irrationality. Marxist reason was like that of Athena "born from the father's mind and therefore deprived of the uterine, maternal, feminine experience."

Notes to Chapter Twenty

1. David Ray Griffin, founder of the Center for a Postmodern World and professor at the School of Theology at Claremont, thus describes "postmodern spirituality" (*In Context* 24 [Late Winter 1990]: 20):

> There are so many ways to describe postmodern spirituality. You can say it is pacific, it's ecological, it's a spirituality of creativity, it's a reenchantment of the universe. But perhaps the best way to get at it, as a summary term, would be *pan-en-theism*: the idea that the world is God—God is something like the soul of the universe—and God is present in all things. As some mystics have said, we swim in God. When I use the words "postmodern spirituality," I mean a spirituality that continues the advances made in the modern period. It is not a desire to go back to some kind of premodern existence, as if that were ideal. Real advances were made in the modern period. But on the other hand, many of those advances were the mirror image of very destructive values. They did not seem destructive at the time, but we can see that they have become so—and that we need to recover some *pre*modern sensibilities, values, and truths. In so doing, we are forging a new synthesis that is *post*modern.

The similarity with Pasolini's positions is striking in more than one respect. For example, Pasolini's much famed "reverential style" (see *Stack*, 83), his desire "to reconsecrate things as much as possible," is nothing but an attempt to reenchant a world which the Enlightenment has disenchanted. His idea of Reality as a language is akin to Griffin's notion of *pan-en-theism* (and both owe much to Eastern spirituality). In a 1971 interview (*Magrelli*, 100), Pasolini remarked: "For some time now, I have been saying reactionary things. In fact, I am thinking of writing an essay entitled: How to recuperate some reactionary stands on behalf of the revolution."

2. See "A Sana'a risanata" (To a Reconstructed Sana'a), *Epoca*, March 27, 1988. The brief description of the work that will be done in Sana'a is followed by the text of Pasolini's documentary in its entirety.

Notes to Chapter Twenty-One

1. "Pasolini sur 'Théorème'," *La quinzaine littéraire* (March 1–15, 1969): 24–25.
2. *Magrelli*, 104–105.
3. "Decameron: intervista con P. P. Pasolini," *Cinemasessanta* 87–88 (January–April 1972): 62–70.
4. "Tetis," in *Erotismo, eversione e merce* (Eroticism, Subversion, and Commodities) (Bologna: Cappelli, 1974), 97–103.
5. *Cinemasessanta*, op. cit., 70.
6. *Willemen*, 77.
7. In the space of a single interview with Giacomo Gambetti, "Il Decameron di Pasolini," *Sipario* 300 (May 1971): 21–23, Pasolini uses the word "authentic" four times.
8. Stephen Heath, *The Sexual Fix* (New York: Schocken, 1984), 3.
9. Pierre Bourdieu, *Distinction*, op. cit., 367.
10. Morando Morandini, "Le responsabilità di Pasolini" (Pasolini's Responsibilities), *Il giorno* (May 13, 1973): 3. For a revealing list of the films making the so-called *filone erotico* (erotic genre) and their box-office turnouts, see Francesco Savio, "Il Boccaccinema,"*Il Mondo* 25, no. 14 (May 4, 1973): 16–19. See also Telesio Malaspina, "I miracoli di San Priapo," *Espresso* (October 10, 1972): 12, which appeared next to an interview with Pasolini conducted by Dacia Maraini. Maraini's feminist perspective exposes Pasolini's contradictions and forces him to acknowledge that "yes, perhaps it is true that I accept a certain condition of inferiority for women." Pasolini's only defense, in this interview, was his "ontological love for the past." The kind of popularity that Pasolini achieved with these "erotic" films is perhaps best defined by the fact that, while he was accusing students and feminists of being petty bourgeois, his longest article on *Il fiore delle mille e una notte* appeared in *Playboy*, "Le mie mille e una notte" (Sept. 1973): 43–126 (the article is eleven pages, but they are not continuously printed). Indeed, the playboy bunny at the end of this article encapsulates the wreckage of "a certain realism."
11. James Roy MacBean, "Between Kitsch and Fascism," *Cineaste* 4 (1984): 12–19.
12. See W. Dynes, *Homolexis* (New York: Gay Academic Union, 1985), 115–116. For a useful assessment of this aspect of Pasolini's work from a gay perspective, see Giovanni Dall'Orto, "Contro Pasolini" (Against Pasolini), in *Desiderio di Pasolini*, op. cit., 149–182.
13. Edward Said, *Orientalism* (New York: Vintage, 1979), 11.
14. Peter Bondanella, *Italian Cinema from Neorealism to the Present* (New York: Ungar, 1983), 289.

15. Michele Mancini and Giuseppe Perella, *Pier Paolo Pasolini: corpi e luoghi* (Roma: Theorema, 1981), ix. Organized around visual topics (e.g., "looks into the camera") and containing an enormous quantity of stills, Mancini and Perella's book is by far the most interesting work on Pasolini to date.

16. For *Il Decamerone*, see Ben Lawton, "Theory and Praxis in Pasolini's Trilogy of Life: 'Decameron,'" *Quarterly Review of Film Studies* 2, no. 4 (November 1977): 395–417; and Millicent Marcus, "The *Decameron:* Pasolini as Reader of Boccaccio," *Italian Quarterly*, op. cit., 175–180. For *I racconti di Canterbury*, Jean Sémolué, "Reflexions sur le Récit" (Reflections on Plot-Structure), *Etudes Cinématographiques*, Paris, 1977: 127–161. For *Il fiore delle mille e una notte*, Barthelemy Amengual, "Le mille et Une Nuits" (The Arabian Nights), *Etudes Cinématographiques*, Paris, 1977, 172–183. For all three films, see *Snyder*, 129–163, who gives his best critical performance in the analysis of *La trilogia della vita*.

17. *Cinemasessanta*, op. cit., 63.

18. Giovanni Boccaccio, *The Decameron*, trans. G. H. McWilliam (New York: Penguin, 1972), 71.

19. I am indebted to Ben Lawton's article, cited in note 16 above, for the recognition of these two paintings.

20. *The Decameron*, op. cit., 493.

21. Millicent Marcus, "The *Decameron*," op. cit., 177.

22. *The Decameron*, op. cit., 367.

23. Jack Babuscio, "Camp and Gay Sensibility," in *Dyer*, 40–57.

24. Geoffrey Chaucer, *The Canterbury Tales* (Middlesex: Penguin, 1958), 255.

25. *Il cinema Italiano degli anni sessanta*, op. cit., 150–161. Quite appropriately, Miccichè adds *Salò* to *La trilogia della vita* and calls these four films "La tetralogia della morte" (The Tetralogy of Death). Miccichè, however, tends to regard Pasolini's fascination with death as a decadent trait and does not adequately explore homosexuality. See "Pasolini: la morte e la storia" (Pasolini: Death and History), *Cinemasessanta* 105 (September–October 1975): 8–19, written shortly before Pasolini's death; and "La tetralogia della morte," *Cinemasessanta* 121 (May–June 1978).

26. Vito Russo, *The Celluloid Closet*, op. cit. See also Philip Bertrand, *L'homosexualité à l'ecran*, op. cit., to which this paragraph is heavily indebted.

27. Vito Russo, op. cit., 52.

28. "Eros e Cultura" (Eros and Culture), *Europeo*, September 19, 1974. It is an interview with Massimo Fini, in which Pasolini reiterates the idea that the ideology of his late films is "deeply hidden."

29. Albert Moravia, "Ma perché tanta passione per l'Oriente?" *Espresso* (September 22, 1974): 143.

30. I said "I must" regretfully, because Carlo Laurenzi wrote his piece in a right-wing newspaper with which I would not like to be associated. "Il fiore delle mille e una notte," *Il giornale nuovo* (Aug 30, 1974): 16.

31. Not surprisingly, the most helpful short text to aid in understanding Pasolini's blend of Oriental philosophy and cine-semiotics is a poem, the preface to the article significantly entitled "Res Sunt Nomina" (Things Are

Names)" (*HE*, 255). In this poem, Pasolini talks about two signifying systems: "a being which never-always-yesterday-tomorrow is" (Reality) and "the Reality-Eater, or the Eye-Mouth" (cinema). While living, we are constantly called to "interpret" and "decipher" Reality, for example, "the eyes, the mouth, the cheekbones, the chin, the skin" of a blond Brazilian boy met on "a real day at the end of March 1970 in the favela on Barra Street." What happens when we see this boy through the "Eye-Mouth" of cinema? Pasolini has no doubt: I still "interpret him (Mestizo? Portuguese? Indian? Dutch? Black?) as in reality." It follows that "the Language of the Reality-Eater is a brother to the language of Reality." Indeed, all this sounds like Pasolini's usual tirade about the code of cinema being equal to the code of reality, but in this poem he hastens to add that both cinema and Reality are "illusion, yes, illusion, here and there." The idea of Reality as the self-manifestation of an impersonal "Being who is and doesn't love" belongs, then, to the Hindu-Buddhist idea that reality, as we experience it (subject-object dualism), is an illusion. All we see are deceptive pictures on *maya*'s veil.

32. See, for example, the recent *Politica e Zen* (Politics and Zen) (Milano: Feltrinelli, 1990), a collectively edited anthology of writings by dissidents of both the sixties and the eighties generation.

33. "Io e Boccaccio" (Boccaccio and I), *Espresso* (November 11, 1970) 14–18.

34. "Questo è il mio scandalo" (This Is My Scandal), *Il tempo illustrato* (May 31, 1974): 47–48.

35. Arthur Schopenhauer, "Transcendent Speculation on the Apparent Deliberateness in the Fate of an Individual," *Parerga and Paralipomena* (Oxford: Clarendon, 1974), 201–223. Schopenhauer's whole essay bears a striking resemblance to the conceptual framework of Pasolini's film. For example, Schopenhauer refers to "the great dream that is dreamed by that one entity, but in such a way that all its persons dream it together," which is precisely the organizing idea of *Il fiore delle mille e una notte*. I am not suggesting that Pasolini knew Schopenhauer (although it is highly possible). I am merely trying to decenter Pasolini's ideas and show how they are part of a discourse—West meets East—dating (at least) as far back as Schopenhauer.

36. *Playboy*, op. cit., 56.

37. On the topic see the following interview-articles: "Dissento" (I Dissent), *Noi Donne*, March 1969, a self-defense by Pasolini; "Dialogo armato con Pasolini" (Armed Dialogue with Pasolini), *Il giorno*, January 31, 1973, an interview with Natalia Aspesi, in which he defines feminists as "petty bourgeois" and denies the possibility of an effective gay movement; "Nella irreligione del mio tempo" (In the 'Irreligion' of My Time), *Aut*, August 4, 1974: 42–46, an interview with Adele Cambria; "Ci dica Pasolini: è con noi o contro di noi?" (Tell Us, Pasolini: Are You with Us or Against Us?), *Amica*, August 8, 1974, an interview with M. T. Clerici; and Pasolini's bitter review of Maraini's book *Donne mie*, in *Il tempo illustrato*, June 14, 1974.

38. *Village Voice*, May 1, 1990: 71.

39. *Duflot*, 89.

40. *Feminine Sexuality: Jacques Lacan and the Ecole Freudienne*, eds. Juliet Mitchell and Jacqueline Rose (New York: Norton, 1982), 84.

Notes to Chapter Twenty-Two

1. *The Dialectic of the Enlightenment*, op. cit., 118.
2. See "Pasolini," an interview conducted by Oreste del Buono, *Europeo*, April 4, 1975: 75–76.
3. After six years of contemptuous silence on Pasolini, *Cahiers du cinéma* 268–269 (July–August 1976) enthusiastically reviewed *Salò*, and, five years later, most members of the editorial board included Pasolini's last work in the list of the ten best films of the decade.
4. "Abiura dalla *Trilogia della vita*" (Abjuration of *The Trilogy of Life*), *Corriere della Sera*, Milan, Sept. 1, 1975; reprinted in *Trilogia della vita* (Bologna: Cappelli, 1975), 11–13.
5. *Scritti Corsari*, op. cit., 58.
6. The first definition is Roland Barthes's, "Sade-Pasolini," *Le Monde*, June 16, 1976, reprinted in *Pier Paolo Pasolini*, ed. Beverly Allen, trans. Verena Conley, op. cit., 102; the second is from a poster advertising the film at the Orson Welles Theater in Cambridge, Mass., December 1985; and the third is Cesare Musatti's "Il *Salò* di Pasolini regno della perversione" (Pasolini's *Salò* as the Reign of Perversion), *Cinema nuovo* 239 (January 1976): 21–23.
7. Pasolini quoted Bernard Berenson by heart during a 1967 interview with Gaetano Stucchi, *Settegiorni* 11 (August 27): 31–33.

> I do not believe that the joy of the image is a joy like the others. The joy of the image can be, is, vitality. I am referring to a sentence by Berenson that more or less goes like this: "If, when you're watching a work of art, reading a poem, or looking at a painting, you feel a sudden surge in vitality, then you must be in front of a work of art. Otherwise, no." When I see an American, commercial film, I get out of the theatre with no vitality whatsoever. I mean, I may have seen joyous images, joyous people, a beautiful spectacle, with beautiful colors, etc. etc.: but no sooner do I get out of the theatre than my vitality is zero. I am talking about average films, let it be clear. Hence, I would like my image to be joyous, but not in the superficial sense: I want my images to cause a surge in vitality.

The English word *vitality* may fail to reproduce all the connotations (energy, zest, desire) of its Italian counterpart, which was, indeed, one of Pasolini's favorite words. Be that as it may, Pasolini's argument is yet another proof that for him the viewer's body is the ultimate recipient and gauge of the image.
8. Fulvio Accialini found it inaccurate with respect to Sade, "La passion selon Sade" (Passion According to Sade), *Cinema e cinema* 7–8 (April–Sept. 1976): 26–27. And, so did Roland Barthes, "Sade-Pasolini," op. cit. Italo Calvino criticized it for its infidelity to both Sade and fascism, "Sade è dentro di noi" (Sade Is Within Us), *Corriere della Sera*, Milan, November 30, 1975, in *Pier Paolo Pasolini*, ed. Beverly Allen, trans. Mark Pietralunga, op. cit., 112–117. Cesare Musatti, op. cit., argued that it represented the failure of Pasoli-

ni's sexuality. Ben Lawton, "The Evolving Rejection of Homosexuality, Sub-Proletariat, and the Third World in Pasolini's Films," op. cit., saw in it a symptom of Pasolini's rejection of homosexuality.

9. *Scritti Corsari*, 289–290.

10. "L'estetica del'osceno per un nipotino di De Sade" (The Aesthetic of the Obscene for One of De Sade's Grandchildren), *Tempo illustrato*, March 8, 1974.

11. *Screen* 15, no. 2 (Summer 1974); now in Colin MacCabe, *Tracking the Signifier* (Minneapolis: University of Minnesota Press, 1985), 33–58.

12. *Screen* 17, no. 3 (1976): 7–27, now in *Tracking the Signifier*, op. cit., 58–82.

13. "Pasolini on De Sade," interview by Gideon Bachmann, *Film Quarterly* 29, no. 2 (1975): 41.

14. De Sade, *The 120 Days of Sodom and Other Writings*, trans. Austrin Wainhouse (New York: Grove, 1966), 427.

15. For a discussion of Sade's *Être unique* (Unique Being), see Maurice Blanchot, *Lautreamont et Sade* (Paris: Minuit, 1963), 17–49.

16. Roland Barthes, *Le plaisir du texte* (Paris: Seuil, 1973); *The Pleasure of the Text*, trans. Richard Miller (New York: Hill and Wang, 1975), 14.

Essential Bibliography Toward a Use of Pasolini's Film Theory and Practice

Works by Pasolini

Books

Le ceneri di Gramsci. Milano: Garzanti, 1957. (Poetry. The homonymous poem is available in English, together with several important poems from this and the other collections, in *Pier Paolo Pasolini, Poems*, trans. Norman MacAfee. New York: Vintage, 1982.)

La religione del mio tempo. Milano: Garzanti, 1961. (Poetry. Contains the seminal poem "In morte del realismo.")

L' odore dell'India. Milano: Longanesi, 1962. *The Scent of India*, trans. David Price. London: Olive Press, 1984. (On his first trip to India)

Poesia in forma di rosa. Milano: Garzanti, 1964. (Poetry, some inspired by cinema)

Teorema. Milano: Garzanti, 1968. (Novel)

Trasumanar e organizzar. Milano: Garzanti, 1970. (Poetry)

Empirismo eretico. Milano: Garzanti, 1972. *Heretical Empiricism*, trans. Ben Lawton and Kate L. Barnett. Bloomington: Indiana University Press, 1988. (Essays on literature, linguistics, and cine-semiotics)

Articles

Le belle bandiere, Dialoghi 1960–65, edited by Giancarlo Ferretti. Roma: Editori Riuniti, 1977. (Short articles, some on cinema, written in response to letters by the readers of the journal *Vie Nuove*, 1960–1965)

"Intellectualism . . . and the Teds." *Films and Filming*, January 1961. (Crucial statement at the outset of his career in filmmaking)

Il Caos, edited by Giancarlo Ferretti. Roma: Editori Riuniti, 1979. (Articles, some on cinema, written for the weekly *Tempo*, 1968–1970)

"L'inutile sforzo di Moravia di dimostrare l'inesistenza della realtà." *Il tempo illustrato*, October 10, 1973. (On his mystical views on reality)

Scritti Corsari. Milano: Garzanti, 1975. (Polemical articles on Italian culture written for various dailies, 1973–1974)

"Tetis." *Erotismo, eversione e merce.* Bologna: Cappelli, 1974. (On the "naked sex = reality" fallacy)

"Abiura dalla *Trilogia della vita.*" Bologna: Cappelli, 1975. (Rejection of the "naked sex + reality" fallacy)

Lettere Luterane. Torino: Einaudi, 1977. *Lutheran Letters*, trans. Stuart Hood. Manchester: Carcanet New Press, 1983. (The pedagogical treatise *Gennariello* plus polemical articles on Italian culture written for the daily *Il corriere della sera* and the weekly *Il mondo* in 1975)

Ecrits sur le cinéma, edited by H. Joubert-Laurencin. Lyon: Presses Universitaires, 1987. (Most of Pasolini's articles on cinema, except those in *Heretical Empiricism*)

Interviews

Con Pier Paolo Pasolini, edited by Enrico Magrelli. Roma: Bulzoni, 1977. (Interviews appeared on *Filmcritica*, from *Accattone* to *Salò*)

"Una lucida passione," with Gaetano Stucchi. *Settegiorni* 11 (August 27, 1967). (Contains reference to "the surge of vitality" which good cinema makes Pasolini's body experience)

"E tu chi eri?" with Dacia Maraini. *Vogue Italia*, May 1971. Reprinted in English, *Pier Paolo Pasolini, A Future Life*. Catalog for the retrospective of Pasolini's films. Roma: Fondo Pier Paolo Pasolini, 1989. (Contains, among other things, one version of the *teta veleta* memory)

Pasolini, with Oswald Stack. Bloomington: Indiana University Press, 1969. (Contains the phrase that gave title to this book)

"Pasolini sur *Théorème*." *La quinzaine littéraire*, March 1–15, 1969. (Ideal companion piece to the paragraph on "a certain realism" in the book above)

Entretiens avec Pasolini, with Jean Duflot. Paris: Belfond, 1970. (Nuggets on cinema and culture, such as "an ideology that is not in crisis is not an ideology")

Published Screenplays

La notte brava. Filmcritica 10, no. 91–92 (November–December 1959).

Accattone (Preface by Carlo Levi). Rome: F. M., 1961.

Mamma Roma. Milano: Rizzoli, 1962.

Il Vangelo secondo Matteo. Milano: Garzanti, 1964.

La ricotta. In *Alí dagli occhi azzurri.* Milano: Garzanti, 1965. This volume also contains *La notte brava*, *Accattone*, and *Mamma Roma*.

La comare secca. Filmcritica 16, no. 161 (October 1965). Subject and treatment of the film directed by Bernardo Bertolucci.

Uccellacci uccellini. Milano: Garzanti, 1966.

Edipo re. Milano: Garzanti, 1967. French translation: *Oedipe Roi* in *L'avant-scene du cinema* 97 (November 1969). English translation: *Oedipus Rex*. London: Lorrimer, 1971.

Che cosa sono le nuvole? Cinema e Film 3, no. 7–8 (Winter-Spring 1969).
Medea. Milano: Garzanti, 1970.
Ostia (written with Sergio Citti). Milano: Garzanti, 1970.
Il padre selvaggio. Torino: Einaudi, 1975. Originally published in two parts in *Cinema e Film* 2, no. 3, and 2, no. 4 (1967).
Trilogia della vita (Il Decamerone, I racconti di Canterbury, Il fiore delle mille e una notte). Bologna: Cappelli, 1975.
San Paolo. Torino: Einaudi, 1977.

Books and Articles on Pasolini

Betti, Laura, *Pasolini: cronaca giudiziaria, persecuzione, morte.* Milano: Garzanti, 1977. (History of persecution/prosecution against Pasolini)
Bruno, Giuliana, "Heresies: The Body of Pasolini's Semiotics." *Cinema Journal,* Spring 1991. (The ultimate reappraisal of Pasolini's film theory)
Casi, Stefano, *Desiderio di Pasolini.* Torino: La Sonda, 1990. (From a gay perspective, with bibliography of works on Pasolini's homosexuality)
De Giusti, Luciano, *I film di Pier Paolo Pasolini.* Roma: Gremese, 1983. (Good film-by-film analysis)
De Lauretis, Teresa, "Language, Representation, Practice: Rereading Pasolini's Essays on Cinema." *Italian Quarterly* 21–22 (Fall 1980–Winter 1981). (First attempt to valorize Pasolini's film theory)
Greene, Naomi, *Pier Paolo Pasolini: Cinema as Heresy.* Princeton: Princeton University Press, 1990. (Contextualizes Pasolini's cinema sociohistorically)
Mancini, Michele, and Perella, Giuseppe, *Pier Paolo Pasolini: corpi e luoghi.* Roma: Theorema, 1981. (Almost entirely made up of stills, excellent)
Naldini, Nico, *Pasolini, una vita.* Torino: Einaudi, 1989. (Best biography, mostly made up of quotations)
Siciliano, Enzo, *Vita di Pasolini.* Milano: Rizzoli, 1978. *Pasolini: A Biography,* trans. John Shepley. New York: Random House, 1982. (Only biography available in English)
Snyder, Stephen, *Pier Paolo Pasolini.* Boston: Twaine, 1980. (Close reading of eleven—"the most important"—films)
Turigliatto, Roberto, "La tecnica e il mito." *Lo Scandalo Pasolini.* Roma: Bianco e Nero, 1976. (Lucid reading of Pasolini's film theory)
Willemen, Paul, editor, *Pasolini.* London: British Film Institute, 1977. (Contains Dyer on Pasolini's homosexuality and Costa's exemplary misreading of Pasolini's theory)
Zigaina, Giuseppe, *Pasolini e la morte.* Venezia: Marsilio, 1987. (Exploration of Pasolini and Jung)

Relevant Books

Adorno, Theodor, and Horkheimer, Max, *Dialectic of the Enlightenment.* New York: Seabury Press, 1972. (Precursor of Pasolini's pirate ideas on culture)

Armes, Roy, *Patterns of Realism*. New York: Barnes, 1971. (Mostly on neorealism, contains useful definition of "realism of attitude")

Armes, Roy, *Film and Reality*. Baltimore: Penguin, 1974. (Survey of realist filmmaking)

Bazin, Andre, *What Is Cinema?* Berkeley, Los Angeles, London: University of California Press, 1971. (Excellent on film and reality in spite of recent realist-bashing)

Bourdieu, Pierre, *La Distinction*. (Paris: Minuit, 1979). *Distinction*, trans. Richard Nice. Cambridge: Harvard University Press, 1984. (Although concerned just with France, it offers an outstanding model for a sociological critique of taste)

Brunette, Peter, *Roberto Rossellini*. New York: Oxford University Press, 1987. (Thorough and theoretically informed, film-by-film analysis of another Italian realist "of attitude")

Deleuze, Gilles, *Cinema 1*. Minneapolis: University of Minnesota Press, 1986. (Among other things, some excellent pages on Pasolini)

Dyer, Richard, editor, *Gays & Film*. London: British Film Institute, 1977. (A historical landmark)

Gramsci, Antonio, *Quaderni dal carcere*. Torino: Einaudi, 1975. (To understand Pasolini's Marxism)

Hillman, James, *Re-visioning Psychology*. New York: Harper, 1975. (Stirs the imagination on what the Jung-Pasolini relationship might have been)

Lovell, Terry, *Pictures of Reality*. London: British Film Institute, 1980. (Against realist-bashers)

MacCabe, Colin, *Tracking the Signifier*. Minneapolis: University of Minnesota Press, 1985. (The quintessential realist-basher)

Marcus, Millicent, *Italian Cinema in the Light of Neorealism*. Princeton: Princeton University Press, 1986. (About a certain realism left as a legacy by neorealism)

Miccichè, Lino, editor, *Il neorealismo cinematografico italiano*. Venezia: Marsilio, 1975. (Interesting anthology, contains Gianni Scalia's "Poichè realismo c'è" with the definition of mimetic and semiotic realisms)

Philbert, Bertrand, *L'homosexualité à l'ecran*. Paris: Veyrier, 1984. (In the wake of Russo, includes European cinema)

Russo, Vito, *The Celluloid Closet* (New York: Harper, 1981). (Homosexuality and repression in Hollywood)

Williams, Cristopher, editor, *Realism and the Cinema*. London: British Film Institute, 1980. (Outstanding, well-commentated anthology of writings on cinematic realism)

Filmography

351

Producer: Alfredo Bini for Arco Film
Running Time: 105 minutes

1963 *La ricotta* (Third episode of *Rogopag* or *Laviamoci il cervello*; other episodes by Roberto Rossellini, Jean-Luc Godard, Ugo Gregoretti)
Screenplay: P. P. Pasolini
Assistant Directors: Sergio Citti, Carlo di Carlo
Photography: Tonino Delli Colli
Art Direction: Flavio Mogherini
Costumes: Danilo Donati
Music: Carlo Rustichelli
Editing: Nino Baragli
Cast: Orson Welles (the Director), Mario Cipriani (Stracci), Laura Betti (the Star), Edmonda Aldini (another Star), Vittorio La Paglia (the Journalist), Ettore Garofolo (Extra), Maria Bernardini (Extra who does striptease), Elsa De Giorgi and Enzo Siciliano (two guests)
Producer: Alfredo Bini for Arco Film-Cineriz (Rome)/Lyre
Film (Paris)
Running Time: 35 minutes

La rabbia (First part; second part by Giovanni Guareschi)
Subject and Verse Commentary: P. P. Pasolini
Assistant Director: Carlo di Carlo
Editing: P. P. Pasolini, Nino Baragli
Commentary spoken by Giorgio Bassani and Renato Guttuso
Producer: Gastone Ferrante for Opus Film
Running Time: 50 minutes

1964 *Comizi d'amore*
Commentary written by P. P. Pasolini
Assistant Director: Vincenzo Cerami
Photography: Mario Bernardo, Tonino Delli Colli
Editing: Nino Baragli
Commentary spoken by Lello Bersani and P. P. Pasolini
Participants: P. P. Pasolini, Alberto Moravia, Cesare Musatti, Giuseppe Ungaretti, Camilla Cederna, Adele Cambria, Oriana Fallaci, Antonella Lualdi, Graziella Chiarcossi (in the role of the bride)
Producer: Alfredo Bini for Arco Film
Running Time: 90 minutes

Sopraluoghi in Palestina
Subject: P. P. Pasolini
Photography: Aldo Pennelli, Otello Martelli
Participants: Don Andrea Carraro, P. P. Pasolini
Commentary and Editing: P. P. Pasolini
Producer: Alfredo Bini for Arco Film
Running Time : 55 minutes

Il Vangelo secondo Matteo
Screenplay: P. P. Pasolini (from The Gospel of St. Matthew)

Assistant Directors: Maurizio Lucidi, Paul Schneider
Photography: Tonino Delli Colli, assisted by Dante Ferretti
Art Direction: Luigi Scaccianoce
Costumes: Danilo Donati
Music: J. S. Bach, W. A. Mozart, A. Webern, S. Prokofiev, Negro spirituals, Russian revolutionary songs (Coordinated by Carlo Rustichelli and Luis Bacalov)
Editing: Nino Baragli
Cast: Enrique Irazoqui (Christ, dubbed by Enrico Maria Salerno), Margherita Caruso (the young Mary), Susanna Pasolini (the old Mary), Marcello Morante (Joseph), Mario Socrate (John the Baptist), Ferruccio Nuzzo (Matthew), Alfonso Gatto (Andrew), Enzo Siciliano (Simon), Rodolfo Wilcock (Caiphas), Francesco Leonetti (Herod II), Natalia Ginzburg (Mary of Bethany), Settimo Di Porto (Peter), Rossana di Rocco (Angel), Otello Sestili (Judas), Giacomo Morante (John the Apostle), Amerigo Bevilacqua (Herod I), Ninetto Davoli (young shepherd)
Producer: Alfredo Bini for Arco Film (Rome)/Lux Cie Cinematographie (Paris)
Running Time: 137 minutes

1966 *Uccellacci uccellini*
Screenplay: P. P. Pasolini
Assistant Directors: Carlo Morandi, Vincenzo Cerami, Sergio Citti
Photography: Tonino Delli Colli, Mario Bernardo
Art Direction: Luigi Scaccianoce, assisted by Dante Ferretti
Costumes: Danilo Donati, assisted by Piero Cicoletti
Music: Ennio Morricone, title song by Domenico Modugno
Editing: Nino Baragli
Ornithological Expert: Pino Serpe
Cast: Totò (the Father, Brother Cicillo), Ninetto Davoli (the Son, Brother Ninetto), Femi Benussi (Luna, the Prostitute), Rossana di Rocco (Friend of Ninetto), Lena Lin Solaro, Gabriele Baldini (the Dantesque Dentist), Francesco Leonetti (Voice of the Crow)
Producer: Alfredo Bini for Arco Film
Running Time: 88 minutes

1967 *La terra vista dalla luna* (Third episode of *Le Streghe*; other episodes by Luchino Visconti, Mauro Bolognini, Franco Rossi, Vittorio De Sica)
Screenplay: P. P. Pasolini
Assistant Directors: Sergio Citti, Vincenzo Cerami
Photography: Giuseppe Rotunno
Art Direction: Mario Garbuglia, Piero Poletto
Costumes: Piero Tosi
Sculptures: Pino Zac
Music: Piero Piccioni
Editing: Nino Baragli
Cast: Silvana Mangano (Assurdina Caí), Totò (Ciancicato Miao), Ninet-

to Davoli (Basciú Miao), Laura Betti (Tourist), Luigi Leoni (Tourist's Wife), Mario Cipriani (Priest)
Producer: Dino De Laurentiis Cinematografica (Rome)/Les Productions Artistes Associes (Paris)
Running Time: 30 minutes

Edipo re
Screenplay: P. P. Pasolini, inspired by Sophocles' *Oedipus Rex* and *Oedipus at Colonus*
Assistant Director: Jean-Claude Biette
Photography: Giuseppe Ruzzolini
Art Direction: Luigi Scaccianoce
Architectural Assistant: Dante Ferretti
Costumes: Danilo Donati
Music: Romanian and Japanese folk songs plus original music coordinated by Pier Paolo Pasolini
Editing: Nino Baragli
Cast: Franco Citti (Edipo), Silvana Mangano (Jocasta), Alida Valli (Mereope), Carmelo Bene (Creon), Julian Beck (Tiresias), Francesco Leonetti (Servant), Ninetto Davoli (Anghelos/Angelo), P. P. Pasolini (High Priest), Luciano Bartoli (Laius), Jean-Claude Biette (Priest)
Producer: Alfredo Bini for Arco Film
Running Time: 110 minutes

1968 *Che cosa sono le nuvole* (Third episode of *Capriccio all'italiana*; other episodes by Steno, Mauro Bolognini, Pino Zac, and Mario Monicelli)
Screenplay: P. P. Pasolini
Assistant Director: Sergio Citti
Photography: Tonino Delli Colli
Sets and Costumes: Jurgen Henze
Music: Domenico Modugno, P. P. Pasolini
Editing: Nino Baragli
Cast: Totò (Iago), Ninetto Davoli (Othello), Laura Betti (Desdemona), Adriana Asti (Bianca), Franco Franchi (Cassio), Ciccio Ingrassia (Roderigo), Francesco Leonetti (Puppetmaster), Domenico Modugno (Garbageman)
Producer: Dino De Laurentiis Cinematografica (Rome)
Running Time: 22 minutes

Teorema
Story and Screenplay: P. P. Pasolini
Assistant Director: Sergio Citti
Photography: Giuseppe Ruzzolini
Art Direction: Luciano Puccini
Costumes: Marcella De Marchis
Music: W. A. Mozart, Ennio Morricone
Editing: Nino Baragli
Cast: Terence Stamp (the Visitor), Silvana Mangano (Lucia, the

Mother), Masimo Girotti (Paolo, the Father), Anne Wiazemsky (Odetta, the Daughter), Andres Jose Cruz (Pietro, the Son), Laura Betti (Emilia, the Servant), Ninetto Davoli (Angelino/the Postman), Susanna Pasolini (Old Countrywoman), Alfonso Gatto, Carlo De Mejo
Producers: Manolo Bolognini and Franco Rossellini for Aetos Film
Running Time: 98 minutes

Appunti per un film sull'India
Subject and Direction: P. P. Pasolini
Collaboration: Gianni Barcelloni
Editing: Jenner Menghi
Producer: Gianni Barcelloni for Italian television (RAI)
Running Time: 32 minutes

1969 *La sequenza del fiore di carta* (Third episode of *Amore e rabbia*; other episodes by Carlo Lizzani, Bernardo Bertolucci, Jean-Luc Godard, Marco Bellocchio)
Screenplay: P. P. Pasolini (from an idea by Puccio Pucci and Piero Badalessi)
Assistant Directors: Franco Brocani, Maurizio Ponzi
Photography: Giuseppe Ruzzolini
Editing: Nino Baragli
Music: J. S. Bach, Giovanni Fusco
Cast: Ninetto Davoli (Youth), Voices of God: Graziella Chiarcossi, Aldo Puglisi, Bernardo Bertolucci, P. P. Pasolini
Producer: Carlo Lizzani for Castoro Film (Rome)/Anouchka Film (Paris)
Running Time: 12 minutes

Porcile
Story and Screenplay: P. P. Pasolini
Assistant Directors: Sergio Citti, Fabio Garriba
Photography: Tonino Delli Colli, Armando Nannuzzi, Giuseppe Ruzzolini
Art Direction and Costumes: Danilo Donati
Music: Benedetto Ghiglia
Editing: Nino Baragli
Cast: Pierre Clementi (Cannibal), Franco Citti (Second Cannibal), Jean-Pierre Leaud (Julian), Alberto Lionello (Klotz, the Father), Ugo Tognazzi (Herdhitze), Anne Wiazemsky (Ida), Marco Ferreri (Hans Gunther), Ninetto Davoli (Young Man/Marracchione), Margherita Lozano (Mrs. Klotz, dubbed by Laura Betti)
Producer: Gian Vittorio Baldi for IDI Cinematografica, Orso Films, INDIEF (Rome)/CAPAC (Paris)
Running Time: 98 minutes

Medea
Screenplay: P. P. Pasolini, based on Euripides and Seneca
Assistant Director: Carlo Carunchio

Photography: Ennio Guarnieri
Art Direction: Dante Ferretti
Costumes: Piero Tosi, assisted by Piero Cicoletti and Gabriella Pesucci
Music: Coordinated by Pasolini with the help of Elsa Morante
Editing: Nino Baragli
Cast: Maria Callas (Medea), Giuseppe Gentile (Jason), Laurent Terzieff (the Centaur), Massimo Girotti (Creon), Margaret Clementi (Glauce)
Producer: Franco Rossellini and Marina Cicogna for San Marco Film (Rome)/Les Film Number One (Paris)/Janus Film and Fernsehen (Frankfurt)
Running Time: 110 minutes

1970 *Appunti per un'Orestiade Africana*
Script: P. P. Pasolini
Photography: Giorgio Pelloni, Mario Bagnato, Emore Galeassi
Editing: Cleofe Conversi
Music: Gato Barbieri
Producer: Gian Vittorio Baldi for IDI Cinematografica
Running Time: 55 minutes

1971 *Il Decamerone*
Screenplay: P. P. Pasolini, based on Boccaccio's tales
Assistant Directors: Sergio Citti and Umberto Angelucci
Photography: Tonino Delli Colli
Art Direction: Dante Ferretti
Costumes: Danilo Donati
Music: Coordinated by Pasolini with the help of Ennio Morricone
Editing: Nino Baragli, Tatiana Casini Morigi
Cast: Franco Citti (Ser Ciappelletto), Ninetto Davoli (Andreuccio), Giuseppe Zigaina (Monk), P. P. Pasolini (Giotto's pupil), Silvana Mangano (the Madonna)
Producer: Franco Rossellini for PEA (Rome)/Les Productions Artistes Associés (Paris)/Artemis Film (Berlin)
Running time: 111 minutes

1972 *I racconti di Canterbury*
Screenplay: P. P. Pasolini, based on Chaucer's stories
Assistant Directors: Sergio Citti, Umberto Angelucci
Photography: Tonino Delli Colli
Art Direction: Dante Ferretti
Costumes: Danilo Donati
Music: Coordinated by Pasolini/Morricone
Editing: Nino Baragli
Cast: Laura Betti (the Wife of Bath), Ninetto Davoli (Peterkin), Josephine Chaplin (May), P. P. Pasolini (Chaucer), Franco Citti (Devil), John Francis Lane (Monk), Hugh Griffith (Sir January)
Producer: Alberto Grimaldi for PEA (Rome)/Les Productions Artistes Associés (Paris)
Running Time: 111 minutes

1974 *Il fiore delle mille e una notte*
Screenplay: P. P. Pasolini, based on the *Arabian Nights*
Collaboration on the Screenplay: Dacia Maraini
Assistant Directors: Umberto Angelucci, Peter Shepherd
Photography: Giuseppe Ruzzolini
Art Direction: Dante Ferretti
Costumes: Danilo Donati
Music: Ennio Morricone
Editing: Nino Baragli, Tatiana Casini Morigi
Cast: Franco Merli (Nur-ed-Din), Ninetto Davoli (Aziz), Franco Citti (the Demon), Ines Pellegrini (Zumurrud), Teresa Bouche (Aziza), Margaret Clementi
Producer: Alberto Grimaldi for PEA (Rome)/Les Productions Artistes Associés (Paris)
Running Time: 148 minutes

Le mura di San'a
Script: P. P. Pasolini
Photography: Tonino Delli Colli
Editing: Tatiana Casini Morigi
Commentary: P. P. Pasolini
Producer: Franco Rossellini for Rosina Anstalt
Running Time: 16 minutes

1975 *Salò o le 120 giornate di Sodoma*
Screenplay: P. P. Pasolini and Sergio Citti, based on the Marquis de Sade's novel *Les 120 Journées de Sodome*
Assistant Director: Umberto Angelucci
Photography: Tonino Delli Colli
Sets: Dante Ferretti
Costumes: Danilo Donati
Music: Coordinated by Ennio Morricone
Editing: Nino Baragli, Tatiana Casini Morigi
Cast: Paolo Bonacelli (the Duke), Giorgio Cataldi (the Bishop), Umberto Paolo Quintavalle (the Magistrate, Curval), Aldo Valletti (the President, dubbed by Marco Bellocchio), Caterina Boratto (Signora Castelli), Elsa De Giorgi (Signora Maggi), Hélène Surgère (Signora Vaccari, dubbed by Laura Betti), Sonia Saviange (Pianist), Ines Pellegrini, Franco Merli
Producer: Alberto Grimaldi for PEA (Rome)/Les Productions Artistes Associés (Paris)
Running Time: 114 minutes

Subjects and Screenplays

1954 *La Donna del fiume* (Dir. Mario Soldati) Co-scriptwriter
1955 *Il prigioniero della montagna* (Dir. Luis Trenker) Co-scriptwriter

1956 *Le notti di Cabiria* (Dir. Federico Fellini) Consultation on Romanesque street jargon

1957 *Marisa la civetta* (Dir. Mauro Bolognini) Co-scriptwriter

1958 *Giovani mariti* (Dir. Mauro Bolognini) Co-scriptwriter

1959 *La notte brava* (Dir. Mauro Bolognini) Subject and scriptwriter
Morte di un amico (Dir. Franco Rossi) Collaboration on subject

1960 *Il bell'Antonio* (Dir. Mauro Bolognini) Co-scriptwriter
La giornata balorda (Dir. Mauro Bolognini) Co-scriptwriter
La lunga notte del '43 (Dir. Florestano Vancini) Co-scriptwriter
Il carro armato dell'8 settembre (Dir. Gianni Puccini) Co-scriptwriter
La dolce vita (Dir. Federico Fellini) Co-scriptwriter

1961 *La ragazza in vetrina* (Dir. Luciano Emmer) Co-scriptwriter

1962 *La commare secca* (Dir. Bernardo Bertolucci) Subject and co-scriptwriter
Una vita violenta (Dirs. Paolo Heusch, Brunello Rondi), based on Pasolini's novel *Una vita violenta*

1966 *Il cinema di Pasolini/Appunti per un critofilm* (Short, dir. Maurizio Ponzi), includes clips from *Comizi d'amore*

1970 *Ostia* (Dir. Sergio Citti) Collaboration on subject and script; supervision of mise-en-scène

1973 *Storie scellerate* (Dir. Sergio Citti) Collaboration on subject and script

Index

Printed in the United States
85775LV00003B/78/A

9 780520 078550